BEFORE THE WAR

Studies in Diplomacy

BEFORE THE WAR
Studies in Diplomacy

By

G. P. GOOCH, D.Litt., F.B.A.,

George Peabody

Vol. I

The Grouping of the Powers

NEW YORK / RUSSELL & RUSSELL

FIRST PUBLISHED IN 1938
REISSUED, 1967, BY RUSSELL & RUSSELL
A DIVISION OF ATHENEUM HOUSE, INC.
BY ARRANGEMENT WITH G. P. GOOCH
L. C. CATALOG CARD NO: 66—24693

PRINTED IN THE UNITED STATES OF AMERICA

PREFACE

THE chronological development of the European situation during the opening years of the twentieth century has been traced by competent scholars in many lands. The purpose of the present work is to survey the familiar scene from a less familiar angle. With the opening of the archives of all the Great European Powers except Italy it has become possible to reconstruct the story of the coming of the war in minute detail from the standpoint of the principal actors. Bismarck used to say that true history could not be written from official documents, since the historian is not always aware what was in the mind of their authors. It is equally true that history cannot be written without them. Moreover in the field of war origins we are no longer dependent on documents intended for publication. With the aid of their private correspondence, their departmental memoranda, their confidential minutes, and the testimony of their associates, we are enabled to watch the makers of history at work, to recapture the *arcana imperii*, to reconstruct the development of ideas. No period in the history of mankind is so intimately known to us as Bismarckian and post-Bismarckian Europe.

Though the personality of a Foreign Minister is a factor of importance, the main element in the determination of his policy is the national tradition, based as it always is on the foundations of geography. Thus the chapters which compose this volume are neither miniature biographies nor essays in psychological interpretation. As the sub-title proclaims, they are studies in diplomacy and nothing more. Though there were six Great Powers in Europe, only five statesmen are selected for treatment. That no Italian is on the list is due, not merely to the lack of official material, but to the absence of an outstanding figure. Italy's main contribution to our story, namely the transfer of her sympathies from the Triple Alliance to the Triple Entente, is sufficiently analysed in the chapters on Delcassé and Bülow.

The studies are in every case preceded by a brief historical retrospect, for a statesman's work is unintelligible unless we can reconstruct the stage on which he is called to play his part. In every instance the general line of advance was more or less clearly marked out by the trend of events. When all the Continental Powers had become members of diplomatic

v

groups, it would have been surprising had Great Britain continued to stand entirely aloof. After consolidating her alliance with Russia, the task of France was to seek further friendships in the hope of redressing the balance tilted against her in 1871. In an age of rampant Imperialism Germany could hardly be expected to remain content with Bismarck's maxim of limited liability. It was as natural that Russia should try her fortune in the Far East as that, on the failure of that adventure, she should resume her activities in south-eastern Europe. And finally it was not astonishing that Austria-Hungary, who, alone of the Great Powers of the world, neither owned nor coveted territory overseas, should desire to consolidate her position in the Balkan peninsula.

In their main decisions and achievements the Foreign Ministers here described were the spokesmen of national aspirations or demands. All of them were men of ability; none of them were supermen. Some worked for change, others for the maintenance of the status quo, according to their reading of the interests entrusted to their charge. All played the same game of *Machtpolitik* with different degrees of skill and success. Nobody dreamed of renouncing war as an instrument of national policy, and the rattle of the sword was never far away; for Europe was nothing but a geographical expression, and there were no recognised rules of the game. The haunting dangers of international anarchy were seldom envisaged, and no sustained attempt to remove them was made. Statesmen of the pre-war world cannot be classified into saints and sinners, and in surveying their performances moral indignation is out of place. It is a wise precept of Professor Pribram that the historian should speak not of war guilt but of war responsibility. No attempt has been made in these pages to prove or disprove a thesis. Their sole object is to explain the formation of policies and the sequence of events. A certain amount of overlapping in a work of this structure is inevitable, but that is not necessarily to be deplored. For it is a bracing intellectual discipline to approach the study of complicated international situations from different points of view, and thus to realise what a strong case every actor in the drama believes himself to possess.

A second and concluding volume, it is hoped, will appear in two or three years, containing studies of Grey, Poincaré, Bethmann Hollweg, Sazonoff and Berchtold.

G.P.G.

CONTENTS

ABBREVIATIONS

B.D. = *British Documents on the Origins of the War*, 1898–1914, edited by G. P. Gooch and Harold Temperley.

G.P. = *Die Grosse Politik der Europäischen Kabinette*,1871–1914.

Ö-U.A. = *Österreich-Ungarns Aussenpolitik*, 1908–1914.

D.D.F. = *Documents Diplomatiques Français*.

LANSDOWNE

CHAPTER I

LANSDOWNE

I

WHEN Lansdowne was transferred from the War Office to the Foreign Office after the General Election of September 1900, he inherited a long and settled tradition of national policy.[1] The two governing principles of British statesmanship have been the development of ordered liberty at home and the utilisation of our island position for expansion overseas. Geography is the mother of history, and our pitch on the fringe of a Continent is the master-key to British diplomacy since the sixteenth century. The Hundred Years War cured us of our grosser Continental ambitions. Sometimes the flag has followed the trader, sometimes the trader followed the hoisting of the flag. This ceaseless activity involved us since the end of the Middle Ages in many wars ; but our aim has been to establish ourselves, commercially or territorially, in the far places of the earth rather than to gain possessions nearer home.

To make and to hold a far-flung Empire it was essential for an island nation to secure and maintain supremacy at sea. " What shall we do to be saved in this world ? " asked Halifax in 1694. " There is no other answer but this, Look to your moat. The first article of an Englishman's political creed must be that he believeth in the sea." Trade was the source of our wealth and our power ; and when the Industrial Revolution transformed a small and predominantly agricultural people into a large and predominantly manufacturing community, we ceased to be able to supply our vital needs. Henceforth we required a fleet not only, like other countries, to avert invasion, but to ensure the unimpeded flow of food and raw materials needed to sustain and employ a rapidly growing population. The whole country stood behind the doctrine enshrined in the crude but forcible eighteenth-century couplet

> " Rule Britannia, Britannia rule the waves,
> Britons never never shall be slaves."

[1] *The Cambridge History of British Foreign Policy* is the best general survey. Headlam-Morley, *Studies in Diplomatic History* ; Algernon Cecil, *British Foreign Secretaries* ; and A. L. Kennedy, *Old Diplomacy and New*, 1876–1922, are useful.

The proudest achievement in our history is the defeat of the Spanish Armada, and the hero of the British people is neither Marlborough nor Wellington but Nelson. What the army was to Prussia, the navy has been to England. We climbed to prosperity behind the impregnable rampart of our wooden walls.

If control of the seas had been accompanied by a large standing army and a commercial monopoly in our widening dominions, England would have been overthrown long ago by a coalition of justly aggrieved rivals in the name of the Balance of Power. We have on the contrary been the leading champions of that principle, which, next to security at sea, has shaped our diplomatic tradition. The phrase has been defined in various ways. To the British people it has meant a determination to resist, by diplomacy or arms, the growth of any European State so formidable as to threaten our national liberties, the security of our shores, or the safety of our foreign possessions. We are too close to the Continent to be indifferent to its concerns. In the words of Lord Grey, " England has always drifted or deliberately gone into opposition to any Power which establishes a hegemony in Europe." She grappled at different times with Spain, France and Imperial Germany ; and the fear that Russia might dominate the Near East drew us reluctantly into the Crimean War. As Palmerston used to say, England has no eternal friendships and no eternal enmities, but only eternal interests.

If our resolve to maintain the Balance of Power led to frequent conflicts, the expansion of the Empire progressively diminished our desire to intervene in the quarrels of the Continent. Since the fall of Napoleon the British people was united in desiring to keep its hands free, to trust to the fleet for the security which other Powers sought in alliances or mighty armies, and only to plunge into the whirlpool if vital interests or treaty obligations were at stake. The policy familiarly known as splendid isolation seemed the obvious course till the end of the nineteenth century. The situation was altered when the five Great Powers of Continental Europe grouped themselves into two permanent alliances, each of them commanding the services of conscript troops. We proclaimed the Two Power standard at sea in 1889 ; but it was politically impossible to increase our army, which, relatively to the expansion of the Empire and the ever-growing hosts of our neighbours, became smaller every year. In the closing decade of the century France and Russia, now allied to one another, appeared incurably hostile ; the Kruger telegram caused the first serious tension with the German Empire ; and a boundary dispute with Venezuela provoked President Cleveland to rattle the American sword. Austria and Italy, it is true, remained friendly, but in drawing up the balance-sheet they scarcely seemed to count.

These novel circumstances convinced the impressionable mind of Joseph Chamberlain that it was no longer safe to stand alone, and inspired his informal approach to Germany in 1898, the critical year of Port Arthur and Fashoda. The views of the Colonial Secretary were shared by some of his colleagues, among them Lansdowne and the Duke of Devonshire ; but Salisbury, who was Foreign Minister as well as Prime Minister, saw no reason to abandon the tradition of the free hand. He was well aware that we had formidable potential foes and no powerful friend, and that our moral isolation was intensified by disapproval of our South African policy. But he felt a robust confidence in the fleet, and a concerted attack, he believed, could always be averted by some minor surrender or timely compromise. Thus in 1898 he yielded for the moment to Russia in the Far East, desiring to free his hands for a duel with France in the Upper Nile, and he made grudging concessions to Germany in Samoa when Kruger's ultimatum set South Africa ablaze. On the other hand he welcomed German co-operation against the Russian domination of the Far East in the Yangtse treaty of 1900. In no direction was he willing to bind himself, for he felt equally little confidence in Russia, Germany or France. The face of Europe, as he knew from long experience, was continually changing. No one could foresee even the immediate future, and the dangers of entanglement appeared in his eyes far greater than the risks of isolation, tempered as were the latter by an unchallengeable fleet. As the old chess-player bent over the board at the turn of the century he congratulated himself on the liberty which he had retained to make any move that he thought best.

II

Such was the situation when Lansdowne succeeded Salisbury at the Foreign Office. The Prime Minister continued to follow every step with the eye of an expert ; but he was growing old, and his grip was slightly relaxed. The new

Foreign Secretary, needless to say, acted with perfect loyalty towards his venerated chief, and no important move was taken without consultation and consent. Yet the retirement of the veteran statesman from the post which he had filled with high distinction for so many years was an event in European history, for Lansdowne brought a younger and more pliable mind to the complicated tasks of the new century. His adhesion to the two governing principles of British policy, supremacy at sea and the balance of power, was unreserved; but he was less convinced than his predecessor of the virtues of isolation, and in consequence less unwilling to respond to approaches from abroad. As Governor-General of Canada, Viceroy of India, and Secretary of State for War he had been accustomed to handling large issues, and he had no fear of responsibility. His unruffled temper, his perfect manners, his spotless character and his irreproachable French accent seemed to make the great Whig aristocrat an ideal occupant of the post, and indeed he proved the outstanding success of the Unionist team which ruled the British Empire from 1900 to 1905.[1]

Chamberlain had been nettled by Bülow's chilly rejoinder to his advances in the autumn of 1899; but the persistent hostility of France and Russia, combined with the exasperating duration of the South African war, still pointed to a rapprochement with Germany. During a visit to Chatsworth in January 1901, Baron Eckardstein, First Secretary of the German Embassy, was assured by the Colonial Secretary that for him and his friends in the Cabinet the time of splendid isolation was over; that the choice lay between the Dual and the Triple Alliance; that, unlike some of his colleagues, he would prefer the latter, and that the first step should be a secret Moroccan agreement.[2] The matter could be taken up when Salisbury left for the Riviera, and the *détente* discussed with Lansdowne and himself. If co-operation proved impracticable they would turn to Russia, despite the high price England would have to pay, perhaps involving China and the Persian Gulf. Dismissing the possibility of a rapprochement between Great Britain and the Dual Alliance as nothing but a spectre, Bülow and Holstein made no response and counselled the Kaiser not to commit himself during his visit to England for the funeral of Queen Victoria. Russian activities in the Far

[1] Lord Newton, *Life of Lord Lansdowne.*
[2] *G.P.* XVII, ch. 109; and *B.D.* II, ch. 10. Eckardstein's *Lebenserinnerungen* Vol. II, contains valuable material but must be used with caution.

East, however, were causing apprehensions in Downing Street, scarcely less than in Tokio, and it seemed clear that, if the domination of China by the Russian bear was to be averted, co-operation with some leading Power was the only way. On February 7 the Foreign Minister informed Eckardstein of the wish of Japan for a joint attempt to secure the repudiation of the agreement concluded by the Chinese commander in Manchuria, and inquired whether Germany would co-operate in strengthening the hands of the Chinese Government. The Wilhelmstrasse politely declined ; for it was anxious not to antagonise Russia, and it believed that a partnership with England at that moment would displease the German people and was indeed intrinsically undesirable. It was an article of faith in Berlin that England would one day urgently require Germany's support, and that in that unhappy hour we should be compelled to accept her terms.

A few weeks later, on March 18, the situation was transformed by a conversation between Lansdowne and Eckardstein, which began with the situation in the Far East and passed on to larger issues. According to the latter the Foreign Minister observed that he was considering the possibility of a long-term defensive alliance between England and Germany, which he believed that several of his most influential colleagues would approve. According to Lansdowne's report, on the other hand, the suggestion of an alliance came from his visitor. " He believed that the German Government, while averse from an agreement entered into solely with reference to the present situation in China, would entertain favourably the idea of an understanding of a more durable and extended character with this country. The kind of arrangement which he contemplated might be described as a purely defensive alliance between the two Powers, directed solely against France and Russia. So long as Germany or England were attacked by one only of the other two Powers the alliance would not operate." After replying that the project was very novel and far-reaching and would require careful examination, Lansdowne proceeded to indicate some of its difficulties. It would involve an identic foreign policy, since every complication of either party might drag the other into the quarrel. Moreover it was often difficult to decide whether a country was acting on the defensive in fact as well as in form. " Baron Eckardstein", concluded the report, " was careful to assure me that his suggestion was not made under instructions, but I feel

B

no doubt that he has been desired to sound me." In a private letter to Lascelles on the same day the Foreign Secretary expressed doubt whether much would come of the plan.[1]

Which of these rival versions are we to believe ? There should be little difficulty in answering the question. The editors of the *Grosse Politik* have illustrated the unreliability of Eckardstein.   Lansdowne, on the other hand, was not only a man of perfect integrity and intellectual precision, but he was bound by every obligation of honour and precedent to provide the Cabinet with an accurate account of a conversation of exceptional significance.   Eckardstein's narrative, moreover, was conveyed in the form of a private telegram to Holstein, who, in a letter of March 17 which reached London on March 19, sent the categorical injunction : " expressly forbid you the slightest mention of an alliance.   The moment, if it ever comes, has not yet arrived."   In face of such an express prohibition he could hardly report that he had suggested an alliance, and even outlined its terms.   To explain that the letter had only reached him after the interview would have been no excuse, for Holstein would have replied that a step of such importance should never have been taken without orders from home.   Moreover Eckardstein, like most other people, was afraid of the *Eminence Grise*, who had broken many promising careers and was terrible in his wrath.   We may add that when Lansdowne, in discussion with Count Metternich at the end of the year, attributed the initiative to Eckardstein, his statement was unchallenged by the new Ambassador.

If we accept the accuracy of the Lansdowne report, how, it may be asked, could Eckardstein dare to make such a far-reaching proposal off his own bat ?   The most probable explanation is that the ardent Anglophil, the husband of an English wife and a *persona grata* at the new Court, was convinced not only of the desirability but of the possibility of such a pact, and was eager to reap the credit were it to be achieved.   Hatzfeldt was old and ill, and the First Secretary possessed a temper that fretted against the shackles of official control.   He had no faith in the statesmanship of the Wilhelm-strasse, and he believed that opportunities should be seized. Moreover he confesses that on March 16—two days before the historic interview at the Foreign Office—when he was the guest of the Foreign Secretary, he had given his host a broad

[1] Newton, 199–200.

hint to come forward with an offer of alliance, remarking :
" If there were a defensive alliance covering all eventualities,
Germany would of course be in a position to localise a war
between Russia and Japan by influencing France." This
passage, he explains in his Memoirs, was omitted from his
telegram to Holstein lest he should be scolded for going too
far.   A diplomatist who confesses to such concealment is as
capable of misreporting a conversation as of exceeding his
instructions.

Bülow replied that the defensive arrangement which he
believed Lansdowne to have proposed appealed to the German
Government which must, however, first consult its allies.
Meanwhile it would be well for England herself to approach
Austria.   If Goluchowsky approved, Germany would be
ready for negotiations, and perhaps Japan might be drawn in.
A second conversation with Eckardstein took place on March
22, of which unfortunately no record is to be found in the
Foreign Office.   After discussing the situation in China the
Foreign Secretary is declared to have said that he had drawn
up a memorandum on the idea of a defensive arrangement,
which he had discussed with Balfour and laid before Salisbury.
The Premier had expressed his concurrence in principle with a
strictly defined defensive alliance, adding that all eventualities
must be considered and a way be found to remove the Parliamentary obstacles to a long term pact.   Lansdowne had
proceeded to ask whether the German Government would be
prepared for a defensive agreement despite the acute anti-
English current of public opinion.   If so, should the alliance
apply in the case of an attack by one Power or only in the
case of two or more ?   Would it desire a secret or a public
agreement ?   Would Japan be included so far as the Far East
was concerned ?   Eckardstein gave his own replies, explaining
that he was unaware of the views of his Government ; and
Lansdowne added that his own remarks were also to be
regarded as personal and academic.   If the conversation
followed anything like the course here indicated, it is a mystery
that no record was preserved by the Foreign Secretary.
That the Prime Minister's supposed approval of the principle
of a defensive alliance contrasts sharply with the uncompromising memorandum which he was shortly to compose suggests a
doubt as to the accuracy of the Eckardstein version of the
whole interview.

On March 29 Lansdowne told Eckardstein that as the

Prime Minister was ill he could not safely say much. His colleagues, while cordially desiring a good understanding directed towards the maintenance of peace and mutual protection against aggressive combinations, were apprehensive of the idea of an international arrangement of the indefinite but very far-reaching character which he had sketched. If the matter was to advance, they should try to form a more precise conception of the contingencies for which they desired to provide. Eckardstein replied that as Salisbury was ill and the Reichstag was irritable, the discussion had better be postponed till after the Easter holidays. " I acquiesced," concludes the report of the Foreign Secretary, " merely adding that I wished him and those with whom he was acting to know that his proposal had not been regarded with indifference or contemptuously put aside." When Eckardstein recurred to the subject on April 9, Lansdowne replied that it must wait till the Prime Minister's return.

The Foreign Secretary was in a difficulty, for he could not be sure with whom he was dealing. " It is not always easy to determine how much of Eckardstein's communications are *de son propre cru*," he wrote to Lascelles. " I doubt whether much will come of the project. In principle the idea is good enough. But when each side comes, if it ever does, to formulate its terms, we shall break down ; and I know Lord Salisbury regards the scheme with, to say the least, suspicion." The next conversation took place on May 15, but here again we have nothing but Eckardstein's report. The Foreign Secretary, we are told, remarked that he and some of his colleagues would welcome a defensive alliance with Germany. He had fully discussed the matter with the Prime Minister, who approved the principle of mutual support against two or more assailants, but saw objections to complicating the issue by the inclusion of Austria and Italy. After pointing out the difficulties arising from such an extension, he expressed his hope that they might be overcome. The time had now arrived when both sides should put their ideas on paper.

A week later Lansdowne discussed the alliance question for the first time with the ailing Ambassador himself, whom he visited at the German Embassy at the latter's request. Here we are on firm ground, for the conversation is minutely described by both parties and their versions closely agree. The foreign policy of Germany, declared Hatzfeldt, must always be based on the closest intimacy with Austria, and it was unthinkable that she should throw over her ally. If there was to be an alliance, it must be between the two " unities "—the one consisting of Great Britain and her Colonies, the other of the Triple Alliance. "Was I then to understand", inquired Lansdowne, " that the proposal was simply that we should join the Triple Alliance?" Hatzfeldt answered in the affirmative. Lansdowne pointed out that we were unaware of its articles, adding that it would be difficult to define aggression. Moreover each of the allies would claim a share in controlling the policy of the rest, a restriction which Great Britain would be most reluctant to accept. Hatzfeldt rejoined that the dangers of isolation were much worse, and that the advantages for England would be immense. It was our interest to join one of the two European groups. We might try Russia and France, but they would demand a high price. As for Germany, if nothing came of these overtures, she might have to look elsewhere for alliances, and Russia could be easily squared. Hatzfeldt smilingly suggested that Salisbury might be a difficulty, which Lansdowne did not contest.

The issue, however it originated, was at last clearly and authoritatively defined. Should Great Britain bind herself to the Triple Alliance? Lansdowne, who was in no hurry to reply, told Eckardstein that the conversation with the Ambassador in no way diminished his desire for the promised memorandum. It never materialised, for the Wilhelmstrasse intervened. "When the first written document in the alliance question leaves our hand," wired Holstein, " the first formal suggestion of an alliance comes from us—exactly what we wish to avoid. To decide on the principle whether an attack on the Triple Alliance should raise the *casus foederis* for England, the English require nothing in writing. When England has expressed herself on the principle, written notes, for instance on the meaning of the word Attack, can be exchanged. Till then, in my opinion, we should give nothing in writing." There was certainly no *empressement* in either camp, which is not surprising if, as was probably the case, neither Government had initiated the discussion.

Though Eckardstein had reported that both parties promised to draw up a memorandum, there is no evidence from the British side that Lansdowne gave any such undertaking. On the other hand on March 27 Sir Thomas Sanderson, the Permanent Under-Secretary, sketched out a Convention between Great Britain and Germany after conversation with his chief, so that the latter might have "something tangible to look at and cut about." Each party was to come to the support of the other if engaged in war with more than one Power. The wording, he explained, would have to be reconsidered when Eckardstein's memorandum or other documents were available. They would have in some way to prevent either party from being dragged into a quarrel of which it disapproved, though such a limitation might enable the Germans to throw us over. "Our public opinion would not allow it—theirs would." "However the Convention may be worded, it seems to me that it will practically amount to a guarantee to Germany of the provinces conquered from France, and that is the way in which the French will look at it. I do not see exactly what Germany will guarantee to us."

From Sanderson's draft it is clear that an agreement with the Triple Alliance was not considered, though Haztfeldt had declared that alone to be the German proposal. Moreover he himself saw no particular advantage even in the Anglo-German treaty of mutual guarantee originally suggested by Eckardstein. That Lansdowne was ready to discuss some limited scheme of association is obvious, for otherwise there would have been no point in drafting a memorandum. He must, however, have realised as clearly as Sanderson that any kind of defensive alliance pledged England in certain eventualities to fight for the retention of the Rhine Provinces by Germany, an obligation which must arouse the fierce resentment of France. The difficulty had been pointed out by Disraeli to Münster in 1879 ; and our relations with Germany were far less cordial in 1901 than when Bismarck was at the helm.

The failure to provide the German memorandum was of little importance, for on May 29, the very day that Holstein was warning Hatzfeldt of its perils, the Prime Minister condemned the whole project root and branch. While the Sanderson draft envisaged an Anglo-German agreement, Salisbury dealt exclusively with the revised proposal of partnership with the Triple Alliance. "The liability of having to defend the German and Austrian frontiers against Russia is heavier than that of having to defend the British Isles against France. Even, therefore, in its most naked aspect the bargain would be a bad one for this country. Count Hatzfeldt speaks of our 'isolation' as constituting a serious danger for us. Have we ever felt that danger practically ? . . . It would hardly be wise to incur novel and most onerous obligations in order to guard against a danger in whose existence we have no historical reason for believing." An even weightier objection was that the British Government could not undertake to declare war for any purpose which the electors might not approve. A secret agreement would thus have no practical validity. There were also very grave objections to submitting an agreement to Parliament, and a defensive alliance with England would excite bitter murmurs in Germany. "Several times during the last sixteen years", he concluded, "Count Hatzfeldt has tried to elicit from me in conversation some opinion as to the probable conduct of England if Germany or Italy were involved in war with France. I have always replied that no English Minister could venture on such a forecast. The course of the English Government in such a crisis must depend on the view taken by public opinion in this country, and public opinion would be largely, if not exclusively, governed by the nature of the *casus belli.*" Whatever life there had been in the plan, either in its limited or its wider form, was trampled out of it by Salisbury's uncompromising sentences. There is no more impressive State paper in our recent diplomatic history than this brief and massive plea for keeping the supreme decisions of peace and war in our own hands.

The opposition of the Prime Minister and the refusal of the German Government to supply a written draft combined with the ill-health of Hatzfeldt to defer further discussion till the autumn. The Ambassador, moreover, was about to leave the public service, and when Lansdowne called on him on June 7 he made no reference to the suggested pact. When King Edward visited his nephew at Homburg at the end of August the Kaiser, as we learn from Lascelles, expressed his regret that negotiations on an Anglo-German alliance had led to no definite result. "The relations between the two countries could only be placed on the satisfactory footing which he most earnestly desired by the conclusion of a definite and binding Treaty. I ventured to reply that, at the risk of being indiscreet, I could assure His Majesty that Your Lordship was in favour of an alliance." Though this sentence of the British Ambassador in an official despatch is more categorical than any evidence emanating from the Foreign Secretary himself, there seems no reason to contest its accuracy. Lansdowne had no more desire than Salisbury to be entangled in the meshes of the

Triple Alliance ; but he was clearly prepared for a partnership of some kind with Germany alone, though the suggestion was not his own.

When the summer holidays were over neither Metternich, the new Ambassador, nor Eckardstein reverted to the subject. The Foreign Secretary, however, was not disposed to let it drop. " Since the English are a practical people ", reported Paul Cambon to his chief on November 9, " they are beginning to appreciate the advantages of good international relations, and they feel the need rather vaguely of showing themselves more conciliatory towards other nations."[1] The Ambassador was a shrewd observer, for the unexpected duration of the South African war was producing a psychological effect. " I have received various indications ", wrote Lansdowne in a long memorandum dated November 22, " that the question is still present to the mind of the German Ambassador, and particularly to that of the German Emperor. Whatever, therefore, be the decision of His Majesty's Government, it seems to me that the time has come for frankly explaining our views to the German Ambassador. Unless some such explanation takes place we shall be accused of not knowing our own mind, and of breaking off negotiations in a discourteous and unfriendly manner. The knowledge that we have been negotiating a Treaty with Japan, an incident of which the German Government is sure to hear, could scarcely fail to add to their irritation in such circumstances."

Lansdowne proceeded to answer some of the objections stated in Salisbury's memorandum of May 29. " I fully admit the force of the Prime Minister's observation that this country has until now fared well in spite of its international isolation. I think, however, that we may push too far the argument that, because we have in the past survived in spite of our isolation, we need have no misgivings as to the effect of that isolation in the future. In approaching the Japanese we have, indeed, virtually admitted that we do not wish to continue to stand alone." Salisbury's reference to the hostility of German opinion is countered by a revealing sentence. " Would it not be true to say that the suspicion and dislike with which we are regarded in Germany are, to a great extent, the result of the ' aloofness ' of our policy, and that an openly declared change in that policy would not be without effect on German sentiment ? " After enumerating the insurmountable objections to

[1] *D.D.F.*, deuxième série, I, 582.

a partnership with the Triple Alliance, he proceeded to sketch out a more limited understanding with Germany in regard to certain matters of common interest. To the recent Far Eastern agreement might be added for instance a similar understanding in regard to the Mediterranean, following the precedent of Salisbury's own pact with Italy and Austria in 1887, and perhaps in the Persian Gulf. " Some similar exchange of declarations as to the objects which Great Britain and Germany have in common and the interests in regard to which they are prepared to afford one another support might be offered to the German Government, the form which such support should take being reserved for consideration when the necessity should arise. The arrangement would, no doubt, fall far short of what was suggested to us, but as a tentative and provisional step it might not be without value."

When the sceptical Prime Minister asked for more details Lansdowne drafted a further memorandum on December 4. The agreement might declare that the two countries had a common interest in the maintenance of the territorial status quo on the shores of the Mediterranean, the Adriatic, the Aegean and Black Seas ; and also in the freedom of commerce and navigation of all nations in the Persian Gulf, and the prevention of any territorial acquisitions on its shores by other Powers which might interfere with that object. The nature of the co-operation in furtherance of this policy would be determined when the occasion arose. " And agreement on the above lines," he concluded, " would amount to little more than a declaration óf common policy and of a desire to maintain close diplomatic relations. Assuming, however, that both sides acted up to it in the fullest sense, it would be distinctly to the advantage of this country that peace should be maintained and that the status quo at Constantinople, in Albania, Macedonia and Bulgaria, in Tripoli and Morocco, and in Egypt, should not be disturbed. It would also be to our advantage to exclude Russia and Germany from establishing themselves strategically on the shores of the Persian Gulf. My own impression is that the German Government (or the German Emperor) desire something much more precise and far-reaching than this, and that they would refuse an overture on the above lines. Should they do this no great harm will have been done, and we shall have put it out of their power to accuse us of having ' dropped ' them."

Even this mild application of the principle of co-operation

with Germany was too much for the Prime Minister, who declared it full of risks and carrying with it no compensating advantage. His unbending opposition was decisive, and on December 19 the Foreign Secretary explained the views of the Government to the German Ambassador, who had been instructed not to speak about an alliance unless it was mentioned. To join the Triple Alliance was impossible for many reasons. Metternich replied that such an agreement was a magnificent opportunity for us, and he wondered why we did not " jump at it ". Our preference for isolation was unintelligible. The German Government, he continued, thought that our failure to reopen the discussions indicated a desire to drop the question, and it believed that something must have occurred. He agreed at any rate with one of Lansdowne's contentions, namely, that the present time was unfavourable for pursuing the question. He feared, however, that so favourable an opportunity as that of the previous summer might not recur, since Germany, he believed, would tend to move more and more towards Russia. " I replied that it would, to my mind, be most unfortunate if there should be any estrangement between our two countries, and I trusted that he would not consider our inability to take so serious a step as that which had been proposed to us denoted any unfriendliness towards Germany. Speaking entirely for myself, I asked him whether, assuming that we could not accept the German proposal as it stood, it might not be possible for the two countries to arrive at an understanding with regard to the policy which they might pursue in reference to particular questions or in particular parts of the world in which they were alike interested." No such minor proposal, replied the Ambassador without hesitation, was likely to find favour in Berlin. It was a case of " the whole or none ".

When Lascelles met the Chancellor a few days after this remarkable conversation, they agreed that nothing more could be done for the present. Bülow, however, expressed the hope that the question would not be dropped altogether, as he was convinced that an alliance between the Triplice and Great Britain would be of the greatest advantage to both countries and secure the peace of Europe for the next twenty-five years. It was a dream. The negotiators had laid their cards on the table and neither of them showed any disposition to give way. The discussions were never resumed, and British statesmen who felt the growing danger of isolation turned elsewhere for support. Barren though they were, the Anglo-German negotiations of 1901 revealed that a more flexible mind was at work in the Foreign Office. The long era of contented isolation was nearing its close.

III

During the months in which an Anglo-German alliance was fruitlessly discussed a very different kind of partnership was being sought and found. When Japan emerged as a Great Power after her defeat of China in 1895 the attitude of England was defined in two far-reaching decisions, the one negative, the other positive. In the first place we stood aloof from the Franco-German-Russian intervention which robbed her of some of the choicest fruits of victory. In the second we surrendered our ex-territorial rights, thereby acclaiming her as a civilised state and setting an example which was speedily followed by the rest of the world. The good will thus suggested or expressed was augmented by a common distaste for Russian hegemony in the Far East, which threatened the economic interests of the one and the political ambitions of the other. The seizure of Port Arthur in 1898 and the prolonged occupation of Manchuria after the suppression of the Boxer revolt in 1900 revealed the intentions of St. Petersburg, and turned the thoughts of Japanese statesmen to the idea of a conflict for the control of Northern China and Korea. The seed sown by the construction of the Siberian railway was ripening to harvest. For the time at any rate Russia had turned her back on Europe and was playing for high stakes at the other end of Asia. While France had surrendered at Fashoda, Russia remained the hostile rival of England that she had been ever since the Crimean war. The appeal of the *National Review* for an Anglo-Russian, rapprochement fell on deaf ears. The latest phase of her expansionist policy seemed scarcely less menacing than her earlier activities in the Near and Middle East. When the new century opened, the silent pressure of events was driving England and Japan towards co-operation.

The first of the conversations between Baron Hayashi and the Foreign Secretary which issued in the Anglo-Japanese Alliance took place on April 17, 1901, a month after Eckardstein's suggestion of an Anglo-German pact.[1] " He told me ",

[1] B.D., II, ch. 11 : *Memoirs of Count Hayashi*, and G.P. XVII, ch. 110.

reported Lansdowne, " that, in his opinion, Japanese interests were seriously threatened by the policy of Russia, and he added that it seemed to him highly necessary that the two Governments should try to reach some permanent understanding for the protection of their interests in that part of the world." Though Hayashi, like Eckardstein, explained that he was merely expressing his own views, Lansdowne rightly assumed that he was being sounded. For Hayashi had reported to Tokio conversations with Eckardstein urging an alliance of Germany, England and Japan, and was authorised to discover the attitude of the British Government without committing his own. Lansdowne cautiously replied that he could scarcely be expected to express an opinion without some substantive proposal. According to Hayashi he added that an agreement need not be confined to the two countries. The Foreign Secretary had not been taken altogether unawares, for a few days previously Eckardstein had informed him of a somewhat similar conversation. Hayashi, he declared, had suggested an agreement between Japan, Germany and Great Britain, pledging the three Governments to support the integrity of China and the maintenance of the open door at the Treaty ports.

A second conversation took place a month later, when Hayashi asked Lansdowne his views on the suggested agreement. The Foreign Minister answered by inquiring what the Ambassador proposed. In anticipation of the interview Hayashi had telegraphed the outlines of an alliance to his Government, which instructed him to discover whether an understanding between England and Germany already existed, but expressed no opinion on the terms he had sketched. Accordingly Hayashi stated that the policy of Japan towards China was unchanged, and that she merely wished to maintain her interests in Korea. He added that, in his opinion, it was of the utmost importance for England and Japan to stand together against a combination. Lansdowne replied that it would be difficult to settle details, but that he would consult the Prime Minister. He reiterated that the proposed agreement need not be confined to the two Powers.

No further step was taken till July 31, when the Ambassador, in the course of conversation, condemned the retention of Manchuria by Russia. Japan's real concern, however, was for Korea, which was too backward to stand alone. Sooner or later it would have to be decided whether it was to fall to Russia or not. To prevent such a fate Japan was ready to

fight. She could deal with Russia alone, and she must therefore endeavour to secure her isolation in the event of war.
This time Lansdowne was ready with a considered reply
which was to make history. It would be most unfortunate if
Korea passed into the hands of another Power, and England,
like Japan, could not regard her fate with indifference. The
policy of the two Governments was so much alike, he continued, both desiring to maintain the status quo, that he was
ready for an understanding in reference to a serious threat to
the balance of power in the waters of the Far East. This time
it was the Foreign Secretary who explained that he was
speaking without authorisation from the Cabinet. Hayashi
was delighted when his Government, to whom he reported
the conversation, instructed him to go ahead. On August 14
he announced that he felt sure that his Government would
welcome an understanding, and asked what conditions would
be required. Since Japan was more immediately interested,
rejoined Lansdowne, it was rather for her to state her wishes.
To the record of this conversation Edward VII added the
words : " The King considers it most essential that we should
give Japan our hearty support on all occasions when it is
possible to do so." Like the majority of his subjects, the
King still regarded Russia as the most dangerous Power in
the world.

The official negotiations began on October 16. At the
outset Hayashi asked whether Lansdowne desired Germany to
be a party to the understanding, which in that case would
" look much more formidable ". Though relations with
Germany were very friendly, replied Lansdowne, he would
prefer in the first instance at any rate a dual agreement. They
could discuss later the question of inviting Germany to join.
Hayashi then argued that it was a matter of life and death for
his country to keep Russia out of Korea, and that it was
interested in Manchuria only because encroachments in that
quarter might lead to encroachments in Korea. Japan, like
England, stood for the open door. She desired our support
if she were obliged to go to war with more than one Power in
defence of these aims, and would assist us if we were at war
with more than one Power in defence of our interests in any
part of China. Lansdowne approved the plan and presented
a draft on November 6, adding that he would have preferred
an agreement of wider scope. The collapse of British naval
power in the Far East would be a calamity if it resulted from a

quarrel originating in the Far East or anywhere else. When the Japanese comments on the British draft were discussed on December 19, Lansdowne reported that his colleagues shared his preference for a wider pact. It seemed scarcely reasonable that, while we must contemplate a war with two Great Powers in consequence of a Russo-Japanese dispute about Korea, we were to receive no help from Japan if involved in war with the same two Powers in regard to India. Such an extension, replied the Ambassador, could not be considered, and Lansdowne realised that it was useless to press the point.

While the discussions were in progress their success was endangered from an unexpected quarter. Prince Ito, the most experienced and the most Russophil of Japanese statesmen, arrived in Europe from America on a semi-official mission to discuss a rapprochement with Russia.[1] Hayashi was alarmed at the possible effect on the British Government of the Prince's visit to St. Petersburg, which Downing Street found very difficult to understand. The negotiations in London, however, had advanced too far to be wrecked, and when Ito reached London at the opening of 1902 he was won for the project of an alliance. Lansdowne pointed out that the agreement was likely to arouse sharp criticism, for it was an entirely new departure. Our policy had been to avoid entangling alliances, and if it was to be cast aside we must receive a substantial price in return. The Japanese proposals asked a good deal more than they gave, an observation which Ito made no attempt to contest. If the agreement were concluded, he asked, should we object to Japan seeking an amicable arrangement with Russia for the protection of her interests in Korea, since peace was her desire? Lansdowne naturally replied that we should have no objection to her obtaining a recognition of the interests which we also were seeking to protect. Though Ito emphasised his unofficial position, Lansdowne's plea for a more generous recognition of British interests in the agreement under discussion was doubtless not without effect in smoothing away the last difficulties of the deal.

The Treaty was signed on January 30, 1902, for a period of five years. In a covering despatch the Foreign Secretary declared that it had been concluded purely as a measure or precaution. " It in no way threatens the present position of the legitimate interests of other Powers. On the contrary, that part of it which renders either of the High Contracting

[1] v. D.D.F. I, 648–651, Lamsdorff's report of his conversations with Ito.

Parties liable to be called upon by the other for assistance can operate only when one of the allies has found himself obliged to go to war in defence of interests which are common to both, when the circumstances in which he has taken this step are such as to establish that the quarrel has not been of his own seeking, and when, being engaged in his own defence, he finds himself threatened, not by a single Power, but by a hostile coalition."

The treaty was received with varying emotions in the different capitals. At the express wish of King Edward it was communicated before publication to the Kaiser, who breezily remarked that the noodles had had a lucid interval. To Cambon, who warned him that England was involving herself in the quarrels of Japan, Lansdowne replied that he had striven in vain for an understanding with Russia in Asia, and had therefore been driven to seek guarantees elsewhere.[1] To Russia, with her memories of the recent visit of Prince Ito, it came as a rude shock. Lamsdorff acidly observed that he knew of no Powers intending to threaten the integrity, independence or interests specified in the agreement. This being so, the publication of the agreement, prepared in such secrecy and published at a moment when everything looked so peaceful, was most discouraging, and the reference to possible hostilities struck a disquieting note. Other Powers, he added, might have to take similar measures of precaution. A month later a Franco-Russian note proclaimed that the two Powers found in the treaty the affirmation of their own principles. But they too, being compelled to envisage the possibility of aggressive action by other Powers or of fresh troubles in China jeopardising the integrity or the free development of that Power, would in case of need consult one another as to safeguarding their interests. In handing the note to the Foreign Secretary, Paul Cambon expressed his personal regret that the treaty diminished the prospect of a good understanding which he had at one time thought might be established between Great Britain and Russia.

Its epoch-making character was recognised by friend and foe, and its significance was soon to be emphasised by events. It was criticised in England both by those who objected to entangling alliances on principle and those who argued that we had got the worst of the deal. Though the ageing Prime Minister accepted the pact, his colleague Hicks Beach ex-

[1] D.D.F. II, 88–91.

pressed the opinion that it would not have been made had he remained at the Foreign Office.[1] The perils of entanglement in the quarrels of another Power were indeed obvious, and the disapproval of the United States was unconcealed. Despite Salisbury's reiterated assertions that no British Government could pledge the country to take part in a war till public opinion had declared itself, here was a conditional surrender of the cherished privilege of self-determination.

The belief in isolation was waning, and most of the criticism was directed against the striking inequality of advantage between the signatories. A clash between Japan and Russia about Korea was only too likely : an Anglo-Russian conflict about China was extremely improbable. Japan received assurance of our support in the only place and in reference to the only problem that really mattered to her, while the promise of Japanese aid was limited to one of our manifold interests. Though Lansdowne put the best face he could on his achievement, his unavailing requests for an extension of Japanese obligations reveal his substantial agreement with his critics. Even in this imperfect form, however, he was proud of his handiwork. The threatened domination of the Far East by Russia would now be opposed with fresh courage and confidence by Japan, whose prestige was enormously enhanced by an alliance with a great European Power. If the two countries came to blows there seemed little danger that we should be involved. The treaty rendered a Russo-Japanese conflict more likely, a general conflict more unlikely. If France would not fight for the valley of the Nile, it was highly improbable that she would draw the sword for Korea. Thus it appeared to safeguard our position in China at a minimum cost, and perhaps our partner might be persuaded to extend the scope of the contract when it came up for renewal. In any case it was useful to possess the friendship of a Power whose strength was certain to grow. Whether it might ultimately increase a little too much to suit British interests was a question that only the future could decide. Statesmen cannot look too far ahead. At the opening of the century the immediate task was to avert Russian domination in the Far East.

In defending the treaty in the House of Lords against Spencer's argument that strong reasons were needed to justify a departure from the policy of isolation, Lansdowne explained the spirit in which he worked from beginning to end of his

[1] *Life of Sir Michael Hicks Beach*, II, 362.

tenure of the Foreign Office.[1] " I do not think that anyone can have watched the recent course of events in different parts of the world without realising that many of the arguments which a generation ago might have been adduced in support of a policy of isolation have ceased to be entitled to the same consideration now. What do we see on all sides? We observe a tendency to ever-increasing naval and military armaments involving ever-increasing burdens upon the people for the defence of whose countries their armaments were accumulated. There is also this—that in these days war breaks out with a suddenness which was unknown in former days, when nations were not, as they are now, armed to the teeth and ready to enter on hostilities at any moment. When we consider these features of the international situation, we must surely feel that that country would indeed be endowed with an extraordinary amount of what I might call self-sufficiency which took upon itself to say that it would accept, without question, without reservation, the doctrine that all foreign alliances were to be avoided as necessarily embarrassing and objectionable. Therefore I would entreat your Lordships to look at the matter strictly on its merits, and not to allow your judgment to be swayed by any musty formulas or old-fashioned superstitions as to the desirability of pursuing a policy of isolation for this country. If considered on its merits I venture to suggest that what you have to take into account in regard to an alliance of this kind is, first, whether the ally is a desirable ally, in the next place whether the objects of the alliance are commendable, and last, but not least, whether the price you pay for the alliance is greater than you ought to pay. If these questions can be satisfactorily answered, then I say the alliance is not a bad thing for the country, but on the contrary is a good thing : for *prima facie*, if there be no countervailing objections, the country which has the good fortune to possess allies is more to be envied than the country which is without them." With the signing of the Japanese alliance and its author's commentary in the House of Lords the Salisbury era came to an end.

IV

The failure of the Anglo-German negotiations of 1901 left the relations of the two countries no worse than before. The

[1] *Parliamentary Debates*, Fourth Series, Vol. CII, 1174. Feb. 13, 1902.

c

hostility of the German people was undeniable : but how deep were its roots ? " I am sanguine enough to hope ", wrote Lansdowne to Lascelles in April 1902, " that the bitter feeling which now prevails against us in Germany may not last for ever.[1] Have we not a right to ascribe a good deal of it to the South African war, and would the Emperor, Bülow, Holstein and others have contemplated as they did an Anglo-German alliance if hatred of Great Britain was to be regarded as for all time inherent in the sentiments of the German people ? Five years hence, before the German naval programme has been carried out, the outlook both in South Africa and in Germany may have altered enormously. And apart from sentiment, I cannot see that it will ever be of advantage to Germany to let us ' go under ' before a great European coalition. Is it not more likely that she will stick to her rôle of the honest broker, taking advantage, if you like, of our difficulties in order to pursue a *politique de pourboire* at our expense, but without pooling her ironclads with those of France and Russia ? " It was an optimistic forecast, shared in the main by Lascelles. On the termination of hostilities in South Africa in the following month it seemed as if something of the old friendliness might be restored. If the peoples continued to say unpleasant things about each other, the Governments at any rate were on fairly satisfactory terms.

The chapter of accidents soon provided an opportunity for co-operation. Venezuela had long enjoyed notoriety for the abnormal frequency of her revolutions, and President Castro showed as little consideration for the Great Powers as for the rebels who challenged his autocratic rule.[2] Incidents and outrages were frequent, and early in 1902 the German Government began to covet British assistance in enforcing its demands. On July 23 Metternich informed Landsowne that in the opinion of his Government the time was approaching when it would be necessary for the Powers interested in Venezuela to put pressure on Castro. He suggested a pacific blockade. Lansdowne replied that he would be quite ready to discuss joint action, but that he must think over the concrete proposal that had been made.

A few days later the Foreign Secretary warned the Venezuelan Government that, unless it amended its ways and paid

[1] Newton, 247.
[2] B.D. II, ch. 12 ; G.P. XVII, ch. 112 ; and Dennis, *Adventures in American Diplomacy*, ch. 11.

compensation, the British Government would proceed to enforce its claims. When Castro declined to yield and brought counter-charges, he invited the Admiralty to suggest the best method of coercion. On October 22 he handed a memorandum to Metternich setting forth the British case and the British plans. He proposed to give Castro a final warning and a final chance before taking action. Germany, concluded the memorandum, might desire to associate herself in this preliminary step by informing Venezuela that the two Governments were determined to co-operate. The invitation to join in the final warning was accepted by the Wilhelmstrasse, and Lansdowne agreed that neither Government should recede till both were satisfied. Germany approved the suggestion that the first step should be the seizure of the Venezuelan gun-boats, and proposed a pacific blockade if further measures were required. Metternich added that the possibility of such a blockade had already been mentioned to the United States, who had raised no objection. On the same day the Foreign Secretary telegraphed a final warning to Caracas, and instructed our Ambassador at Washington to explain the British grievances and the steps in contemplation. John Hay replied that, though he regretted that European Powers should employ force in Central or South America, the United States could not object to their obtaining redress for injuries, provided that they aimed at no acquisition of territory. When Castro again refused satisfaction and reiterated his counter-claims, the British and German Governments renewed the discussion of coercive measures. In view of our objections to a pacific blockade as a measure unjustifiable in international law, Germany consented to a blockade of the normal kind.

The truculent intransigence of Castro swept away the last hesitations, and on December 7 the British and German Ministers at Caracas presented ultimatums. Even now Castro merely repeated his previous reply, adding that the Treasury was empty. When the warships in the harbour of La Guayra were seized and the coast blockaded, he arrested British and German subjects in Caracas, but liberated them on the intervention of the United States. After denouncing the attack as cowardly and barbarous, he invited the American Minister to propose that Great Britain and Germany should submit their claims arising out of the insurrection in Venezuela to arbitration. Since the offer only covered a portion of the Allied demands, the coercion continued; but the partners accepted arbitration in principle, and expressed the hope that President Roosevelt himself would act as arbitrator.

Co-operation with Germany, though useful in overcoming the resistance of Venezuela, was not without its disadvantages. A disturbing telegram from our Ambassador at Washington on December 16 reported a growing feeling in Congress against coercion. " The Administration is not suspicious of us, but it is undoubtedly apprehensive as to German designs. The impression prevails in Washington that Germany is using us, and our friends here regret, from the point of view of American good feeling towards us, that we are acting with her." A fortnight later Sir Michael Herbert described the situation at greater length. From resentment of British co-operation with Germany opinion had veered round to satisfaction that we should hold our partner in check. Our fidelity to the Monroe doctrine was universally recognised, whereas suspicion of German designs in the Caribbean Sea was shared by the Government, the public and the press. Indeed the Venezuelan incident seemed more likely to improve than to impair the relations between Great Britain and the United States. The irritation against Germany was intensified by the bombardment of San Carlos, which, so Metternich explained, was merely a reply to an attack on a German ship engaged in the blockade.

The growing excitement of the United States intensified Lansdowne's desire for a speedy conclusion of the discussions at Washington, where Bowen, the American Minister at Caracas, was acting on behalf of Venezuela. On February 7, 1903, Sir Michael Herbert telegraphed that a settlement could be reached that day if we stood alone. German and Italian claims were the stumbling block, and he hoped that Lansdowne could secure their modification. A great change for the worse had taken place in the feeling towards England in the last few weeks, and our relations would be seriously impaired if the partnership with Germany continued much longer. The concluding sentence was ominous. " The time has almost come, in American opinion, for us to make the choice between the friendship of the United States and that of Germany." Lansdowne pointed out to Metternich the gravity of the situation and the importance of immediate settlement. Our position would be intolerable if, after securing our own claims, we were to break off negotiations on account of extreme German demands ; and the position of Germany under such circumstances would hardly be enviable. We had no intention of deserting her, but it was absolutely necessary to find some solution. This plain speaking produced the desired result. On February 13 the protocol was signed and the blockade was raised.

The material objects of Anglo-German co-operation had been secured. But the enterprise was viewed throughout by a large section of British opinion with profound distaste, and Lansdowne found it far more difficult to run in double harness than he had reckoned. Moreover the intense suspicion of German aims entertained in America fortified the dislike and distrust surviving in England from the South African war. To the end of his life Metternich spoke gratefully of the loyalty and courage with which Lansdowne had played his part during these trying days, whereas Balfour, who had succeeded his uncle as Prime Minister in the previous summer, became chilly as the opposition developed. Certain ministers took pains to minimise their commitments. There was no alliance, declared Cranborne, the Under Secretary for Foreign Affairs ; and Balfour of Burleigh spoke truthfully but slightingly of " a mere casual co-operation for a specific purpose and a limited time ". In Lansdowne's tones, on the other hand, there was no note of apology or regret. Replying to Tweedmouth's contention that we should have acted alone, he pointed out that we were approached by Germany, and that it would have been very inconvenient if measures of coercion had been employed without an understanding. " The blockade took place under a prearranged scheme ; each Power took its own sphere of operations and the result was that within a fortnight the Venezuelan Government, which had turned a deaf ear to our remonstrances, proposed that our disputes should be submitted to arbitration."[1] The sharp hostility of the British press was noted in Germany with resentful surprise, and both countries realised that the experiment in co-operation had been a political failure, though Lansdowne in after years expressed the opinion that " the Germans on the whole ran straight as far as we were concerned".[2]

If the worsening of Anglo-German relations was in no sense the fault of the Foreign Secretary, the growing friendliness of the United States owed much to his skilful efforts. Our

[1] *Parliamentary Debates*, Fourth Series, Vol. CXVIII, 1059–1069. March 2, 1903.
[2] Newton, 260.

avowed sympathy in the Spanish war, followed by the voluntary surrender of our rights under the Clayton-Bulwer treaty in the Panama Canal, had healed the smart of the Venezuelan crisis, and made it possible for controversies, old or new, to be settled in an amicable mood. When the blockade of Venezuela was over, the discussion of the treaties relating to the Alaska boundary was resumed. Roosevelt warned the British Government that, if the negotiations again fell through, he would establish a boundary as the United States claimed it. He added that, while ready to discuss the minor issues, he would not agree to arbitration on the large sections of Alaska demanded by Canada, and that the Canadian claim to deep water was indefensible. The British Government, undeterred by these blustering tones, appointed Lord Alverstone as our Commissioner, who, while the two Canadians maintained their full claims, was compelled by the evidence to accept the main American case. The adoption of the American standpoint by the Lord Chief Justice in October 1903 confirmed the growing belief in British good will, and, in the President's words, removed the last obstacle to agreement between the two peoples. The *détente* inaugurated by Salisbury and Pauncefote had been fostered by Landowne's faultless temper and tact.

The Venezuelan adventure was scarcely concluded when the British Government was faced with the far more formidable issue of the Baghdad railway.[1] Konia had been reached in 1896, and in 1899, when the joint efforts of the Kaiser and Marschall had won the confidence of the Sultan, a concession extending to the Persian Gulf was secured in principle. London financiers had been associated with the German *concessionnaires* in 1888, and in 1899 Chamberlain remarked to the Kaiser, on his visit to London, that he would like to see Great Britain co-operating with German enterprise in Hithér Asia. French financiers took shares in 1899, but German efforts to secure British assistance were unavailing. On January 1, 1902, the Company received a concession for ninety-nine years to build a railway from Konia to the Gulf with a kilometric guarantee. As the security was not specified and no terminus was selected, the document was merely a sketch; but it appeared to the Foreign Secretary that the time had come to explain the position of the British Government. On March 18, accordingly, he informed Metternich that we did

[1] *B.D.* II, ch. 12, and *G.P.* XVII, ch. 114.

not regard the project with unfriendly eyes. If it was to be carried out with our support and good will, we should expect a share, at least equal to that of any other Power, in respect of capital, management and orders for materials. The Ambassador replied that, so far as he was aware, the door was open. Thus began the discussions which, after many intervals and vicissitudes, were satisfactorily concluded twelve years later on the eve of the world war.

In the previous summer Sir Nicholas O'Conor, British Ambassador in Constantinople, had reviewed the situation in a despatch. It was unpleasant to contemplate the construction of a railway through Asia Minor to the Persian Gulf in which Great Britain would have no share. This opinion was shared by his chief, who was far more favourable to participation than his cautious words to Metternich in March appeared to suggest. " It would be a great misfortune ", he wrote a month later in a minute, " if this railway were to be constructed without British participation. The line will be a most important highway to the East with a débouché on the Persian Gulf. It is clearly for our interest that the enterprise should be given an international character and that we should have our full share in the control of the line as well as of any advantages to be derived from its construction and maintenance." He had made inquiries in the City and had learned that the financiers were not likely to come forward unless the Government showed its confidence in the enterprise by material support.

The final Convention between the Turkish Government and the Anatolian Railway Company was signed on March 5, 1903, extending the line from Konia to Basra, via Adana, Mosul and Baghdad, with branches to Aleppo, Urfa, Khanikin and other cities north and south of the main track. The concession included conditional permission to work all minerals within twenty kilometres each side of the line, to construct ports at Baghdad and Basra, and to navigate the rivers in the service of the railway. It was a glittering prize which required British good will to turn to the fullest account. Discussions with Sir Ernest Cassel and with the houses of Rothschild, Baring and Morgan led to the selection of Lord Revelstoke to represent the British group ; and on March 23 the Foreign Secretary conveyed the desired assurances to the head of the Baring firm. The Government would agree to a reasonable increase of the Turkish Customs, part of which would go towards the kilometric guarantee. If the new route offered substantial advantages for the carriage of mails and passengers to India, use would be made of the line. Thirdly the Government would help to secure a terminus at or near Koweit. The proposal of Dr. Gwinner, Chairman of the Anatolian Railway Company, was that the French, German and British groups should each have twenty-five per cent. of the capital of the Baghdad Railway Company, and the Anatolian Company ten per cent., while the remaining fifteen per cent. would be held in Austria, Switzerland and other countries.

At this point, when the goal seemed to be in sight, a sharp attack was opened by a section of the Conservative press. On April 7 the Foreign Secretary told Revelstoke and Cassel that, until the strength of the movement could be judged, the Government must hold its hand. He added that in his view the campaign was founded on misapprehension, and he strongly deprecated any change of attitude. The financiers replied that they had in no way committed the Government, adding that if the negotiations were continued the constitution of the Board of Directors and other details would not be settled without official approval. In their view the participations should take place on the basis of absolute equality between the British, French and German interests. On the same day the Prime Minister, in reply to anxious inquiries in Parliament, announced that conversations were in progress with British capitalists. The suggestions for equality of capital and control, the raising of the Turkish tariff, the carriage of the Indian mails, and the provision of a terminus near Koweit, would be carefully considered. Whether we co-operated or not, he added, the railway would be built. French and German financiers were in agreement. We had to consider whether it was desirable that the shortest route to India should be entirely in foreign hands ; whether the terminus should be at Koweit, within our own sphere of influence, and finally whether British trade would benefit if British capital were represented. " I think that this great international artery ", he concluded, " should be in the hands of three Powers rather than of two or one. It is to our interest that countries which we cannot absorb should not be absorbed by others."

The Foreign Secretary remained unaffected by the attacks in Parliament and the press, and in a comprehensive memorandum of April 14 he expressed his hope that the Cabinet would authorise the British group to continue negotiations. " Although our abstention may have the effect of retarding the completion of the line, I feel little doubt that it will eventually be made. That it should be made without British participation would, to my mind, be a national misfortune. It will be a most important highway to the East. It will shorten the journey to India by about three days. It will open up new regions, some of which will certainly prove rich and productive. It will have a terminus on the Persian Gulf, in which our interests are supreme. I submit that we ought not to let such a line be made over our heads, and that we should insist upon having our full share in its control, as well as in any advantages to be derived from its construction. But for the anti-German fever from which the country is suffering, I am convinced that we should be unanimously supported in holding and acting upon these views, nor, so far as I am able to judge, has the attempt to discredit us for having consented to examine the project with an open mind produced much effect on the public. . . . My strong conviction is that, in all cases such as this, the best plan is to treat the question as one of common and international interest."

Despite this vigorous advocacy and the sympathy of the Prime Minister it proved impossible to secure the assent of Chamberlain and other members of the Cabinet. Balfour announced on April 23 that the proposals from the German side failed to provide the international control of the enterprise and the equality of status for the British group that was desired. The decision was greeted by the bulk of Unionist opinion with relief as an escape from the embrace of a Power which for years had been growing steadily more unpopular. On the other hand it was deplored by the director of the Ottoman Bank, who considered that the participation of British and French groups would have insured the international character of the enterprise, and by O'Conor, our Ambassador in Constantinople, who regretted that a question of such importance should have been decided by a temporary surge of opinion. "We have had a sharp recrudescence of the anti-German fever over the Baghdad Railway question," reported the disappointed Foreign Secretary to the Viceroy of India on April 24. . . .[1] "I believe, however, that we had the game very much in our own hands, and that we might have done a great stroke by getting rid of the existing Anatolian Railway as a German enterprise, and substituting for it an international line from sea to sea upon conditions which would have

[1] Newton, 254.

permanently secured for it and for its terminus on the Persian
Gulf an international character. . . . Whether we shall ever
again have as good a chance of insisting on our own terms I
do not know." The failure of the negotiations with the
British group was followed by the refusal of the French Government to sanction the participation of the French group in an enterprise which was in any case notoriously distasteful to Russia.

In talking over the matter with the British Ambassador at
Constantinople at the end of the year, Dr. Gwinner attributed
the breakdown of the negotiations with the British syndicate
entirely to the outburst of public opinion. He had practically
accepted the terms, but the British financiers had not cared to
expose themselves to the ill-feeling of political circles and the
City. A frank minute on O'Conor's report of the conversation reveals that the attitude of the Foreign Secretary was
unchanged. " It is to be observed that he admits frankly that
the insensate outcry which arose against the scheme had the
effect of choking off the British financiers quite as much as the
British Government. If it had not been for the ' scuttle ' of
the financiers, I should have been in favour of sticking to our
position." It was the principal disappointment of Lansdowne's memorable term of office. It was not only, in his
eyes, the loss of an excellent opportunity for co-operation in a
desirable enterprise, but a symbol of the growing estrangement
between two great nations. It was equally regretted, both at
the time and in later years, by that unflinching champion of
Anglo-German understanding, Sir Frank Lascelles, the
British Ambassador at Berlin, who saw in it a needless widening
of the gulf that had already begun to yawn. Writing in 1905
Lord Esher expressed the opinion that, if the Committee of
Imperial Defence had been in full working order in 1903, the
decision would have gone the other way.[1] Though the fact
was not grasped at the time, it was the last real chance of a
détente before the Moroccan controversy and the Flottenpolitik
combined to drive the countries and the peoples apart.

The Baghdad discussions were quickly followed by the
revival of a troublesome controversy. The grant by Canada
in 1897 of a preference on imports from the mother country
had elicited protests from Germany and Belgium against the
breach of most-favoured-nation treatment.[2] Salisbury had
replied by giving the year's notice required to terminate the

[1] Journals and Letters of Viscount Esher, II, 82.
[2] v. Correspondence with the Governments of Belgium and Germany, 1903.

Treaties and suggested a new agreement, allowing the self-governing Colonies to make their own arrangements for inter-imperial trade. According to German law the general or higher tariff came automatically into force on the termination of a commercial treaty ; but the Wilhelmstrasse, in order to afford time for negotiations, continued most-favoured-nation treatment for a year to every part of the British Empire except Canada. This provisional arrangement was annually renewed till 1901, when it was prolonged till the end of 1903.

On March 18, 1903, Lansdowne inquired what action Germany intended to take. Richthofen, the Foreign Secretary, replied that he hoped to prolong most-favoured-nation treatment to Great Britain, but that, if Germany were differentiated against in important parts of the empire, or if, in particular, South Africa followed the example of Canada, public opinion might object. At this point a new element of discord was introduced by the insertion of a clause in the Canadian tariff imposing a surtax of ten per cent. on the goods of any country which discriminated against imports from Canada. In explaining this decision Lansdowne pointed out that it was only taken after the failure of every effort to secure fair treatment of Canadian produce, and would be revoked if Germany restored most-favoured-nation terms. Should the German Government persist in its attitude, and extend to the products of other British Colonies, and even to those of Great Britain, the discrimination enforced against Canada, a very serious issue would be raised.

Each country had a grievance against the other, and on June 27 Richthofen set forth the German case in a lengthy despatch. The maintenance of the lower tariff, he argued, revealed a special desire to meet the wishes of Great Britain, and the application of the general tariff to Canada, far from inflicting a penalty, was merely the automatic consequence of the expiration of the Treaty. If the British Colonies were free to determine their own Customs policy, other countries must be allowed to treat them as separate units. The responsibility for the conflict could not be laid on Germany ; but the Government was ready for an exchange of ideas, and would leave it to Great Britain to make suitable proposals. To this apologia Lansdowne launched a spirited rejoinder. Canada had not increased the duties on German goods or treated Germany differently from other countries. She had been made to suffer because she refused to extend to Germany, as to all other Powers, a special concession made to the mother country. If it were true that the Colonies were independent Customs units, which foreign Powers were at liberty to treat as such, Great Britain could not be held responsible for their acts. Having thus given vent to his indignation at the threat to chastise the mother-country for the generosity of one of her children, the Foreign Secretary concluded by promising to approach any discussion of the difference in a most conciliatory spirit. Since, however, the British market was too valuable to risk for considerations of logic or pride, and since German trade with Canada continued to increase despite the preference, no more was heard of retaliation. The Canadian controversy, none the less, had added to the store of ill will accumulating between the two nations. The dream of finding in Berlin an escape from the perils of isolation had vanished, as the Kaiser fully realised when he visited his uncle at Sandringham at the end of 1902.

V

With the conclusion of the South African conflict warmer airs began to blow across the Channel. The Dreyfus case was liquidated, and the memories of Fashoda were growing dim. Salisbury had gone, and Chamberlain's eyes were no longer riveted on Berlin. Though Monson's despatches still bewailed the prevailing Anglophobia, he gratefully recognised the friendliness of Delcassé and President Loubet. On August 6, 1902, the French Ambassador, after one or two informal exchanges, officially explained the ideas of his chief.[1] The French Government were " partisans du statu quo partout ". Their colonial dominions were as large as they required. French colonial policy was therefore essentially conservative, and Delcassé believed that it would be possible for the two countries to keep in step. The only points where the position was insecure were Morocco and Siam. In the latter the rights of France needed to be clarified. In the former, with her Algerian frontier, France could not allow any external influence. She did not desire the Moroccan question to reach an acute stage, but it would be desirable for the two Governments to discuss their action if the country passed into liquidation. Spain, who would have to be reckoned with, must have the hinterland of her coast possessions. Tangier should be internationalised. Lansdowne deprecated the raising of the

[1] B.D II ch. 14.

question, for Italy, Spain and Germany were also concerned. Any attempt to deal prematurely with the liquidation of Morocco would lead to serious consequences. He could, however, make no official reply to so important a communication without consulting his colleagues.

When the conversation was renewed after the holidays Cambon explained the new Franco-Siamese agreement, on which Lansdowne reserved his judgment. In reference to Morocco the Ambassador, after reiterating his suspicions of Kaid Maclean, renewed his plea for an understanding. England, he assumed, was concerned with Tangier, not with the interior. Lansdowne refused to accept such a simplified conception of British interests, adding that the proposed French terms for a possible " liquidation " of Morocco seemed unacceptable. The French Government, replied the Ambassador, had no desire to bring about a premature liquidation, but they wished by an agreement to diminish the chances of it becoming necessary. Lansdowne gave no encouragement, and a rebellion in Morocco at the close of the year led him to fear that the French might take advantage of a catastrophe and renew their overture for an arrangement.

British policy at this moment was defined in a memorandum drawn up for Kaid Maclean. The Sultan proposed that Great Britain, with or without Germany, should guarantee the integrity of Morocco for seven years,—the guarantee to lapse if the Sultan did not thoroughly reform the administration and develop the resources of his country. The memorandum replied that the integrity of Morocco concerned other states in addition to Great Britain and Germany, and that no disturbance of the status quo appeared to be in contemplation. " As for ourselves we have always regarded and still regard the Moorish question as one in which we have a special interest ; but any attempt to interfere with the integrity and independence of Morocco would be a matter of general concern, and there is not the slightest chance of any one Power being given a free hand in that country. Great Britain will not acquiesce in such an attempt." The memorandum concluded by approving the proposals to offer the Moorish loan in England, France and Germany and to distribute railway concessions between the three Powers. It was a striking declaration of policy, both in its repudiation of the policy of a free hand for France and in its acceptance of Germany's equality of status.

On the last day of 1902 Cambon again explained the desire of the French Government to maintain the status quo and to abstain from interference in Moroccan affairs. If, however, intervention became inevitable, only the interested Powers should participate. When Lansdowne asked the meaning of this phrase, the Ambassador replied without hesitation that Germany was the Power which his Government desired to exclude. Had Italy no interest in Morocco? inquired Lansdowne. " He replied unhesitatingly that she had none, and his manner left me in no doubt that a clear understanding upon the point exists between France and Italy." It was the first hint of Delcassé's secret agreement which reached Downing Street. Lansdowne was relieved that the proposal of dividing Morocco into French, British and Spanish spheres of influence explained to him in August had not reappeared, and that France was back on the platform of the status quo. His own policy was perfectly clear,—to maintain the status quo as long as possible, to prevent any attempt to deal with Morocco without regard to British interests, and to keep in close touch with Spain.

In March 1903 the improvement in Anglo-French relations led King Edward to propose an official journey to Paris. Lansdowne favoured the plan, and the visit broke the rapidly thinning ice. The British Ambassador described its success as more complete than the most sanguine optimist could have foreseen.[1] The speech which won the heart of France breathed a warmth rare in royal utterances. " It is scarcely necessary to tell you with what sincere pleasure I find myself once more in Paris, to which, as you know, I have paid very frequent visits with ever-increasing pleasure, and for which I feel an attachment fortified by so many happy and ineffaceable memories. The days of hostility between the two countries are, I am certain, happily at an end. I know of no two countries whose prosperity is more interdependent. There may have been misunderstandings and causes of dissension in the past, but that is happily over and forgotten. The friendship of the two countries is my constant preoccupation, and I count on you all, who enjoy French hospitality in this magnificent city, to aid me to reach this goal."

The royal share in the momentous transformation which followed has been exaggerated by foreign observers, ignorant

[1] Monson's description of the visit is printed in B.D. VI, 762–8. cp. Lee, King Edward VII, II, 236–243.

of the working of British institutions.   " The King ", writes
Lord Sanderson, " did much to promote an atmosphere of
good will; but he did not start the notion nor take any active
part in the details."   " His visit gave a great impetus to the
movement," declares Lansdowne in his official survey of the
influences which were to produce the agreements of 1904.
These guarded tributes secure for Edward VII the honourable
mention which is his due among the architects of the *entente
cordiale*, and the importance of the visit to Paris was obvious
from the first.   The tide that had been flowing in one direction
ever since the British occupation of Egypt in 1882 had turned.
" A new Triple Alliance is in process of formation ", wrote
Eckardstein from Paris to the German Chancellor.   They
were prophetic words.

Three months later President Loubet returned the visit, the
first French Chief of the State to cross the Channel since
Napoleon III.   The royal host welcomed his guest with an
exuberance unusual on such ceremonial occasions.   " I hope
that the welcome you have received to-day has convinced you
of the true friendship, indeed I will say the affection, which my
country feels for France.   I shall never forget the reception
that was recently given to me, and the sentiments which I now
express are those which I have always entertained.   I hope
our countries will always retain the most intimate relations and
the deepest friendship."   In crediting his subjects with
affection for France the King overshot the mark.   Yet the
atmosphere had certainly changed, and now it was possible for
the diplomatists to get to work.   Edward VII had taken no
Minister with him to Paris ; but the situation had developed,
and Loubet was significantly accompanied by Delcassé.   The
latter had sent a message through Cambon that he would be
glad to discuss certain questions which had formed the theme
of conversations between Lansdowne and the Ambassador.

A full dress rehearsal of the performance took place on July
2, when Etienne, the leader of the French Colonial group,
called at the Foreign Office.[1]   Though not at that time a
Minister and making no claim to speak with official authority,
his conversation anticipated that of Delcassé five days later so
closely that he may be reasonably regarded as sent to explore
the ground.   He was paying a short visit to England, he
explained, in the hope of promoting a good understanding
between the two countries.   There seemed to him no really

[1] *B.D.* II, ch. 15.   The French material is in *D.D.F.* Vols. III and IV.

serious points of divergence, and the moment appeared
particularly propitious for a rapprochement. He laid special
stress on the necessity of coming to terms with regard to
Morocco, where France, owing to her position in Algeria,
must have a preponderating influence. The Tangier coast
could be neutralised and the trade of Morocco should be free
to all. The Newfoundland dispute could be settled; the
New Hebrides might be partitioned; France had abandoned
the idea of annexing Siam; a slight territorial revision was
needed in West Africa. The gravest menace to peace came
from Germany, and a good understanding between France and
England was the only means of holding her designs in check.
If it could be reached, England would find that France would
be able to exercise a salutary influence over Russia. While
non-committal in regard to details, Lansdowne warmly welcomed the prospect of a reasonable " give-and-take " arrangement. If the French Government would put their cards on
the table, we should be ready to meet them in a similar spirit.

When the two Foreign Ministers met in Downing Street for
the first time on July 7 each knew a good deal of the mind of
the other, not only from the Etienne conversation but from
the previous exchanges with Paul Cambon. These discussions, began Lansdowne, though they had led to no definite
result, had convinced him that the points at issue between the
two Governments were few in number and by no means
incapable of adjustment. Delcassé replied that this view was
shared not only by himself but by the Chamber. The French
Government had ceased to desire a wide extension of their
colonial possessions, wishing rather to consolidate them and
to remove all sources of future trouble within them and on
their frontiers.

The first topic of the historic conversation was Newfoundland. France, explained Delcassé, was chiefly concerned with
the supply of bait for her fishermen. The fish, which had of
late deserted the French Shore, might return, and any surrender
of French rights would be resented unless sufficient compensation was secured. Lansdowne replied that the Newfoundland
fishermen complained of the French system of bounties. He
had discussed with Cambon a settlement on the basis of the
withdrawal of the French from the French Shore, with compensation to the persons engaged in the fishing industry, while
the French fishermen would receive facilities for a free supply
of bait on the Newfoundland coast. The Ambassador had

suggested territorial as well as financial compensation, and the demand, though surprising, had not been altogether rejected. Though the surrender of Gambia was out of the question, concessions might perhaps be made elsewhere. It was for the French to make proposals.

Delcassé was ready with his plan, and indeed he had sought the conversation in order to press it. An understanding about Newfoundland, he explained, depended on the British attitude to French interests in Morocco. An agreement on Morocco would remove all other difficulties or render them comparatively easy to liquidate. There was no desire to get rid of the Sultan or to annex the country. The French Government wished to maintain his rule and had no desire to force the pace, as they had shown by their self-denying policy on the Algerian frontier. His authority, however, was waning rapidly and was incapable of maintaining order. France could not tolerate chronic disorder in Morocco, and it was her business to regenerate the country. She desired an assurance that England would not obstruct her policy.

The British Government, replied Lansdowne, had shown in the last two years that it recognised her right to take measures for the pacification of the Algerian frontier, and had accepted the assurances that the recent operations had been merely punitive in character. It was unlikely that England would ever take a leading part in the pacification of the interior of Morocco in the event of anarchy. Sir Harry Maclean was indeed the Sultan's military adviser, but the resulting suspicion that England was trying to interfere in the internal affairs of Morocco was unfounded. The Sultan, doubtless alarmed by French activity on the Algerian frontier, had naturally turned to England for assistance and had frequently sought her advice. Our counsel had been of a kind to which France could not object. The British Government had urged him to give reasonable facilities for trade and to avoid extravagance. When he had needed money, he had been advised to apply not to any one country but to the three Powers most interested in preserving his authority. On the other hand England could not be indifferent to the fate of Morocco. We were largely interested in the Mediterranean seaboard, particularly Tangier and the neighbouring coast. Secondly we could make no arrangement affecting the balance of power in Morocco without considering and consulting Spain. Thirdly equality of opportunity for British commerce must be retained. The

D

three conditions were unhesitatingly accepted by Delcassé. The Tangier seaboard would be neutralised ; a satisfactory compromise would be reached with Spain ; and there would be no difficulty about the open door.

Turning to Siam Delcassé claimed that the agreement of 1886 involved the recognition of French claims in the valley of the Mekong and of England in the Malay peninsula. Salisbury, rejoined Lansdowne, had rejected this interpretation, for England had treaty rights in the Mekong valley. There was no desire, replied the French statesman, to contest her right to most-favoured-nation treatment. France merely wished for a preference if railways were to be made by some foreign Power in that region. There was no desire to obstruct French railway enterprise in the Mekong valley, rejoined Lansdowne ; but railways were not commerce, and for commerce the door must be kept open. When he asked for his visitor's solution of the problem of French and British interests in the New Hebrides, Delcassé replied that, if an agreement on Morocco was reached, the New Hebrides question could be easily settled. In regard to Sokoto he pleaded for a revision of boundaries which would enable French convoys from the Niger to reach Lake Chad by a shorter route—a request which was promised favourable consideration as a part of a general settlement.

At this point Lansdowne introduced the question of Egypt, to which he had made no reference in his interview with Etienne. No one believed that we were likely to retire from that country, and Lord Cromer reported that the French and British representatives in Egypt were on excellent terms. But it might still be possible for France, if she chose, to give us trouble in matters of detail, and this possibility would need to be considered if a general settlement were to be sought. Delcassé replied that he was entirely in favour of a comprehensive settlement, and that the Egyptian question formed part of the larger African question which, he felt sure, could be satisfactorily settled if only an agreement on Morocco could be reached.

" Throughout our conversation ", concluded Lansdowne's report on the most important interview in his life, " M. Delcassé spoke apparently with the utmost sincerity, and he did not attempt to disguise from me the immense importance which the French Government attached to obtaining from us a recognition of the predominance which they desired to obtain in Morocco. The impression which he evidently desired to leave upon my mind was that, in order to secure our acquiescence, they would, in regard to Morocco itself, accept conditions upon which we should probably desire to insist, whilst they would at other points go very far indeed to comply with our requirements." Here, indeed, were the firm outlines of a world-wide settlement acceptable to both sides. The conversations with Etienne and Delcassé were promptly reported to Cromer, who was as delighted as he was surprised.[1] The negotiation, he advised, should proceed on the basis of recognition by the French that Egypt fell within our sphere of influence, as Morocco would fall within theirs. "What it really amounts to is this : that everything depends on our attitude as regards Morocco."

On July 29 Cambon presented Delcassé's views in further detail, but to Lansdowne's surprise he made no reference to Egypt. When the Foreign Secretary observed that it could not be excluded, the Ambassador replied that he had no instructions on the subject, and suggested that it should be left alone for the present—a plan promptly dismissed by the Foreign Secretary. It was the first indication of formidable difficulties ahead. A week later the conversation was confined to Morocco, which for the first time was thoroughly discussed. His chief, reported Cambon, believed no difference of opinion to exist. The difficulties, rejoined Lansdowne, would begin when they came to details. The French proposals for commercial freedom, the neutralisation of a part of the coast, and the recognition of Spanish interests were merely outlines which would have to be filled in with the utmost care. Moreover, he had consented to deal with Morocco only as part of a general settlement of outstanding questions. The British Cabinet, which he had informed of the negotiations, was unanimous on the inclusion of Egypt, where the regularisation of the British position must be reached. Delcassé, replied Cambon, had understood Lansdowne to refer merely to the removal of inconvenient financial restrictions : a formal recognition of the British position was a much more serious affair. France felt strongly on the matter. She had missed her opportunity in Egypt. The English had seized theirs, but they had announced that the occupation was not to be permanent. The French nation clung to this pledge, though without a very definite expectation that it would be fulfilled.

[1] Zetland, *Lord Cromer*, ch. 24.

A government proposing to recognise its permanence would require plenty of nerve. His chief was not lacking in courage and was prepared to try. If France removed this big thorn from the foot of Great Britain, she would look for a commensurate compensation such as greater liberty of action in Morocco than she had hitherto proposed. Moreover the Egyptian question concerned other Powers. If England wanted concessions in Egypt, she should say what they were. Lansdowne promised a statement of his demands, adding that, if the British Government were to satisfy the French in Morocco, it would also require nerve to justify its proposals to the British people.

In speaking of Spain the Ambassador declared that negotiations had been opened a year ago, but that the approach, though favourably received, had led to no agreement. If a partition of Morocco became inevitable, Spain was to receive a considerable slice of the coast and hinterland near her possessions, including Tangier. She would, however, be bound not to fortify or alienate her zone. Complete neutralisation of any part of the coast was impossible, as it would involve the adhesion of other Powers. It would suffice if England, France and Spain agreed not to fortify or allow other Powers to fortify within certain limits. What would Germany say to such an arrangement ? inquired Lansdowne. Germany, replied Cambon, had at one time wished for a coaling station, but nothing had recently been heard of German designs in Morocco. At the close of the conversation Lansdowne announced his intention of telling the Spanish Government that he would do nothing behind its back, and would see that its interests were adequately secured. Cambon agreed that Spain might be told that both Governments fully recognised the necessity of giving her satisfaction. A few days after this conversation the Foreign Minister instructed his Ambassador at Madrid to inform the Spanish Government of the negotiations and to obtain its views. He was also to deny the idle rumours attributing to England aggressive designs on Spanish possessions.

After the summer holidays Lansdowne gave Cambon, " unofficially and confidentially ", the promised statement of his views under eight heads. The Morocco section elaborated the three conditions laid down on July 7. Our commercial rights under a treaty of 1856 must remain intact, for British trade with Morocco was double that of France. The seaboard from the Algerian frontier to Mazaghan should remain unoccupied and unfortified by any Power. The interests of Spain should be first discussed between the French and Spanish Governments, but a certain amount of territory adjoining her possessions should be recognised as destined to fall under her influence. If the Sultan's authority collapsed, she should administer, though not fortify or alienate, the seaboard from the Algerian frontier to Mazaghan.

The section on Egypt, the most important part of the memorandum, stated British claims in unambiguous terms. " His Majesty's Government have no desire to alter the political status of Egypt, or, so far as Powers other than France are concerned, to raise at this moment questions affecting the international position of Great Britain in that country. They desire, however, that the Government of the French Republic should recognise that the British occupation of Egypt, which was originally intended to be temporary, has, under the force of circumstances, acquired a character of permanency. It would therefore, as between Great Britain and France, be understood that the period of its duration should be left entirely to the discretion of His Majesty's Government." Passing to details, the memorandum asked for the termination of the Caisse de la Dette and for a free hand at a later date, so far as France was concerned, in regard to the Capitulations. The British Government would be ready to give France the same freedom in Morocco if and when she became so predominant as to assume responsibility for the good government of the country. In regard to Newfoundland Lansdowne put forward proposals for dealing with bait and bounties, and accepted the principle of a modest territorial compensation for the surrender of French treaty rights. In Siam the Declaration of 1896 should be supplemented by a further Declaration, disclaiming all idea of annexation but defining the zones of influence of the two Powers. The French plan of a partition of the New Hebrides would be unacceptable to Australia and New Zealand, but the request for a revision of the boundary of Sokoto was accepted as part of a bargain, for instance in return for the surrender of treaty rights in Newfoundland. Some trifling differences in the Sultanate of Zanzibar should be settled, and the British Government would discontinue its claims and protests arising out of the annexation of Madagascar. Lansdowne had now laid all his cards on the table, slightly widening the field of discussion in the process, and confronting France with the necessity of an unpopular decision in the valley of the Nile. A few days later Cambon, who had seen Delcassé in the interval, commented caustically on the British terms. The two questions which really mattered were Morocco and Egypt. His chief had not expected the whole Egyptian question to be raised, and he found the proposals very far-reaching. France, he argued, would not receive in Morocco a sufficient equivalent for the immense concessions which she was asked to make ; for England's gain would be immediate, while she only gave France a hope. Lansdowne rejoined that France would also receive immediate advantages, while she was merely invited to recognise existing facts. Cambon retorted that in the field of Egyptian finance France had the same rights as England, and she was being asked to abdicate in favour of the latter. Moreover in Morocco, after England had made way for her, she would have to deal with other Powers. Spain would be difficult, for she was already suspicious, while German pretensions must be taken into account. Why should not France and England carry out their programme of reform of the Capitulations and the Egyptian Debt gradually and *pari passu* ? Lansdowne politely but firmly rejected the suggestion of gradual and parallel advance. To the request for the recognition of the permanence of the occupation of Egypt he expected an immediate Yes or No. England, he added, would also have other Powers to reckon with in Egypt, like France in Morocco. In taking such a firm line he reckoned on the ultimate willingness of Delcassé to pay a high price for his aims. When Cambon complained that the British plan gave Spain far too much seaboard in the event of a liquidation of Morocco, Lansdowne replied that there were hardly any important ports in that area. In closing the conversation he begged for a speedy reply, mindful of Cromer's shrewd advice to settle before the French mood had time to change.

The French reply was set forth in a letter from Cambon on October 26. After an uncontroversial section on Morocco, Delcassé conveyed the assurance which, from the British point of view, formed the essence of the deal. " Le Gouvernement du Roi ayant reconnu la tâche qui incombe à la France au Maroc et pour laquelle pleine liberté d'action lui est laissée, le Gouvernement de la République se déclarera disposé à ne point entraver l'action de l'Angleterre en Egypte et à ne pas

demander qu'un terme soit fixé à l'occupation Britannique."
France, he added, would allow the proceeds of the conversions
of 1890 to be used for public works in Egypt and accepted
reciprocity in the ultimate abolition of the Capitulations.
When she had established effective financial control in
Morocco, she would renounce her part in the financial control
of Egypt and her right to oppose conversion of the debt. The
letter proposed the cession of Gambia, an enclave in French
West Africa, in return for the surrender of French rights in
Newfoundland, and expressed regret that the partition of the
New Hebrides was ruled out.

Lansdowne's maxim throughout the most momentous
discussions of his life was firmness in Egypt and pliability
elsewhere. His reply of November 19 flatly refused to defer
the surrender of France's rights in the financial control of
Egypt till her effective control of the finances of Morocco was
secured. The suggested cession of Gambia was also categorically declined, and a revision ·of the boundaries of Nigeria
offered in its place. The French refusal to abolish bounties to
the French fishermen in Newfoundland provoked the reply
that in that case they could not purchase bait in the island
outside the French Shore. It was clear from the slight under-
tone of annoyance in the letter that the negotiations were
proving more troublesome than he had expected. The chief
difficulties, it was now clear, lay in Egypt and Newfoundland.

Cambon returned on December 9 after a visit to Paris,
bringing copious notes of the conversations with his chief.
While complaining that France was asked to surrender her
financial rights in Egypt without delay, he made advances
towards the British standpoint which Cromer, who was consulted at every turn of the path, pronounced very satisfactory.
Delcassé emphasised his responsibility for the interests of the
French bondholders, which Lansdowne was ready to help him
to fulfil. Once more Gambia was demanded, and once again it
was refused. The tone of the conversation, however, was
warmer than on the previous occasion, and Cambon's earnest
desire for a settlement was evident throughout. For the
first time the Ambassador referred to German designs on
Morocco, which Delcassé proposed to thwart by including in
the Anglo-French settlement the maintenance of the status quo
within a radius of 500 miles from the Straits of Gibraltar, which
would include the Balearic Isles. After a Cabinet discussion
Lansdowne rejected the plan as outside the scope of the

proposed arrangement. On the other hand, in a memorandum of December 24, he explained his plans for securing the interests of the French bondholders, and suggested the issue of a Khedival decree embodying the final arrangement.

When agreement in regard to Morocco and Egypt appeared within sight, the problem of compensation in West Africa for the surrender of French rights in Newfoundland loomed up as a formidable obstacle. Though Lansdowne had accepted the principle, he felt that a small sacrifice was enough. He had rejected the insistent demand for Gambia, and on January 5, 1904, he declined the request for a large tract on the Niger in the hinterland of Lagos which had been assured to England in the agreement of 1898. A week later Cambon reported Delcassé's great regret at the decision, as there was a strong feeling in France on the subject of Newfoundland, and observed that it would be a grievous misfortune if the negotiations, which had proceeded so satisfactorily, should break down on this point. The Egyptian part of the question, he added, was virtually settled since Sir Eldon Gorst's visit to Paris at Christmas. The British offer of a rectification of the frontier north of Sokoto was quite unsubstantial. Could not the Foreign Minister propose something else? Lansdowne replied that he had no authority from the Cabinet to do so. Five days later Cambon reported Delcassé's dissatisfaction with the Sokoto offer, and Lansdowne gravely rejoined that the decision seemed to bring the negotiations to a deadlock.

At this moment Cromer, who was terrified at the possibility of losing the glittering prize that was almost within his grasp, intervened with an urgent telegram from Cairo. " I have little doubt from what I hear on the spot that the danger of a breakdown of the negotiations is serious. I venture to urge most strongly the necessity either of making concessions which will enable the Newfoundland question to be settled or of dealing with Morocco and Egypt separately. The former is by far the best solution but the latter is preferable to doing nothing. To allow negotiations to break down now would in my opinion be little short of a calamity, whether from the general or the local Egyptian point of view. Also I cannot but think that it would be severely criticised by the public who already know more or less what is going on. It has to be borne in mind that the French concessions to us in Egypt are in reality far more valuable than those we are making to them in Morocco, and moreover that they can hamper us greatly here, whereas if they choose they can carry out their Morocco policy without our help. They are perfectly well aware of this. Further, the recognition of the Occupation removes what must otherwise always remain a source of danger to peace. I cannot but think that this point, which appears to me of the utmost importance, would be understood in England and would serve as an adequate justification for some concessions elsewhere."

It is hardly fanciful to connect this forcible appeal from Cairo with the altered tone of the Foreign Secretary two days later. The Cabinet, he told Cambon, would grant facilities for French trade on the Niger or the Gambia river in addition to the Sokoto plan, and the Ambassador expressed a desire for the Isles de Los, opposite the capital of French Guinea. The new British plan, set forth in detail in a letter of February 5, offered to cede the islands, but on condition that France should allow British protection over the New Hebrides. Lansdowne can scarcely have expected acceptance of such a scheme, which Delcassé promptly rejected. The cession of the Isles de Los eased the situation, and the next fortnight was devoted to elaborating the West African settlement. On March 11 Cambon, just back from Paris, reported the view of his chief that, subject to one or two details, the negotiations were complete. The French Government would probably make a declaration to Germany, but did not propose any public announcement of its intentions in the event of the existing régime in Morocco breaking down. To this plan of a secret document dealing with the liquidation of Morocco Lansdowne saw no objection. The Foreign Minister was in high spirits. "The French negotiations", he wrote to Cromer on March 14, "after sticking in all sorts of ignoble ruts, suddenly began to travel at the rate of an express train. I attribute Delcassé's desire to get on quickly partly to doubts as to the stability of his own Government, and partly to similar suspicions of the stability of ours."[1]

At the eleventh hour, to Lansdowne's surprise and alarm, Delcassé strove to reopen the question of the Newfoundland fisheries and to evade a formal recognition of England's right to remain indefinitely in Egypt. He was quite unable to understand the Minister's attitude, telegraphed the Foreign Minister to Monson at midnight on March 30. Both sides had agreed months ago to restrict the right of French fishermen to buy bait on the French shore. "The French Government

[1] Zetland, *Lord Cromer*, 281.

now reinsert a clause giving them the right of obtaining bait
throughout the whole coast. We shall certainly break off the
negotiations if this demand is pressed. Do you think M.
Delcassé really knows the history of the case or understands
the utter unreasonableness of making this demand at the
eleventh hour after concessions on each side have been carefully balanced ? " He had been scared by the prospect of
a deputation representing the Newfoundland fisheries and
capable of stirring up serious Parliamentary trouble, but on
receiving Lansdowne's sharp protest he gave way. On the
British occupation of Egypt the Foreign Secretary also held
his ground. On the New Hebrides no agreement could be
reached.

The agreements were signed by Lansdowne and Cambon on
April 8, and were published with a full explanatory memorandum by the Foreign Secretary. A settlement, he began, had
been notoriously desired on both sides of the Channel. The
movement had received a powerful impetus from the visit of
the King to Paris, and the return visit of the President accompanied by Delcassé to London. The conversation with " the
distinguished statesman who has so long presided over the
French Ministry of Foreign Affairs " had left no doubt that a
mutually advantageous settlement was within reach. The
wide knowledge and diplomatic experience of the French
Ambassador had been of the greatest assistance throughout.[1]

The survey opened with Egypt and Morocco. British
interests in the latter, argued Lansdowne, had been fully
safeguarded, and the importance of the agreement in regard
to the former could not be overrated. " It is true that the
other Great Powers of Europe also enjoy, in virtue of existing
arrangements, a privileged position in Egypt ; but the interests
of France—historical, political and financial—so far outweigh
those of the other Powers, with the exception of Great Britain,
that so long as we work in harmony with France there seems
no reason to anticipate difficulty at the hands of the other
Powers." After explaining in detail the nature of the settlement he ended on an optimistic note. The arrangement,
taken as a whole, would be to the advantage of both parties.
" And it may, perhaps, be permitted to them to hope that, in
thus basing the composition of longstanding differences upon

---

[1] Hallmann, *Methoden Paul Cambons, Historische Zeitschrift*, Vol. CL, 290–305,
accuses the Ambassador of arousing Lansdowne's suspicions of Germany in
order to facilitate the rapprochement.

mutual concessions and in the frank recognition of each other's legitimate wants and aspirations, they may have afforded a precedent which will contribute to the maintenance of international good will and the preservation of the general peace." These sentences were more than mere words. For Lansdowne it was a colonial agreement, nothing more. The Treaty was the greatest of his achievements, its signature the crown of his career. The intention of encircling Germany never entered his head. Cromer, whose counsel had been beyond price, shared his chief's satisfaction to the full, declaring that it was the happiest day of his life. Except for a shrill protest from Rosebery against handing over Morocco to a great military Power, the settlement was greeted with general acclaim.

The most important of the agreements was the Declaration respecting Egypt and Morocco. Great Britain declared that she had no intention of altering the political status of Egypt, and France undertook not to obstruct our action by asking that a limit of time be fixed to the occupation or in any other way. France, in turn, declared that she had no intention of altering the political status of Morocco, and Great Britain promised not to obstruct her action. In both countries commercial liberty was to prevail for at least thirty years. No fortifications were to be permitted on the coast opposite Gibraltar. France was to come to an understanding with Spain in regard to Morocco, and the contracting parties agreed to afford one another diplomatic support in carrying out the Declaration. A Khedival Decree, annexed to the Declaration, laid down regulations relating to the Egyptian debt, and, subject to acceptance by the Powers, gave the Egyptian Government a free hand in the disposal of its own resources so long as the punctual payment of interest was assured.

Next in importance was the settlement of the Newfoundland fishery dispute, France surrendering certain privileges in return for three British concessions in West Africa. The frontier fixed in 1898 between Gambia and Senegambia was slightly modified to give France access to the navigable portion of the river; the Los Islands were ceded; and the 1898 boundary between British and French Nigeria, which compelled French convoys from the Niger to Lake Chad to follow a circuitous and waterless route or to pass through British territory, was improved. France thus obtained 14,000 square miles and uninterrupted access from her territories on the Niger to those on Lake Chad. A third document contained a Declaration concerning Siam, Madagascar and the New Hebrides. In the former the two Powers confirmed the agreement of 1896, in which they undertook to refrain from armed intervention or the acquisition of special privileges in the basin of the Menam. France now recognized that all Siamese possessions on the west of this neutral zone and of the Gulf of Siam, including the Malay Peninsula and the adjacent islands, should come under British influence, while Great Britain recognised all Siamese territory on the east and southeast of the zone as henceforth under French influence. In Madagascar the British Government abandoned its protest against the tariff introduced after the annexation of the island in 1896. The difficulties in the New Hebrides arising from disputes as to land title and the absence of jurisdiction over the natives were referred to a commission, which in due course established an Anglo-French condominium.

In addition to the treaty announced to the world there were five articles which remained a secret till the crisis of Agadir. The first provided that, if either Government found itself constrained by the force of circumstances to modify its policy in Egypt or Morocco, their published engagements towards each other should remain intact. The second declared that the British Government had no present intention of proposing changes in the Capitulations or the judicial organisation of Egypt. If, however, it were considered desirable to introduce reforms, France would not refuse to entertain the proposals on the understanding that Great Britain would entertain similar French suggestions for Morocco. In the third article the two Governments defined the territory which should come under Spanish influence if the Sultan's authority over it were to cease ; but Spain would have to assent to the treaty and to promise not to alienate any part of her sphere. The fourth declared that the agreement should stand if Spain declined to accept the provisions of the third. The fifth referred to the payment of the Egyptian debt. The important articles were the first and the third, which contemplated the eventual partition of Morocco into French and Spanish zones of influence. To one school of thought these secret transactions were a reasonable precaution in view of the notorious fragility of the Sultan's rule. To the critics of Delcassé, on the other hand, they embodied the goal of his ambition, the public articles merely serving to keep the tree alive till the fruit was ready to pluck. However innocuous they might seem at the time, their makers were playing with fire. There was nothing dishonourable or selfish about them so far as Lansdowne was concerned, for the public treaty gave him all that he wished. They remain nevertheless the feature of his work which it is most difficult for his admirers unreservedly to approve.

VI

For several months after the signing of the treaties of April 8, 1904, there was no immediate cause for anxiety in Downing Street except in regard to the Russo-Japanese war. The Khedival Decree embodying the liberation of Egyptian revenues was promptly accepted by all the Powers concerned except Germany, whose consent was obtained by guarantees for her commerce and her schools. In the long negotiations between France and Spain no international complications were involved, but Lansdowne's good offices proved of the utmost value to the weaker side. He had made consideration of Spain's interests a condition of his assent to French preponderance in Morocco, and in the elaboration of details he insisted that she should have a fair deal. In giving moral support to Spanish claims he was at the same time acting in the interests of France ; for it was essential to the success of Delcassé's Moroccan policy that his southern neighbour should regard it with friendly eyes.

When the Anglo-French treaty was published the Spanish Ambassador confided to Lansdowne that his countrymen were alarmed.[1] They did not relish the prospect of fighting matters out with France, and would have greatly preferred negotiations à trois, in which Spain would have depended on the advice and the assistance of England. Lansdowne replied that it had taken nearly a year to reach agreement with France, and that a triangular discussion would have failed. To the Ambassador's complaint of the danger of allowing France a free hand in preserving order in Morocco and financing the Sultan's Government, Lansdowne retorted that it was virtually bankrupt and that neither Spanish nor British financiers were inclined to help. He had done nothing to prejudice the rights of Spain, having merely promised in certain respects not to stand in the way of France. Friendly and helpful though he was, he did not feel at liberty to reveal to his visitor the provisions of the secret treaty.

[1] B.D. III, ch. 17.

Though the first French proposals for the delimitation of the spheres of influence were enlarged at Lansdowne's wish, the memory of the larger concessions offered by France in 1902 was a sore point at Madrid. Since the reconciliation with England Delcassé's position was immeasurably stronger, and the weaker Power had now to take what it could get. Lansdowne's mediation was most useful, but he could not press France too hard. Throughout the negotiations runs a recurring note of Spanish resentment and alarm. When an agreed delimitation of zones was in sight, the Ambassador visited the Foreign Secretary on July 2 in a state of acute distress. Delcassé wished to prevent Spain taking any action within her sphere of influence until the status quo in Morocco had come to an end. In other words France would be able for an indefinite period to establish her influence in Morocco, and she would so act that Spain could not claim that the status quo had been changed. Nothing would induce her to sign such an article. If she were pressed to do so, she would probably appeal to the Powers,—an observation which Lansdowne interpreted as an attempt to obtain German support.

The Foreign Secretary tactfully advised Delcassé to show a little more consideration. Even if it were recognised that Spain might at once exercise a kind of peaceful penetration within her zone of influence, it was unlikely that she would be able to turn her opportunities to account. It would be a pity not to recognise her aspirations, in theory at all events : a peremptory refusal would have a bad effect and possibly lead to international difficulties. A conciliatory response arrived from Paris, expressing readiness for her to share in the economic development of the country. At a later stage Lansdowne intervened on the other side in regard to a question directly affecting British interests. Delcassé wished Spain to undertake not to alienate any portion of her sphere. The Spanish Government, considering such an obligation beneath her dignity, proposed to give France a preference if she decided to alienate the whole or part. Lansdowne strongly disapproved the refusal to renounce the right of alienation, and the Spanish Government promptly gave way. The summer holidays interrupted the discussions, but the Franco-Spanish agreements were signed on October 3. The published Declaration recorded the adhesion of Spain to the Anglo-French Declaration of April 8, 1904, and the devotion of the signatories to the integrity of the Moroccan Empire under the sovereignty of the Sultan. The most important and the most satisfactory article of the unpublished convention from the English point of view was that in which Spain promised not to alienate, even temporarily, any portion of her zone. In announcing the agreement the Ambassador told Lansdowne that the close watch kept by the British Government on the proceedings had been of the greatest service, and his Government was extremely grateful. It was a well-deserved compliment. Lansdowne had needed all his tact to smooth away the many difficulties, to counsel concessions on both sides without hurting national pride, and to safeguard British interests where directly involved. His countrymen knew nothing of his share in a treaty whose stipulations remained a secret for seven years, but among his diplomatic achievements it takes high rank.

While the Franco-Spanish discussions on Morocco were in progress Lansdowne received indications that another Power might have something to say. The German Chancellor had received the Anglo-French treaty calmly, but on June 1 Metternich expressed serious apprehensions as to the Franco-Spanish negotiations. Germany, he explained, could not remain indifferent if France obtained access to the Mediterranean coast in the neighbourhood of the Straits of Gibraltar. Moreover if the rights and reversionary interests of Spain were to be ignored, Germany might have to give her diplomatic support. The Ambassador described his observations as unofficial, but in the serious exchanges of diplomacy such assurances carry little weight. It was the first rumbling audible in London of the coming storm. The Foreign Secretary replied that nobody proposed to oust Spain from the position she occupied in Morocco, and her negotiations with France were likely to lead to an acceptable agreement. His assurances produced little effect, and on August 15 Metternich returned to the charge, explaining once again that he spoke unofficially. The German Government was anxiously watching events in Morocco. They desired that the status quo so far as possible should be maintained, that the Sultan should remain independent, and that the policy of the open door should prevail. Markets were being closed to German trade all over the world, and they were anxious to keep the Moorish market open. Their commercial treaty with Morocco entitled them to most-favoured-nation treatment without limit of time. This was doubtless enough to prevent unfairness to their trade, but they were not so sure about concessions and industrial enterprises. They detected monopolistic symptoms on the part of France, and they wondered how England would regard such attempts. Did the promise of diplomatic support mean that she would support unfair French treatment of a German concessionaire ? Lansdowne replied that both Powers, as announced in Article IV, were equally attached to the principle of commercial liberty in Egypt and Morocco, and no attempt had been made to dispose of the rights of other Powers. The Ambassador, concluded Lansdowne's report, made it clear that Germany intended to uphold her treaty rights. Similar hints were conveyed to France as the year advanced.

Though the authors of the treaties of April 8, 1904, were delighted to have cleaned the slate, they had no thought at that stage of a political partnership. The agreement, however, of the two Governments " to afford to one another their diplomatic support, in order to obtain the execution of the clauses of the present Declaration regarding Egypt and Morocco ", was an elastic formula the full implications of which were scarcely realised in England at the time. When France, emboldened by her agreement with Great Britain and her secret pacts with Italy and Spain, pushed forward in Morocco with a programme of reforms at the close of the year, Germany, whom Delcassé had unwisely omitted to consult, sharply asserted her rights and her claims. The announcement of the Kaiser's intention to visit Tangier in the spring of 1905 sounded the alarm bell, and his challenging declarations in that city created an international crisis of the first magnitude. In a moment the slumbering embers burst into a flame, and Lansdowne's anxiety was scarcely less than that of Delcassé himself. Convinced as he was that the Anglo-French agreement contained nothing detrimental to the interests of other Powers, he feared that the German Government was out for mischief and might at any moment present an unacceptable demand.

On April 22 the Foreign Secretary despatched an important telegram to Paris.[1] " It seems not unlikely that German Government may ask for a port on the Moorish coast. You are authorised to inform Minister for Foreign Affairs that we should be prepared to join French Government in offering strong opposition to such a proposal and to beg that if question is raised French Government will afford us a full opportunity of conferring with them as to steps which might be taken in

[1] B.D. III, ch. 18.

order to meet it. The German attitude in this dispute seems to me most unreasonable having regard to M. Delcassé's attitude and we desire to give him all the support we can." In expressing his gratitude for this communication Delcassé replied that he had not heard of any step by Germany to obtain a port on the Morocco coast. He would inform the French Minister in Morocco of the possibility of an attempt to secure a concession and instruct him to warn the Sultan. He promised to communicate any information and to consult the British Government as to steps to be taken. Whence Lansdowne received the information that Germany might ask for a port we do not know. A suggestion from the French Ambassador at Madrid that Lascelles might speak privately to the Kaiser about Morocco was forwarded by Lansdowne to Berlin for the Ambassador's opinion on April 23. "I feel considerable doubts as to the wisdom of this suggestion," added the Foreign Minister. "If it were possible for you to say anything which might help to convince the Emperor that German interests were in no way threatened French Government would be grateful, but nothing has yet been said to me on the subject by M. Delcassé." Lascelles thought a personal approach to the Kaiser undesirable, and the project was dropped.

While Lansdowne attributed to Germany the plan of securing a port on the Moorish coast, the Kaiser confided to Roosevelt his fear that England was about to support France in some important declaration of policy concerning Morocco. The British Ambassador in Washington was informed of the President's desire to create better feeling between England and Germany. Roosevelt, it seemed, wished to know Lansdowne's views for communication to the Kaiser. "We have not and never have had any idea of attacking Germany", telegraphed the Foreign Minister in response, "nor do we anticipate that she will be so foolish as to attack us. There is at this moment so far as I am aware no subject of dispute between the two Powers, nor any reason why their relations should not be of a friendly description. As to Morocco we are quite unable to understand why any trouble should arise. Anglo-French agreement contained nothing detrimental to interests of other Powers, and in spite of provocative talk of German Emperor and officials, attitude of French Government is most forbearing and conciliatory. I cannot see why any international complication should be created, unless German

Government is determined to take advantage of what was at most a diplomatic oversight in order to make mischief or to disturb the status quo by demanding cession of a Moorish port." The Ambassador was instructed to say nothing which could be interpreted as an invitation to the President to act as mediator between England and Germany.

On May 3 Cambon attempted to obtain more light on the significance of Lansdowne's declaration of April 22.[1] He did not suppose that the situation would grow worse, though they did not know what the Kaiser had at the back of his mind. He had been annoyed by the agreements in which he did not share, and he disliked Delcassé, whom he hoped to overthrow. "That is true", remarked Lansdowne, "but M. Delcassé is stronger than ever." German designs on Mogador, he added, were beyond dispute. What measures did he contemplate, inquired the Ambassador, if the Kaiser secured such a concession or revealed some design of a still more menacing character? "We are not there yet," replied Lansdowne. "For the moment we must wait and let Germany show her hand. It is enough that she knows we are in complete accord." During these weeks of growing tension ominous reports reached Downing Street from Spain and Italy. On May 5 the British Ambassador at Madrid reported a threat that, if the Spanish Minister in Morocco proceeded to Fez, the German Government would regard it as an unfriendly act. On the same day the British Ambassador at Rome reported menacing language by the German Ambassador. It was no wonder that Downing Street was alarmed, for it looked as if at any moment the situation might get beyond control.

On May 17 a conversation of historic importance took place between Lansdowne and Cambon. The Ambassador complained of German attempts to sow discord between England and France. His chief regarded the situation not as profoundly dangerous, but as a cause of serious preoccupation. The Kaiser, he thought, was calming down, but the German officials were ominously reticent when Morocco was mentioned. "I observed", reported Lansdowne, "that the moral of all these incidents seemed to me to be that our two Governments should continue to treat one another with the most absolute confidence, should keep one another fully informed of everything which came to their knowledge, and should, so

---

[1] D.D.F. VI, 459–61. Lansdowne's report makes no mention of his own observations.

far as possible, discuss in advance any contingencies by which they might in the course of events find themselves confronted. As an instance of our readiness to enter into such timely discussions, I reminded His Excellency of the communication which had recently been made to the French Government by you at a moment when an idea prevailed that Germany might be on the point of demanding the cession of a Moorish port." Cambon's report closes with the words : " Je peux écrire à M. Delcassé que si les circonstances l'exigeaient, que si, par exemple, nous avions des raisons sérieuses de croire à une aggression injustifiée, le Gouvernement britannique serait tout prêt à se concerter avec le Gouvernement Français sur les mesures à prendre. Vous le pouvez, me dit Lord Lansdowne, nous sommes tout prêts."[1]

A week later, desiring to secure written confirmation of the spoken word, Cambon addressed a brief letter to Lansdowne summarising the interview of May 17. " At our last conversation on Morocco you recalled the Memorandum presented to M. Delcassé on April 24 by Sir Francis Bertie, and you added that henceforth, if circumstances required it, if for instance we had serious reasons to believe in an unprovoked aggression on the part of a certain Power, the British Government would be quite ready to discuss with the French Government what measures to take. I have informed M. Delcassé of this communication, the importance of which he has gratefully recognised." In thanking the Ambassador for his letter Lansdowne asked to be allowed to repeat in his own language the substance of his remarks on May 17, and proceeded to quote the chief passage from his report to Bertie. " I do not know", he concluded, "that this account differs from that which you have given to M. Delcassé, but I am not sure that I succeeded in making quite clear to you our desire that there should be full and confidential discussion between the two Governments, not so much in consequence of some act of unprovoked aggression on the part of another Power, as in anticipation of any complications to be apprehended during the somewhat anxious period through which we are at present passing." The letter seems to breathe a slight uneasiness as to the impression produced at Paris by Cambon's report of the interview of May 17. There was more ground for anxiety than he realised, for Cambon and Delcassé had read into the words more than he had intended to convey. " I suppose

[1] D.D.F. VI, 520–3.

this was the origin of the offensive and defensive alliance ", minuted Lansdowne at a later date on a copy of his record of the interview. His letter of May 25, wrote Cambon to his chief on May 29, suggested a general entente which would in fact amount to an alliance.[1] Delcassé accordingly informed his colleagues at the decisive meeting on June 6 that an alliance had been offered, and he reiterated the statement to the end of his life.

That an alliance had been proposed was energetically denied by Lansdowne at the time and ever after. On June 12 Bülow and Holstein told Lascelles that unofficial but reliable information had reached them shortly before Delcassé's fall that England had offered France an offensive and defensive alliance against Germany. France had refused, but the offer proved the unfriendliness of the British Government. Lascelles expressed his surprise and disbelief, and King Edward minuted : " This is nearly as absurd as it is false ! " Lansdowne at once sent for the German Ambassador and expressed his surprise at the statements about Anglo-German relations. " With regard to the alleged offensive and defensive alliance, the offer of which was cited as a proof of our unfriendliness, I could scarcely believe that the assertion was seriously made or that the story was worth contradicting. If, however, His Excellency thought that a contradiction from me would serve a useful purpose, I was glad to assure him that no offensive and defensive alliance had ever been offered or even discussed on either side." Metternich. added Lansdowne, accepted unreservedly the contradiction of the rumour. In reporting the conversation the Ambassador added ; " I regard Lord Lansdowne as incapable of tricking me with his clear declaration."[2]

On June 27 Eckardstein, now a free lance, came to Metternich with a sensational tale.[3] He knew for a fact that Delcassé had had the offer of an offensive and defensive alliance in his pocket. In the last ten days the British Government had told the French that they could count on diplomatic support under all circumstances, and that, if they wished for an alliance, the English fleet would if necessary support French policy. The British Government, he added, was trying every means to bring about an alliance. Since France would have to choose between England and Germany, England, though wishing to avoid war, would not shrink from an alliance and even a war,

[1] D.D.F. VI, 557–8.   [2] G.P. XX, 631.   [3] ibid. 634–5.

in order not to sacrifice the entente.   His informant, Armand
Lévy, knew from Rouvier himself that the English plan was
being energetically pressed.   The Premier was vacillating, but,
if Germany's attitude continued to be uncompromising, he
would close with the offer.   On the following day Metternich,
acting on his own responsibility, informed Lansdowne of what
he had heard.[1]   He would not have mentioned it, after the
Foreign Minister's assurances, did it not come from French
sources which he could not ignore.   He had been categorically
assured that within the last fortnight the English Government
has promised not only diplomatic support but also, if France
concluded an alliance, the support of the fleet.   Diplomatic
support within the limits of the treaty, replied Lansdowne,
was assured to the French Government.   This naturally
involved discussion of the means of carrying out the various
points of the agreement.   An alliance, on the other hand, had
never been discussed by the Cabinet or offered to the French
Government, either in the last few days or before.   He must
add, however, that in the utterly improbable event of Germany
light-heartedly launching a war, he could not foretell how far
public opinion would drive the Government in support of
France.   Curiously enough there is no record of this weighty
declaration in Lansdowne's version of the conversation,
though he had no reason to conceal it.   For it was neither a
confession of hostility nor a hypothetical declaration of war,
but a timely warning to Berlin.
   Though the offer of an alliance by the British Government
is a legend, the situation had undoubtedly changed, and the
contingency of joint resistance to a common foe had been
envisaged for the first time.   In the words of Clausewitz,
war is the continuation of policy by other means.   The Treaty
of 1904 had removed the grounds of enmity and distrust.
The Tangier crisis created the *Entente Cordiale*, and inaugurated
a working partnership which was soon to extend far beyond the
problem of Morocco.   The development was due to the
blunders of French and German policy rather than to the will
of the British Government.   To recognise French predominance in Morocco and to promise diplomatic support in that
particular field seemed harmless enough.   And so it would
have been had Delcassé taken the same pains to purchase the
acquiescence of Berlin as he had taken to secure the consent of
England, Italy and Spain.   It was Lansdowne's misfortune,

[1] *G.P.* XX, 635–7.

not his fault, that a welcome reconciliation should have been accompanied by our entanglement in a wholly unnecessary Franco-German quarrel about Morocco. We can scarcely blame him for failing to warn Delcassé of the danger of ignoring his formidable neighbour, for it was the business of France to look after herself.

Lansdowne's assurances satisfied Metternich, who liked and trusted him, but they were not enough for the Ambassador's countrymen. Moreover in an interview with Delcassé published in the *Gaulois* of July 12, the ex-Minister declared that he had told his colleagues that he was sure of English support in the event of war and had laid before them the outline of an alliance.[1] Metternich called the Foreign Secretary's attention to the matter, remarking that, though the alliance story had been disposed of in their private conversations, no *démenti* had appeared.[2] The trouble recurred in an aggravated form in October, when the *Matin* published three articles on the fall of Delcassé by Lauzanne, an influential champion of the late Minister.[3] England, he declared, had given a verbal promise in the event of a German attack on France to mobilise the fleet, occupy the Kiel Canal, and land 100,000 men in Schleswig-Holstein. Since Lansdowne was away Metternich called on Sir Thomas Sanderson, the Permanent Under-Secretary, who said that the Government had never promised military help. A conflict between France and Germany had not been discussed by the Government, and the landing of troops in Schleswig-Holstein was a fairy-tale. "To begin with", he observed with a jest, " we have not got 100,000 men to land anywhere." Perhaps, suggested Metternich, the promise of armed help came from an influential quarter outside the Government. The Ambassador's hypothesis was shared by the Kaiser, who minuted on the report : " The King gave Delcassé the promise, not the Government." When the *Figaro* confirmed the story of an alliance the Kaiser suggested asking the British Government for a *démenti*, and in case of an unsatisfactory reply proposed withdrawing his Ambassador for an indefinite period. Bülow rejected the plan, and Metternich expressed the opinion that the offer of armed support had come either from Bertie acting without instructions or from the King himself. Whence it came remains unknown to this day. So far as diplomacy was concerned the incident was closed by a statement in the *Norddeutsche*

[1] *G.P.* XX, 637–8.   [2] ibid. 639–640.   [3] ibid. 662–70; *B.D.* III, 83–7.

Allgemeine Zeitung on October 15 that Lansdowne's denial was accepted.

Lansdowne agreed with Delcassé that the invitation to a Conference from the Sultan of Morocco should be declined. "Inform Moorish Government", he telegraphed on June 5, " that proposal to invoke assistance of all Governments having representatives at Tangier to take part in discussion of reforms so urgently needed for improvement of administration is in our opinion wholly undeserving of encouragement.[1] Such a discussion would involve participation of a large number of Powers many of them having no interest worth speaking of in Moorish affairs. We could not take part in it, and we desire to dissuade Sultan from pressing upon the Powers a project which we consider most ill-advised and contrary to interests of his country." On the day following the despatch of this uncompromising telegram Delcassé resigned, and Germany announced her acceptance of the Conference. The new situation was discussed by the Cabinet on June 8, after which Lansdowne invited Metternich to see him.[2] Though considering a Conference undesirable, he explained, the Cabinet had decided to reserve its decision and to exchange ideas with France. He proceeded to argue that Germany had no ground of complaint. " The acquisition of that influence which a civilised Power naturally exerts over a barbarous one when the two are in close contact must, I thought, always tend to place the civilised Power in a privileged position, but that influence did not seem to me to involve any wrong to others." Metternich rejoined that he recognised the necessity for France to act as " policeman " in regions adjoining the Algerian frontier ; but if the policeman proceeded to lay hands on the whole country and its administration the other Powers could not be indifferent. He thought the French Government would come to terms " if England did not stiffen their backs". Lansdowne replied that England had no reform programme for Morocco. The Ambassador reported that, despite his dislike of a Conference, the Foreign Secretary had no wish to see the situation become more acute. He was right. " The fall of Delcassé is disgusting", wrote Lansdowne to a friend, "and has sent the Entente down any number of points in the market."[3] But he realised that it was no use crying over spilt milk.

A week later Cambon reported on the discussions between Rouvier and Radolin. If France would accept the idea of a

[1] *B.D.* III, 89.   [2] ibid. 92-3, and *G.P.* XX, 422-4.   [3] Newton, 341.

Conference in principle, Germany was ready for an understanding which might make it unnecessary. The German Ambassador had added that, if a Conference was ruled out, Germany would probably give trouble in Morocco. Lansdowne replied that he had declined the Sultan's invitation. France, who was suspected by Germany of designs on the integrity of Morocco and on the commercial rights of other Powers, should explain her ideas. Till an exchange of views had taken place he saw no reason for admitting the theoretical necessity of a Conference. The British attitude, he concluded, would naturally depend on that of the French ; " but if they maintained their refusal, so most certainly should we ". After further discussions between Rouvier and Radolin, France accepted the Conference on July 8 and England followed suit.

Rouvier's surrender in no way involved a flirtation with Berlin. After all that had happened, explained Cambon, the French Premier was more convinced than ever of the necessity of a close understanding with England.[1] It was essential that the two Governments should treat one another with the fullest confidence, and that no further steps should be taken without previous discussion. The Premier's eyes had been opened, for he had been led to suppose that with Delcassé's resignation German irritation would disappear. Lansdowne replied that the British Government would continue its loyal support. " At the same time I was bound to tell him that the apparent sacrifice of M. Delcassé in the face of German pressure had created an unfavourable impression in this country, and I therefore thought there was a good deal to be said for M. Rouvier's view that it would be as well to avoid any action calculated to bring about fresh complications." After the Franco-German agreement of September 28 on the programme of the Conference the Moroccan problem slumbered till Lansdowne had left office. He had faithfully carried out the treaty obligation to afford France diplomatic support, and the fall of Delcassé only momentarily cooled the cordiality of the relationship. The Entente had been tried in the furnace without melting away. A new factor of immeasurable significance for Europe and the world had emerged. Though bound neither by formal alliance nor secret guarantee England, it was generally understood, would support France if she were attacked by Germany. At last, after decades of isolation, we had transformed a dangerous rival into a powerful friend.

[1] B.D. III, 118–119.

It was an immense achievement, but it was not an unalloyed gain. For the price of partnership with a Great Power is entanglement in its feuds.

VII

That our outspoken support of France should be interpreted in Berlin as hostility to German interests and aims was inevitable. The new orientation of British policy had been no secret since the spring of 1903. In discussing the Morocco question with Metternich in the autumn of that year Lansdowne remarked that, owing to her long Algerian frontier, France must ultimately obtain a preponderating influence, as always happened when a civilised state collided with an uncivilised community.[1] Would this preponderating influence confine itself to the districts on the Algerian frontier, inquired the Ambassador, or would it extend to the whole country ? It would begin with the frontier districts, answered Lansdowne, and eventually no doubt spread to the interior. " These important declarations", reported Metternich to the Chancellor, " contradict his previous utterances to me, which scouted the notion of leaving Morocco to France. We must assume that a new and important step has been taken on the road to an Anglo-French understanding about Morocco." Nothing could be done by Germany to prevent or delay the consummation, and the Wilhelmstrasse nervously awaited the result of the negotiations. Lansdowne was also a little anxious. " I have felt from the first", he confided to Cromer, " and so has Cambon, that we shall have to reckon with Germany."[2] She might even ask for a port.

Bülow's first public comment on the treaty of April 8, 1904, was all that could be desired. " We have no reason to suppose that it contains a point against any other Power. To this attempt to remove differences we have no objections from the point of view of German interests to raise." A reassuring despatch from Bernstorff, the German Chargé in London, analysed British policy and opinion.[3] Government and people were anxious for peace with all the Great Powers. England had rejected the jingoism of the Chamberlain era. If the French believed she would support them in a war of revenge against Germany they would be disappointed. Public opinion was hostile owing to the German fleet, but not so

[1] G.P. XVII, 362–3. November 25, 1903. [2] Newton, 285.
[3] G.P. XX, 14–21.

hostile as might be inferred from the press, and the Government was friendly. An arbitration treaty would be a good beginning. Some weeks later Lansdowne assured Metternich, in answer to his inquiries, that the rumour of secret clauses relating to a rectification of the Rhine frontier was a mare's nest.[1]

The necessity of securing the adhesion of the Powers to the Khedival Decree seemed to the Wilhelmstrasse to provide a lever for wider discussions. If England displayed a readiness to consult German interests in Egypt, thought Bülow, other colonial questions might be discussed : an arbitration treaty might be concluded, and perhaps at a later stage an agreement about the fleet.[2] When the British Government formally requested the acceptance of the Decree, the German Foreign Minister raised a number of colonial questions. Lansdowne, annoyed by what he regarded as a great piece of effrontery, replied that some of them could not be treated as part of the Egyptian settlement, which must be dealt with on its own merits. The British Government was willing to maintain German rights in Egypt, and to sign an arbitration agreement similar to those recently concluded with France, Italy and Spain ; but without further inquiries it could not discuss an agreement under which disputes regarding colonial frontiers would be submitted to arbitration. While ready to examine in the most friendly spirit any questions unconnected with Egypt, they hoped that no further concessions would be demanded as the price of consent.

Germany dropped her non-Egyptian demands, and the British claim that commercial equality in Egypt should be matched by a similar equality in the German colonies was declined. Each side felt a slight grievance against the other, the Germans arguing that their consent was worth a price, the English replying that the German share of the Egyptian debt was infinitesimal, and that Russia, Austria and Italy had accepted the change without any fuss. The problem was amicably solved in the middle of June. Germany's commerce in Egypt was guaranteed most-favoured-nation treatment for thirty years ; her treaty rights would be respected ; her schools would retain their liberty unimpaired ; and her officials in the Egyptian service should be as well treated as the British. In return Germany assented to the Khedival Decree, undertook not to obstruct the British occupation, and accepted the change

[1] G.P. XX, 27-30.   [2] ibid. XX, ch. 143, and B.D. III, ch. 16.

in the administration of the Suez Canal already approved by France and the other Powers. Bülow was well satisfied with the result of the negotiations, which had secured German interests in Egypt at the cost of trifling concessions. And Lansdowne was glad to remove the last difficulty in a matter to which, as he confided to Metternich, the British Government attached overwhelming importance. So far the Anglo-French treaty seemed to have inflicted no damage on Anglo-German relations.

A few days after the Egyptian agreement Edward VII visited the Kaiser at Kiel.[1] The toasts were cordial and the King's conversations with Bülow were satisfactory to both sides. The understanding between England and France, the Chancellor was assured, was not directed against Germany. There was nothing on the surface to show that the Anglo-French rapprochement was resented by the hosts. A fortnight later, on July 12, an Anglo-German arbitration treaty was signed. The situation, however, was very different from what it seemed. Germany was deeply stirred by the action of France in attempting to settle the affairs of Morocco without consulting her, though for the time she kept her feelings to herself. The Franco-Spanish negotiations, wrote Bülow to Radolin on July 21, must be completed before action was taken.[2] With England, he added, relations were less tense. Agreement had been reached about Egypt, and she would probably not take too seriously her promise of diplomatic support of France in Morocco. In a word our part in the conclusion of the Anglo-French treaty was not censured, for Egypt meant little to Germany. Delcassé, not Lansdowne, was the villain of the piece.

Before leaving for his summer holiday Metternich˙ complained to Lansdowne of French action in Morocco.[3] They were aiming at commercial monopoly, which Germany could not allow. She might soon have to defend her commercial interests, and it was important to know if she would have to deal with one or two antagonists, in other words if England would feel bound to give diplomatic support. Would the Foreign Secretary in confidence explain how he interpreted this duty? The British Governments, replied Lansdowne, were very unwilling to answer hypothetical questions. The promise of diplomatic support would certainly not operate

[1] Lee, *King Edward VII*, II, 292–7.   [2] *G.P.* XX, 210–14.
[3] ibid. XX, 219–22. August 15.

against the legitimate rights of third parties. Moreover the French Government, he believed, would proceed very cautiously in Morocco, as it wished to avoid trouble with other Powers. " My impression ", concluded Metternich, " is that Lord Lansdowne will try to narrow rather than to expand the obligation of support. He will stand aside when we challenge French hegemony on the basis of our treaties with Morocco, even when commercial concessions are concerned which the Morocco Government can give without diminution of authority, for instance lighterage in the harbours. If, however, we try to secure control over a harbour on the west coast England, I believe, would honour her obligation under Article IX. If we have treaty rights on our side we can stand up to France without troubling our heads about England. . . . England will do nothing to quicken the tempo of French penetration, but equally she will do nothing to endanger the good understanding with France about Morocco. . . . Yet if any Power were to challenge the predominance of France, English diplomacy and above all English public opinion would be found on the side of the French." The Foreign Secretary himself could not have defined more accurately the new attitude of the British Government towards Morocco. There was nothing in it at which Germany could take offence, and indeed no trouble with the Wilhelmstrasse from this source arose till the Kaiser's visit to Tangier brought Franco-German rivalry to the boil.

"I am afraid", wrote Lansdowne to Lascelles, " that we can hardly regard this Tangier ebullition as an isolated incident.[1] . . . We shall, I have little doubt, find that the Kaiser avails himself of every opportunity to put spokes in our wheels." In his first interview with Lansdowne after the Tangier demonstration Metternich explained once again the German attitude.[2] To the contention that France was trying to make Morocco a second Tunis the Foreign Minister replied that that would contravene the Anglo-French pact. To the statement that the French Minister had claimed in Fez to be the mandatory of Europe, Lansdowne rejoined that he doubted the accuracy of the report : if correct, he had acted very unwisely, for he possessed no such mandate. When Metternich observed that Germany merely wanted the maintenance of commercial freedom for all in Morocco, he was assured that it was laid down in the treaty. Lansdowne was obviously on his guard, but in the Ambassador's opinion he wished to keep out

[1] Newton, 334. [2] G.P. XX, 608-9.

of the Morocco game as long as he could. Events, however, might easily force him to diplomatic support of the French, whom England would under no circumstances leave in the lurch. In two elaborate surveys of British opinion written at this critical moment Count Bernstorff, the German Chargé, reported that no one wanted England to fight.[1] German policy in Morocco was regarded not as the defence of legitimate economic interests but as a wanton attack on the *Entente Cordiale*. The Jingos, however, were in a small minority, and the Liberals, who would oppose a war, were gaining strength.

After the fall of Delcassé Lansdowne continued to express his distaste for a Conference ; but he realised that the attitude of France had changed, and that Rouvier was less Anglophil than Delcassé. " I do not think ", telegraphed Metternich on June 15 after a talk with Lansdowne, " that the Government wishes to stiffen the French in their opposition to us.[2] On the contrary I believe that leading circles would prefer to see an understanding between us and France which enabled British policy to get closer to us again." Metternich's optimistic reading of Lansdowne was not shared by Bülow, who falsely charged him with encouraging France to a conflict.[3] Though the German Ambassador knew that Lansdowne had no wish for war, he faithfully reported the angry mood of the public.[4] The King was deeply incensed, particularly against his nephew. If the French lost their heads and went to war, England would fight on their side even in the absence of an alliance. The Morocco question had become a symbol of the struggle to keep the friendship of France. To retain it and to avert complete German hegemony in Europe, England would be ready to fight. Neither the King, the Government nor the incensed English people wished for a war with Germany. But under certain circumstances it might occur, and the Morocco question had brought it a step nearer. The King and British policy, added the Ambassador in a private letter to Bülow after a friendly reception at Cowes, were dominated by the rapprochement with France.[5]

While Lansdowne was involved in the Moroccan antagonism, the Japanese war opened up new vistas of trouble beyond the North Sea. Though Germany was an ally of neither belligerent, the unconcealed sympathies of her Government were

---

[1] *G.P.*, XX, 609–15, and 618–19.
[2] ibid. XX, 441–2.
[3] ibid. XX, 461–3.
[4] ibid. XX, 646–8. July 22.
[4] ibid. XX, 651–9, Aug. 14.

on the side of Russia and her neutrality was benevolent in the extreme. Her readiness to help was indeed greater than that of France, who resented the locking up of her ally's resources in the Far East. Englishmen naturally wished their ally to win, while Germany endeavoured to strengthen Russia's hands. If the Russian fleet was to play its part in the struggle at the other side of the world it required generous supplies of foreign coal ; and the coaling of the ships raised questions not only of legality but of high politics. On August 15, 1904, Lansdowne informed Metternich of his fear lest Japan, on the basis of the treaty, might look to England if she believed that Germany violated her neutrality in dealing with Russian ships of war.[1] In reporting the declaration Metternich added that the Foreign Minister had in no wise intended a veiled threat to Germany, but the agitated Chancelleries breathed a sigh of relief when Admiral Rojdesvensky sailed out of European waters.

Morocco and the Japanese conflict were not the only causes of Anglo-German friction during the last two crowded years of Lansdowne's tenure of office. Commercial rivalry was an annoyance, but never a determining factor in the shaping of British policy. The construction of a formidable High Sea fleet, on the other hand, created an alarm which grew from year to year. The first Navy Law of 1898 was nothing to trouble about, but that of 1900 was a very serious affair. Having always thought of British security at sea in terms of the naval strength of France and Russia, it was a shock to Englishmen to realise that danger threatened from a new quarter as well. Though the German fleet was never mentioned in the Morocco negotiations, its rapid growth was continually present to Lansdowne's mind, and it was one of the reasons which prompted him to favour close association with France. When Edward VII visited the Kaiser at Kiel and inspected the fleet, Tirpitz records that he saw the King and Lord Selborne, the First Lord of the Admiralty, exchange knowing glances.[2] The German battleships and the German Navy League began to cast their shadow in 1904, though they only became a nightmare in 1909.

It was in 1904 that certain English journals suggested the destruction of the German fleet before it grew too strong.[3] *Vanity Fair* was not a gun of large calibre, but the *Army and Navy Gazette*, though entirely unofficial, was more alarming as

[1] *G.P.* XIX, 321.   [2] Tirpitz, *Memoirs*, 200.   [3] *G.P.* XIX, ch. 136.

a symptom of unrest.[1] The transfer of ships from the Mediterranean fleet to home waters was frankly explained by the First Lord of the Admiralty on December 10, 1904, on the ground that a powerful German navy had been created. The concentration, itself a product of fear, aroused a corresponding apprehension of British attack in Germany, and the Kaiser desired ships to be brought home in anticipation of a possible attack in the spring of 1905. Tirpitz, Bülow and Holstein pointed out that such a measure would increase the tension and lead England to station still more ships in the North Sea. Holstein, however, now believed for the first time in the possibility of a British attack. The Military Attaché in London, asked for his opinion, replied that a deep hatred of Germany existed, but that there was no immediate danger of war. On the other hand an incident like the Dogger Bank or Fashoda would compel the Government to fight. Metternich, whose advice was also sought, reported that there was no thought of attack. A German alliance with Russia, however, would be dangerous, and to ignore protests from England and Japan in regard to the coaling of the Russian fleet would be madness.

On January 11, 1905, Lansdowne discussed the situation with Metternich. He had heard that the Ambassador had combated the alarmist rumours in Berlin of hostile British plans against Germany. He could not understand how they arose. There was not the slightest cause of friction. No one in England dreamed of a conflict. No one took the society journal *Vanity Fair* seriously, and the *Army and Navy Gazette* was used by retired officers to attack the Government. It was not the mouthpiece of the Admiralty or the War Office. Metternich replied that his Government did not believe in a coming attack ; but the press campaign was a danger, for some incident, unimportant in itself, like the Dogger Bank, might cause an explosion. The Foreign Secretary replied that the press had been quieter the last few weeks, and Metternich agreed. On the same day the Ambassador in a private letter to the Chancellor reported that the situation was improving. A few days after Metternich's reassuring report, a speech by Arthur Lee, the Civil Lord of the Admiralty, in his constituency caused the smouldering embers to shoot up in flame.[1] For the first time Germans could quote or misquote a British Minister for their fears of a sudden attack. In the following

[1] G.P. XIX, 568-9.

years the *Saturday Review* article of 1897 *Delenda est Germania* and Arthur Lee's ill-advised utterance proved the most effective recruiting agents for the drummers of a big fleet. The launching of the Dreadnought increased the sense of danger and inevitably provoked the construction of German battleships of equal size. Fisher was ranged against Tirpitz. The naval race had begun. With two such apples of discord as Morocco and the fleet it was beyond Lansdowne's power to mend the wire to Berlin.

VIII

It was inevitable that the reconciliation with France should raise the question of a rapprochement with Russia, and no one knew better than the Foreign Minister that the first was bound to remain precarious in the absence of the second. The road to St. Petersburg, however, was blocked by many obstacles, new and old. The Anglo-Japanese alliance proclaimed aloud our suspicions of Russian aims in the Far East. The occupation of Manchuria by Russian troops long after the suppression of the Boxer rising was almost as distasteful to London as to Tokio. Salisbury's attempt in 1898 to delimit spheres of influence in Asia had failed, and Lansdowne had not felt inclined to renew the experiment. Russia's tightening political and economic hold over Persia and her feeble Shah filled the Viceroy of India with angry alarm, and prompted the Foreign Secretary to a statement in the House of Lords in May, 1903, which ranks in importance with the Grey declaration on Egypt in 1895.[1] The policy of the British Government was to protect and promote British trade in the Persian Gulf, but not to exclude the legitimate trade of others. " In the third place—I say it without hesitation—we should regard the establishment of a naval base or a fortified port as a very grave menace to British interests, and we should certainly resist it with all the means at our disposal. I say that in no minatory spirit, because, so far as I am aware, no proposals are on foot for the establishment of a foreign naval base in the Persian Gulf." The emphatic warning was reinforced by the Viceroy's imposing naval demonstration in the Gulf in the autumn of the same year.

A conversation with Chamberlain during Delcassé's historic visit to London in July 1903 may be taken as the starting point of the discussions which culminated in the Anglo-Russian

[1] *Parliamentary Debates*, Fourth Series, Vol. CXXI, 1343-1353. May 5, 1903.

Convention of 1907.[1] The French statesman was struck by the remark that England was not opposed to the idea of an understanding with Russia, but that it was rendered difficult by Russian opposition in the Yangtze valley. The reference to the Yangtze valley, declared the Russian Ambassador in London a few days later, was unintelligible to his Government, which had no desire to oppose in that quarter, and was by no means averse to an understanding with England. Lansdowne doubted whether Chamberlain could have referred to the difficulties with Russia as being confined to the Yangtze valley. There were other questions at issue, particularly Manchuria. He had always desired an amicable arrangement. The British Government would not repel any overture ; but in that case Russia would have to display more confidence, particularly by explaining her dealings with China concerning Manchuria. "If Russia would put us in full possession of her ideas, and if she would bear in mind that for any concessions which she obtained from us we should expect corresponding concessions from her, I believe that we might put an end to the unfortunate rivalry which had so long prevailed between us in China and in other parts of Asia."

After the summer holidays the Foreign Secretary spoke to Cambon of a forthcoming visit of Lamsdorff to Paris, for dark clouds were rolling up in the Far East.[2] "I said, explaining that I was expressing merely my personal sentiments in the most unofficial manner possible, that I could not help hoping that Count Lamsdorff's discussions with M. Delcassé might indirectly have an effect upon the attitude of the Russian Government towards this country. The exchange of ideas which had recently taken place between the French and British Governments had been, I rejoiced to think, characterised by the utmost frankness on both sides. It seemed to me most unfortunate that we had hitherto entirely failed in establishing the same kind of diplomatic relations with the Russian Government. I did not think the fault lay on our side, for I had more than once made proposals in that direction, but without success. On the other hand it certainly seemed to me that the Russian Government had been far from open in their dealings with us. Their conduct placed us in a very embarrassing position. We had more than once received from them specific pledges, for example with reference to Manchuria, which we had loyally accepted and upon which we had relied when we

[1] B.D. II, 212. [2] ibid. II, 217-18.

were questioned in Parliament. Those pledges remained unfulfilled, and I was afraid that a feeling of impatience and mistrust had obtained possession of the public mind in this country." Cambon listened sympathetically and promised to report to his chief. Lamsdorff, he pointed out, was in a position of extreme difficulty, as he was not master in his own house. When Lamsdorff reached Paris and expressed his fear that the attitude of Japan was being stiffened by the hope of British support, Delcassé assured him that the British Government were far from desiring to follow a provocative policy, but that they complained of having been left in the dark concerning the policy of Russia.[1] A little more frankness would be useful. The Russian statesman took the hint in good part and authorised Delcassé to say that he was ready for explanations of the frankest kind. He also assured his French colleague that Russia was genuinely anxious for a peaceful solution of her differences with Japan.[2] With an unaccustomed warmth of tone Lansdowne charged Cambon to thank his chief for this friendly service. "Your Excellency", commented the Ambassador, " has been asked to act as mediator between St. Petersburg and London, and your intervention has had the happiest results."[3]

A friendly talk with Benckendorff—the first since the summer holidays—took place a few days later.[4] His chief, declared the Ambassador, felt strongly that an effort should be made to remove all sources of misunderstanding, and that there should be a " change for the better " in the relations of the countries. He was therefore instructed to discuss frankly the various outstanding issues and the manner in which they should be handled. Meanwhile the Russian Government would avoid any seemingly hostile action. The Ambassador was to visit St. Petersburg early in the new year and report the result of his discussions. Lansdowne expressed his pleasure at the prospect, all the more because he was seriously concerned at the position. He proceeded to complain of Russia's attitude in Afghanistan and of the continued occupation of Manchuria. Benckendorff explained that the creation of the Viceroyalty of the Far East had made difficulties, and that his chief was not responsible for all that occurred. The excuses filled the Foreign Secretary with alarm. How could a satisfactory understanding be reached with a Foreign Office where conflicting influences were at work ?

[1] D.D.F. IV, 66–7. [2] ibid. 80. [3] ibid. 81–3. [4] B.D. II, 222–4. November 7.

At the end of the conversation Lansdowne mentioned that the Younghusband expedition would advance further into Tibet, but that there was no intention of annexing or permanently occupying territory. At their next meeting ten days later Benckendorff complained of the announcement.[1] The invasion of Tibet by a British force involved a grave disturbance of the situation in Central Asia, and it was most unfortunate that, on the eve of an amicable discussion of their interests, an event so calculated to create mistrust in Russia should have occurred. Lansdowne expressed his great surprise at the excitement of Russia. Tibet was close to India and remote from Russian possessions. The provocations had been gross. The Russian Government would not have shown such patience and would have been in Lhassa by this time. Such protests from a Power which had never hesitated to encroach upon its neighbours were strange indeed. If the Russian Government had a right to complain of England taking steps to obtain reparation by advancing into Tibet, what kind of language ought the British Government to use about Russian encroachments in Manchuria, Turkestan, Persia and elsewhere? This sharp rejoinder by a statesman who kept his feelings so well under control reveals the formidable difficulties of an Anglo-Russian rapprochement in 1903.

After this unpromising start Lansdowne asked whether Benckendorff could suggest a convenient way of examining the other questions which he was authorised to discuss. The Ambassador replied that the questions seemed to group themselves into those concerning China, in which Russia had a special interest, those concerning India, in which Great Britain had a special interest, and those concerning Persia, in which both Powers were concerned. Russia did not favour an arrangement which would place northern Persia under Russian and southern Persia under British influence ; but she recognised our predominance in the Persian Gulf, though she would probably require a commercial port. After a few words on Manchuria and Afghanistan, Lansdowne asked Benckendorff if he could put his own views on current issues on paper. The Ambassador feared that he had not the materials at hand. Lansdowne then inquired if he had authority to make any specific proposals. Benckendorff replied that he had not, but that he was instructed to discuss them. The Foreign Secretary was disappointed by this

[1] B.D. IV, 306–7, and 183–4.

beating about the bush, and he concluded that the discussions were unlikely to have much result.

A day or two after this interview the Ambassador, during a visit to Windsor, discussed with Hardinge, then an Assistant Under-Secretary in the Foreign Office, the outlines of an Asiatic settlement, and a further conversation took place in the Foreign Office in which Lansdowne sketched out an arrangement.[1] Afghanistan and Tibet should be recognised as within our sphere of influence. We would recognise Russia's predominating interest in Manchuria, though our trade must receive equal treatment. We could also accept Russian preponderance in the north of Persia : but Seistan must be entirely under British influence, and if a railway to the Gulf were to be built we should claim control of the southern section. Benckendorff promised consideration for these suggestions, but the outbreak of war severed the threads before they could be woven into a pattern.

As 1903 drew to a close Lansdowne's anxieties rapidly increased. On December 11 he asked Cambon if he knew the intentions of the Russian Government.[2] " Our treaty with Japan does not oblige us to intervene if she is engaged with a single Power, and in a conflict of our ally with Russia we should be entirely within our rights in remaining neutral ; but I am afraid of a wave of opinion in England. Russia's silence is inexplicable, and I sense the first symptoms of trouble. If the conflict broke out and Japan suffered a check, I do not know whither we might be dragged." He asked the Ambassador to beg his chief to work at St. Petersburg for peace, as he himself would work at Tokio. They were on the eve of events which might become very serious. Joint action was needed to avert a catastrophe. Delcassé was as anxious as Lansdowne to keep the peace, and, after receiving soothing assurances from Russia, he urged the British Foreign Minister to moderate the Japanese demands.[3] Lansdowne replied that he had abstained from encouraging the Japanese, but that he could not advise them to abandon just demands which were also in the interest of all the Powers, including England. These well-meant exhortations to moderating action were fruitless, for neither Russia nor Japan was in the mood to listen to advice. The storm broke on February 9, 1904, with a sudden attack on the Russian fleet.

[1] B.D. IV, 184-8.   [2] D.D.F. IV, 175-6.
[3] ibid. 271-2. January 18, 1904.

IX

The position of England as the ally of one of the belligerents was bound to cause friction with the other, and the sympathies of the British people with Japan was unconcealed. " The Anglo-Japanese Alliance", wrote Lansdowne to King Edward, " although not intended to encourage the Japanese Government to resort to extremities, had, and was sure to have, the effect of making Japan feel that she might try conclusions with her great rival in the Far East, free from all risk of a European coalition such as that which had on a previous occasion deprived her of the fruits of victory."[1] The Foreign Secretary had made no real attempt in Tokio to avert the war, and when it came, made no attempt to end it. He complained to Cambon, who dreaded complications, that Japan never consulted her ally.[2] During the opening phases of the struggle, however, the relations of the British and Russian Governments remained friendly enough. A cordial conversation in April 1904, between King Edward and Iswolsky, the Russian Minister at Copenhagen, gave the greatest satisfaction at St. Petersburg,[3] but could not remove the deadlock created by the war. Agreeing with Lansdowne that negotiations for a general settlement must wait, Benckendorff pleaded for the amicable adjustment of such minor differences as might arise.[4] Could the Foreign Secretary for instance say something to allay the apprehension in regard to Tibet ? Lansdowne referred the Ambassador to recent declarations in Parliament, which, he thought, should be highly satisfactory to the Russian Government.

A few days later Benckendorff brought a message from his chief in reference to the King's conversation at Copenhagen.[5] The Russian Government would welcome a complete understanding on all questions as soon as the war was over, assuming of course that the attitude of England during the crisis in the Far East conformed to her assurances. Lansdowne seized the opportunity of asking for Russia's assent to the proposed Khedival Decree, in return for which he promised to repeat his declaration that neither occupation nor permanent intervention in Tibetan affairs was contemplated.[6] The deal was promptly

[1] Newton, 308–9.   [2] D.D.F. IV, 377–9.
[3] Lee, King Edward VII, II, 284–7.   [4] B.D. IV, 188–9. April 22, 1904.
[5] ibid. 189–190.
[6] For the declaration of policy on November 6, 1903, see B.D. IV, 305.

carried out, and the signature of a treaty at Lhassa on September 7, 1904, ended an incident which had created a good deal of bad blood. Lamsdorff complained that portions of the agreement contravened the assurances of the Foreign Secretary. Colonel Younghusband had in fact exceeded his instructions, and the settlement was modified by the Cabinet.

Lansdowne did not seriously expect to be drawn into the struggle by our obligations under the Japanese alliance. A less remote cause of anxiety was the temptation of a sorely pressed belligerent to send the Black Sea fleet to the scene of action in the Far East.[1] On the eve of hostilities he assured Japan that we should regard the passage of the fleet through the Dardanelles as a grave violation of treaty engagements, though he could not say what action we should take. The contingency, he added, was unlikely to arise. To the French Ambassador, who at a later stage inquired as to Anglo-Russian relations, he spoke more freely. The passage of the Straits for the purpose of attacking our ally could not be tolerated, and a collision might be inevitable. He spoke in similar terms to the Russian Ambassador, and Turkey was reminded of her duty to prevent armed vessels from passing the Dardanelles.

The prospect of annihilation by superior British vessels kept the Black Sea fleet idle throughout the war, but friction threatened from another quarter. The so-called Volunteer Fleet had been created during the conflict with Turkey in 1877–8. The ships carried the mercantile flag in time of peace, but the crews were subject to naval training and the chief officers were commissioned by the Government. When the war had been in progress for some months Russia requested Turkey's permission to send ships from the Volunteer Fleet, adding that they would not change their commercial flag or transport munitions. On this understanding they were allowed to pass, but when the *Petersburg* and the *Smolensk* were safely through the Dardanelles the mischief began. On July 13 the P. & O. steamship *Malacca*, which included in her cargo a few tons of munitions for the Government dockyards at Singapore and Hong-Kong, was seized in the Red Sea, the passengers and crew being landed at Port Said. Lansdowne demanded immediate release, and the *Malacca* was restored to her owners when she reached Algiers on her way to Russia. Orders were sent from St. Petersburg to prevent further captures, and the

[1] B.D. IV, 41–60

two other British vessels which had been seized were promptly released. Meanwhile a far more serious incident occurred in the Far East, where the *Knight Commander*, bound from New York to Yokohama, was stopped and sunk after a very perfunctory examination of her cargo, the crew being taken to Vladivostock. The act was described by Lansdowne in the House of Lords as an outrage and a serious breach of international law.[1] A wave of indignation swept over the country. Lansdowne spoke very gravely to Benckendorff, and Delcassé urged caution at St. Petersburg.[2] The Russian Government, as anxious as the British to avoid a rupture, made the necessary promises ; but Lansdowne solemnly warned the Ambassador of the effect on public opinion of further operations against neutral commerce. Happily the caution proved effective.

When the temper of the British people had been ruffled by the activities of Russian vessels, and the Russians had been hurt by the refusal to allow their warships to coal in British ports, an incident of the kind particularly dreaded by diplomatists occurred. On the night of October 21–2 the Russian squadron on its way to the Far East opened fire on a Hull fishing fleet on the Dogger Bank.[3] " A most dastardly outrage ", minuted the King on the first telegram ; " an unspeakable outrage", cried Rosebery. "Inform Count Lamsdorff of what has occurred", telegraphed Lansdowne to the British Ambassador in St. Petersburg, " and say that it is impossible to exaggerate the indignation which has been provoked. It is aggravated by the callousness of the Russian Commanding Officer, who must have known before resuming the voyage that his fleet had fired upon and seriously injured innocent and defenceless people. It will be the duty of His Majesty's Government to require ample apology and complete and prompt reparation as well as security against the recurrence of such intolerable incidents. They prefer however not to formulate their demands until they have received the explanations which the Russian Government will no doubt hasten to lay before them. The matter is one which admits of no delay." The Foreign Minister spoke in the same strain to the Russian Ambassador.

It was the most critical moment in Anglo-Russian relations since the Penjdeh incident of 1885, but the two Governments kept their heads. Delcassé pleaded in both capitals for

[1] *Parliamentary Debates*, Fourth Series, Vol. CXXXVIII, 1433–6. July 28.
[2] *D.D.F.* V. 221–9.   [3] *B.D.* IV, 5–41.

moderation and received the thanks of both sides.[1] Regrets were expressed by Lamsdorff and the Tsar before the offending Admiral telegraphed his report. In a friendly interview on October 25 Lansdowne informed Benckendorff that we should expect an ample apology, the fullest reparation to the sufferers, a searching inquiry followed by adequate punishment of the persons proved responsible, and security against a repetition of the incident. Who would be safe, asked the Foreign Secretary, and what was to prevent the Russian fleet, during its long journey to the Far East, from carrying death and destruction with it throughout its course ? Prompt action was needed, else the British Government would be obliged to take its own measures to prevent a repetition of these acts. Never before had the Foreign Secretary spoken to an Ambassador with such severity. Danger arose, not from the Russian Government which expressed its profound regret for the untoward incident, but from the exasperating silence of the offending Admiral. On the following day Lansdowne plainly warned the distressed Ambassador of the danger of war. " We could not admit that the Russian fleet should be allowed to proceed upon its voyage, carrying with it the persons who were responsible for the North Sea incident : their departure would not only enable them to elude justice but would also render it impossible to obtain conclusive results from the inquiry which the Russian Government had promised to undertake. It was my duty to tell him that unless our demands in this respect were complied with, it might be necessary for us to take measures for the purpose of enforcing them." Orders, in fact, were given to the British fleet to be ready for emergencies.

The Admiral's report, which arrived on October 27, stated that the fleet had seen and fired on two torpedo boats steaming at full speed and without lights. Every effort had been made to spare the trawlers. The version, observed Lansdowne to Benckendorff, bristled with improbabilities. How could Japanese torpedo boats be found in the North Sea ? Before the fleet left Vigo, the person responsible for the attack must be discovered and left behind. The inquiry, he proposed, should be held by an international Commission as provided by The Hague Convention. The tension diminished with the news that the officers responsible for the incident and other material witnesses would be disembarked at Vigo. At this point Cambon, with whom Lansdowne had been in constant touch

[1] D.D.F. V, 468–477.

throughout the crisis, urged a conciliatory attitude in view of Russia's concessions. He did not believe that, in the event of a war, France would join Russia, but the Anglo-French entente would inevitably suffer.

The view of the Cabinet was expressed in a speech on October 28 by the Prime Minister, whose references to the Russian Government Benckendorff described to Lansdowne as better than he had ventured to expect. Balfour's caustic comments on the Admiral's story, on the other hand, seemed to him needlessly offensive. After defending his chief the Foreign Secretary spoke gravely of the future. He foresaw no difficulty in dealing with the further phases of the actual crisis, but he lived in dread of new troubles. Count Lamsdorff no doubt realised that a conflict had only just been avoided. The British Government had gone as far as it dared—further than many of its friends approved. In these circumstances he would not dwell upon the results of a repetition of the North Sea incident. A wholesale seizure of vessels suspected of carrying contraband would also render public opinion uncontrollable. " I was not making any complaint or asking for any further pledges, but merely giving a friendly warning in the interest of those good relations which Count Lamsdorff was, I knew, as anxious to preserve as myself." After the failure of Russian attempts to limit the inquiry the agreement was signed at St. Petersburg on November 25. The report of the Commission, which sat at Paris, courteously rejected the Admiral's story. Russia's face was saved, and the incident closed with a payment of compensation to the sufferers. A single word of menace, confessed Lamsdorff to Hardinge, would have made war inevitable. Never before nor after did Lansdowne experience such acute anxiety as in those dark October days, and never had he displayed greater skill. It was some consolation that the entente with France had begun to bear fruit, and the King sent a message of thanks.[1] " As for M. Delcassé tell him that I have absolute confidence in him, and that I count on his loyalty and experience to spare us the horrors of a conflict."

The Tsar had regretted the North Sea incident, and was glad to see it liquidated without war. But the alliance of England with his enemy rankled, and the British veto on the employment of the Black Sea fleet aroused a resentment which waxed as the chances of victory waned. Germany stood ready to turn

[1] D.D.F. V, 540.

Russian Anglophobia to her own account, and when the Kaiser presented the Björkö pact it was promptly accepted by the Tsar. Though the secret was well kept, Russia's sentiments were fully understood in Downing Street. From the mediatory activities of Roosevelt and the Kaiser which preceded the conclusion of peace Lansdowne stood aloof, for his services were not requested by Tokio. At intervals throughout the conflict Japanese statesmen expressed their entire satisfaction with the manner in which England carried out her obligations as an ally.

While the Kaiser and the Tsar were planning changes in the diplomatic map of Europe, Great Britain and Japan were tightening their bonds of friendship.[1] The alliance of 1902 had been concluded for five years, and its authors were well satisfied with their handiwork. The delicate machinery had operated without a hitch. It had kept the ring for a victorious war, and Russian domination in the Far East had been overthrown without spilling a drop of English blood. If, however, the ground which had been won was to be maintained, it was clear that the partnership would have to be prolonged. The struggle was still in progress, but its issue was not in doubt. In celebrating the completion of the third year of association at the opening of 1905, the Japanese Foreign Minister expressed a wish both for the extension and the enlargement of the contract. He was knocking at an open door. On March 24 Lansdowne referred to the matter in conversation with the Japanese Minister. " What was meant by the suggestion that the alliance might be given a wider scope ? " Hayashi replied that his Government had been too occupied with the war to formulate plans. He added that some eminent soldiers were prepared for the employment of Japanese troops in India in return for adequate concessions. There were, however, cross currents in Tokio, and at their next meeting the Ambassador reported that his Government would be glad to renew the alliance for seven years without extending its scope.

Now was the opportunity to redress the balance, and Lansdowne argued persuasively for amplification of the partnership in two directions. Firstly the parties might help each other if either were attacked without provocation by one or more Powers. Secondly Japan might undertake to help Great Britain by land or sea within certain geographical limits. In asking our ally to enlarge her responsibilities, the Foreign

[1] B.D. IV, ch. 24.

Minister pointed out that Russia, after recovering from her defeat, might renew her attack with irresistible force. The knowledge that in such an event she would confront Great Britain as well as Japan would probably cause her to abandon the idea of reprisals in the Far East, and turn her eyes to other parts of Asia, such as the Indian frontier. The alacrity and unanimity with which the Japanese Government accepted the new demands in principle were a measure of the utility of the alliance and came as an agreeable surprise. On May 26 Hayashi handed in a draft, and after ten weeks of earnest discussion the treaty was signed on August 12, 1905, when peace was at last in sight.

The new arrangement, embodying the two British suggestions and valid for ten years, corresponded far more closely to the desires of British statesmen and the needs of the British Empire than the old. Each Power was to help the other against unprovoked attack wherever it arose. England recognised the right of Japan to take any measures of " guidance, control and protection " in Korea compatible with the commercial equality of all nations, and Japan recognised our right to safeguard the frontiers of India. This time there was no criticism in the British press. Once again Lansdowne had set his hand to a pact which was to make history on a larger scale than he could guess in 1905.

When the Anglo-Japanese treaty was signed, the Russian and Japanese plenipotentiaries were sitting round a table at Portsmouth in Maine. On the conclusion of the war a fortnight later it was announced to the world. A reassuring despatch from Lansdowne endeavoured to make an unwelcome announcement as palatable in St. Petersburg as he could contrive. " The Russian Government will, I trust, recognise that the new Agreement is an international document to which no exception can be taken by any of the Powers interested in the affairs of the Far East. . . . H. M. Government believe that they may count upon the goodwill and support of all the Powers in endeavouring to maintain peace in Eastern Asia, and in seeking to uphold the integrity and independence of the Chinese Empire and the principle of equal opportunities for the commerce and industry of all nations in that country. On the other hand the special interests of the Contracting Parties are of a kind upon which they are fully entitled to insist, and the announcement that those interests must be safeguarded is one which can create no surprise and need give rise to no misgivings." In communicating this despatch to Lamsdorff the British Ambassador read extracts from a conciliatory private letter from his chief, and did his utmost to convince the Minister of the absolute sincerity of the British Government in their desire to live on friendly terms. Reserving the treaty and the despatch for subsequent perusal Lamsdorff remarked that the Ambassador was well aware of his desire for good relations, and added that they must now work strenuously together to remove points of dissension based solely on unreasoning prejudice. In the course of the conversation Hardinge casually alluded to the possibility at a future date of the renewal of negotiations for an agreement which had been interrupted by the war. Lamsdorff replied that he was most anxious that they should be brought to a successful issue, but they ought not to be rushed. The interview proved more satisfactory than might have been expected, and the comments of the Russian press were comparatively restrained. The ending of the war had removed the main obstacle to a rapprochement, and the reconciliation with France rendered the prospects far more promising than in 1903.

The ice was broken on October 3 when the Russian Ambassador asked Lansdowne his views on the possibility of an understanding.[1] The new treaty with Japan had been rather a shock ; but the Russian Government was not unfriendly, and Lamsdorff was ready for a discussion. It would be wise, however, not to say too much at the moment. He was about to visit Russia and would be better able to explain the ideas of his Government on his return. Lansdowne rejoined that it would be a mistake to attempt too much or to aim at a comprehensive transaction on the Anglo-French model. His idea was to seek the solution of outstanding differences and then to pass on to others if the work proceeded successfully. The Foreign Secretary had in mind, though he did not refer to it, the relations between Russian and Afghan officials. Two days later he told Benckendorff that he was about to meet the King and the Prime Minister at Balmoral and was extremely anxious to learn his views. The Ambassador replied that his Government and an influential section of the public were strongly in favour of an understanding, but advised that the matter should not be hurried. The recent pact with Japan had been a blow from which it would take time to recover. In his view the Persian question was the only difficulty, though it was not

[1] B.D. IV, 204-8.

insurmountable.   Russia did not want to annex Persian territory or acquire a post on the Gulf, though she might need an
outlet for her trade.   Lansdowne replied that we too had no
desire to infringe the integrity of Persia, and that our policy
in regard to commerce was well known.   Benckendorff added
that any arrangement should avoid a spirit of hostility to
Germany, to which the Foreign Minister rejoined that nothing
was further from his thoughts.   The situation was developing
as healthily as could be wished ; but before the Ambassador
returned from Russia the Balfour Ministry had resigned.
Lansdowne had smoothed the way for a rapprochement, but
he was not himself to enter the Promised Land.

X

The Unionist Ministry, though well aware that the tide was
running against it, desired to remain in power long enough to
bring the revised Japanese alliance into port.   On its conclusion Balfour's resignation was in sight, but there was still
time for the Foreign Secretary to add another feather to his
cap.   He had watched the boiling cauldron of Balkan politics
with growing impatience and disgust.   For the misrule of
the Turk not only produced chronic exasperation among its
Macedonian victims, but encouraged the neighbouring Christian states to peg out claims for the future.   Complaints at the
Balkan capitals of the outrages of the bands were as fruitless as
appeals to the Sultan to set his house in order.   Austria and
Russia were recognised to be the most interested Powers and
to possess the most effective means of enforcing their demands.
But the statesmen of Vienna and St. Petersburg cared far less
for the victims of an intolerable system than Lansdowne, who
inherited the Gladstonian tradition and awaited the opportunity
to emerge from his tent.

At the opening of 1903 the Foreign Secretary informed the
Austrian Ambassador that he was watching with close interest
the efforts of the two Powers to arrange with Turkey for the
reform of Macedonian government, to which we attached
immense importance and which we earnestly desired to assist.[1]
Three days later, in a despatch to our Ambassador at Constantinople, he advocated the appointment of European experts of
tried ability and integrity in the departments of Justice and
Finance, and of a number of carefully selected European

[1] B.D. V, chs. 31-2.

officers to reorganise the gendarmerie and police. " It is of course obvious that without adequate financial arrangements for the payment of the various branches of the administration no reforms can be carried into practical effect." A month later a scheme was worked out by Lamsdorff and Goluchowsky. An Inspector-General was to be appointed, irremovable for three years, except by agreement with the two Powers. Foreign experts were to reorganise the police and the gendarmerie, the latter to contain Christians as well as Mussulmans. A budget was to be drawn up for each of the three Macedonian vilayets, and local revenues were to be assigned in the first place to the local administration. Lansdowne accepted the scheme in principle and undertook to recommend it to the Sultan ; but he reserved the right of recommending modifications and suggesting alternative proposals in the event of it proving inadequate.

Before the new system was inaugurated Macedonia, tormented by intolerable sufferings, burst into flame. The revolt was quickly suppressed, and the Foreign Ministers of Austria and Russia met at Mürzsteg to revise their earlier scheme. Lansdowne seized the opportunity to forward suggestions. Either a Christian Governor, unconnected with the Balkans and the Great Powers, or a Mussulman Governor assisted by European Assessors selected by Austria and Russia, should be appointed ; and European officers in adequate numbers should be engaged to reorganise the gendarmerie. In thanking him for his proposals the Austrian and Russian Governments added that they were in accord with the decisions already reached. Civil Agents of Austria and Russia were to be attached to the Inspector-General and to report to their Governments. A foreign General, with foreign officers, was to command the gendarmerie, dividing up the country into zones. After the pacification of the country Turkey was to modify the administrative boundaries with a view to the grouping of the nationalities, and the courts were to be reformed. The Sultan offered the customary opposition, but ended by accepting the scheme in principle. An Austrian and a Russian Assessor were appointed ; an Italian General was selected to command the gendarmerie, and Great Britain undertook responsibility for the Drama zone.

The Mürzsteg programme was an improvement on its predecessor, but Lansdowne never believed in its adequacy, even were it to be carried out. After watching without

surprise the evasions and delays throughout 1904 he determined
to force the pace. On January 11, 1905, he outlined bolder
measures in a memorable despatch. No part of the reform
scheme, he complained, had been carried out except the organisation of the gendarmerie, in which the European officers
were still too few. The first necessity was the immediate
reduction of the troops in and near Macedonia to the number
required for the preservation of order, while Bulgaria was to
make a corresponding reduction and prevent the organisation
of bands. The second was the appointment of a Commission
of Delegates, nominated by the Powers and under the presi-
dency of the Inspector-General, possessing administrative and
executive authority. Financial reforms should provide for a
fixed payment to the Porte by each vilayet, the balance remaining for local purposes. The Inspector-General, assisted by
the Commission, might command the troops.

It was too large a mouthful to swallow whole ; but on May
8 the six Powers demanded the appointment of four Financial
Delegates, nominated by France, Germany, Great Britain and
Italy, to co-operate with the Inspector-General and the two
Civil Agents. After waiting for nearly four months for a
satisfactory reply, the Powers informed the Porte of the names
of the four Delegates. When the Sultan refused recognition
they were instructed to join the Civil Agents at Uskub. Since
Turkey continued intransigent, Austria and Russia proposed a
naval demonstration in case of need. In welcoming the
proposal Lansdowne suggested that, if the Powers were to be
put to so much trouble and expense, they should secure acceptance not only of the Financial Commission but of the *Réglement*
which it had drawn up. The Sultan should also agree that the
reforms to be worked out by the Commission should include
the reorganisation of the Courts. It was most important,
explained the Foreign Secretary to the Russian and Austrian
Ambassadors, to convince the Sultan that obstructive tactics
were useless. If after weeks and months he was allowed to
escape with the original conditions he would be encouraged
to repeat his familiar tricks.

The threat of coercion proved unavailing, and the Sultan
only yielded after the occupation of the custom-house and
telegraph office in Mitylene by the ships of all the Powers
except Germany. When Lansdowne left office in December
11, 1905, he had the satisfaction of knowing that the Financial
Commission and the *Réglement* were safe. During his last

year his vigorous policy had placed Great Britain at the head of the European Concert and secured at least partial control of the finances of Macedonia, in which he had always discerned the key to reform. That the new machinery brought neither prosperity nor peace to a distracted province was the fault not of the British statesman but of the incurable inertia of Turkey and of the ferocious rivalries of the Balkan states. In Macedonia as in the Belgian Congo, where he initiated the movement for reform which his successor brought to fruition, he had no national axe to grind. He was aware that these humanitarian crusades, which were commonly attributed to selfish political motives, did not add to our popularity abroad. It was his consolation that his efforts were not wholly in vain.

Lansdowne regarded his rule at the Foreign Office as the most memorable chapter in his life, and Liberals agreed with Conservatives that he had justified his appointment. By his breadth of conception, his firmness, his conciliatory temper, his skilful technique, he had won high rank among British Foreign Secretaries. His undeviating principle was *suaviter in modo, fortiter in re*. He had taken the helm at a moment when Great Britain was morally no less than politically isolated, and he had steered the ship through five eventful years. When he laid down his burden the position of the country appeared far safer and stronger. The Japanese Alliance and the defeat of Russia had removed all danger in the Far East. The reconciliation with France had secured a free hand in Egypt. London and Washington were on excellent terms. A rapprochement with Russia was in sight. The only cloud on the horizon was the growing tension with Germany. No one at this stage in Downing Street or elsewhere could forecast the results of the abandonment of isolation, for the British Empire only gradually came to realise the significance for good or evil of the immense change that had taken place. How Lansdowne would have reacted to the varying moods and phases of French, German and Russian policy in the ensuing years it is idle to guess. The custodian of national interests in the field of foreign affairs can only act as seems to him best during the brief hour that he is called to take a hand in the most perilous of political adventures.

DELCASSE

CHAPTER II

DELCASSÉ

I

AMONG the shining merits of Albert Sorel is that of establishing the continuity of French foreign policy.[1] In no country of modern Europe have the changes of régime been more frequent, yet nowhere have such revolutionary transformations exerted less influence on the governing principles of diplomacy. France, like Great Britain, has instinctively endeavoured to make the most of her geographical position. Surrounded on three sides by the sea, her land frontiers have been her main concern. For centuries her army has been to her what our navy has been to us. Her national heroes are her soldiers, from Condé and Turenne to Napoleon and Foch. To attain, to defend, to regain her " natural frontiers "—the Pyrenees, the Alps and the Rhine— was the dream of her statesmen, since the consolidation of her unity and the rise of the Absolute Monarchy in the sixteenth century enabled her to play for the highest stakes. Under Louis XIV and Napoleon she threw caution to the winds and learned the lessons of adversity. In the pursuit of her goal she has displayed a tenacity of purpose and a resilience after defeat worthy of one of the foremost nations of the world.

The Second Empire crashed to the ground in a clumsy attempt to secure compensation in the Rhineland for the unification of Germany under Prussian control. After the Treaty of Frankfurt the military hegemony of Europe passed from Paris to Berlin, and for the first decade of the Third Republic internal reconstruction was the imperative task of France. The occupation of Tunis in 1881, which inaugurated a new phase of colonial expansion, announced that she had recovered her breath and was preparing to resume her activities as a Great Power. Ten years later partnership with Russia ended the quarantine in which Bismarck had kept her since

[1] Emile Bourgeois, *Manuel historique de politique étrangère*, 4 vols., and René Pinon, *Histoire Diplomatique* 1515–1928, forming Vol. IX of *Histoire de la Nation Française* edited by Gabriel Hanotaux, are the best general surveys. *Histoire diplomatique de l'Europe*, publiée sous la direction de Henri Hauser, 2 vols.; Bourgeois et Pagès, *Les Origines et les Responsabilités de la Grande Guerre*; Tardieu, *La France et les Alliances*; Recouly, *De Bismarck à Poincaré*; and E. M. Carroll, *French Public Opinion and Foreign Affairs* 1870–1914, are useful for the Third Republic.

her defeat. The Dual Alliance confronted the Triple Alliance, and Frenchmen reflected with pride and gratitude that the days of humiliation were at an end. France had hitherto been compelled to wait on the smiles and frowns of Berlin. Henceforth she could once again have a policy of her own. Though no one imagined that the Dual Alliance was the stronger of the rival groups, she would at any rate cease to be treated as of no account.

The new orientation was a rejoinder to the Triple Alliance ; for though Alexander III had not the slightest intention of shedding Russian blood for the recovery of Alsace and Lorraine, the problem of the lost provinces assumed a fresh aspect and the inferiority complex disappeared. The future was open and dreams became possibilities. The strength of Russia was overestimated in Paris as in all the other capitals of Europe. Ribot and Freycinet, who had made the alliance, agreed with Hanotaux, who steered the ship of state with a short interval from 1894 to 1898, that the paramount duty of the Quai d'Orsay was to maintain the new pact. In the exhilaration of the moment no one suggested that the partnership might be used for purely Russian aims. If British policy could be summarised as Naval Supremacy and the Balance of Power, French statesmanship at the close of the nineteenth century was inspired by the old tradition of *les frontières naturelles* and the new factor of the Russian alliance.

Delcassé, like Thiers and Gambetta, was a *méridional*.[1] Like most clever young provincials, after serving his apprenticeship in law and journalism, he determined to seek his fortunes in Paris. His idol was Gambetta, as was natural to a young man who had reached the age of eighteen when the Franco-German war broke out ; and he never ceased to speak of the great tribune with affectionate regard. He was happy in finding employment on the staff of the Gambettist organ, *La République Française*, where he quickly attracted the attention of his chiefs. His duties constantly took him to the Chamber, and " le petit journaliste " soon became a well-known figure in the lobbies. From the outset he specialised in foreign and colonial affairs, accepting the maxim of his master that, since the Rhine provinces could not at present be reconquered,

[1] André Mévil, *De la Paix de Francfort à la Conférence d'Algésiras*, and Georges Reynald, *La Diplomatie Française, L'Oeuvre de M. Delcassé*, defend him. René Millet, *Notre politique extérieure de 1898 à 1905*, is a sharp attack. Graham H. Stuart, *French Foreign Policy* (1898-1914) is more detached. Charles Benoist, *Souvenirs* III, 115-123, gives a vivid portrait of the man.

compensation should be sought in expansion overseas. In a vigorous pamphlet published in 1882, *Alerte ! Où allons nous ?* he warmly eulogised Gambetta, lamented his fall, and denounced the weakness of Freycinet's policy in Egypt.[1] He supported Ferry, the heir of Gambetta, not only in the hour of his popularity but when a trifling reverse in the Far East swept him away. " The European Powers are partitioning the world ", he wrote on March 30, 1885, the day of his fall. " The duty of every Government is marked out in advance. It will be no slight claim to glory for the Republic to have refashioned for France a colonial empire to replace that which the Monarchy had lost."

Delcassé was among the first of French journalists to proclaim the need of a partnership with Russia. " To France and to Russia alike ", he wrote in 1887, " a common peril calls imperatively for the closest co-operation.[2] . . . Each acts as a counter-weight, one in the East, one in the West, to the Teutonic giant, just as they act as bulwarks in Asia, one in the north, one in the south, against the encroachments of China and Great Britain. Everywhere they confront the same enemies, share the same interests, cherish the same aspirations. The astonishing thing is that an Entente of such obvious mutual advantage should have taken so long to fructify." When the seed was sown at the end of the 'eighties it ripened rapidly to harvest.

From lobby correspondent and leader-writer to Member of Parliament was only a step, and in 1889 Delcassé was elected a Deputy in his own Department of Ariège, which he continued to represent for the rest of his political life. Appointed a member of the Budget Commission, he vigorously defended the increase of the colonial credits before a Chamber which either doubted the colonial capacity of France, or, like Clemenceau, resented the dispersion of her energies. His competence in his chosen field was recognised by his appointment as Under-Secretary for the Colonies in the Ribot Cabinet of 1893, and he retained his post in the Dupuy Ministry which followed. Largely owing to his efforts, the Colonial Office was made a separate department under a Cabinet Minister ; and when, after a short interval, a second Dupuy Ministry was formed in May 1894, he returned to the scene of his labours as chief. It was during his official connection with the

[1] A copy is in the British Museum.
[2] Quoted in Michon, *The Franco-Russian Alliance*, 2c.

Colonial Office that Liotard was sent as Commissioner to the Upper Ubanghi; and the Liotard Mission was the parent of Marchand's eastward journey, which began in 1896 and aimed at securing an outlet for the French Congo on the Nile. The fall of the Méline Ministry in June, 1898, removed the masterful Hanotaux from the Quai d'Orsay and brought the Radicals back to power. Delcassé was appointed by Brisson to the Foreign Office,[1] which he was to hold for a far longer period than any other Minister of the Third Republic. Before he left it seven years later he had changed the face of Europe and won new friendships for France.[2]

II

Delcassé's handling of his first problem was a significant indication of his life-long attitude. On June 17, 1898, the French Ambassador in Berlin told Bülow that he heard from Paris that suspicious negotiations were on foot between Portugal and England concerning a lease of Delagoa Bay in return for financial aid.[3] Bülow answered evasively, believing that more could be secured in this matter from England than from France. " Perhaps the English statesmen ", he added in reporting the conversation to Hatzfeldt in London, " will become more favourable to our modest claims when they know that France is seeking support against England." On the following day he also reported the incident to Münster in Paris. Germany and France had the same interest either in preventing or in sharing in such a breach of the political and economic status quo. If France continued to be hypnotised by the gap in the Vosges, the Russian alliance would hardly be able to prevent England expanding everywhere outside Europe without consideration of her interests. The diplomatic co-operation of Germany and France would be aimed not directly against England, but against Portugal. Lisbon should be informed that the German and French Governments, whose nationals had important interests in Portugal, must consider by what economic or other pressure an international financial control might be established. " His

---

[1] According to Auguste Gérard, *Mémoires*, 316, he was recommended to Brisson by Paul Déroulède.

[2] The First Series of the *Documents Diplomatiques Français* has not yet reached 1898. The Second Series begins in 1901. Interpretations of his first years in office are therefore provisional.

[3] *G.P.* XIV, 266–9. cp. *D.D.F.* II, 188.

Majesty the Emperor ", concluded the despatch, " instructs you to speak earnestly with M. Hanotaux in this sense. The chief object of the conversation is to discover whether a practical co-operation between Germany and France in current questions of every kind is excluded as a matter of principle, as it was at the time of the Jameson incident. I need not say that the clearing up of this point is of far-reaching importance for the shaping of our foreign policy."

When this remarkable communication reached Paris the Méline Ministry had resigned ; and Hanotaux, who carried on till the appointment of his successor, was unable to give an official reply. He was, however, strongly of opinion that energetic resistance should be offered to the Portuguese plans. He could not bind the Government, but he had made it clear in Lisbon that Portugal must reckon on energetic resistance from France. He hoped that similar representations would be made by Germany. More he could not say, as the Ministry had ceased to exist. " I gathered from a long talk ", concluded Münster, " that personally he would be much inclined to co-operate with us in questions of common interest like this." To the surprise of the Ambassador the new Foreign Minister made no reference to the subject, though Hanotaux at a later period publicly stated that he had transmitted the German approach to his successor.[1] Delcassé himself, when challenged at a later date, declared in the Senate ; " No proposition from Germany concerning the Portuguese Colonies and inviting a decision about them was addressed to my predecessor in June 1898. So far as I am concerned it has been impossible for me to decline the proposals for the simple reason that no proposals were made to me." This is surely an economy of truth. Delcassé's apologists have argued that the German approach was too vague and embodied no formal proposition. But we have only to read the telegram, with the Kaiser's express instructions to speak to Hanotaux, in order to realise that this is no valid excuse. Rarely do Governments address one another so directly and on matters of such far-reaching significance. To make no reply, either formal or informal, was an astonishing début, and the Wilhelmstrasse drew its conclusions as to the new spirit beyond the Rhine.

" I greatly regret the departure of Hanotaux ", wrote Münster to Hohenlohe.[2] " My relations with him were of the best. Though he was bound to follow the course of Russian

<hr>

[1] G.P. XIV ,268-9, note.   [2] G.P. XIII, 241.

policy, he desired to entertain good relations with us and to improve them. The suspicion of this Minister that I noted in Berlin I find on close acquaintance to be unfounded. On the other hand I fear that Delcassé will deserve our mistrust. He has busied himself with politics both as a writer and behind the scenes. He has throughout endeavoured to work for the Russian alliance. He is said to dream of a Russo-Slav-Austrian alliance. He was a disagreeable Colonial Minister both for us and for England, and he has no experience of foreign affairs. I knew him as Colonial Minister, and did not like him." Ten days later Münster described the new Minister as the Russian candidate. " Why Delcassé was desired for that post I am not quite clear, as he has played no part either with his pen or in Parliament, and did nothing particular as Colonial Minister. He has always passed for a keen supporter of the Russian alliance, and perhaps Muraviev is glad to have a man here inferior to himself." If Münster was wrong in his disparaging estimate of the Minister's abilities, his prophecy that Delcassé would earn the mistrust of Germany was speedily fulfilled. Only once during the seven years of office on which he was embarking did he envisage co-operation with Berlin, and that was in a moment of exasperation. In a marginal comment on Münster's eulogies of Hanotaux the Kaiser described him as the most dangerous man for Germany that France possessed. He was soon to discover that Delcassé was very much worse.

III

The appointment brought as little satisfaction to the British as to the German Ambassador. " I cannot say ", wrote Monson, " that his antecedents at the Ministry of the Colonies inspire one with any other expectation than that H.M. Government will find him a very combative Minister.[1] M. Denis Gilbert, the Anglophobe writer in the *Figaro*, welcomes his advent at the Quai d'Orsay in the confident hope that he will signalise it by vigour in dealing with the Egyptian question. It is at any rate generally believed that his selection for the portfolio of foreign affairs is very acceptable at St. Petersburg." The new Minister, in a word, was a dark horse, and what little was known was far from reassuring. Hanotaux and Delcassé agreed that the Russian alliance was

[1] *B.D.* I, 158.

the sheet-anchor of French policy and that France could afford
no more than one rival or potential enemy at a time. They
differed, however, on the vital question which Power that
rival should be. It is probably doing Hanotaux no injustice
to suggest that, like Gambetta in his later years, he had given
up any real expectation of regaining Alsace-Lorraine by force ;
for on any other hypothesis it would have been madness to
risk a conflict with the British Empire by challenging her
position in the valley of the Nile. To the Grey Declaration
of 1895, reiterated by the Unionists on their return to power
shortly afterwards, he replied that the Sudan belonged to the
Sultan of Turkey and the Khedive, and that France had as
much right there as England. Rejecting the new Monroe
Doctrine, as she had a perfect legal right to do, France despatched the Marchand expedition from the French Congo in
1896, hoping that it would reach the Upper Nile before the
reconquest of the Sudan brought the British flag south of
Khartoum. It was a risky game, and it was Delcassé's misfortune that it fell to him to capitulate when France's bluff
was called.

On July 10, 1898, a few days after the new Minister was
installed at the Quai d'Orsay, Marchand reached Fashoda with
8 officers and 120 native soldiers after an adventurous journey.[1]
His arrival was unknown in France till two months later. On
September 7, after the battle of Omdurman, Delcassé offered
the British Ambassador his congratulations on a brilliant feat
of arms, despite the difference of opinion between the two
countries about Egypt. He supposed a flotilla would push
up the river and it might fall in with Captain Marchand, who
had been instructed to consider himself " an emissary of
civilisation ", without authority to decide on questions of
right, which would have to be discussed by the two Governments. He added that he hoped that the British Commander
would be instructed to avoid a collision. When Monson
inquired as to the whereabouts of the expedition the Minister
replied that he did not know. " The moderation of Delcassé's tone and manner ", reported the Ambassador, " inspires

[1] B.D. I, 158–193, and Affaires du Haut Nil et du Bahr-el-Ghazal, 1898. The
Livre Jaune is very incomplete. The most authoritative presentation of the
French case is in Hanotaux, Fachoda. cp. Freycinet, La Question d'Egypte ;
Kossatz, Untersuchunden über den französisch-englischen Weltgegensatz im Faschoda-
jahr ; and Riker, " British Policy in the Fashoda Crisis," Political Science
Quarterly, March 1929. André Maurois, Édouard VII et son Temps, 87–92,
prints some private letters of Delcassé.

me with a certain hope that, if the French are going to discuss this question at once, they will do so with calmness. No doubt the Government will be questioned upon the subject when the Chamber meets, and will be forced to maintain in public that French policy does not and cannot vary in regard to it. But as the whole country is aware that under existing circumstances that policy must remain unsupported by action, I trust that there is no danger that the Government will compromise itself by any talk of entering upon impracticable engagements." Monson was so penetrated with the consciousness of the strength of his country's position that he could hardly conceive a French Cabinet ignoring the stern realities of the situation. Delcassé's report of the conversation, as published at the time, is much shorter. Both the Sirdar and Marchand, he argued, were struggling against barbarism in the interests of civilisation. As a consequence of the battle of Omdurman they might come face to face ; but political questions could only be dealt with between the two Governments.

Salisbury replied firmly that all the territories lately subject to the Khalifa passed to the British and Egyptian Governments by right of conquest. " H.M. Government do not consider that this right is open to discussion, but they would be prepared to deal in the manner suggested by his Excellency with any territorial controversies now existing in regard to those regions which are not affected by this assertion." Delcassé merely remarked that the expression " territories which were subject to the Khalifa " was vague. Meanwhile a British flotilla was steaming up the Nile, and Kitchener reached Fashoda on September 19, where he was welcomed by Marchand " in the name of France." When the gallant French officer was informed that his presence was regarded as a direct violation of the rights of Egypt and Great Britain, he begged that the matter should be referred to Paris. Thus the French flag continued to fly, while the Egyptian flag was hoisted a few hundred yards away. It was an unstable equilibrium, and Delcassé sadly remarked : " We have only arguments down there, and they have soldiers."

On the day before the meeting of Kitchener and Marchand an important interview took place between Delcassé and the British Ambassador. Assuming Marchand to be at Fashoda, as the British newspapers asserted, was it maintained, asked the Minister, that he had no right to be there ? Fashoda, replied Monson, evading the question, had passed into the hands of Great Britain and Egypt. The Minister was well aware of the British declaration that any incursion into the Upper Nile basin would be considered an unfriendly act. Why, then, did they send this mission, when they must know what serious results its success in reaching this point must inevitably produce? France, rejoined Delcassé, had never recognised the British sphere of influence in the Upper Nile regions, and Hanotaux had openly protested against it in the Senate. But, as a matter of fact, there was no Marchand mission. Marchand had received his orders from Liotard, who had been sent as Commissioner to the Upper Ubanghi when the region of the Bahr-el-Ghazal had long been outside the influence of the Khalifa, and, if the newspapers were to be believed, Fashoda itself was unoccupied when Marchand arrived. If the British Government would meet the French in a friendly spirit, a satisfactory arrangement could be quickly reached.

At this point the British Ambassador brought the conversation back to realities. " I said to his Excellency that I must tell him very frankly that the situation on the Upper Nile is a dangerous one. I must refer him again to your Lordship's telegram of the 9th instant, and I must state distinctly that Fashoda falls within the territories therein designated as dependencies of the Khalifate, and that H.M. Government are determined to hold to the decision already announced to him. It was right that I should state to him categorically that they would not compromise on this point. For the rest we had no desire to pick a quarrel ; but having long ago given a warning, I could not see how we could now cause surprise if we resent a step which we had cautioned France not to take." Delcassé's report stresses the argument that France had as much right in the Sudan as England, who had never received the Sultan's authorisation of her claims. Moreover the Liotard Mission dated from two years before the Grey Declaration. Though the conversation was conducted with perfect courtesy, there was thunder in the air.

After a Cabinet Council Delcassé invited the British authorities to convey his instructions to Marchand to send his report via Cairo as the quickest route, since it would be difficult for the Government to act without their agent's view of the situation. Had the French Government, rejoined Monson, decided not to recall him till they had received his

report ? " His Excellency after some few minutes' consideration said that he was ready, and he believed that his colleagues
would be ready, to make great concessions but that if I asked
him for the impossible there would be but one answer. He
would be ready to enter into discussion, negotiation, or whatever it might be called, without receiving the report, but this
was all he could do. I reminded him that he knew from
your Lordship's telegram of the 9th instant that H.M. Government considered that there could be no discussion upon such
questions as the right of Egypt to Fashoda. His Excellency
replied that, if there was to be no discussion, a rupture could
not be avoided." He hoped his request would be granted,
for the press was already suggesting that Marchand was
abandoned and holding up the Foreign Minister to execration.
Delcassé's carefully edited report gives little indication of the
strained situation that had been reached. Salisbury consented
to forward the message to Marchand, but added that if the
existing situation were prolonged great uneasiness would be
caused.

The crisis was now acute, and Delcassé returned to the
charge on the following day. The Cabinet, he declared,
wished to make a friend of England, and he added the curious
confession that " between ourselves " he would much prefer
an Anglo-French to a Franco-Russian alliance. " Do not ask
me for the impossible : do not drive me into a corner." He
knew that feeling in England was strong, but Englishmen
were not so excitable as the French, and they felt sentimental
considerations less deeply. Monson stoutly replied that he
could not exaggerate the strength of feeling in England, both
on the part of the Government and the public. " You surely
would not break with us over Fashoda ? " exclaimed Delcassé.
That was exactly what he feared, rejoined Monson. "' In such
an event we shall not stand alone", came the retort ; " but I
repeat I would rather have England for our ally than that
other." There seemed little hope of Marchand's recall, added
the Ambassador's report ; but the Foreign Minister had
several times mentioned the possibility of a " transaction".
The brief and colourless French version of this interview
conveys no idea of its exciting character.

There was no hint of surrender two days later when Delcassé asked Monson to tell his chief unofficially that it was
impossible for the French Government to give up Fashoda.
" Neither this nor any other Ministry could submit to what

would be the humiliation of France.   Any formal demand of
this nature would be considered as an ultimatum and rejected.
The whole country would resent as an insult to the national
honour the proposal to recall Marchand and to treat the
occupation of Fashoda as an unjustifiable act.   He could not
think that England wished to go to war over such a question ;
but France, however unwillingly, would accept war rather
than submit."   On this occasion Delcassé's report makes no
attempt to conceal the tension of the hour.   " We reached
Fashoda first, I said, and we took it from barbarism, as you
were to take Khartoum two months later.   To ask us to
surrender it without any discussion would be to present an
ultimatum.   To know France is to know her reply.   You
are aware of my desire for an entente with England—as
advantageous to England as to France—and my conciliatory
sentiments.   I have only affirmed them so frankly because I
knew, and you too were sure, that they would not lead me
beyond the limits of national honour.   I can make material
sacrifices for the sake of the entente, but in my hands the
national honour will remain intact.   Nobody in my place
could speak otherwise, and perhaps they might be less
conciliatory."

On October 3 Monson's communication of the contents of
the forthcoming Blue-book moved Delcassé to set forth the
French case once again in a despatch to his Ambassador in
London.   There was no Marchand Mission organised after
and in opposition to the Grey declaration.   There was only a
Liotard Mission dating from 1893.   " C'est moi qui ai envoyé
M. Liotard dans l'arrière Oubangui et en lui désignant le Nil
comme le terme de sa mission.   How could I have supposed
that I was trespassing on Egyptian territory, since Egypt, by
the advice of England, had long abandoned these old Sudanese
provinces, particularly the equatorial province and that of
Bahr-el-Ghazal, and since at the same moment Great Britain
was pocketing Equatoria ? "   These and other arguments were
repeated by the French Ambassador in a long conversation
with Salisbury on October 5, but the dispute was too grave
to be settled by argument.   The decisive factor was the
British fleet.   While France was prepared for conditional
evacuation, England insisted on unconditional surrender.
Punch expressed the growing impatience of the man in the
street in a contemptuous cartoon.   " What will you give
me if I go away ? " asks the little organ-grinder.   " I will

give you something if you don't", replies a muscular John Bull with a menacing frown. There could no longer be the slightest doubt that England was ready for the fray.

On October 11 the British Ambassador found Delcassé in a very serious mood. He spoke of the possibility of resignation, and added that his successor would not be so accommodating. Describing the conversation as unofficial he declared that he would be conciliatory in substance if things were made easy for him in form. He was willing to discuss the evacuation of Fashoda in connection with the delimitation of the Franco-Egyptian frontier. When Monson replied that he had no authority to modify the British attitude, Delcassé was very despondent. He was tired of saying how anxious he was to avoid a rupture, and the knowledge of his friendly disposition towards England was injuring his position. Despite his excitement and complaints the Minister, reported Monson, was likely to retreat if a golden bridge could be built for him. The relentless logic of facts was beginning to tell. His strategy incurred the criticism of Münster. He had complicated his thankless task by failing to disclaim responsibility for Marchand's proceedings, and this would make it very difficult to yield as he would have to do. Muraviev, on the other hand, warmly praised his attitude, and declared that he had preached moderation in Paris. At his next interview with Monson on October 21 Delcassé—once more " unofficially "—complained of the speeches of British Ministers. He was accused of being weak. But, imbued as he was with the conviction that war between England and France over such a question as Fashoda would be an unparalleled calamity, he had always been ready to discuss Marchand's recall, provided he was not presented with an ultimatum. The French Government, concluded the Ambassador, now realised that they would have to withdraw Marchand, but only if they could announce negotiations on their claims to the west of the Nile.

A Parliamentary crisis at the end of October arising out of the Dreyfus case threatened the position of Delcassé, who told Monson on October 28 that his fate depended on the British attitude. He could not continue in office if an outlet by the Bahr-el-Ghazal, as a condition of the immediate evacuation of Fashoda, was refused. The feeling in his favour in the Chamber caused by the publication of the Livre Jaune was

practically universal, and he might have counted on a long
term at the Quai d'Orsay. " It is you who make it impossible
for me to remain." The humiliation of France, if persisted
in, would produce a feud which would take long to heal.
She would be driven to cultivate other Powers, which would
be only too glad to co-operate against English colonial policy,
and even Germany would be ready for such an understanding.
He produced a telegram stating that Russia entirely approved
French views and procedure in regard to the Upper Nile, and
would associate herself in any step which might become
necessary. This telegram he had omitted from the Yellow
Book in order to avoid excitement, though his popularity was
waning from his inability to give his countrymen proof of
Russian sympathy and encouragement. He was, however,
now only a *Ministre démissionaire*, and the conversation was
therefore private. On October 30 Münster telegraphed that
Delcassé would not join the new Ministry, as he declined to
order the unconditional evacuation of Fashoda.[1] Muraviev,
on the other hand, believed that he would.

At this moment the news reached Paris that Marchand had
left Fashoda without permission and had reached Khartoum
on his way to Cairo. Monson found the Minister angered
by this escapade, for the papers were already accusing him
of having ordered the officer to withdraw. He was going to
send him back to his post. He then reiterated his declarations
of the previous day. He would not accept the humiliation
involved in the evacuation of Fashoda without the promise of
negotiation on an outlet for French commerce to the Nile.
And as a war with England, which was the only alternative,
would be contrary to policy and repugnant to his principles,
he would be obliged to resign. Monson was disappointed,
for he had hoped that the Minister would have hailed Marchand's journey as facilitating a retreat from an untenable
position. Delcassé's pertinacity appeared to be invincible, he
reported, and the best chance of a solution would be his
resignation. The storm was still at its height, yet the end was
not far off.

On November 2 Delcassé unbosomed himself to Münster.[2]
He would never have sent Marchand to Fashoda, which had
little value, and he would not fight for the place. He added
that he had resolved to evacuate and would advise the Cabinet
in that sense. " Trop tard", commented the Ambassador in

[1] *G.P.* XIII, 311–12.   [2] *G.P.* XIV, 384, 391.

his telegraphic report. Had he not declared that he would not yield, he would have avoided humiliation to France and himself. Returning to the theme on November 9, after the crisis was over, Münster contended that a trained diplomatist or a real statesman would have played his cards differently. Delcassé had not understood English feeling and had ignored Monson's warnings. Münster forgot that the Foreign Minister could do nothing without the consent of the Cabinet, and that no French Cabinet can ignore public opinion. The crisis ended on November 3, when it was decided to evacuate Fashoda with the least possible delay. In his interview with the British Ambassador, Delcassé displayed considerable emotion. It had cost him much to continue in office after adopting this step, and he had only yielded to urgent appeals to his patriotism. His popularity would suffer, and it would be a very disagreeable task to defend the decision in the Chamber. France, reported Monson, was staggered, and Delcassé was profoundly depressed. He had stood out for terms, but Salisbury had refused to bargain. He had referred to assurances of Russian help, but Salisbury remained unimpressed. The humiliation, personal and national, was complete and unconcealed. France had hauled down her flag before a threat of war.

Never since 1871 had a Great Power received such a staggering blow to its pride. Yet the Cabinet had taken the only possible course, for England had all the winning cards in her hand. " A conflict", explained Delcassé in the Chamber, " would have involved sacrifices disproportionate to the object." Even the super-patriots could not contest this disagreeable truth. The fleet was weak, and the whole colonial empire lay at the mercy of the strongest navy in the world. Moreover, to quarrel with England was to play straight into the hands of Germany and to destroy any chance of recovering the Rhine provinces. The momentous resolve shaped the future of France. Delcassé had approved the policy of the Marchand Mission, though he was not in office when the decision was made. He now realised that it was a mistake and turned back on the brink of the abyss. It was not a question of legal right but of material strength. With that belated discovery he set out on a new and more promising course. On his return to St. Petersburg Moraviev warmly praised the French Ministers who had had the courage to realise the mistakes of their predecessors in Africa and to

climb down.[1] Delcassé, indeed, had told him in Paris that
he would think twice before he lifted a finger if the English
contemplated a permanent occupation of Egypt. The burnt
child feared a second touch of the scorching flame. Some
time had to elapse before French policy could adapt itself to
the new situation or Delcassé could swallow the bitterness of
defeat. When, a week after the surrender, Monson asked his
opinion about Russian and Italian proposals in regard to Crete,
he replied that France would agree to anything accepted by
the other Powers.[2] " In fact his tone seemed to be pitched in
the ' humiliation ' key, and his meaning to be—' What is
the use of France having an opinion of her own about anything
nowadays ? ' " Münster reported that there was a good deal of
talk about a coming rapprochement with Germany, though
he himself was sceptical on the subject.[3]

Delcassé's mood found expression in an astonishing interview with Huhn, the well-known Berlin Correspondent of the
Kölnische Zeitung, which took place at the suggestion of the
former.[4] England had known France would have to give
way and had made the surrender as humiliating as possible.
If the English wanted anything and were sure of its attain-
ment, they demanded it with brutal public threats so as to
make retreat more difficult. France had given up Fashoda
and now she was to be chucked out of the Bahr-el-Ghazal.
" Ils me font avaler un crapaud par jour et ça ne finit pas et ne
finira jamais." England seemed resolved to drive her
neighbour into war. A rapprochement with Germany was
extremely desirable, and need not interfere with the Russian
partnership. Without using the word " alliance", the two
states should pursue a common policy in view of English
encroachments. France was satiated, and was ready to support Germany's colonial aspirations everywhere, especially in
China and in securing stations for the sea route to Eastern
Asia. " Il faut refaire la politique suivie depuis seize ans."
At this point Huhn brought the embittered statesman back to
solid earth. A French Ministry could not bind its successor,
and would any Ministry have the courage to announce to the
Chamber that it had concluded far-reaching agreements with
Germany ? The Revanche, replied Delcassé, had lost ground

[1] *G.P.* XIV, 401 and 404.
[2] *B.D.* I, 192.
[3] *G.P.* XIII, 242-3.
[4] ibid. 251-4. Huhn's report, written for the German Foreign Office after
his return to Berlin, is dated December 5, 1898.

H

in recent years, as the younger generation was not interested. He saw no reason why a French Minister should not present the Chamber with a pact. " J'y irai, demain, si vous voulez." Germany could rest assured that he and a great majority of his countrymen were in earnest. The Wilhelmstrasse took no notice of this emotional outburst. Delcassé's attitude to Germany only a few weeks before the Fashoda crisis was unforgotten, and the Minister was speaking to a private individual.

A conversation with the British Ambassador on December 8 showed that the angry Minister's thoughts were still running on Germany.[1] Monson had heard that the French Government was about to propose a settlement of disputed questions ; and Delcassé, without referring to any such plan, reiterated his belief that the best interests of the two countries demanded good relations. He was troubled, however, by the fact that the naval preparations recently made in England had not been modified, which suggested the existence of a party in the Cabinet for war at any price. Monson reminded him of his statement that France would be backed up by Russia, a combination which required precautionary measures. The reply astounded the Ambassador. Speaking very deliberately he said that if France had to fight she would seek and find support not from Russia alone but from Germany as well. " He had frequently told me, he said, of the overtures indirectly made by Germany to the French Government. He was convinced that the rival commercial interests of Germany and England would strongly dispose the former to identify her action with that of Russia and France for the purpose of destroying England's maritime and commercial superiority, and he could affirm that recent events had caused in France a very marked turning towards Germany, which might easily be increased to an extent which probably I would not consent to believe. At any rate, I must be aware that public sentiment is by no means favourable to England." Delcassé, concluded Monson's report, possessed the vivacity and fluency of the *méridional*, and was easily carried away by the attraction of his theme. That the majority of Frenchmen were looking towards Germany the Ambassador declined to believe.

All this talk came to nothing, and Delcassé gradually reverted to his normal Germanophobia. In January 1899, Paul Cambon, the new French Ambassador in London,

[1] *B.D.* I, 196–7.

initiated the discussion which the situation required.[1] His manner was described by Salisbury as exceedingly conciliatory. He formally announced the evacuation of Fashoda, and made no demand that the French flag should fly in any part of the valley of the Nile. He sketched out a line separating French from Anglo-Egyptian territory which Salisbury believed to contain the elements of a settlement. Madagascar and Newfoundland were also mentioned, but these thorny topics were not followed up, and the agreement signed on March 21 related to North Africa alone. The territory of the Upper Nile, including the Bahr-el-Ghazal region, was allotted to Great Britain; France received the Central Sudan; and commercial equality throughout these enormous territories was proclaimed. The cession of the Bahr-el-Ghazal, in which posts had been established, was a blow to French pride, but Delcassé was ready with his defence. Now that British troops could be brought down from Cairo in twenty days, to claim that remote province was like crying for the moon. The Minister was pleased with the agreement and Münster found him in excellent spirits. It was fair to both sides, he said, and would leave no desire for revenge. He had escaped from a great danger, and, though the English war party still existed, it would now hardly be able to find a pretext for a fight.[2] It was the end of the Fashoda crisis, though a national reconciliation was still far away. When Cambon suggested the discussion of certain questions in a friendly spirit, he met with no response. " I have the greatest confidence in M. Delcassé and your present Government", replied Salisbury, " but in a few months time they will probably be overthrown and their successors will do exactly the contrary. No, we must wait a bit." Owing to unexpected events over which the French statesman exerted no control, the period of waiting was to last four years.

IV

A few weeks after Delcassé's appointment the Russian Government invited the Powers to meet at The Hague in 1899 to discuss the limitation of armaments. In welcoming the

---

[1] B.D. I, 197-8, January 11. Cambon's report is summarised by Paul Mantoux in his lecture " M. Paul Cambon in England," Studies in Anglo-French History, 154-7.
[2] G.P. XIV, 423-4.

initiative in the Chamber the Foreign Minister declared that the idea was good in itself, and that at various times France had cherished the same lofty design. She also supported the proposal because the Tsar was the head of a great nation, " an ally and a friend with whom the accord has never been more complete nor relations more confident." It was the first duty of every French statesman to win the confidence of his Russian counterpart, and in discussing the coming conference with the German Ambassador at Vienna, Muraviev paid Delcassé a high tribute. He had gone to Paris to win support for the Conference. To his great joy he had found the new Minister an exceptionally quiet, sensible, peaceful man, with whom Germany could be well content. " Please tell your Government so in my name." He greatly preferred him to Hanotaux, who was eaten up by vanity. Delcassé had money, was quite independent, and not in the least afraid of Parliament. " They will do exactly what I wish."[1] The Foreign Minister, however, was not quite so docile as his colleague believed. On April 21, 1899, he criticised the policy of the Russian statesman with a cynical frankness that astonished Münster and urged Franco-German co-operation at the approaching Conference.[2] They had the same interests in the matter—to resist the reduction of armaments. The Tsar's feelings must be spared, but nothing should be allowed to weaken their respective strengths.

While The Hague Conference was in session the Minister visited the Russian capital for the first time. " People are wondering what is the meaning of Delcassé's sudden journey to St. Petersburg", reported Münster.[3] Official circles explained that he had to return Muraviev's visit. " Le petit homme n'avait qu'une idée dans sa tête", observed his colleague Galliffet, " c'est celle de faire shake-hand avec notre ami Nicholas." Galliffet's disdainful words were telegraphed from the Wilhelmstrasse to the German Ambassador in St. Petersburg, who declined to believe that the visit was without political purpose.[4] Its object, Radolin believed, was to strengthen the alliance, which had been weakened by Russia's chilly attitude in the Fashoda crisis and other incidents, and to buttress Delcassé's personal position. No one discovered or guessed that its aim was nothing less than a revision and extension of the alliance itself. The Military Convention of

[1] G.P. XV, 162–4. October 23, 1898. [2] ibid. 186–7.
[3] G.P. XIII, 273. [4] ibid. 276–8. Aug. 8.

1893, which had been limited to the duration of the Triple Alliance, was now declared operative so long as the diplomatic accord of 1891 continued. The new agreement was embodied in an exchange of letters between the Foreign Ministers on August 9, 1899, and on his return Delcassé explained the transaction in a report to the President.[1]

After recalling the discrepancy between the diplomatic agreement, to which no time limit was assigned, and the Military Convention, which was to possess the same duration as the Triple Alliance, the French statesman proceeded to ask a question. What would happen if the Triplice were to break up ; if, for instance, Francis Joseph, who seemed the only bond of union between rival and even hostile races, were suddenly to die ? What was more capable of disturbing the peace and upsetting the equilibrium of Europe ? What pointed more clearly to the need of finding France and Russia, not only united in the same policy, but ready for its execution ? At the very moment when the Military Convention ought to come into play, it would have ceased to exist, swept away with the Triplice to which it owed its life. " Here was a gap which had not ceased to occupy my thoughts since my appointment, and it was my firm intention to fill it. The approval I obtained from your lofty and far-sighted patriotism has been a powerful support. Counting on a friendly welcome from the Emperor Nicholas I decided to return the visit which Count Muraviev, with whom I have always found myself in complete agreement, paid me last October." The Minister proceeded to describe his conversation with the Tsar, who praised his conduct in the Fashoda crisis. When the host had approved the proposal to alter the Military Convention, Delcassé submitted a declaration. " The arrangement of 1891 is solemnly confirmed, but its scope is strikingly enlarged. While in 1891 the two Governments merely describe their solicitude for the maintenance of peace, my project involves that they equally consider the maintenance of the balance of power in Europe." The extension was approved by the Tsar, and the draft was read to Muraviev, whom his master had summoned. The Foreign Minister had already been won, and the words were embodied in the letters exchanged. The change remained a secret till after the fall of the Russian Empire.

---

[1] The documents were published for the first time in 1918 in the Livre Jaune L'Alliance Franco-Russe, 129–132. The letters, but not the report, are printed in Pribram, Secret Treaties of Austria-Hungary, II, 218–221.

Delcassé had not merely correlated the pacts of 1891 and 1893 but widened the scope of the Alliance itself. In the eyes of some of his critics the latter was infinitely more important than the former. If we are to believe the latest historian of the Alliance,[1] he had secured the approval of the President for his plans, but without notifying most of his colleagues. On the plea of merely extending the duration of the Military Convention to correspond with the main diplomatic instrument, argues Michon, he had completely altered the character of the pact. " Delcassé had taken a defensive treaty, which only came into operation in the event of aggression on the part of the Triple Alliance, and imposed upon it as its chief aim the maintenance of the Balance of Power in Europe "— a phrase, he argues, capable of serving as an excuse for intervention in almost any modification of the status quo. This view is shared by Mathiez, the historian of the French Revolution, who argued that the seeds of the world war lay hidden in the agreement of 1899. Delcassé, he suggests, desiring to detach Russia from Germany, virtually promised armed support for her Balkan ambitions. " Thus the agreement was the price that France—or rather M. Delcassé—paid for the abandonment of the policy of amicable relations with Germany which M. Hanotaux had pursued. . . . It was a bargain—the Straits for Alsace." These comments overshoot the mark, for the Balance of Power was a recognised principle long before 1899, and the *casus foederis* remained unaltered. But Renouvin, one of the fairest of French historians, admits that the spirit of the alliance was changed, and that Delcassé was not afraid of increasing the responsibilities of France.[2]

This was not the end of the chapter, for in the summer of 1900 and again in February 1901 the Chiefs of the French and Russian General Staffs considered the hypothesis of a conflict with England. If the latter attacked France, the Russian army might make a diversion against India with 300,000 men after the completion of a railway from Orenburg to Tashkent. If England attacked Russia, France would mass 150,000 men on the Channel coast and threaten invasion. This was merely a military plan contingent on the decision of the Governments. But it assumed importance on the occasion of Delcassé's second visit to Russia in the spring of 1901. The atmosphere

[1] Michon, *The Franco-Russian Alliance*, ch. 5.
[2] Les engagements de l'alliance franco-russe 1891–1914," *Revue d'Histoire de la Guerre Mondiale*, Oct. 1934.

was no less cordial than in 1899.[1] The Tsar repeated several times the comforting words : *Comptez sur moi, ma politique est invariable.* Agreement with Russia was complete, telegraphed the Foreign Minister to Loubet, and he was entirely satisfied. Among the topics discussed was the co-operation of France in the Baghdad railway, which Delcassé described as a genuinely international enterprise.

The most substantial incident of the visit was the ratification of the military arrangements in regard to a conflict imposed on France and Russia by England alone or by England with the support of the Triple Alliance. The Tsar's approval was recorded by Delcassé in a letter to Lamsdorff.[2] The monarch added that he was giving orders for the construction of the strategic railway which was considered indispensable to the simultaneous movement of the Russian and French armies in the event of a war with Germany. Delcassé's letter proceeded to state that President Loubet also approved the military arrangements. "For the future, in accordance with Your Excellency's suggestion, the Government of the Republic agrees with the Imperial Government that the measures concerted between our General Staffs will be regarded as definitely adopted if the. Russian and French Ministers, to whom they will be immediately communicated, do not expressly notify within a month that their Governments cannot adopt them."

Lamsdorff's reply on the following day poured water into Delcassé's wine. The Tsar had approved the substance of the military agreements. He had also said that the strategic railway was approved in principle, though certain financial matters would have to be cleared up before the work could be commenced. "As for the future studies of the General Staff, I do not think a change desirable. Our diplomatic accord of 1891 and the ensuing military arrangements assumed a continuous exchange of ideas between the General Staffs, whose conclusions would inevitably depend on circumstances and could be modified at any moment. The purpose was to be always ready to pass from discussions to action directly the political situation demanded it. If every plan of the Chiefs of Staff has to be immediately communicated to the Foreign Ministers and is to be considered as definitely adopted unless

[1] *D.D.F.* I, 246, April 25, and 338–9, June 21 ; Zaiontschkovsky, " Relations Franco-Russes, avant la Guerre de 1914," in *Les Allies contre la Russie* ; and Combarieu, *Sept Ans à l'Elysée*, 129–130.
[2] *D.D.F.* III, 601–3.

repudiated within a month, it might gravely embarrass the liberty of the discussions." The present system of reports was more in the spirit of the makers of the alliance, and approval by the Ministers of War was enough.

Lamsdorff's qualifications did not seriously diminish the significance of the achievement. The co-operation of the armies was decided in principle in the event of a struggle with England, and the French Government proceeded to authorise a loan for strategic railways, in particular the Orenburg-Tashkent line. The success of the visit encouraged hopes in the Quai d'Orsay of a still further advance.[1] The strategic arrangements only envisaged land operations. But the two Admiralties had recently and independently made plans for the eventuality of a naval war. " These dispositions being so to speak the corollary of those of 1900 and 1901 for a continental war, it would be very desirable that the Naval Chiefs of Staff should be authorised to confer, so as to harmonise the efforts of the fleets." A plan of naval strategy worked out by the Ministry of Marine in the event of war with England or the Triple Alliance was appended to the Note of the Department. A naval agreement, however, had to wait till 1912, when a war with England no longer needed to be taken into account by either of the allies.

Shortly after this very satisfactory visit Delcassé was incensed by the news that the Tsar had accepted the Kaiser's invitation to the German naval manœuvres at Danzig.[2] If it was really impossible to decline, he argued, the only way to reassure public opinion was for Nicholas II to come and witness the French manœuvres. The French Ambassador in St. Petersburg explained that the Tsar, in accepting the pressing invitation to Danzig, had evaded a visit to Berlin.[3] The French Government, replied Delcassé, fully recognised the demands of the family ties between the two Courts ; but if on certain matters France was peculiarly sensitive, Russia had no ground of complaint.[4] For Muraviev had once declared to the French Ambassador that the alliance would be meaningless on the day that France came to regard the loss of the Rhine provinces as definitive. " And I think that the alliance, not less than family ties, has its rights, and that the Emperor, in resigning himself to the German naval

[1] D.D.F. III, 603–5. " Note of the Department." December 21, 1901.
[2] D.D.F. I, 325, June 12, 1901.
[3] ibid. 336–7.　　　　　　　　　　　　　　　　　　[4] ibid. 348.

manœuvres, would be happy to review the army of his ally and to satisfy himself of its spirit, its unity, and its strength." The Tsar was surprised and annoyed by the anxiety of France. " I cannot help feeling hurt by this apparent mistrust of me ", he complained to Lamsdorff—a sentiment which Delcassé promptly repudiated.[1] After taking time for reflection he accepted an invitation to a naval review at Dunkirk and a militaiy review at Rheims. Delcassé was delighted at the favourable development of a situation which had caused him considerable alarm. In a circular telegram to French representatives abroad he emphasised the significance of the promised visit.[2] " If one connects it with my own visits to the Tsar in 1899 and 1901 and with the military missions of the Chiefs of the Staffs, it will be seen that the original instruments of the alliance have been further defined and enlarged." In September the journey passed off without a hitch, and the Foreign Minister was a happy man.

Delcassé's policy of combining loyalty to his ally with friendliness to England bore the strain of the Anglo-Japanese alliance, which came as a disagreeable shock to his ally. The Franco-Russian Declaration of March 20, 1902, demanded by Lamsdorff soothed the ruffled feelings of St. Petersburg without causing Downing Street to be alarmed. The essential principles of the Anglo-Japanese treaty, namely the status quo in the Far East, the independence of China and Korea, and the open door, were accepted as the affirmation of the policy of the signatories.[3] " Being compelled, however, to envisage either the aggressive action of third Powers or new troubles in China, threatening her integrity or free development, which might become a menace to their own interests, the two allied Governments reserve the right to discuss the means of their defence." Since such discussions would in any case take place between allies, the new formula did not appear to augment his responsibilities.

Delcassé deeply regretted the entanglement of Russia in the Far East, but he was powerless to arrest the drift towards war. Knowing Lamsdorff to be a man of peace, reassured by his optimism on the occasion of his visit to Paris in October 1903,[4] and unaware of the strength of rival influences in the entourage of the Tsar, he underestimated the danger of a catastrophe. Asked by a Senator on December 26, 1903,

[1] D.D.F. I, 376, 380.   [2] ibid. 460–1.
[3] D.D.F. II, 177–8.   [4] D.D.F. IV, 68 and 106–8.

whether a Russo-Japanese conflict was probable, he replied
that it was not for him to pronounce on the negotiations.[1]
Since, however, the pacific dispositions of the two Governments were not in doubt, he saw no reason to credit alarmist
rumours. It was an optimistic response. He has been
blamed for his inactivity in regard to the development of a
situation so closely concerning the fortunes of France, but
there is no reason to believe that another statesman could have
done better. The Tsar had no desire for war, but he was in
the hands of men whose forward policy led straight to the
abyss. Pressure at St. Petersburg would have produced
indignation, not a change of course, and would have weakened
the solidarity of the alliance. We must never forget that
France was regarded by Russia and regarded herself as the
junior partner in the firm.

V

Two days after his return from Russia in August 1899
Delcassé complained to the British Ambassador " in a
studiously impressive manner " of the impossibility of friendly
relations with England, the rejection of all France's justifiable
demands filling Cambon and himself with profound discourage-
ment.[2] He had that morning received from Cambon most
unsatisfactory reports respecting a coal depôt at Muscat and
the extension of the French cemetery at Shanghai. He began
to believe that the politicians who argued that there was
nothing to be done with England were right, for the British
Government seemed to show a deliberate unfriendliness in
every possible way. Monson warmly retorted that, as he had
raised the question of " mauvais vouloir ", we had numerous
complaints against the " mauvais vouloir " of France. After
a sharp exchange, which he begged to be treated as unofficial,
Delcassé asked his visitor to do his utmost for a good understanding. The Ambassador was not hopeful, for the press
was hostile, the adulation of Germany continued, and the
Transvaal crisis was looming up.

The outbreak of war in South Africa opened the floodgates,
and Monson's despatches for the next three years are filled
with monotonous complaints. It was a golden opportunity
to hurl back the darts that had been aimed at the Dreyfus trials
and the Marchand Mission, and the French press seized it

[1] D.D.F. IV, 204.   [2] B.D. I, 212-213.

with both hands. The hostility of Chamberlain to France was notorious, and to attack his South African policy was to pay off old scores. In France, as in Germany, the attitude of the Government remained correct, and Monson, who was not easy to please, believed that Delcassé was doing his best. Yet there was no surprise in Downing Street when rumours of unfriendly intervention began to spread. Muraviev, who had been spending his holidays at Biarritz, had spoken to the Spanish Premier, Silvela, of a league against the aggressive expansion of England, and urged Spain to join if the plan took shape.[1] The difficulty, he had added, would be to persuade France and Germany to run in double harness, for though the French Government desired co-operation with Berlin it was afraid of public opinion. Muraviev's visit to Paris at the end of October on his way home set tongues wagging. No authoritative account of his conversations with Delcassé could be obtained ; but a few days after his departure Monson heard that he had tried to persuade the French Government to pursue a course hostile to England.[2] " M. Delcassé, according to my informant, maintained in opposition to Count Muraviev that France's true policy is to keep on a friendly footing with England, and in this view he has been supported by his colleagues and by the President. The Count has gone away greatly disappointed at the non-success of all the arguments he employed." He anticipated an early change of Government. With the growing bitterness towards England, he calculated, it would be easy to force another Minister to steer a new course. This unfriendly testimonial from the colleague who had welcomed his appointment suggests that Delcassé was learning the bitter lesson of Fashoda. Dr. Leyds, the agent of the Transvaal, was no more successful in his efforts to convert him to the idea of mediation.[3]

The danger, as Monson explained, lay not in the Government but in the mob.[4] " With an excitable people like this it will, I fear, be at any moment easy to arouse such a current of opinion as would carry away all the checks which a sensible Ministry, such as I believe is now in office, would seek to interpose against the forcible rupture of amity." At the end of November Delcassé told him that the Government entirely dissociated itself from the press attacks, and denied that they

[1] Muraviev's conversations with Silvela are described by Monson on the basis of a report from the Austrian Chargé in Spain. cp. G.P. XV, 133-4.
[2] B.D. I, 239. [3] G.P. XV, 430.
[4] B.D. I, 236.

represented the real feelings of the majority of Frenchmen.[1]
On the latter point Monson was unconvinced. The Government, he reported, was powerless to prevent the insults, but
it was doing its best. On the other hand, though reserved
in his official utterances, the Minister shared the resentful
feelings of his countrymen.   " The hostility to England grows
ever stronger ", reported Münster at the end of the year, "and
is fostered by Russia.[2] It is greatly hoped the Russians will
soon be in Herat. Delcassé told me with obvious pleasure
that the Transasiatic railway is within a hundred kilometres of
Herat." He would have been more than human had he not
watched the embarrassments of the haughty victors of Fashoda
with malicious delight. Monson was never attracted to him,
but after the great surrender he never doubted his good faith.
When on January 17, 1900, the *Times* Correspondent brought
tales of negotiations between France, Germany and Russia for
combined pressure on England, he declined to believe them.[3]
Two or three hours later he attended the weekly reception at
the Quai d'Orsay and was welcomed with the usual cordiality.
" I, of course, did not address him any direct question on the
subject ; but his manner and his language were both of a
character so friendly and straightforward that I could detect
no symptom of his having entered into an international con-
spiracy against us ; and my experience of M. Delcassé is that
he is by no means so consummate an actor as to be able to
conceal absolutely any sentiment which would naturally cause
emotion."

In February, after a series of disasters had revealed the
magnitude of the British task in South Africa and the stopping
of the *Bundesrath* had set German opinion aflame, Muraviev
returned to the charge. The Russian Ambassador suggested
joint intervention to prevent further shedding of blood, basing
the proposal on Article III of The Hague Convention and on
the proviso that Germany should take the first step. Delcassé
agreed on condition that Russia should approach Berlin.
Germany replied that she could not expose herself to complications so long as she had to reckon on French hostility, and
that, since the enterprise might prove a serious affair, a mutual
guarantee of their respective European territories was an
essential preliminary. Russia rejoined that such a step was
needless, since nothing beyond a friendly *démarche* was planned,
and that in any case France would never confirm the Treaty of

[1] *G.P.* XV, 242.   [2] ibid. 508.   [3] *B.D.* I, 247-8

Frankfurt. The attitude of the Wilhelmstrasse resembled that of the Quai d'Orsay. The ringleader was Russia, not Germany nor France. André Mévil testifies that Delcassé's sole motive in following the lead of his ally was that of humanity. It would probably be more correct to say that he desired to humour French opinion and his Russian ally without angering England.

Determined to limit his risks Delcassé toyed with the idea of associating the United States.[1] But the difficulties of joint mediation proved insuperable as soon as they were closely explored. When Muraviev remarked that a guarantee of the status quo would require long negotiations, the Kaiser wrote on the despatch : " Nonsense ! A telegram from Delcassé to Noailles is enough. Le Gouvernement reconnait sans arrière-pensée les frontières de l'Allemagne comme elles sont délimitées par le traité de Francfort."[2] Such a declaration, as the Kaiser should have known, was no less unobtainable than a guarantee. Delcassé, we may surmise, was relieved to see the whole dangerous edifice crumble away. It was impossible to propose arbitration, he explained to the Senate on March 15, for Salisbury had ruled it out. France had not refused to associate herself with a *démarche* which, without violating neutrality, would have constituted a friendly and disinterested effort towards the cessation of hostilities ; but after so many harsh experiences her duties towards the world must not make her forget her duty to herself.

Delcassé felt no tenderness for England at any period of his life, but he was free from the angry suspicions of the crowd. " You say that after finishing with the Transvaal ", he remarked at a dinner party, " the English will turn against us. Frankly, I do not think so."[3] A governing consideration was discreetly indicated in a speech to the Senate on April 3, 1900. If a conflict with England were to occur, he reminded his hearers, it was not to the conqueror that the principal benefits of the victory would accrue. When Lord Carrington visited Paris in March 1901 on a special mission to announce the accession of King Edward, he was warned by Lansdowne that his reception might not prove very cordial, owing to French sympathy with the Boers. He found the atmosphere at the Élysée friendly and almost cordial.[4] Delcassé, " a sharp, clever, dark man of about 45, sociable and civil ", asked him

[1] G.P. XV, 517–8.   [2] ibid. 520.
[3] Stuart, *French Foreign Policy*, 43.   [4] Lee, *King Edward VII*, 14–15.

to assure the King that no effort would be spared on his part to foster and maintain happy relations between France and England. Loubet added that he and his Ministers would consider it a crime if anyone were to make mischief between the two countries. " Please tell your King this and say I said so." Carrington reported that his impressions of Paris were most favourable, and that the President and all his Ministers were willing and anxious to talk openly on every subject. He felt certain that there would not be much difficulty in coming to a very friendly understanding. Sir Thomas Barclay also testifies in his *Reminiscences* to the steady support given by Delcassé to his efforts on behalf of Anglo-French reconciliation. He encouraged the plan of the annual meeting of the British Chamber of Commerce being held in Paris in 1900, and told Barclay that he would welcome nothing more than the growth of a sentiment which would allow the Governments to reach a balanced settlement of outstanding questions. When Kruger passed through the capital after his flight from the Transvaal, no French Minister, however Anglophile, could have refused to receive him ; and in London the obligatory courtesies aroused neither resentment nor surprise.

Though at no moment during the South African war did Delcassé suggest or desire a risky intervention, Lamsdorff deeply regretted the impotence of Europe.[1] Russia, he complained to the French Ambassador at the opening of 1902, could not act alone, and he had tried in vain to save a people from annihilation by collective action. Perhaps a joint appeal from the branches of the Red Cross in different countries might have better luck. Delcassé had no such illusions. "Mediation to be effective", he declared in the Chamber, " must be imposed—which means making war to stop the war."[2] It was impossible, however, to return a blank negative to an ally, and, while accepting Lamsdorff's plan in principle, he asked how it was to be carried out. Nothing came of the scheme, for the British Government knew it could win, and Delcassé knew it too. Throughout the distracting years of the South African conflict he handled Anglo-French relations with a good deal of skill, avoiding provocation on the one hand and subservience on the other. The door was kept ajar, so that in due course it could be opened wide.

The intense unpopularity of England produced a slight *détente* between Paris and Berlin. The placing of French

[1] *D.D.F.* II, 39–40. [2] ibid. 50–1. January 20.

troops in China under Waldersee was a bitter pill to swallow, but Delcassé put the best face on it and the ordeal was of short duration. " Our co-operation in China has one good side ", he observed to Münster, " as I am convinced that French and Germans who fight together get on well, and that it will contribute to a better relation between the nations."[1] An interesting series of despatches from Radolin, who succeeded Münster in Paris, reveals the very natural desire of the Foreign Minister to turn the South African war to account, though he was not quite certain how it could be done.[2] Since the surrender of Fashoda the main lines of his policy never varied ; but the moods of statesmen, as of lesser mortals, are subject to atmospheric change.

On June 5, 1901, Radolin reported a talk with the Spanish Ambassador. Delcassé had often told Castillo that Münster never tried for a Franco-German rapprochement. " I ask nothing better than to enter into relations with the German Ambassador to reach an understanding on all questions and arrive at an entente, but Prince Münster does not give me the least encouragement and never mentions the subject." Ten days later Castillo resumed the conversation with Radolin. " I have asked Delcassé if he was still animated by the same conciliatory sentiments towards Germany as eight months ago. Yes, he replied, but the initiative must come from the German Ambassador." Castillo urged Radolin to strike while the iron was hot, for his welcome in Paris had been wonderful and he was now the most popular of the Ambassadors. Delcassé explained that no French Minister could renounce Alsace-Lorraine, but Castillo thought that France was giving up the idea of revenge. The Spanish diplomatist had taken Delcassé's references to Germany too seriously, as Bülow immediately perceived. It was useless and academic on account of the Rhine provinces, replied the Chancellor. Hatzfeldt was instructed to tell Lansdowne that France might use the South African entanglement to effect a *fait accompli* in Morocco. Leading French journals suggested that now was the time for Germany to show her good will to France in Morocco in tangible form. The Wilhelmstrasse made no response, and Delcassé told Radolin that he had no intention of adventures in that quarter.

This was not the end of the story. In October, Radolin reported a talk with Jules Hansen, who was in close touch

[1] *G.P.* XVI, 44-5. July 7, 1900.　　　　　[2] ibid. XVIII, ch. 126.

with Delcassé. The Foreign Minister had passed through
Berlin in April on his way to Russia without paying the
Chancellor a visit. He was, however, anxious to meet him.
But where and how ? If Bülow would visit Paris incognito,
he would return the compliment at Berlin. In a private letter
Radolin supported the plan. " It would be useful ", replied
Bülow, " but not at present. Please prepare the way for a
visit and a rapprochement." Like Gambetta's romantic
scheme of a visit to Friedrichsruh, it came to nothing, for it
was a dangerous game and Delcassé had other irons in the fire.
In May 1902 Castillo reported him as cooling off since the
rapprochement with Italy. In the autumn he told Radolin of
a further talk with Delcassé, who desired a rapprochement,
though he argued that Berlin must begin. Richthofen
replied that no concrete proposal had come from France.
There had indeed never been much life in the project, for both
sides knew that the Rhine provinces barred the way. In
April 1903 the German Secretary of Legation in Paris reported
a complete change in Delcassé since the previous year. He
avoided political talk and only saw Radolin for a few minutes.
Once again it had been proved that a genuine Franco-German
approach was impossible. Delcassé's gestures had been
vague ; the response from Berlin had been cool ; and when
the relations of France with Italy and England improved the
flirtation was quietly dropped. He has been blamed for his
inertia while our army was tied up for nearly three years at
the Cape. But what could he do without infuriating the
British lion ? The Morocco pear was not yet ripe. The merit
of his policy was precisely that he resisted the insidious
temptation to blackmail. The vision of a profitable and not
very distant reconciliation filled his mind, and it was vital
during the long period of waiting to give England no serious
cause of complaint.

In one direction alone did Delcassé manifest a willingness
to co-operate with Berlin. The Baghdad railway needed
French co-operation, and an agreement signed at Berlin on
May 6, 1899, provided for equal shares in stock and management. The enterprise, however, possessed its political as
well as its economic aspect. The Foreign Minister informed
the Chamber that French diplomacy had not interfered. The
Anatolian Company had negotiated with French financiers,
and he was of opinion that, if satisfactory arrangements could
be made, France would do well to participate. Russia, how-

ever, must be able to join, and France must have equal rights with the most favoured foreign unit. Unfortunately the project was viewed in Russia with profound mistrust, not only on the ground that it would bring German influence into Asia Minor, but because it would strengthen the Turkish Empire. Delcassé's attempts during his visit in 1901 to induce his ally to co-operate were without success. Russia would not make difficulties, but beyond that she could not go. Rouvier, the experienced Minister of Finance, and Constans, the French Ambassador in Constantinople, favoured co-operation ; but the frowns of St. Petersburg and London were too much for Delcassé. The French Cabinet refused to allow quotations of Baghdad Railway shares on the Bourse, and on November 19, 1903, the Foreign Minister informed the Chamber that the Government could not advise investment without guarantees of full equality in the direction and construction of the line. This change of attitude did not prevent the French syndicate from taking part ; but the official repudiation of the scheme marked the end of the mild Franco-German *détente* engendered by the excitements of the South African war.

VI

During the period between Fashoda and the end of the South African war Delcassé scored his first resounding triumph in the reconciliation with Italy.[1] Since the occupation of Tunis relations had been dangerously strained. The fortification of Bizerta stirred the fiery Crispi to wrath, and the tariff war inaugurated in 1888 was both an expression and an aggravation of the feud. When the disaster of Adowa hurled Crispi from power in 1896 a *détente* became a possibility, and the new Foreign Minister, Visconti Venosta, consented to the abolition of the capitulations in Tunis. In 1898 the appointment of Delcassé to the Quai d'Orsay and Barrère to the Embassy at Rome brought on the stage two men whose joint labours were to change the orientation of a Great Power. The first task was to end the senseless economic war. Negotiations begun by Hanotaux were resumed, and on November 21, 1898, a commercial treaty was signed. The path was now open for a further advance.

[1] For the estrangement and reconciliation of France and Italy see Crispi's *Memoirs*, Billot, *La France et l'Italie*, 1881–1899 ; Tardieu, *Questions diplomatiques de l'année* 1904, ch. II. ; Italicus, *Italiens Dreibundpolitik*, 1870–1896.

I

The Anglo-French treaty of March 21, 1899, delimiting boundaries in Central Africa, aroused resentment in Rome. Italians of all parties looked forward to the ultimate domination of the Turkish province facing their southern coasts ; and Tripoli, without control of her caravan routes into the interior, would be in Crispi's phrase an empty jewel-case. The treaty recognised the larger part of the hinterland to be under French influence. The Italians complained of the neglect of their interests by Great Britain, but without result. Unless some agreement could be made with Paris Tripoli would be hardly worth having, if indeed it ever became Italian at all. Happily there was now good will on both sides, and the delimitation of French and Italian possessions on the Red Sea and the Gulf of Aden prepared the way for more comprehensive agreements nearer home. Since France had been suspected of wishing to extend her rule not only to Morocco but to Tripoli, Delcassé decided to provide assurances that she had no designs in that quarter. Italy, it was hoped, would give France a free hand in Morocco in return.

The secret agreement was recorded in an exchange of letters dated December 14 and 16, 1900.[1] Barrère's letter announced that France regarded Tripoli as outside her sphere of influence. The reply of Visconti Venosta declared that if the political or territorial status of Morocco were to be modified, Italy would reserve to herself, as a measure of reciprocity, the right eventually to develop her influence with regard to Tripoli. In the opinion of the Ambassador, France had the best of the bargain. It was improbable, he argued, that Italy would take action in Tripoli even if France were to occupy Morocco. Italy would need soldiers, money, a satisfactory political situation, and the good will of the Powers, particularly of her allies, none of which she possessed at that moment. If, however, she moved, she would imperatively require not only the consent but the benevolence of France, and thus any extension in the Mediterranean would place her under an obligation to France. The agreement further removed a cause of fear and jealousy on the part of Italy, which prevented any sincere and serious rapprochement. Finally it barred the way to further Mediterranean coalitions between Italy and England with a point against France. " In a word it modifies profoundly and to our advantage the position of the active forces in the Mediterranean." Delcassé was equally

[1] Pribram, *Secret Treaties*, II, 240–5, and *D.D.F.* I, 22–23.

delighted.   The text remained secret, but the existence of an agreement was known.[1]   France and Italy, it was realised, had liquidated their rivalry in the Mediterranean.   It was the first stage on the road which led one of the signatories to a memorable decision in 1915, and the first step towards the domination of Morocco by the other.

The changed relations were announced to the world when an Italian squadron under the Duke of Genoa, the King's uncle, visited Toulon in April 1901 and was welcomed by President Loubet.   The King, who referred in his telegram to *La France, amie de l'Italie*, was delighted, and Barrère reported that the Italian press was admirable.[2]   French papers, on the other hand, grumbled that the Triple Alliance was incompatible with friendly relations between France and Italy.   Barrère advised that, in congratulating the Italian Ambassador on the Toulon meeting, his chief should say that France expected Italy to harmonise her engagements with her friendship for France.   " I allude to the clause which obliged Italy to draw the sword if Germany is attacked by France. In this defensive form such a clause is clearly offensive for us. There can be no equivocation on this vital point."   Here was the second and more difficult item of the programme of reconciliation of which the Tripoli-Morocco agreement had been the first, and the indefatigable Barrère now girded himself for the greatest fight of his life.

The visit of the Italian fleet to Toulon aroused almost as much excitement throughout Europe as the visit of the Russian fleet to the same waters in 1893.   Berlin and Vienna frowned but were powerless to intervene.   Barrère described " the feeling of relief, satisfaction and almost joy " throughout the peninsula.[3]   The Italian Government made no attempt to hide its delight, even at the risk of displeasing its allies.   The young King, whose growing share in the shaping of policy rendered his attitude of exceptional significance, only regretted that the speech of the Duke of Genoa had not been warmer. The Triple Alliance, which would fall to be renewed in two years, would have to be adjusted to the new mentality.   Many Italians believed that Italy would not fight against France, and Barrère agreed with them.   In the region of high politics, however, hypotheses are not enough.

[1] Despatch of Barrère, March 10, 1912.   *D.D.F.* II, 692.
[2] *D.D.F.* I, 227.   cp. Combarieu, *Sept Ans à l'Elysée*, 122–7.
[3] *D.D.F.* I, 239–241.

In a despatch to Barrère Delcassé formally expressed his satisfaction at the Morocco-Tripoli pact.[1] The letters had embodied the conservative character of the agreement. It diminished the temptation to precipitate action which would oblige France to quicken her pace. Italy had realised the necessity of leaving the Mediterranean equilibrium undisturbed, except for a legitimate compensation " if one· day circumstances compelled us to renounce the policy of the status quo which we pursue with entire sincerity in Morocco, and obliged us to establish our direct sovereignty or a Protectorate". If Italy were to seize the occasion of harmonising her international engagements with her new friendship, France would be delighted. In the mind of the Foreign Minister, no less than of the Ambassador, the Morocco-Tripoli agreement was only the prelude to the main plot. France, explained Barrère, could not consider the friendship consecrated by Toulon compatible with the maintenance of an obligation to join in a war against her provoked if not declared by a third Power.[2] Prinetti replied that he could not say whether the alliance would be renewed in two years. If it were, " I could not admit for a moment that it should contain anything at which France could take umbrage, arouse mistrust, or directly or indirectly menace her security." What had induced Prinetti to make such a grave and definite declaration? Because, replied Barrère, he was intelligent enough to realise the importance of the good will of France. A revision of the Triple Alliance seemed almost in sight.

On July 21 Prinetti proposed the publication of the substance of Barrère's letter of December 16, 1900, in order to fortify public opinion against false alarms.[3] The plan was supported by the Ambassador in view of the approaching renewal of the Triplice. The susceptibilities of Turkey, he suggested, might be assuaged by a confidential explanation at Constantinople. Italy, it might be pointed out, could not be indifferent to the possibility of France extending her African Empire, and the profession of disinterestedness would thus appear as a new guarantee of the integrity of Turkey. Such a one-sided revelation made no appeal to Delcassé, who noted his opinion on the despatch. " A revelation in regard to Tripoli involves a revelation in regard to Morocco, which seems to me altogether inopportune, at any rate at the present moment."

[1] *D.D.F.* I, 299–300.   [2] ibid. 352–3 and 369–71.   [3] ibid. 397–8.

In November Prinetti returned to the charge.[1] The King eagerly desired publicity for the part of the compact concerning Tripoli. Delcassé might arrange an interpellation, and he himself would then confirm his words. Conversations on the renewal of the Triple Alliance would soon have to begin, and a revelation was virtually indispensable. Delcassé reiterated that the Tripoli engagement could not be announced without its Morocco counterpart, and the veil on future action in Morocco could not be lifted. Prinetti, however, might make a general allusion to the agreement in language which he proceeded to suggest. After a good deal of discussion the final draft was approved at Paris.[2] The French Government, ran the essential passage, had declared that the Anglo-French convention of 1899 marked for France in regard to the regions adjoining the eastern frontier of her African possessions, particularly in the Tripoli vilayet, a limit which she had no intention of passing, and that she had no thought of cutting the caravan routes from Tripoli to Central Africa. " Since then the friendly relations of the two countries have been such that they have enabled the two Governments to exchange explanations, as precise as they are satisfactory, on their interests in the Mediterranean." Prinetti's declaration to the Chamber on December 14 was welcomed with delight in Italy, and with corresponding disquietude by her allies. Bülow spoke lightly of the " extra dance", but he meant more than he said. While approving the rapprochement, Lansdowne feared that Italy might be encouraged to move in Tripoli. The reverberation was profound, and it was recognised that a new factor had entered into European politics.

At the usual reception of the French colony in Rome on New Year's day, 1902, the triumphant Ambassador used language so cordial that his words echoed through Europe, all the more since Delcassé had not yet found an opportunity of confirming Prinetti's declaration.[3] Barrère reported that the Triplice was no longer taken as a matter of course, and he turned the advertised meeting of Bülow and Prinetti at Venice to good account.[4] " We shall not make a pact", remarked the Minister ; " and as for the future rest assured that I shall sign nothing which France could regard as contrary to the bonds of friendship which unite us, or as a menace,

[1] D.D.F. I, 598–602.   [2] ibid. 651.
[3] ibid. II, 6–8.   [4] ibid. 202–7.

direct or indirect, to her security." " I quite understand", rejoined the Ambassador, " but the point is how you will carry out this loyal promise." " If we renew the Triple Alliance", replied the Minister, " I will give you and I will give Parliament categorical assurances as to the character of this act." " Quite so ; but the act itself must be in harmony with your declarations. Is it so at present ? We, at any rate, do not think so. It must therefore be harmonised with our new relations. Any equivocation would be deeply regrettable. We are free from any engagement against Italy. It must be the same for France." Pressed thus vigorously by the importunate diplomatist Prinetti answered that he would be delighted to introduce a formula into the text if he could. Moreover, the point against France was to be found not in the treaty itself but in the annexes, which would have to disappear. Barrère reported that Prinetti was visibly impressed. " I was determined to make him understand that we should not content ourselves with vain words." He was not a Visconti Venosta, and it would have been well if Italy could have been represented by a stronger personality. The words of the Ambassador in Rome, he suggested, should be reinforced by the voice of the Minister in Paris. Prinetti had explained that Italy reserved the right of pronouncing on the *casus belli*, and hinted that she would not fight in a quarrel which was not her concern. In Barrère's opinion her military obligations to Germany were a dead letter, and he could not imagine the Government carrying the Italian people into a war against France.

On returning from his meeting with Bülow, Prinetti explained that nothing had been decided or prejudged, and Barrère discovered that he had urged a modification of the text of the treaty, though in vain.[1] Steady pressure, commented the Ambassador, would have to be continued, and, learning that conversations had begun, he had another heart to heart talk.[2] Rather than accept an agreement which he did not approve, declared the Minister, he would resign. The treaty itself, he repeated, was purely defensive ; but annexes relating to France had been added at the instigation of Crispi which had now lost their *raison d'être* and must disappear. Assuming the principal clause to be general in character and purely for mutual defence, replied Barrère, might not Italy possibly find herself in an anti-French group in a war which

[1] D.D.F. II, 217–220.   [1] ibid. 267 and 270–3.

France was forced to declare even if it had been provoked by one of Italy's allies ? The moment had not come to talk of that, replied Prinetti after some hesitation, but he would be ready to discuss the question of provocation.   The Ambassador was delighted at the prospect, and told his chief that they were practically certain of securing a satisfactory agreement.   In May Prinetti confided to Barrère that the renewal of the Triple Alliance was decided in principle and that he was ready for conversations with France.[1]   The Ambassador submitted to his chief the terms he proposed to ask, and a draft declaration was drawn up in Rome.   Delcassé reminded Barrère that the main point was neutrality in case one of the parties issued a declaration of war to which it had been provoked in defence of its honour and security.   Prinetti was naturally anxious that Delcassé should say nothing to arouse the suspicions of his allies that secret arrangements were on foot.

The declarations were signed on June 30, Barrére having hurried on the affair.   The Germans were suspicious, and till the last moment he dreaded a peremptory intervention from Berlin.   Prinetti assured Delcassé " that, in the renewal of the Triple Alliance, there is nothing directly or indirectly aggressive towards France, no engagement binding us in any eventuality to take part in an aggression against her, finally no stipulation which menaces the security and tranquillity of France."[2] He added that the annexes to the Triple Alliance, which altered its completely defensive character and might even have an aggressive character against France, did not exist.   The text of the declaration remained a secret till it was published by the French Government in 1920[3] ; but Delcassé promptly revealed its existence to the Chamber.[4]   In view of the natural anxiety of France on the occasion of the renewal of the Triple Alliance, the Italian Government had explained the situation.   " En aucun cas et en aucune forme l'Italie ne peut devenir ni l'auxiliaire ni l'instrument d'une aggression contre notre pays."   The words echoed round the world.   The Triple Alliance was renewed on June 28, but it was now, to use the exultant expression of Barrère, a negative and discredited pact.   The wheel had indeed come full circle.

[1] *D.D.F.*, II, 286.
[2] Pribram, II, 244-7.
[3] It was not communicated to the Chief of the French General Staff till June 10, 1909, and a large French army was kept in the Alps during those years. Joffre's *Memoirs*, I, 37.
[4] *D.D.F.* II, 386, note.

Crispi's additions had been swept away. The stampede of
Italy into the Austro-German camp had been the result of the
French seizure of Tunis. Twenty years later the feud was
healed at the prospective expense of Turkey and Morocco.

An exchange of letters further defined the novel situation.[1]
" In case France should be the object of a direct or indirect
aggression from one or more Powers", wrote Prinetti, " Italy
will maintain a strict neutrality. The same shall hold good
in case France, as the result of a direct provocation, should find
herself compelled in defence of her honour and security to
take the initiative of a declaration of war. In that eventuality
the Government of the Republic shall previously communicate
its intention to the Royal Government, which will thus be
enabled to determine whether there is really a case of direct
provocation." He added that no military compact conflicting with this declaration existed or would be made. The
Ambassador's letter was to a similar effect. On the following
day at the desire of Barrère Prinetti defined the meaning of
" direct provocation." In a despatch of July 10 Barrère
explained why the two copies of these letters bore different
dates.[2] Prinetti disliked the idea of signing them at the same
time as the renewal of the Triple Alliance, to which they were
a counterpart and which they undermined. He had therefore
suggested the date of November 1, 1902. Since, however,
the death or retirement of one of the signatories before that
time would annul the agreement, duplicates had been dated
July 10, which would be destroyed when no longer required.

Barrère was satisfied at last. He had been the equal partner
of his chief, and his work ranks in importance with that of
Paul Cambon. Delcassé was fortunate indeed to possess two
diplomatists of the first rank to aid in transforming potential
foes into friends. Barrère's task was the more difficult of the
two, since Italy, unlike England, had to be enticed away from
a rival diplomatic group. Looking back on the struggle ten
years later, when the Tripoli war momentarily clouded the
friendship of the two countries, he recalled the stages of the
reconciliation and emphasised its enduring worth.[3] Italy,
he argued, made no engagement in contradiction with her
alliances as renewed in 1902 without the military protocols,
and she was never invited to do so. The scope of the partnership was limited, and France never asked her to leave the

[1] Pribram, II, 249-257. [2] D.D.F. II, 390, July 10.
[3] Despatch of March 10, 1912. D.D.F. II, 692-9.

Triplice itself. " The pact was not a counter-treaty but a counterpart to the Triplice, which it reduces to very small proportions in the part which concerns us most. . . . Before 1902 a fit of jealousy or temper was enough to dispose Italy to listen to the suggestions of our adversaries, and to interpret or even to modify her alliances in a sense dangerous for us and without our knowledge. That is absolutely forbidden." Whatever may be thought of Italy's loyalty to her allies, from whom the secret was carefully hidden, there can be no doubt that she derived as much benefit from the pact as France herself. Like Bismarck with his re-insurance treaty of 1887, she had made the best of both worlds. The conventions of 1900 and 1902 had cut the cords which bound Rome to Vienna and Berlin. Well might Rouvier declare at the Cabinet which decreed Delcassé's fall : L'Allemagne vous reproche d'avoir débauché l'Italie.

All the world could see that a decisive event had occurred. The visit of the King and Queen of Italy to Paris in October 1903 was justly described as " the natural result of the rapprochement happily accomplished between our two countries." In a circular despatch Delcassé retraced the phases of the reconciliation. The King had suggested the visit, and the popular welcome had ratified the friendship.[1] The impression left on Victor Emmanuel was profound. He discovered a France that he had not known, reported Barrère, a nation full of vitality.[2] His prejudices had disappeared. France had won his confidence. Well aware that his decision involved a return journey to Rome, he expressed his hope and belief that the President would be received by the Pope. The year ended happily with the signing of the Franco-Italian treaty of arbitration.

The visit of President Loubet to the Italian capital in April 1904, accompanied by Delcassé, placed the seal on the new association.[3] Barrère promised him such a welcome, both from the people and the Government, as no chief of a foreign state had ever received,[4] and the prophecy was fulfilled to the letter. What made the Presidential journey a unique event, reported the Ambassador, was the people's share.[5] Governing circles expected something exceptional. But the intensity of the affirmation came as a surprise, and for some it was a

[1] D.D.F. IV, 75–7.   [2] ibid. 196–8.
[3] Combarieu, 276–283.   [4] D.D.F. V. 57.
[5] ibid. 132–4.

revelation. Italy had ceased to be a military instrument at the disposal of the Central Powers. "If a war broke out to-morrow between France and Germany, even if Germany was not the aggressor, no Government would have the power, even if it had the intention, to constrain Italy to side with our adversaries. That is one of the stubborn facts against which statesmen and international pacts are of no avail." Barrère in no way exaggerated when he declared that Rome had passed out of the German orbit. The annoyance and alarm of the Wilhelmstrasse were a proof that the situation was well understood in Berlin.

Loubet's visit to the King of Italy in Rome was the first paid by the head of a Catholic state since the downfall of the Temporal Power. Such a journey would have been inter-preted at any time as a challenge to the Holy See, and with the unbending Pius X in the Vatican an explosion was inevitable. There was, however, no flinching at the Quai d'Orsay or the Élysée. Delcassé accepted the breach as the price of his policy, and French Republicans were prepared for the shock by memories of incessant friction with the Church. Its activities in the Dreyfus case had filled the cup, and the Law of the Associations was the first retort of the angry State. For a time the feud was kept within bounds by Waldeck-Rousseau who, like Delcassé, agreed with Gambetta's maxim that anti-clericalism was not an article of export; and when the Socialists urged the abolition of the Embassy at the Vatican, the Foreign Minister resisted the demand.

When the credits for the President's journey were voted, the Foreign Minister explained to the Chamber that no offence was intended.[1] "To discharge an evident duty, to return a visit, to convey to Italy in the person of her Sovereign the greeting of France, to strengthen for the good of both countries the ties formed by sentiments and interests alike—who could take exception to such a natural step?" He ended with a pointed warning to the Vatican. "Take care not to make France believe that she can only maintain good relations with the Holy See on condition of neglecting her duties and interests elsewhere." The hint was in vain, for on the departure of the guests the Pope passionately denounced both Governments. The visit, he declared in a note to the French representative, had filled his soul with bitterness. Delcassé's declaration that there was no hostile intention could not alter

[1] *D.D.F.* V. 86.

the fact that the offence was inherent in the act itself. The Italian Government had sought the visit in order to weaken the rights and offend the dignity of the Holy See. Against such a painful occurrence he protested in the most explicit way. He also addressed a note to the other Catholic Powers, hinting that the Nuncio in Paris might soon be recalled.

Delcassé telegraphed a reply that, having explained to Parliament the character of the visit, he could only repudiate in the name of the Government both the arguments in the note and the form in which they were conveyed.[1] The French Ambassador to the Vatican was promptly recalled, and the reply of the French Government to the interpellations was as sharply phrased as the Vatican's note itself.[2] The President, declared Combes, had been scolded for returning the friendly visit of the King of Italy in the recognised capital of his Kingdom, and for declining to accept the ultramontane doctrine of the Papal prerogatives. The recall of her Ambassador indicated that France would not tolerate the interference of the Vatican in her international relations, and that she desired once for all to finish with the outworn fiction of a Temporal Power that had vanished more than thirty years before. The final rupture occurred a few weeks later when the Pope ordered a French bishop to resign his see. The French Government called attention to the breach of the Concordat, and on July 30, 1904, official relations with the Papacy were terminated. The Concordat was dissolved, and the separation of Church and State was an accomplished fact. The breach with Rome was the almost inevitable conclusion of an embittered struggle of thirty years, but its proximate cause was the reconciliation with Italy. In the eyes of Delcassé and the majority of his countrymen the effective neutralisation of a member of the Triple Alliance was well worth the loss of the traditional guardianship of the Catholics in the East and the angry frowns of the Church.

VII

A few months after the Morocco-Tripoli agreement, Delcassé turned to the problem which was to dominate his policy for the rest of his term of office and ultimately to

---

[1] *D.D.F.* V, 112.   [1] ibid. 198–9.

determine his fall.[1] The conquest of Algeria had made
France a neighbour of Morocco with a long, ill-defined and
ill-defended frontier largely peopled by raiding tribes. In the
closing decades of the nineteenth century she had her hands
full of colonial enterprises elsewhere, and a vigorous Sultan,
Muley Hassan, kept foreign influences at bay. Fourteen
Powers met at Madrid in 1880 and signed the Convention
relating to Moroccans under foreign " protection ", but no
intervention in internal affairs was attempted or desired. The
partition of Africa was in full swing, but the advancing wave
sought the lines of least resistance. With the accession in
1894 of Abdul Aziz, an irresponsible child who never grew
up, the door was opened wide. The lad developed a craving
for mechanical toys and inventions, and he lacked the strength
of will to keep his turbulent subjects in control. At the dawn
of the twentieth century Morocco lay like a tempting morsel
before the hungry eyes of Europe, and the world began to
wonder who would get the largest slice.

Tangier, where Révoil, the French Minister, laid the
foundations of French influence while Sir Arthur Nicolson
watched over British interests, was a hot-bed of intrigue.
The Sultan's favourite, Sir Harry Maclean, a British soldier
of fortune, who had been employed first as instructor and
later as Commander-in-Chief of the army, was always at his
side to represent England as the only friend. France had the
best strategic position for exerting pressure, but just for that
reason Abdul Aziz watched her proceedings with suspicious
eyes. The occupation of the Tuat oasis in 1900, which
Delcassé regarded as falling within the French sphere, filled
him with alarm. He asked Nicolson to convey an autograph
letter to Queen Victoria requesting her to persuade the
French to fix a frontier beyond which they would not advance.
Accordingly Monson told Delcassé " incidentally " that the
British Minister at Tangier reported apprehensions of French
designs on the Eastern frontier. Delcassé replied that he had
no intention of attacking Morocco, and indeed he had limited
the reinforcements that had been sent. In March 1901 he
telegraphed to Révoil that he was very anxious to continue

[1] The fairest account is by Eugene N. Anderson, *The First Moroccan Crisis*,
1904–1906. E. D. Morel, *Morocco in Diplomacy*, states the case against Delcassé.
Harold Nicolson, *Lord Carnock*, chs. 5–6, is useful. Taillandier, the French
Minister at Tangier, tells his story in *Les Origines du Maroc Français*.
O. J. Hale, *Germany and the Diplomatic Revolution*, 1904–6, studies the
press.

his policy of caution.[1] If, however, the Government were compelled by the force of events to give the military authorities the latitude they claimed, the Makhzen should not be surprised or alarmed. He was well aware that for French troops to pass beyond the line marked out by the Government would produce a very bad effect in Morocco and Europe.[2]

The apprehensions of French encroachments were not allayed. For the second time the Sultan turned to England, and Menebhi, his Francophobe Minister of War, was despatched on a special mission to London and Berlin. On the advice of Nicolson, tendered through Kaid Maclean, not to treat France with suspicion and discourtesy, the Sultan decided to send his Francophil Foreign Minister Ben Sliman to Paris and St. Petersburg at the same time. Menebhi was ceremonially received by King Edward, and such minor issues as roads, harbours and telegraphs were discussed. High politics were eschewed, and the envoy received the sensible advice to reform his country and to consider the French. The first report from Paul Cambon was reassuring.[3] " The English are keeping their eye on us in Morocco, but they distrust the Germans just as much." Lansdowne gave the French Ambassador a memorandum on his conversations with the Mission, in the course of which he had obtained promises of administrative and economic amelioration from which all the Powers would benefit. When the Sultan's representative expressed his apprehensions of French policy, Lansdowne had replied that it was for the Moroccan Government to keep order on the Algerian frontier. If it failed to do so, it had no right to complain of the action of France. The Ambassador reiterated both the disinterested intentions of his Government and its determination to protect its Algerian subjects. " M. Cambon assured me that the measures taken by the French Government were inevitable on account of the lawless conduct of the tribes.[4] His Excellency, however, laid earnest stress on the fact that nothing was further from the intention of the French Government than to raise serious questions in Morocco. They were well aware of the warlike character of the people, and an entanglement in that part of Africa— necessitating military operations on a large scale—was the last thing in the world they desired." The situation was further improved by Delcassé's declaration in the Senate on

[1] *D.D.F.* I, 153, March 2. [2] ibid. I, 215–216. April 5.
[3] ibid. I, 322–3. [4] *B.D.* II, 261.

July 5 on the Moroccan Mission, of which Lansdowne said that he had read and weighed every line.[1]

Sliman's journey to Paris was far more important. His main object, to complete the delimitation of the frontier begun in 1845, was not achieved, since France argued that to fix a frontier in nomad country was impossible ; but an agreement for the joint policing of the district was signed.[2] Delcassé seized the opportunity to emphasise the predominant rights and interests of France, while endeavouring not to arouse the apprehensions of his visitor. It was the first time that such plain language had been used. Contrary to the expectation and desire of the Sultan in appealing to Europe, the result of his Missions was to diminish the chance of being allowed to misgovern his country in his own way. When at the end of July Lansdowne tactfully inquired about the doings of the envoy at Paris, Cambon replied that France had nothing to hide.[3] The chief question was the frontier. There was, however, disquieting talk in Paris, echoes of which doubtless reached Fez. " I am aware that rumours are current of the possible assumption by France of the protectorate of Morocco ", wrote Monson.[4] " This rumour was discussed in my presence by the Ambassadors of Germany and Italy the day before yesterday. I took no part in that discussion, but I noticed with pleasure that Count Tornielli characterised the step as absolutely improbable. I myself cannot believe that the moment is propitious for such a new departure." The situation, he added, required to be watched. " The temptation to round off the French possessions in North Africa by repeating on a larger scale in Morocco what has been done in Tunis is evidently very great. The hints given by M. Cambon of the high value which France would attach to the permission of Great Britain to use a free hand in Morocco cannot but raise a certain suspicion. But the audacity required for springing such a surprise upon the world as that to which I have alluded would, in my opinion, be certainly foreign to the spirit now directing the policy of the Government of the Republic." Monson knew a good deal, but Delcassé's long-range plans were beyond his ken.

When the Moroccan Mission had come and gone, Delcassé signed elaborate instructions to Saint-René-Taillandier, the new Minister to Tangier.[5] He had explained to Ben Sliman

---

[1] *D.D.F.* I, 382–3. [2] ibid. I, 444. [3] ibid. I, 413–414.
[4] B.D. II, 260–1, June 14. [5] *D.D.F.* I, 402–7. cp. Taillandier, 13–14.

—and the Minister was to inform the Morocco Government—
the unique situation of France which made Morocco an *enclave*
in French Africa.   From her geographical position France
derived interests and rights which made her either the best of
friends or the most formidable of enemies.   When Morocco
decided to enter on a new path, France would have a right to
expect that she would look first to her great and friendly
neighbour, who was always ready to supply her needs.   The
French Minister was to make the Sultan understand that it
depended on him to keep " the most reliable of his friends, the
most careful of the integrity of his power, the most capable of
preserving it in the event of certain dangers.   Our loyalty and
our interest are guarantees that we shall not infringe it unless
he compels us."   The duty of the Minister was to increase
French influence and gain the entire confidence of the ruler.
Spanish interests should be carefully considered, and particular
attention should be given to the activities of the British
Legation.   The rival in Delcassé's eyes was to be sought in
London and nowhere else.   Had the Sultan and his Ministers
read these instructions, they would have sensed the iron hand
beneath the velvet glove ;   and Lansdowne would not have
been overpleased.

"I brought with me an essential idea ", writes Taillandier
in his Memoirs, " the résumé of my instructions and the soul
of my actions :   France intended to reserve the future in
Morocco for herself.   I had to avert all foreign enterprise
which would have limited her authority in advance.   I had
also, by winning the confidence of the Sultan and the Makhzen,
to open the way for our own initiative when our agreements
with the Powers should give us a free hand."   It required
careful steering, for the waters were full of cross currents and
shoals.   Great Britain stood for the status quo, which allowed
her to dominate the Straits.   Her commerce was expanding,
but she desired neither commercial privilege nor influence at
Court.   The state of the country was deplorable, but it was
not her business to clean it up.   The policy was simpler in
idea than in execution ;   for Fez was besieged by touts, and
the Moroccan Government tried to play off Great Britain
against France.   Nicolson's conduct was straightforward and
disinterested throughout.   Frankly recognising the superior
interest of France, he advised the Sultan to give her no cause
for complaint.   Yet, despite the entire absence of competitive
intrigue, there was an open conflict between the British

principle of equal opportunity and the French desire for
political preponderance. The Sultan's monkey-tricks ruined
his finances and destroyed his prestige ; and as the grip of the
central Government relaxed, the growing anarchy on the
eastern frontier stirred France to new demands. While the
Governor of Algeria naturally longed to extend his frontier
in a district where the Sultan's authority was a fiction, Delcassé
was bound to view the problem from a wider angle. Only
the authority of the ruler, feeble though it was, held the
country together, and through him alone could competing
influences be warded off. Before undertaking the task to
which he believed France to be called, it was essential for her
to obtain the leave of the Powers principally concerned.
Meanwhile the Moroccan Government must be taught to lean
on Paris. A frontal attack would spoil the game. Delcassé
knew where he was going and refused to be rushed.

At the opening of 1902 the new French Minister was
presented to the Sultan at Rabat.[1] In view of the dangerous
activities of British agents at Court he had secured permission
to accentuate his warnings.[2] " You may say ", telegraphed
Delcassé, " that we are resolved to proceed to action in case
of need, either to secure the withdrawal of any scheme involving the alienation of Moroccan independence for the benefit
of another Power, or to obtain compensation for ourselves.
. . . We have always refrained from encouraging organic
innovations, knowing that they would involve the delicate
task of explaining to the Sultan and the Powers that, except
in the special case of the Spaniards, neighbours of Morocco
like ourselves, we cannot allow them to be carried out under
the direction of any Power but France." Armed with
extended powers the French Minister explained the policy of
his chief.[3] The French and Moroccan Governments were like
two friends, he began, owners of two beautiful contiguous
gardens. Neither coveted the heritage of the other : each
was ready to help his neighbour. But if one of them allowed
strangers to instal themselves in his garden his authority was
endangered, and in causing his neighbour anxiety he obliged
him to take precautions. Foreign loans or concessions for
railways, telegraphs or large public works, the employment of
foreign military instructors or administrators would, in the
eyes of the French Government, compromise his independence

[1] Taillandier, ch. 3, and D.D.F. II, 74.   [2] ibid. II, 25, and 34–5.
[3] ibid. II, 92–5.

and consequently the security of Algeria. In such case France would be forced to act. The envoy asked for nothing, but warned the Sultan that it would be dangerous to trifle with France. It was the same message that Sliman had brought home from Paris. " Our warnings could not be welcome ", reported Taillandier.[1] The ever-growing importance of Kaid Maclean was a danger. Menacing projects had been scotched, but the outlook was anxious. The hostility of Sultan and Makhzen was unconcealed. He feared some decision in favour of England which would force France to a rupture or an abdication, and he counselled his chief to act.

On July 23 Cambon informally mentioned to Lansdowne his uneasiness in regard to Morocco.[2] The British Government, he believed, was perfectly sincere in its desire to maintain the status quo ; but some British subjects were not equally discreet. He was particularly alarmed at the position acquired by Kaid Maclean, who had become virtually Commander-in-Chief of the army, which he was organising and equipping and which could only be intended for use against France. Lansdowne expressed his belief that Maclean did not interfere in politics, but failed to convince the Ambassador, who suggested a frank discussion of the situation. The attitude of the tribes had become extremely threatening. " It was not enough that we should declare our desire to maintain the status quo. We should both be prepared for eventualities. He apprehended that what we really cared about was Tangier, and an arrangement with France for its neutralisation could easily be reached." These were only his personal opinions, but he intended to ask permission to mention them officially at some future time. Cambon's report adds that Lansdowne, in proof of his loyalty to the status quo, mentioned that he had recently declined a request from the Sultan for an English Military Mission. The Ambassador sketched an arrangement for England to obtain security by the neutralisation of Tangier, recognising in return the influence of France and the right in case of need to police the south. He pleaded for an exchange of views on all questions of common interest, among them Siam. Lansdowne reflected a moment, and said that he was ready to talk when Cambon received instructions.

A fortnight after this revealing conversation the Ambassador reappeared. He had seen Delcassé and was authorised to

[1] Ch. 4, and *D.D.F.* II, 146-150.
[2] *B.D.* II, 263, and *D.D.F.* II, 439-40.

K

explain his ideas on Siam and Morocco, the only two points where the position of France was insecure.[1] He desired that the Morocco question should not become acute ; but he thought it desirable that the two Governments should frankly discuss and agree on their action in the event of the country passing into liquidation. Spain, who would have to be considered, must receive a sufficient allowance of hinterland. Tangier should become an international port. Beyond the Spanish line France would expect to exercise exclusive influence. Great Britain, Delcassé believed, had no interest in those regions. Lansdowne's response was to pour water into the foaming wine. " I told his Excellency that I regarded with the greatest apprehension the idea of provoking an international controversy with regard to the future of that country : as he must be aware, France and England were by no means the only Powers concerned in Morocco. Italy, Spain and Germany had all of them at one time or another manifested an interest in its affairs. Any attempt to deal prematurely with the ' liquidation ' of Morocco would be sure to lead to serious complications."

Cambon's report fills in and enlarges the outlines. Speaking throughout in the name of his chief he defined Morocco as a prolongation of Algeria, the open gate of France's African Empire. It was impossible to permit the gathering of a force independent of French influence. England's interests would be met by the neutralisation of Tangier, and, if France was led to extend her domination, England could have commercial liberty for a certain period. A zone round her settlements should be reserved for Spain in the event of a general liquidation of Morocco. South of this zone France would have a free hand. " M. Delcassé hopes that this hypothesis will not occur for a long time. He hopes the status quo will last for generations and he will work for its preservation. But he thinks that the best way to preserve it is a free exchange of views on the future and the removal of the rivalries which threaten it." Lansdowne expressed his gratitude for the clarity of the declarations, but could not inform the Cabinet till after the holidays. Cambon did not press the matter, knowing that his chief desired to conclude his discussions with Spain. At the close of the interview Lansdowne expressed the hope that the conversation might be continued. " But could we not round it off by talking of Newfoundland ? "

[1] B.D. II, 264-6, and D.D.F. II, 440-3.

Cambon replied that he had already explained the view of his chief on that subject, namely that France must obtain territorial compensation, but there had been no response.   " I told you", rejoined Lansdowne, " that we could not give you Gambia ; but if you like to look round and ask for something else we will see."

On receiving the report of the conversation Monson expressed the greatest surprise that Delcassé had gone so far as to propose, under the device of spheres of influence, a practical partition of Morocco.[1] " For such a professed adherent of the principle of the maintenance of the status quo as applicable to all delicate territorial questions to sanction the immediate and radical operation which the proposed solution would necessitate is certainly a step which I should never have thought M. Delcassé would decide upon taking." An exaggerated version of this conversation reached the Sultan, who sent Maclean to London with a letter to the King asking England to guarantee the integrity of his country. If his request were refused he would apply to Berlin. He also asked for a loan. The envoy was received at Balmoral, but once again the British Government declined to hold its shield over the Sultan. It was explained that other Powers would have to participate in a loan. The French Minister in Tangier pressed for action, and his chief had to remind him that there was a European side to the question.[2] His plan was to settle with each Power in turn in order to obtain a free hand. Negotiations with Spain, he added a little later, were in an advanced stage,[3] and they must not be upset by an explosion which might open the Morocco question before certain Powers could be won. Already assured that Italy would not oppose, France would be in a good position after a deal with Spain to undertake the discussion with England which the latter appeared to desire. The chief obstacle in the path appeared to be Kaid Maclean, whom Cambon, despite the denials of Lansdowne, persisted in describing as a semi-official agent of the British Government, and whose visit to King Edward and his Ministers confirmed his suspicions.[4]

The growing discontent in Morocco made further discussion inevitable, and on December 30 Delcassé furnished his Ambassador with instructions.[5] France desired to see the

[1] B.D. II, 267.
[2] D.D.F. II, 458–9.
[3] ibid. II, 473–4.
[4] ibid. II, 514–15.
[5] ibid. II, 682–3.

crisis terminate without the action of any Power. If Lansdowne referred to the exchange of views between Paris and Madrid, of which he was doubtless aware, an explanation could be given. Certain eventualities had to be considered, but the loyal desire to maintain the status quo had never changed. Cambon was reminded that the wish of the Quai d'Orsay was to retain a privileged position for France, and he was instructed to avoid opening the door to intervention by other Powers. " Being nearer to Morocco than other Powers we must be ready to act ; but we must avoid initiatives which our contiguity and the importance of our interests would themselves render an object of suspicion."

The French Government, declared the Ambassador to Lansdowne on the last day of 1902, strongly desired that there should be no disturbance of the status quo, even if the Sultan were to be overthrown by his subjects.[1] They also wished to abstain, if possible, from interference with the internal affairs of the country. Thirdly they desired that, should intervention become inevitable, the Powers with a distinct interest in Morocco should consult as to its nature and scope and should rule out single-handed intervention. No other Powers should be allowed to participate, for it would be a great mistake to internationalise such action overmuch. He emphasised this point, which indeed proved to be the core of his declaration. For when Lansdowne asked the meaning of the phrase " Puissances intéressées " Cambon answered without hesitation that Germany was the Power which the French Government would like to exclude. Germany had no concern with Morocco. The only Powers really interested were Great Britain, France, and Spain. It would be most desirable that, if Germany were to try to play a conspicuous rôle, she should be told that she had no *locus standi*. Lansdowne replied that the question of what Powers should intervene was a delicate one, on which he could not without further consideration commit himself. For instance, was it safe to assume that Italy had no interest in Morocco ? The unhesitating response that she had none convinced him that a clear understanding on the point existed between the two countries. Cambon's report amplifies the reference to Germany, and asserts Lansdowne's agreement that it was the common interest of the two Powers to prevent her intrusion. The best way of averting the danger, added the Foreign

[1] *B.D.* II, 274–5, and *D.D.F.* II, 686–9.

Secretary, was to cling to the status quo, since partition would involve competition, and it would be difficult to refuse the Kaiser his morsel. "This consideration", comments Cambon, "perhaps explains his hesitation in committing himself on the future of Morocco."

In reporting the conversation to Monson the Foreign Secretary contrasted it with that of August 6, when the French Government looked forward to a "liquidation" under which Morocco would be, if not partitioned, at any rate divided into spheres of influence under the control of France, England and Spain. "To-day he made no reference to any such possibilities, and represented the French Government as the leading advocate of non-intervention and of the maintenance of the status quo." The change noted by Lansdowne was one of tactics rather than strategy, for the policy outlined in the summer had received a cold douche in London. The scheme itself was being pushed steadily forward. Lansdowne guessed at the Franco-Italian pact, and the emphasis on the exclusion of Germany pointed to a definite plan of campaign. The acceptance by Great Britain of the forward policy, of which Monson regarded Cambon rather than his chief as the sponsor, had to wait for a more favourable breeze; for Lansdowne had not moved an inch. Meanwhile Delcassé was busily tilling another portion of the coveted field.

VIII

The loss by Spain of her empire in the West Indies and the Pacific increased the relative importance of her possessions nearer home. Since the maintenance of the status quo in Morocco[1] appeared to be improbable, a section of opinion led by the Conservative Silvela advocated a deal with France, whom he described as the natural ally. Visiting the French Ambassador in Madrid in July 1902, he argued that the two countries had common interests and common apprehensions —an obvious allusion to England.[2] "If I return to power in a few months, as I hope to do, you will find I hold these ideas more strongly than ever." His conviction, he added, was shared by almost all the political leaders.

---

[1] For Spanish views see Gabriel Maura, *La Question du Maroc*; Romanones, *Las Responsabilidades des Antiguo Regimen* 1875–1923, 39–52; Leon y Castillo *Mis Tiempos*, II, ch. 19.

[2] *D.D.F.* II, 387–8.

A remarkable Memorandum drawn up in the Quai d'Orsay at this moment explained the situation as it appeared to official eyes.[1] However advantageous the status quo in Morocco, circumstances beyond the control of France might render it impossible to maintain, and it would be imprudent not to look ahead. If Italy took action in Tripoli on the strength of the recent pact, France would have to seek compensation in Morocco. Moreover the Sultan might favour other Powers to the detriment of France, and the Morocco question might thus be reopened. Next to France, Spain was the most directly interested; and now that she had lost her distant possessions, her ambitions were concentrated on Morocco. A partition of territory or influence was the obvious course—first an entente for the maintenance of the status quo, secondly an agreement as to the zones of influence or action if it broke down, and thirdly a concerted diplomacy for the further stages. France and Spain, thus united, could approach England and offer to place the Tangier zone under a collective guarantee. The critical hour of liquidation might thus be postponed, and when it arrived France and Spain could avow their intention to play a preponderating part. A final phase would be needed to secure the assent of the Powers to the programme by the maintenance of commercial liberty and in other ways. They could rely on the good will of Italy and Russia, while Germany and England would require special compensation. It was a well-planned scheme, and Delcassé's reputation as a diplomatist would stand higher if he had carried it out in full.

Sagasta, the veteran Liberal leader, was now a convert. In September Delcassé wired to Taillandier that the negotiations with Spain were in an advanced stage, and it was important not to endanger them by anything which would reopen the Morocco question before France had won over the Powers whose interests could be harmonised with her own.[2] " Assuming that Italy would not oppose us, and in agreement with Spain, we should be in a good position to converse with England." A draft secret convention, dated November 8, 1902, embodied the French programme.[3] By the first article the two Powers undertook not to favour any other foreign influence. The second agreed that if, owing to the weakness of the Morocco Government, its inability to keep order, or

[1] D.D.F. II, 397–400. [2] ibid. II, 473–4.
[3] ibid. II, 583–6.

for any other cause, the maintenance of the status quo became impossible, the two Governments would have the exclusive right to restore order within their respective zones. The third delimited the spheres of influence, the old kingdom of Fez falling to Spain and the old kingdom of Marakesh to France. The Spanish sphere in the extreme south was to be extended. Article 4 envisaged the neutralisation of Tangier. Article 5 bound each signatory to inform the other in advance if it were compelled to use force for the protection of its interests in its own sphere. The sixth promised mutual diplomatic support in questions arising out of the convention. Articles 7 and 8 dealt with trade, navigation and fisheries. Article 9 forbade the alienation of territory within the respective zones without the assent of the other party.

Ten days later the French Ambassador at Madrid urged the prompt conclusion of the negotiations. The only obstacle, in the opinion of Silvela, lay in the pretensions of Great Britain, with whom Spain had no wish to enter into conflict. This was indeed a difficulty, as was pointed out by the Spanish Ambassador in Paris, who contended that in the absence of an arrangement with England complications would quickly arise.[1] At this critical point of the negotiations, of which Delcassé had not informed the Cabinet, Silvela returned to power, Francophil as ever, but aware that there were lions in the path. " It was good—too good", he declared. " Could we accept it without the approval of England ? " That Downing Street had not been consulted is a revelation of Delcassé's curious lack of vision ; for it was a gamble to negotiate a settlement of such dimensions without informing the Power which held Gibraltar and whose friendship he was hoping to win. The attempt to keep the secret in Paris broke down, for the Spanish newspapers furnished their readers with maps of the promised zone. Warnings were heard in France, where René Millet urged caution in the press and Ribot raised the question in the Chamber.

On January 2, 1903, Abarzuza, the new Spanish Foreign Minister, in conversation with the British Ambassador, declared that, though Spaniards had no wish for a policy of adventure, they claimed some influence " in a part at least " of Morocco.[2] He refrained from entering into details and desired to know the view of Great Britain on this point. A thorough understanding with England was vital to Spain.

[1] *D.D.F.* II, 611–13.   [2] *B.D.* II, 276–7.

There was no Franco-Spanish alliance, he stated explicitly, and so long as he was in office there never would be. The French, he believed, were less attached to the status quo than they professed. The Ambassador was not sure how far the Minister represented the view of the Government, for Silvela had not yet spoken to him about Morocco. Lansdowne replied by telegram that in the event of a catastrophe Spain must have a voice in any new international arrangements ; that a discussion of such contingencies seemed premature ; and that he believed the French Government sincerely desired to avoid the disturbance of the status quo. Abarzuza was pleased with the message, and declared that, whatever proposals the French might make, Spain would refuse to do anything displeasing to England. " He evidently wished me to suppose that the French were inclined to make proposals for some secret agreement ", commented the Ambassador, " though he was somewhat indefinite in his language with regard to this point. . . . My belief is that Señor Silvela now sees the danger of the course he advocated eighteen months ago, and that, for the present, all likelihood of a French alliance is at an end."

At this moment Delcassé signed the elaborate instructions to Jules Cambon, the new Ambassador to Madrid, which betray his mortification at the failure of his plan.[1] The relations of the two countries were good, and the memory of French services in the conclusion of peace with the United States was fresh. These good relations made it a duty to prevent mistrust in regard to Morocco. Accordingly, at the reiterated wish of the Spanish Ambassador, the French Government had tried to discover a basis of reciprocal concessions in view of certain eventualities, though both parties sincerely desired to maintain the status quo as long as possible. No firm agreement was reached ; but it would clearly be possible, when the time arrived, for the two Governments to attain a settlement equally satisfactory to both. France had always thought it wise in co-operation with Spain to prepare a solution of the territorial problem which events in Morocco might at any moment present. The Spanish Cabinet had at first appeared to share this attitude, but at a later stage it feared the displeasure of England and advocated an understanding with her. France must now await an approach by Spain, which seemed extremely probable. Spanish sym-

[1] D.D.F. III, 15-18. January 8.

pathies with France had been growing in recent years, and some day it might be possible to join in settling the future of Morocco.

Shortly after Jules Cambon's arrival in Madrid Silvela confessed that he thought it unwise to make an arrangement with France without informing England, and he asked to be relieved of the obligations of secrecy.[1] His own preference was for France, backed up by Russia. The danger of isolation in a European or African conflict was so strongly felt that, if France and Russia were unresponsive, Spain would be forced to the side of England. He distrusted the English, " who, while embracing you, try to steal your watch". He himself would never make an arrangement with them, but others would. " If Spain does not go to France, she will go to England." In the recent draft France merely promised diplomatic support, but in case of difficulties with England Spain would be dangerously exposed to her wrath. She was gradually recovering her strength, and if France was insulted by England Spanish forces could easily threaten and invade Portugal. Thus to conclude an agreement without informing England, and with a mere promise of diplomatic support from France, would be unwise. Here was the Premier's new programme, dictated not by any affection for England but by fear of her might.

Delcassé's reply was distinctly cool.[2] The plan resulting from numerous conversations undertaken at the initiative of Spain had been submitted for the definite approval of the Sagasta Ministry, but without result. The principle of an arrangement remained, but the details were unsettled. He had no objection to England being informed that France and Spain had exchanged views on Morocco ; that they desired to preserve the status quo as long as possible ; and that, if changes became inevitable, they had recognised that their interests need not conflict. Silvela was grateful for permission to make a guarded communication. " We must be on good terms with England and on still better terms with France." How did they stand in regard to the recent project ?[3] " It is not a reality, but it was more than a sketch. Shall we sign it, or negotiate afresh, or consider it annulled ? " The discussion, replied the French Ambassador, must wait till he had informed London as had been proposed.

[1] D.D.F. III, 70–1, 76–83. [2] ibid. III, 89–90.
[3] ibid. III, 92 and 97–8.

Abarzuza now revealed the secret to the British Ambassador.[1] Before the fall of the Liberal Government the French Ambassador had proposed the division of Morocco into two zones of influence, Spain to have the coast with a strip of hinterland, and France the rest. Fez was to fall within the Spanish zone. The French were pressing for an immediate reply when the change of Government occurred, and they had now raised the matter again. He had replied that he could make no such arrangement without the approval of England. He added that he was strongly in favour of maintaining the status quo, and of avoiding the question of zones of influence till it was forced upon them. Moreover the suggested plan was very unfavourable to Spain. A clear intimation that England would refuse to recognise it would put an end to the matter once for all. He was greatly surprised that Delcassé should have proposed such a plan. Lansdowne telegraphed in reply that it was of the utmost importance that Spain and Great Britain should act together in regard to Morocco. " We share his views, and I have more than once informed the French Ambassador here that we deprecated attempts to bring about a virtual partition of Morocco. We could of course recognise no such arrangement unless we were parties to it." This unequivocal Spanish declaration, so much more detailed than Delcassé had authorised, might have been expected to end the discussions between Paris and Madrid. But Abarzuza told the British Ambassador that Paul Cambon had persuaded Delcassé that England was not interested in the Morocco question, and that France and Spain could deal with it as they pleased. This view had become prevalent in Madrid; for though he had tried to combat it, Cambon's assurances were positive. Lansdowne wired that the reports were absolutely groundless, and that an attempt to deal with Morocco without regard to British interests would not be allowed.

Even this was not the end; for while the Foreign Minister was a convinced Anglophil, his chief never wavered in his attachment to France. The Spanish Ambassador in Paris informed Delcassé that the King and the Queen Mother were more than ever convinced of the utility of a close understanding with France.[2] Silvela had declared that any other policy, such as an alliance with England, was inconceivable. That these were no empty words was proved by the fact that

[1] B.D. II, 279–280.   [2] D.D.F. III, 149.

on the same day Silvela dispatched a Note to the French Ambassador.[1] The most obvious duty for Spanish statesmen, he began, was to deliver Spain from isolation. It had been decided to strengthen the army and navy. The Government desired to know whether Spain would be admitted to an *entente cordiale* with France and Russia, with the object of securing a guarantee of her coasts and possessions or at any rate the neutrality of the African littoral opposite the Straits of Gibraltar, and perhaps ultimately forming an alliance. In forwarding the note Cambon added an elaborate memorandum. Her isolation in 1898 had taught Spain the need of friends, and she looked to France and Russia to save her from the hostility or the domination of England. Cambon warmly supported the plan, which involved no obligation in regard to Morocco. Delcassé was naturally pleased with Silvela's advances and authorised the continuation of the discussions.[2] But he pointed out the extreme disparity between the advantages to Spain and the obligations of France and Russia, and remarked that the latter was unlikely to commit herself in the Western Mediterranean. Nothing more indeed was heard of the plan.

Delcassé had been as unsuccessful with Spain as he had been successful with Italy. The rebuff necessitated a change of tactics though not a change of policy. The road to Madrid, he had discovered, passed through London. An arrangement with Spain was inescapable, but it would have to follow instead of preceding a deal with England. No ground had been lost, for Spain remained predominantly Francophil. On July 17 Silvela made a declaration of almost passionate attachment to France.[3] " We must remain the friends of all nations. But who can deny that an intimate union binds us to our neighbour, the French Republic, and that the harmony of our interests and our aspirations for the maintenance of the status quo as long as possible leads us to maintain a complete friendship, a union of interests, a harmony of thoughts with this nation, our sister by race ? " A few days later, he was succeeded by Villaverde, who, though he thought the declaration rather premature, contemplated no change in policy.[4] When, however, he expressed his desire to resume the discussions, the French Ambassador tartly explained that the situation had changed.[5]

[1] *D.D.F.* III, 192–8.   .[2] ibid. III, 219–221. April 6.
[3] ibid. III, 462–3.   [4] ibid. III, 476–7.
[5] ibid. III, 564–5.

Spanish statesmen had made a great mistake in not showing more *empressement*. The negotiations of which the Premier spoke were only a prolonged conversation, and the French Cabinet had never been informed. Though the intentions of France were unchanged in their main outlines, important modifications would have to be made, and the question of Fez could no longer be decided in the old way. The change of tone reveals the confidence of Delcassé in the success of the negotiations with England which had just begun. Spain would indeed still have to be squared, but it was no longer necessary to pay a fantastic price. Recognising that Fez was lost, Spain asked for Agadir. Delcassé replied that in that case France must have the territory of the Sus. The deal was refused by Spain, and Delcassé switched his attention from Madrid to London.

IX

On February 8, 1902, at a party at Marlborough House, Eckardstein saw Chamberlain and Cambon in animated conversation, and overheard the significant words Egypt and Morocco. It was a false dawn, for Lansdowne's reiterated declarations to France and Spain throughout the year revealed his reluctance to open the Morocco question. The violent hostility to Germany during the brief Venezuela partnership made France by comparison more popular, but at the beginning of 1903 Cambon warned his chief not to count on the permanence of the anti-German mood.[1] Chamberlain, for instance, changed his views with incredible facility, and might change them again. A week later he reported cordial conversations during a visit to Windsor, in which King Edward argued emphatically for keeping the Morocco problem in the hands of England, France and Spain.[2] Italy might be associated if necessary, for she had interests in the Mediterranean. The King's desire to exclude Germany was unconcealed, and Queen Alexandra's outburst against the Kaiser showed how strongly the tide was running.

On February 4, after discussing the loan desired by the Sultan, Cambon reminded Lansdowne of their previous conversations on the future of Morocco, adding that, though there was no urgent need of dealing with the question, France was

---

[1] *D.D.F.* III, 47-8.   January 22, 1903.
[2] ibid. III, 65-8.

ready to do so at any moment.[1] Invited to recapitulate his ideas, the Ambassador summarised four points : recognition of the hinterland of the Spanish possessions, neutralisation of Tangier, commercial liberty, and French influence to the south of the Spanish zone. All this, he added, had been frequently discussed with Spain, but the exchange of views must remain academic till England joined in. Lansdowne listened attentively but made no response ; and Cambon felt that the Morocco question would not be solved without British demands for large compensation. Happily the tone of the British press had become more friendly,[2] and the British Minister in Tangier had changed his note.[3] His recent attitude towards his French colleague, reported the latter, seemed to say : " It is you and we who are concerned. The major issues in Morocco are for England and France."

After the visit of Edward VII to Paris Delcassé issued a circular despatch to the representatives of France throughout the world.[4] The Russian alliance, he declared, remained the corner stone of French policy, and the *démarche* of the King would alter none of the principles of French policy. It was, nevertheless, of considerable importance. The satisfaction at the change was all the greater owing to the large volume of commerce and to the fact that France and England touched in every quarter of the globe. Hence an antagonism of interests and inevitable difficulties involving the danger of conflicts unless handled in a conciliatory mood. " It is from this point of view that we are justified in congratulating ourselves on the visit of King Edward and in hoping that it will not be without advantage to our policy." With the royal visit the atmosphere of chill suspicion had passed away. When Delcassé accompanied the President in July on a return visit, the battle was won. The long-deferred reward for his surrender at Fashoda and for his steady neutrality during the South African war was in sight. He was delighted with the cordiality of the welcome, and Cambon declared that never for fifty years had such ovations greeted the head of a foreign state.[5]

Delcassé's report of the historic conversation of July 7 is far less detailed than that of Lansdowne.[6] " I laid most stress on Morocco, explaining that the possession of Algeria and

[1] *D.D.F.* III, 85-8. [2] ibid. III, 183-5.
[3] ibid. III, 170-1. [4] ibid. III, 321-3.
[5] Ibid. III, 502-5. [6] Ibid. III, 471-3

Tunis commands us to allow no one but France to control the affairs of that country ; that it possesses for us a capital interest, and that England ought to recognise it." After readily agreeing to British wishes for the neutralisation of the Straits, commercial liberty, and consideration for the interests of Spain, he exclaimed : " On these conditions give France a free hand in Morocco, and she will be conciliatory on other matters." When Newfoundland, Siam, and the New Hebrides had been discussed, Lansdowne mentioned Egypt, but " in view of my extreme reserve he did not touch on the political question." Here alone the two accounts differ ; for Lansdowne describes himself as saying that nobody could imagine that England would withdraw, and his visitor as replying that the problem could be satisfactorily solved as part of the African question if Morocco could be settled in accordance with the wishes of France. On his return to Paris Delcassé expressed to Monson his deep satisfaction at the warmth of his reception and the genuine friendliness of the public towards France.[1]

In a conversation on July 29, after discussing various matters, Lansdowne referred to Egypt, which found no place in a draft treaty communicated by the Ambassador.[2] Cambon replied that he was not authorised to open up this question, which involved many points concerning other Powers, such as the Canal and the international institutions. It seemed impossible to assimilate the Egyptian question to those which the two Governments could settle. Lansdowne reported that there had never been a better opportunity of settling the matter. " There is the chief point for England ", commented Cambon, " and Lansdowne's declaration was not lightly made. It embodies some decision of the Government. If we recognise the Occupation we should have to ask more in Morocco or elsewhere." Delcassé replied that he was willing to examine suggestions on Egypt, but that French concessions in that quarter would demand equivalent sacrifices elsewhere.[3] In his eagerness to secure a free hand in Morocco he had unintentionally reopened the Egyptian question.

On August 5 Lansdowne and Cambon held their last conversation before the summer holidays.[4] For the first time German designs were mentioned, Lansdowne remarking

[1] B.D. II, 302–3.   [2] D.D.F. III, 485–7 and 497–9.
[3] ibid. III, 510–11.
[4] ibid. III, 516–520, and B.D. II, 306–7.

that he believed they had shifted from the Mediterranean to the Atlantic, Cambon replying that the German Legation at Tangier desired some concession at Rabat or Casablanca as a pretext for interference in a matter concerning France, England and Spain. When he remarked that Spain would receive a title to the hinterland of her settlements, Lansdowne rejoined that the concession would only materialise in case of a general liquidation and that the preservation of the status quo remained the programme. " Assuredly ", replied Cambon, " but in this zone recognised as falling eventually to Spain, she should not be hindered in her action." " Just as you desire not to be hindered in the rest of Morocco ", replied Lansdowne, " nor to be thwarted in your economic enterprises or in your directions to the Sultan." " Precisely ", replied the Ambassador.

When the conversation turned to Egypt, Cambon argued that the question was in a different category, that it had agitated French opinion for twenty years, and that it would have to be treated with infinite care. " You expect us to recognise your Occupation. I know of nothing which France would find it more difficult to accept. I know that M. Delcassé sincerely desires to liquidate all our affairs, even Egypt, if it is possible. I believe him to be courageous enough to ignore clamour. But, if I may use a familiar expression, he would need a lot of *d'estomac* to assume responsibility for a settlement of the Egyptian question." " Do you think we do not need *d'estomac* to give you Morocco ? " retorted Lansdowne. Cambon pleaded that the cases were different. " If M. Delcassé was led to recognise the existing situation in Egypt, it would be such a considerable concession, and one on which French opinion is so sensitive, that he could not accept it without effective compensations and without a more favourable settlement of the other questions under discussion. In Morocco for instance he would have to ask for more definite advantages. He told me so, and I beg you to take note." Such are the complications of diplomacy. It was now clear that his aims in Morocco could only be attained at a price which he had never intended to pay. On the other hand it opened up the prospect of a richer harvest of concessions. Russian apprehensions at the talk of an *Entente Cordiale* were calmed by reassuring explanations from Paris.[1] The ground had been mapped out and success

[1] *D.D.F.* III, 501–2 and 527–8.

seemed to be assured. Where each party possesses grievances
and aspirations, the method of give and take can be applied.
The *détente* was quickly felt in Tangier. Early in September
Nicolson spoke of the future to Taillandier for the first time.[1]
The inhabitants of Morocco, he observed, needed reforms,
and they could not reform themselves. " To help them is
decidedly not our business, but it might well be yours." The
phrase was joyfully registered as the turning of the tide.
The years of rivalry were at an end.

When negotiations were resumed after the holidays Lansdowne presented a detailed memorandum, of which Delcassé's first impressions were not altogether favourable.[2]   To
the Foreign Minister's argument that he gave France a free
hand in Morocco, the Ambassador replied that he was giving
what he did not possess—a hope, not a tangible reality.
England possessed nothing in Morocco, yet she asked France
to abandon her advantages and rights in Egypt. Delcassé
would have to consider the complicated issue with care. A
more exhaustive discussion took place on October 21, when
Cambon, after a visit to Paris, brought a preliminary reply to
the statement of October 1.[3]   Delcassé, he explained, could
not forthwith surrender France's position in Egypt, but he
was prepared for withdrawal by stages in return for compensations. On the other questions the Ambassador touched
lightly, but he indicated that the only suitable territorial
compensation for French rights in Newfoundland would be
Gambia. The Colonial Office, rejoined Lansdowne, would
never abandon that colony, to which Cambon sturdily retorted
that his chief would maintain his demand. Lansdowne then
spoke of the financial embarrassment of the Sultan, who
was unable to suppress the insurrection. He proposed that
England and France should participate in a small loan, as the
need was urgent, and France's claim to be the only lender
could not become operative till the negotiations were completed. In reporting the suggestion Cambon argued for its
adoption, on the ground that otherwise Germany might offer
her services or Morocco might collapse before France was
ready to deal with the situation. The project was accepted by
the French Government.

Delcassé's detailed response to the memorandum of October
1 was accompanied by a despatch to Cambon dealing with

---

[1] Taillandier, 150.   [2] *D.D.F.* IV, 15–16.
[3] ibid. IV. 42–5.

two points.[1]   In Egypt, he frankly confessed, time had worked against France.   England had gradually transformed a precarious possession into a veiled Protectorate, and evacuation would only occur after a lost war.   French rights and privileges became each year more theoretical as England consolidated her position.   Rights, however, must be surrendered in return not for hopes but for realities, and surrendered by instalments synchronising with the acquisition of similar rights and advantages in Morocco.   To secure the safety of the Straits of Gibraltar, to reassure Spain and to prevent a German settlement on the Morocco coast, he proposed that no territorial change should be made within a radius of 500 miles of the Rock.

The memorandum of October 26 is mainly of interest in reference to Egypt ; for the success or failure of the whole transaction, it was now clear, turned on the readiness of Delcassé to pay the British price in the valley of the Nile.[2] His formula was quoted in the preceding chapter.[3]   The outlines remained to be filled in, but it was a promising start. Less hopeful was the reiteration of the demand for Gambia, " surrounded as it is by French possessions and possessing above all a sentimental value for Great Britain ".   Lansdowne remarked to Cambon that at first reading the document suggested that an agreement would be very difficult ; that French demands seemed rather excessive ; that the cession of Gambia was impossible ; and that the surrender of French advantages in Egypt by instalments was unsatisfactory.[4] Cambon hoped that a second reading would change his views, and added that no French statesman except Delcassé would have the courage to liquidate the question of Egypt.

A week later a similar brief conversation took place.[5]   " You will never have such an opportunity again ", argued Cambon. " You are in an irregular situation.   You lack resources   You are at the mercy of changes in French opinion.   You are negotiating with the only French Minister capable of taking the responsibility of such an agreement.   You suffer more than we from the prolongation of the present position, and it is important for you to end it.   Who knows what the future will bring ? "   Who knows, rejoined Lansdowne, that other Powers may not oppose ?   The cession of Gambia, he added,

[1] D.D.F. IV, 50-1.   [2] ibid. IV, 55-60.
[3] v. supra, 44.   [4] ibid. IV, 69.
[5] ibid. IV, 83-4.

L

was vetoed by the Colonial Office. Cambon confessed that
his impressions were none too sanguine.[1] The British Foreign
Office discussed questions as they were discussed in a counting-
house in the City. " My advice is to stand firm, to take our
time, not to appear in a hurry. We have the right to be
difficult. It is more important for the English to arrange
with us about Egypt than for us to arrange with them about
Morocco. They will become intransigent if they think us too
anxious to settle." It was, in truth, a contest of wills no less
than of wits. Both parties were eager for a deal, and each
gambled on the unwillingness of the other to miss a glittering
prize.

It was a great encouragement to Delcassé to receive the
blessings of the Tsar on the occasion of Lamsdorff's visit to
Paris at the end of October.[2] " In charging me with his best
wishes ", declared the Russian Foreign Minister, " the
Emperor desires you to know that he is more than ever
attached to our alliance." Far from disapproving France's
rapprochement with England and Italy, he was very pleased.
England's attitude towards Russia had already changed, and
Russia was grateful to France for her share in bringing it
about. These views, which were officially conveyed in a
letter from the Tsar to the President, were fully shared by
Lamsdorff himself. So delighted was Delcassé that he sent
a full account of the visit in a circular despatch to French
representatives all over the world.

Lansdowne's written reply to the French memorandum was
received on November 19.[3] The plan of a 500-mile zone was
rejected ; the cession of Gambia was once again declined ;
the methods of securing financial liberty in Egypt were
precisely defined. The document could hardly be said to
bring agreement nearer, for the wide range of differences
requiring adjustment was now fully apparent. Cambon
renewed his advice to go slow.[4] England, he pointed out,
would benefit immediately by the removal of financial control
in Egypt, whereas in Morocco France would still be faced
with the Sultan and the Makhzen. Experience showed that
in dealing with oriental governments only two instruments
availed—money or menace. Delcassé's elaborate reply dealt
mainly with Egypt and Newfoundland.[5] Realising at last

[1] D.D.F. IV, 115-116.   [2] ibid. IV, 68 and 106.
[3] B.D. II, 324-7.   [4] D.D.F. IV, 127-31.
[5] ibid. IV, 162-8.

that the whole of Gambia was unobtainable, he suggested that England should cede the hinterland, contenting herself with the town and port—a suggestion which Lansdowne promptly dismissed.[1] Two days later, after a Cabinet meeting, the Foreign Minister replied in detail, buttressing his previous contentions with the authority of his colleagues.[2] At the close of the year Delcassé hinted to the Chamber the steady advance of France towards her Moroccan goal.[3] No military expedition, he announced, was in contemplation, and the Government believed in supporting the Sultan. " When people talk nowadays of a Moroccan question, the idea that the last word rests with France has become almost an axiom, and seems almost natural even to those who previously would have felt bound to oppose it with fury. Everyone sees that the action which our situation summons us to take not only consolidates our preponderating interests but is equally advantageous to Morocco and to foreign interests."

The opening of 1904 found Delcassé in high spirits. " If Russia keeps her hands free in Europe ", he remarked to Paléologue, " and if I conclude my agreements with England, Italy and Spain, you will see Morocco fall into our garden like ripe fruit."[4] A month later he was in a still more expansive mood. The negotiations with England would liquidate all the quarrels of the past. " But believe me, I shall not stop there. This liquidation should lead us, and I desire that it shall lead us, to a political alliance with England. Ah ! my dear friend, what beautiful horizons would open before us ! Just think ! If we could lean both on Russia and on England, how strong we should be in relation to Germany ! A Franco-English alliance has always been my dream, even during the Fashoda crisis. Now I believe I am near the goal." After a moment's pause he added : " It would be difficult to combine with the Russian alliance. But each day has its task." When the dreaded war in the Far East broke out a week later it was more than ever necessary to make sure of England, though France could not anticipate the sensational defeat of her ally.

The Moroccan negotiations as a whole were held up by the question of the territorial compensation for the surrender of French rights in Newfoundland. Convinced at last that Gambia was beyond his reach, Delcassé asked for access to

[1] D.D.F. IV, 169–171.
[2] ibid. IV, 172–5, and B.D. II, 333–4.
[3] D.D.F. IV, 145.
[4] Paléologue, Un Grand Tournant de la Politique Mondiale, 2, 11–12.

the lower Niger, but asked in vain.[1] At his first meeting with Lansdowne in the new year Cambon expressed the disappointment of his chief.[2] The French proposals having been rejected, he awaited a British offer. But it was useless to continue the conversations on other points till the question of territorial compensation was settled. Lansdowne rejoined that in the opinion of his colleagues France's gains in Morocco and Siam would be large, and that only a small compensation was due for her slender sacrifice in Newfoundland. Cambon smiled at his presentation of the case, and reiterated his conviction that the French sacrifices in Egypt were immense. At this point Lansdowne offered territory in the region of Sokoto, which, as Cambon unkindly reminded him, Salisbury had once described as light soil. " My impression", reported the Ambassador, " is that Lord Lansdowne would go farther than his colleagues. There was a touch of sadness when he spoke of Sokoto, for he could not imagine that it would content us." The best hope, in Cambon's view, lay in pressure from Cromer, who, he believed, would willingly give Gambia and access to the Niger to obtain a free hand in Egypt. The French Chargé in Cairo was accordingly instructed to tell him, as if the warning came from himself, that the Egyptian settlement depended on compensation for Newfoundland.[3] The plan developed like clockwork. Cromer replied that he would do his best, and promptly telegraphed home that a breakdown of the negotiations would be a calamity.[4] Lansdowne accordingly made a slightly more extended offer of concessions in Africa, which Cambon considered insufficient.[5] Delcassé asked for details, and suggested the cession of the Los islands, which he described as useless to England, and which commanded the French port of Konakry.[6] Lansdowne rejoined that the Los islands could only be ceded to France in return for some fresh concession, such as a British Protectorate over the New Hebrides.[7]

Delcassé expressed surprise at the British reply about the Los islands.[8] " He fears that certain departments of the British Government are not sufficiently animated by the spirit of the cordial understanding which has made conversation on Newfoundland possible." " Our demands ", concluded the

[1] D.D.F. IV, 225–6. [2] ibid. IV, 248–251.
[3] ibid. IV, 274.
[4] ibid. IV, 277–8 and B.D. II, 339–340. [5] D.D.F. IV, 286–8.
[6] ibid. IV, 295. [7] B.D. II, 341–3. Feb. 5.
[8] D.D.F. IV, 372–5.

despatch, " are as moderate as they are equitable, and I hope
a fresh examination will allow us to reach the understanding
which my government warmly desires." When Lansdowne
relented on the Los islands,[1] the goal at last seemed in sight.
On March 11 the negotiators discussed the date and method of
announcing the agreement in the two countries.[2] While
Delcassé desired to keep the terms secret and to confine himself to a vague declaration, Lansdowne explained that in
England such a course was impossible. Arrangements contingent on the termination of the status quo in Morocco, he
added, could be made in a secret article. It was agreed that
Spain should now be informed, and Delcassé decided to make
the same declaration on commercial liberty to Germany as he
had done to England. In accepting the demand for publication, he insisted that France's freedom of action should be
established beyond doubt and that Moroccan susceptibilities
should be considered.[3] After a final fruitless attempt to
secure better terms for the Newfoundland fishermen, the
treaties were signed on April 8.

The Livre Jaune, issued on May 26, expounded Delcassé's
view of the bargain. Both Governments, he declared,
recognised that great moral and material interests demanded
an amicable settlement. In Newfoundland France had only
abandoned privileges which were difficult to maintain and in
no way necessary, while the essential right of fishing in territorial waters was preserved, and the right of fishing for and
purchasing bait along the whole extent of the French Shore
was explicitly recognised. In West Africa the gains were of
considerable importance. The Niger-Chad frontier had been
improved, and the keys of Konakry were now in French
hands. " Under our influence Morocco would be a source of
strength for our North African empire. If subject to a
foreign Power, our North African possessions would be
permanently menaced and paralysed. The moment had
arrived to decide who was to exercise preponderant influence
in Morocco. The present state can only last on condition that
it is sustained and improved. On the importance of securing
from England the promise not to hamper us it is superfluous
to insist. We should complete our work of civilisation, thus
showing ourselves the best friends of Morocco, since we are
the nation most interested in her prosperity. This will greatly
strengthen French power without prejudice to acquired rights,

ibid. IV, 417-19.   [2] ibid. IV, 448-451.   [3] ibid. IV, 465-72.

and will ultimately benefit everybody." The sacrifice in
Egypt was small. No change was to be made in her political
status, and all necessary guarantees for French financial
interests had been obtained. The adhesion of England to the
execution of the Suez Canal Convention of 1888 was noted
with special pleasure. It was, in a word, a splendid bargain,
purchased at little cost.

It could hardly be expected that Delcassé's satisfaction with
his handiwork would be shared by all his countrymen.[1] It
was unreservedly approved by President Loubet, and by
politicians so different in outlook as Etienne and Jaurès. But
the sacrifices in Newfoundland were so keenly resented that
the Minister was reluctantly compelled to promise the reopening of negotiations, and the acceptance of the British
occupation of Egypt was a bitter pill for impenitent Anglo-
phobes. In replying to his critics in the Chamber when the
agreements were submitted for approval in the autumn,
Delcassé set Morocco in the foreground of his defence. The
prosperity of Algeria and Tunis, he argued, depended on the
fate of Morocco. The problem had been to establish the
preponderance of France in Morocco, and in consequence to
increase her strength in the Mediterranean, without alienating,
but on the contrary conciliating, the Powers concerned. It
was now for France to persuade Morocco by acts rather than
by speeches that she had the will as well as the power to carry
out her task of co-operating in the establishment of order and
the development of her resources. What each had surrendered was of peculiar value to the other. Fundamental
interests were safeguarded on both sides, and both parties had
reason to be content. Less opposition was encountered in
the Senate, where the Minister repeated his spirited apologia.
By the end of the year Parliamentary approval of the agreements had been secured.

It was a personal triumph for Delcassé and the proudest
moment of his life. Since the retirement of Waldeck-
Rousseau he had ploughed a lonely furrow. Combes was
absorbed in his struggle with the Church, and the Foreign
Minister never troubled about his colleagues. Now he was
on the top of the wave. King Edward sent him a message
through Cambon that he regarded him as a true friend.[2]

---

[1] Full summaries of the debates in the Chamber and the Senate were sent
home by the British Ambassador. *B.D.* III, ch. 16.
[2] *D.D.F.* V, 55-6.

Never for a moment throughout the remaining years of his life did he see cause to repent of his policy in 1904. In a revealing conversation with Sir Donald Mackenzie Wallace after his fall he said that during the early years in office Germany desired an understanding with France ; but no definite terms were offered and he regarded the approach as a trap.[1] With England on the other hand it was possible to conclude a business arrangement on the principle of give and take. The abandonment of Egypt distressed many Frenchmen ; but as practical politicians they had to choose between their Egyptian dreams and the claim to recover some day the lost provinces of Alsace and Lorraine. Here indeed was the governing consideration. Partnership with Germany meant the end of the *revanche*. Partnership with England, in addition to its material advantages, kept the door open for the realisation of the dearest hopes. In his ardour for colonial expansion he never forgot the draped statue on the Place de la Concorde. The recovery of the lost provinces, records Paléologue, who worked with him throughout seven eventful years, was his darling dream, the master-key of his thought, the unavowed goal of all his efforts.[2] Moreover he had won the confidence of England without forfeiting that of his ally, thereby creating the possibility that the two friends of France might one day make up their feud. Nothing could be achieved in this direction during the Russo-Japanese war, which complicated his task and filled him with anxiety ; but nobody can contest his title to be regarded as one of the principal architects of the Triple Entente.

X

Article VIII of the Anglo-French Declaration respecting Egypt and Morocco ran as follows : " The two Governments, inspired by their feeling of sincere friendship for Spain, take into special consideration the interests which that country derives from her geographical position and from her territorial possessions on the coast of the Mediterranean. In regard to these interests the French Government will come to an understanding with the Spanish Government. The agreement which may be come to on the subject between France and Spain shall be communicated to His Britannic Majesty's

[1] Lee, *King Edward VII*, II, 254, note.
[2] Paléologue, 164.

Government." In other words the negotiations were to be carried on between Paris and Madrid, with England holding a watching brief for the weaker party. The Queen Regent was annoyed and alarmed at a settlement in which Spain had not been consulted, for Morocco was a vital question not only for the country but for the dynasty itself.[1] The Spanish press complained more bitterly of France than of England, for it had believed France to be a friend.[2] Delcassé had secured British assent to French preponderance in Morocco, and there was no need to offer Madrid such a high price again.

At their first interview on April 19 Delcassé explained to the Spanish Ambassador the concessions he was prepared to make, adding that beyond them he could not go.[3] " I have reason to believe", he telegraphed to Jules Cambon, " that the Spanish Ambassador, who had perhaps created extravagant expectations, will be led to disparage the concessions I have made and to attribute to unfriendliness what is merely his own misreading of the situation. It would be regrettable if the Spanish Government failed to realise that I have gone to the extreme limit permitted to me by the interests in my keeping." When the Spanish Foreign Minister sadly contrasted the new terms with the old, Jules Cambon stiffly replied that the earlier conversations were more or less private ; that he had repeatedly declared that France could not abandon Fez ; that the new concessions largely exceeded what public opinion in France would approve ; that they could not be enlarged ; and that they embodied the deep friendship of his chief for Spain.[4] The Premier rejoined that they expected compensation for the loss of Fez, but that the proposals of 1904 reduced instead of extending the other concessions of 1902 both in the north and the south.

Well aware what views would reach Lansdowne from the Spanish side, Delcassé explained to Paul Cambon that his concessions were considerable.[5] The Spanish Ambassador in Paris, he added, had held out impossible hopes and was fighting for his post. On the same day the Ambassador complained to Monson that the tentative agreement of 1902 was now repudiated by Delcassé, who offered greatly diminished advantages. The Foreign Minister, he considered, had been guilty of bad faith. Castillo poured out his heart to the

[1] G.P. XX, 170–2. Radowitz to Bülow, May 6.   [2] D.D.F. V. 34–5.
[3] ibid. V, 40–1 and 45.   [4] ibid. V, 62–4.
[5] ibid. V, 57.

German Ambassador in Paris.[1]   Spain had been treated during the Anglo-French negotiations as a *quantité négligeable*, and now Delcassé magnanimously threw her some crumbs of the cake. He added that she had lost her opportunity by not protesting at once against the one-sided agreement.   The complaint was renewed by the Spanish Ambassador in London, who declared that an agreement had been reached in 1902, though not signed, since France vetoed its communication to England. The new offer of spheres of influence was less extensive both in the north and south, and France even claimed a portion of the Mediterranean seaboard.   It seemed to him quite wrong that Spain should be asked to accept less merely because England had entered upon the scene.

On April 29 Cambon gave Lansdowne the French version of the negotiations of 1902.   Delcassé had put forward his plan for a Spanish sphere of influence as a basis of discussion, and he could not make official proposals till he knew the terms on which Spain was prepared to deal.   This he had explained at the time.   His suggestions had been " noted " and referred to Madrid, but without result, for a new Ministry had declared that it could go no further without consulting England and Germany.   When Cambon proceeded to defend the latest French offer, Lansdowne expressed a hope that France would make a concession in regard to the Mediterranean seaboard.   Delcassé gave way to some extent on this point and extended Spain's southern sphere farther to the north ; but these concessions were conditional on acceptance of the remainder of the French plan.   His nerves were becoming frayed.   " Since Lord Lansdowne's opinions are invoked every moment", he telegraphed irritably to Jules Cambon on May 16, " I beg you, in presenting these important and absolutely final concessions, to invoke Article 9 of the Franco-English Declaration, which I have already carried out on England's behalf in regard to Russia, and to ask Lord Lansdowne to make Spain feel that she has reached the extreme limit of our good will."[2]   It is not surprising that the Spanish Ambassador in Paris complained to his German colleague that he had never known a Minister so difficult to deal with.[3]

It was clear to Delcassé from the outset that the pact he was seeking to make must remain a secret.   Publication, he argued,

[1] G.P. XX, 169-170.   [2] D.D.F. V, 152-3.
[3] G.P. XX, 180.

would exasperate the Sultan, or, if it did not, would infuriate his subjects, who were already reproaching him with handing over his country to foreigners.[1] Since Spain confessed her inability to share in an expedition, the whole burden of repressing a revolt would fall upon France. " But nothing is more opposed to our views, frequently proclaimed, than a military expedition. It is by pacific means, by financial support, by administrative organisation, by public works, by material prosperity that we desire to implant our influence in Morocco. We wish to gain the Sultan, and, through him, the population. When our assistance has produced results, when the Sultan and the people have felt the benefits, then will be the time with the minimum of inconvenience to make our arrangements known." At the moment it would be enough to issue a declaration that an agreement had been reached and that the interests of both countries had been safeguarded. To this decision the Spanish Government, after pleading that the Cortes should see the text of the pact, was forced to submit.

Spain experienced another shock when Delcassé indicated that she would have no influence over her zone till the Moroccan Empire came to an end, a proviso which was regarded as utterly inacceptable. Lansdowne passed on the complaints to Cambon, who denied the accuracy of the information and reported further French concessions. On July 22 Lansdowne was informed that Delcassé had come to terms with the Spanish Ambassador, except in regard to the undertaking not to alienate any part of the respective zones. This time Spain gave way at the suggestion of Lansdowne, who thus deserved the title of honest broker which Bismarck had claimed at the Congress of Berlin. The value of his influence was gratefully recognised by the Spaniards, who repeatedly complainted of Delcassé's intransigence. At the end of July Castillo told Radolin that he could not reach an agreement and that the negotiations were temporarily suspended.[2] He accused the Foreign Minister of great untrustworthiness. Concessions made one day would be twisted on the next and given incorrectly in the protocol. " M. Delcassé est absolument de mauvaise foi", he cried excitedly. France's policy in Morocco was to take everything for herself. Countless French speculators and financiers lay in wait like hungry wolves to seize all enterprises and concessions. They were

[1] D.D.F. V, 203-4.   [2] G.P. XX, 188-9.

supported by the Colonial party and Creuzot, and Delcassé could not resist the pressure. Spain was unhappily not in a position to take a stronger line.

The negotiations dragged on through the summer. Jules Cambon complained to his chief of the habitual indecision and prodigious obstinacy of Spain, while the Spaniards were incensed by the treatment they received. Castillo told Monson that he had found Delcassé hard and unsympathetic from the first.[1] He despaired of getting him to take a fair view of the position and claims of Spain, who counted mainly on the support of England in frustrating the evident aim of France to exclude Spain from all participation in the work of civilising Morocco. It was the complaint of an angry diplomatist outmatched in a game in which his opponent held the strongest cards. Delcassé, like other negotiators, demanded as much and conceded as little as he could. Spain had missed her chance in 1902, and in 1904 she had to take what she could get.

The Franco-Spanish Declaration signed at Paris on October 3, 1904, ran as follows : " The Government of the French Republic and the Government of His Majesty the King of Spain, having agreed to fix the extent of their rights and the guarantee of their interests which flow, for France from her Algerian possessions, and for Spain from her possessions on the coast of Morocco, and the Government of His Majesty the King of Spain having in consequence adhered to the Anglo-French Declaration of April 8, 1904, respecting Morocco and Egypt, which was communicated to them by the Government of the French Republic, declare that they remain firmly attached to the integrity of the Moorish Empire under the sovereignty of the Sultan." This was all that the world was allowed to know of the negotiations between Paris and Madrid which had filled the summer months.

On the same day a secret Convention was signed. In the first article Spain repeated her adhesion to the Anglo-French Declaration. The second defined her sphere of influence, and pledged her not to take action within it for fifteen years without the consent of France. The third was the core of the transaction. " In case the continuance of the political status of Morocco and of the Shereefian Government should become impossible, or if, owing to the weakness of that Government and of its continued inability to uphold law and order or to any other cause the existence of which is acknow-

[1] B.D. III, 47.

ledged by both parties, the status quo can no longer be maintained, Spain may freely exercise her right of action in the territory defined in the previous article, which henceforth constitutes her sphere of influence." Other articles recognised the special position of Tangier and bound Spain not to alienate any portion of her zone. The Convention was officially communicated to Lansdowne with a request to keep it secret. The Spanish Ambassador in London expressed the extreme gratitude of his Government for the close watch he had kept on the negotiations, which had been of the greatest service. The compliment was thoroughly deserved, for without British mediation there would have been a one-sided agreement or none at all. Castillo, who was not easy to please, confessed to Radowitz that Spain had got all she wanted, namely full equality of rights with France in their respective spheres.[1] Delcassé was equally satisfied. Indeed he confessed to Paléologue that he would have made even greater sacrifices to prevent Spain becoming the instrument and the champion of Germany in Morocco.[2]

The Franco-Spanish Convention, like other unavowed commitments, brought difficulties in its train. Its existence was guessed, and the mystery bred suspicion both at Fez and Berlin. " This treaty", wrote Tardieu when it was revealed to the world, "encumbered French policy with a grave contradiction. For while we publicly affirmed our attachment to the integrity of Morocco, we made secret engagements for eventual partition. Moreover it went beyond the Anglo-French treaty, which merely obliged us to have regard to the interests of Spain deriving from her geographical position and her possessions on the Moroccan coast of the Mediterranean. For we now recognised two Spanish zones on the Atlantic, at Larache and at Ifni. Thus the pourparlers of 1902 were reflected in the agreement of 1904."

The object of the Convention was to remove a further impediment to French predominance in Morocco. In the opinion of his closest collaborator, however, Delcassé had created more obstacles than he had overcome.[3] Consulted at the beginning of the negotiations, Taillandier argued vigorously against the recognition of the Spanish zone, which would break up the unity of the Moroccan Empire and limit the sphere of French reformatory action. Spain, he declared,

---

[1] G.P. XX, 190.   [2] Paléologue, 133.
[3] Taillandier, ch. 10.

should be offered satisfaction in the economic field. He
seemed unable to realise that this course had been rendered
impossible by the negotiations of 1902. He was in Paris
when the Convention was signed, and he was shown the text.
The friendship of Spain was a necessity, explained the Foreign
Minister, and a zone was the price. He had tried to meet his
subordinate's objections by keeping secret the details which
might excite the Sultan to wrath. Though a warm admirer of
his chief, Taillandier could not conceal his dismay. The
bleak simplicity of the public treaty would make the Sultan
and everyone else suspect a secret which its authors dare not
reveal. This suspicion would destroy the confidence in the
sincerity of France which he had laboured to build up at Fez.
In formally communicating the Franco-Spanish Declaration
to the Moroccan Minister of Foreign Affairs, the French
representative was instructed to explain that France had desired
to associate Spain with her own promises in regard to the
sovereignty of the Sultan and the integrity of Morocco, and
would view with keen satisfaction the efforts of the Makhzen
to consolidate its authority, particularly in the north where
French aid was available if desired.[1] These soothing words
produced little effect, and Taillandier's apprehensions were
speedily confirmed.

XI

The first response of the Sultan to the Anglo-French treaty
was to draw up a protest to the Powers. The letters, however,
were never sent, for Saint-Aulaire was despatched by Taillandier from Tangier to Fez just in time. Delcassé, declared
Abdul Aziz, had always been a faithful friend of Morocco,
and thanks to him relations had improved. He recognised
the need of reform, and knew that he could count on the
co-operation of France. " But I intend to act freely", he
added with a slight trembling of the hands. " As for submitting to pressure, never ! " The visit was followed by a
loan, and when Saint-Aulaire left the capital in July 1904 he
carried away an invitation to Taillandier to come and talk over
the necessary reforms. The outlook seemed promising, and
in September the Minister discussed the next moves with his
chief at the Quai d'Orsay. Their conclusions were recorded
in a letter from Delcassé to the Prime Minister. The Makhzen

[1] D.D.F. V, 437.

was ready to discuss the organisation of the frontier on the basis of the agreements of 1901 and 1902, and if the results proved satisfactory the system could be extended to other parts. The negotiation of these preliminary reforms must be carried on in a manner to confirm the confidence of the Moroccan Government in France.

The Sultan's invitation preceded the Franco-Spanish agreement, and on his return to Tangier Taillandier noticed without surprise a chill in the atmosphere. It was ominous that the Sultan decided to dismiss his foreign advisers and employees, including the French Military Mission. A vigorous and successful protest came from the Quai d'Orsay; but in Taillandier's judgment the Moroccan Government was convinced that France would shrink from the use of force. Accordingly when the time arrived to draft the instructions for his visit to Fez, he urged his chief to combine the iron hand with the velvet glove. " Our energy", he wired, " should if necessary equal our moderation."[1] If all the resources of persuasion were exhausted, the interest and dignity of France demanded a change of course. " The temporary occupation of Ujda and of all the maritime customhouses would beyond doubt lead the Makhzen to submit." For long its resistance had been inspired by the belief that England would resist French aims. Now it believed that in no case would coercion be applied. The first supposition had been destroyed by the Anglo-French treaty. The second could be overthrown by a resolute attitude.

In his elaborate instructions dated December 15, 1904, Delcassé approved the attitude of his representative.[2] It was the interest of France to serve the interests of Morocco, and the tranquillity of French possessions involved assistance to Morocco in the establishment of order. The prosperity of France would increase by furnishing Morocco with the means of developing her abundant resources. Continuing to live its own life, retaining its customs, its laws, its chiefs under the Sultan whose authority would be fortified and enhanced, Morocco would learn the power of France only through the benefits that it brought. The success of this entirely pacific policy depended on the close union of the two Governments, based on the one side on confidence, on the other on consistency, loyalty and tact, not excluding firmness when necessary. A later passage in the instructions was rather more

[1] *D.D.F.* V, 576-8. December 12.   [2] ibid. V, 581-591.

blunt. " It is absolutely necessary that you should energetically push on the execution of arrangements seriously thought
out and repeatedly promised. There are several roads to the
goal—either loyal co-operation on a footing of apparent
equality and the maintenance of the dignity of the two parties,
or a forward march by the strongest, limited only by considerations of policy."

Delcassé's programme presupposed a free hand in Europe.
Such elbow-room he did not possess. Though Italian,
British and Spanish obstacles had been successively removed,
he had omitted to deal with Germany, and the omission was
his undoing. Franco-German relations, though never more
than correct, had been uneventful during the earlier phases of
his long reign. Well aware that neither could compromise
on the Rhine provinces, Bülow made no attempt to force the
pace. Receiving the French Ambassador at the opening of
1903 with his usual smiling courtesy, he expressed his sympathy for France and his desire for a rapprochement.[1] The
understanding, he discreetly hinted, must be limited to certain
issues. " We cannot go too fast." The Kaiser, he added,
had been impulsive in words but not in deeds. Passing to
foreign affairs he expressed the hope that the rising in Morocco
would cause no difficulty among the interested Powers, all of
whom, including France, seemed to favour the status quo.
" As for Germany she has so to speak no interests in Morocco,
so insignificant are they up to now." The Anglo-French
détente could hardly be welcomed at Berlin, even though the
Wilhelmstrasse was slow to penetrate its full significance.
After King Edward's visit to Paris Eckardstein reported that
French haute finance was endeavouring to push Delcassé, not
only towards an Anglo-French, but towards an Anglo-Russian
rapprochement, and that the seed had fallen on very fruitful
soil.[2] A new Triple Alliance, he added, was in the making.
" Eckardstein", commented Bülow with his usual short-
sightedness, " stands alone so far in his expectations of a
Franco-Anglo-Russian regrouping." At the opening of 1904
Loubet expressed to the Prince of Monaco his admiration for
the Kaiser and his desire to meet him, though he was aware of
the difficulties.[3] Asked by Bülow for his opinion, Radolin
advised against the plan. It was very doubtful, he explained,
if the project would be approved by Delcassé, who could

[1] D.D.F. III, 30–31, January 13, 1903.   [2] G.P. XVII, 567–572.
[3] G.P. XX, 109–113.

scarcely afford to present his many enemies with new grounds of attack. The question was discussed during Loubet's visit to Rome, and Luzzatti told the German Ambassador that Delcassé and Barrère raised no objection in principle.[1] Despite the desire of Italy for such a meeting, the French Ministry abandoned the scheme as likely to endanger its life. That it was considered at all shows that the relations of Paris and Berlin were at any rate correct enough.

A fortnight before the signing of the Anglo-French Treaty, the German Ambassador asked Delcassé if he might put an indiscreet question.[2]

Radolin : Is it true that an agreement between England has been or is on the point of being signed ?

Delcassé : Neither one nor the other. But we have been discussing with the London Cabinet for some time the friendly settlement of questions which interest our two countries. An understanding has been recognised as a possibility and will probably be reached.

Radolin : People say that it concerns Newfoundland.

Delcassé : Yes, we have talked about that.

Radolin : And Morocco ?

Delcassé : That too. But you already know our standpoint on that subject, and I have repeated to you what I said in the Senate and the Chamber. We desire to preserve as long as possible in Morocco the political and territorial status quo, but if this is to last it must obviously be sustained and improved. During last year Morocco's repeated aggressions gave us strong and legitimate grounds for intervention. Each time I resisted, though with increasing difficulty, the natural demands of those who desired to avenge bloodshed and those who proposed to seek in the country itself guarantees for the respect of our Algerian frontier and the tranquillity of the adjacent populations. We have had to reinforce our posts and create new ones, incurring considerable expenses which only a reform of internal conditions will enable us to reduce. The Sultan has already experienced the value of our aid where he asked for it. We must continue to give it. But it will be supplied in such a way that everyone will benefit, particularly as regards commercial undertakings which the establishment of a much needed security can only encourage. I need not add that, in whatever manner we assist the Sultan, commercial liberty will be vigorously and integrally respected.

[1] *G.P.* XX, 118–119.   [2] *D.D.F.* IV, 509–510.

Radolin : And Spain ?

Delcassé : I said in the Chamber that Spain knows we are friends and can count on friendly conduct. I am not the man to ignore her positive interests and legitimate aspirations.

" Prince Radolin", concluded Delcassé's report, " found my declarations very natural and entirely reasonable and thanked me warmly for making them."

Radolin's report combines this historic conversation with a talk at dinner a few days before.[1] Various matters in dispute, Delcassé explained, needed solution. The question of the Newfoundland fisheries contained the elements of a deal. In the Egyptian question there was plenty of scope for discussion, though the disposal of the savings of the Dette concerned other countries as well as France. His chief wish in Morocco was to maintain the status quo as long as possible. He must insist, however, that the Algerian frontier should be secured against raids. The insecurity of trade for all nations in Morocco resulted from the weakness of its Government and demanded a change in the general interest. As her neighbour this was primarily the task of France, who, he believed, deserved the gratitude of all commercial nations in striving for orderly or at any rate tolerable conditions. The seaboard opposite Gibraltar must be neutralised, and the historic rights of Spain must be recognised. France desired no special privileges, but it was her task to suppress anarchy. An agreement, he hoped, would soon be reached. The word Protectorate, commented Radolin in his report, was carefully avoided ; but the influence desired by France might amount to the same thing—a reflection to which the Kaiser added " Yes". The conversation, as Delcassé subsequently informed the Ambassador, had no official character.[2]

After signing the Treaty Delcassé ordered the French Ambassador to inform the Wilhelmstrasse that Lansdowne and himself had been concerned exclusively with the interests of their own countries, without detriment to those of any other Powers, and that he did not think it necessary to present a copy since it was known to all the world. " We have no cause to imagine that the Treaty has a point against any other Power", declared the Chancellor in the Reichstag. " As to Morocco, we have commercial interests which we must and shall protect. We have, however, no ground to fear that they will be overlooked or infringed." On his visit to the Kiel

[1] G.P. XX, 5–7.   [2] ibid. XX, 330. April 14, 1905.

M

regatta in June the Kaiser remarked to King Edward that Morocco had never interested him. The barometer seemed equally steady at Tangier. At a dinner at the German Legation on July 25 Taillandier met Tattenbach, the German Minister at Lisbon, and the fact that the latter had served in Morocco gave point to his friendly words. " You have a difficult task, but you alone can undertake it. We hope you will have regard to our commercial situation. German business men here, as in Indo-China and Algeria, will not make difficulties for you."

The mood of acquiescence was too good to last, and indeed it was only a pose.[1] Visiting the Wilhelmstrasse on April 26 to express his appreciation of the Chancellor's declaration in the Reichstag, the French Ambassador was struck by the glacial attitude of Richthofen, the Foreign Minister.[2] " More and more", he telegraphed to his chief, " I believe that Bülow's declarations dissemble his profound dissatisfaction." The Franco-Spanish Declaration—obviously a mere blind for a secret treaty—aroused the same uneasy suspicions at Berlin as at Fez. It was in vain that Delcassé charged the French Ambassador to explain that the new pact, by securing the adhesion of Spain to the principle of commercial liberty enshrined in the Declaration of April 8, had strengthened the guarantees of international commerce in Morocco.[3] At the same time the victories of Japan were visibly sapping the power and prestige of the Dual Alliance. When Kühlmann took over the Legation at Tangier as Chargé d'Affaires in October, a new attitude was assumed. The grievances of the German Colonial party, he declared, were meeting with more attention in the highest quarters. The principle of French political preponderance in Morocco was uncontested, but Germany must safeguard her trade. Bülow was being reproached for not obtaining the commercial advantages secured to England and Spain. Taillandier was uncertain how far these sentiments were those of the German Government. In any case they were ominous enough as the first indication by a German diplomat of a challenge to the unconcealed ambitions of France.

In January 1905 Taillandier journeyed to Fez in response to the Sultan's invitation in the previous summer, and commenced the conversations which were to last nine months. Once

[1] G.P. XX, ch. 145. [2] D.D.F. V, 72.
[3] ibid. V, 445. October 12.

again he argued that there was a community of interest between France and Morocco and that reforms would be advantageous to all. Never for a moment, however, according to his account, did he suggest that he was speaking in the name of the Powers.[1] The Sultan replied that he accepted some of the demands ; others he would discuss with his Ministers. He was courteous but reserved, and the Minister sensed the chill shadow of the Franco-Spanish pact. Persuasion, he reported, could go no farther : if it failed, coercion must be applied.

While Taillandier was pleading the French cause at Fez, a storm was brewing at Tangier. On February 7 Kühlmann expressed his surprise to Chérisey, the French Chargé, that France had not notified Germany of the recent arrangements concerning Morocco, and broadly hinted that she would regret it.[2] Most Germans, he added, thought solely of economic interests in that country ; but the influential Colonial party had other ideas, and the Kaiser might act. Four days later he returned to the charge. He had received instructions to declare that there was no recognition since there had been no official communication. Delcassé's reply was to recall his conversation with Radolin on March 23, 1904.[3] Only Germany and Russia, he explained, had been informed before the signature. Moreover on October 7 the French Ambassador in Berlin had communicated the terms of the Franco-Spanish declaration before its publication. Neither England nor Spain had officially notified any Power. These explanations fell on deaf ears at Berlin, where a forward move was being resolutely engineered.

The repercussion of the new German policy was quickly felt both at Paris and at Fez. Taillandier's elaborate reports indicated a stiffening of the Makhzen. The Sultan was polite but elusive. The French Minister complained that his chief wished to continue the method of persuasion when it had become insufficient. The Makhzen and the Sultan believed that France would not go beyond words, and they acted accordingly. Delcassé, however, had to think of difficulties nearer home which his representative in distant Fez could not visualise. Bülow spoke in firm tones of Germany's interest in Morocco and France began to be alarmed. On March 19

[1] This assertion the Sultan sharply denied to Vassel, April 21, 1905. *G.P.* XX, 339–340.
[2] *D.D.F.* VI, 92–3 and 108–9.   [3] ibid. 129–132.

Delcassé wired to Taillandier that public opinion desired a peaceful policy ; the collapse of Russia and the declarations of Berlin rendered the situation uncertain ; and though hostile German action was unlikely, it was not impossible. " Bref, il nous importe moins d'avancer rapidement que d'avancer sans secousse."[1] Never indeed had he known such acute anxieties ; for the long sojourn of the Russian fleet in the French territorial waters of Madagascar and Indo-China exposed him to the dread possibility of an ultimatum from Tokio.

At this moment the Kaiser's forthcoming visit to Tangier was announced—an unambiguous reply to Delcassé's attempt to obtain an explanation of Kühlmann's complaints. Taillandier was instructed not to risk a rupture by pressing demands likely to meet with a categorical refusal. Time was on their side.[2] Delcassé complained to Monson that he could not understand what Germany desired to obtain by the Emperor's move. There was no response, for the situation had passed beyond his control. The contrast between the smooth acquiescence of 1904 and the menacing gestures of 1905 has been generally attributed by French and English writers exclusively to the disasters of Russia in the Far East and to a desire to dissolve the newly-formed Anglo-French entente. The creeping paralysis of France's ally undoubtedly encouraged Bülow to rattle the sword. But the proximate cause of the change was the despatch of the French Minister to Fez with a comprehensive programme of reforms which, to suspicious minds, suggested that Morocco was destined to become a second Tunis, and for which the Wilhelmstrasse believed him to have claimed a European mandate. An article in the official *Norddeutsche Allgemeine Zeitung* declared that the French negotiations at Fez did not harmonise with the avowed policy of maintaining the political status quo ; and the Kaiser complained to Roosevelt that France and Spain wished to divide up Morocco and close her markets to the world. On March 30, the German Chargé in Paris reported that Delcassé was surrounded by critics, including some of his own colleagues, and that public opinion was beginning to feel that he was too dear at the price.[3]

The anxiously awaited telegram from the French Chargé at Tangier reached Paris on March 31, a few hours after the

[1] *D.D.F.* VI, 206–7.   [2] ibid. 216–17.
[3] *G.P.* XX, 288.

Kaiser had re-embarked.[1] After a few commonplaces he remarked ; " Yes, Morocco is a fine country, especially from the commercial point of view. I hope all the European nations will take care to safeguard their commercial interests. As far as I am concerned, I am quite determined to secure respect for the interests of German commerce." That was also the sincere desire of the French Government, replied the Chargé. This was harmless enough ; but the Kaiser's address to the Sultan's representative, stressing the complete independence of Morocco, claiming equal treatment for all nations, and uttering a warning against precipitate reforms, was an unambiguous challenge to the policy and aims of the Quai d'Orsay.[2]

The demonstration aroused resentment in France and England precisely as the Mansion House speech of 1911 was to create indignation in Germany. In each case a Great Power proclaimed with shrill emphasis that it was not going to be elbowed aside. If France desired to turn the country into a French Egypt, she would have to compensate Germany, as she had compensated Great Britain, Italy and Spain. Germany, declared Bülow, had not moved at first, as the Treaty recognised the status quo, and she had assumed that France would consult the Treaty Powers if she aimed at changes limiting their rights. " It was necessary to act when the Moroccan Government asked us if France was the mandatory of the Powers, when we learned of parts of the programme, and when great papers pointed to Tunis as a model." The Moroccan issue had become a European problem, for the prestige of a Great Power was at stake. When the news of the Tangier visit reached Fez Taillandier knew that at any rate for the present the game was up. Delcassé instructed him not to press for exclusive economic advantages, but it was now useless to ask for anything at all. The Sultan had found a powerful protector and could snap his fingers at France. The projected agreement concerning military reform, it was announced, was unofficial, and must be discussed by the Notables. Tattenbach, the German envoy, who reached the capital on May 11, told Abdul Aziz that Delcassé's policy was not that of France, and that Germany could supply financial support in case of need. He suggested a Conference, and demanded that Germany should be no less favoured than other Powers in every sphere. The official invitation to the

[1] *D.D.F.* VI, 265-6.   [2] ibid. 283-4.

signatories of the Treaty of Madrid was received by Taillandier on the day before Lowther, the British Minister, arrived in Fez on a fruitless quest. German influence was supreme, and the Sultan counted on the Conference restoring to him the freedom he had abused.

By this time the Foreign Minister was thoroughly alarmed. " Nous ferons tomber M. Delcassé," said the German Ambassador in Rome to Luzzatti, who repeated it to Barrère.[1] After a dinner at the German Embassy on April 13 he asked his host with a tremor in his voice for a moment's conversation.[2] He had gathered from the press, he began, that the German Government was annoyed. Before he could go further Radolin coldly interjected that he could not speak of this subject as he had no instructions : he could merely report. " I declare formally", resumed Delcassé with emotion, " that if there is any misunderstanding, despite all my declarations, I am ready to remove it. I beg you to inform the Imperial Government, and I shall instruct M. Bihourd to make the same declaration." He proceeded to contradict the assertion that Taillandier had spoken in the name of Europe. The idea of formally communicating the Anglo-French Convention to the German Government had never crossed his mind. In informing Radolin confidentially of the Anglo-French discussions on March 23, 1904, he had desired to show his special confidence, for he had spoken to the German and Russian Ambassadors alone. Radolin rightly believed that Delcassé spoke at the express wish of Rouvier, and he gathered from his excitement that he realised it would have been wise to inform the German Government officially of the Anglo-French Convention. After this explanation had been repeated to the Wilhelmstrasse by the French Ambassador in Berlin, Delcassé felt he could do nothing more.[3] Radolin reported the general opinion in Paris that it was the most critical emergency in Franco-German relations since the Schnaebele incident of 1887.

Delcassé was attacked in the Chamber from the Right as well as from the Left, by Deschanel no less sharply than by Jaurès himself. He appealed to his record—to his treaties with Italy, England and Spain, to his seven arbitration agreements. He had spoken to the German Ambassador, and he

[1] D.D.F. VI, 305.
[2] G.P. XX, 328–330 ; and D.D.F. VI, 360–2.
[3] D.D.F. VI, 377–9.

reiterated his readiness to supply further explanations. At this moment, when he most required help, it was not to be had. The happy days of Waldeck-Rousseau's friendship and the indifference of Combes were over. Rouvier, who had been Premier since the beginning of the year, had ideas of his own, and was determined to keep the country out of war. His defence of the Foreign Minister was so lukewarm that the latter offered to resign. He was persuaded to remain by Loubet, who never wavered in his affectionate support, and by Rouvier himself; but he realised that his days were numbered, and he was no longer master in his own house. Caring nothing for domestic politics, he was out of touch both with the Chamber and the Cabinet, and he frankly despised most of the Ministers. Moreover he had neglected to satisfy himself that France was prepared for war. " I do my duty", he remarked testily, " and I assume that my colleagues do theirs." Yet this was the man who often told Paléologue that the actions of the impulsive Kaiser were unpredictable, and that he felt sure he would sooner or later attack. The unreadiness of France was as notorious as the crushing superiority of the German army. The conclusion was inescapable. In 1905, as in the dark days of Fashoda, he would have to yield.

The situation filled Rouvier with alarm. Dining with Radolin on April 26, he declared with emotion that France would do her utmost to live on good terms with Germany and that war over Morocco would be a crime. On the same day the Ambassador heard that the Premier had said he was not in agreement with Delcassé, since English ships had no wheels. He made no secret of his distrust, and on April 30 he spoke to Radolin with surprising freedom. He disapproved much that had occurred. The Foreign Minister's task was to carry out the decisions of the Cabinet, but he had gone beyond his commission. After this discovery he had cut his wings and he now saw all the papers himself. It had cost him an effort to save Delcassé in the Chamber, but he thought it the wisest course. Meanwhile he sent Betzold, a financier, on a secret mission to Berlin, where Holstein explained Germany's opinion of Delcassé and was told that Rouvier had lost all confidence in his Foreign Minister.[1] About the same time Delcassé sent Paléologue to Berlin to study the situation, and the emissary brought back the worst possible news. The French

[1] Schwabach, *Aus Meinen Akten*, 290–3.

Ambassador had lost his nerve, and moaned that Delcassé's policy was leading straight to war.

In the first Morocco crisis of 1905, as in the repetition of 1911, the Premier and the Foreign Minister were working independently of one another. In both cases the Premier justified his unusual conduct on the ground that his colleague was playing with fire. Delcassé discovered that his chief desired his resignation and that the Wilhelmstrasse had been informed of the wish. He was *persona grata* in St. Petersburg, but the Tsar was far away. Loubet's confidence was undiminished, but the President was powerless. Paul Cambon and Barrère approved his policy, but they were subordinates. Even the unconcealed sympathy of Edward VII, who telegraphed from Algiers his consternation at the thought of his fall, was of no avail.[1] On passing through Paris on his way home from the Mediterranean, the King dined at the Élysée, and, in conversation with the Foreign Minister, strongly supported his views.[2] Before leaving the capital the two men had another long talk at the house of an old friend. Delcassé declared himself very satisfied; but he gave his staff no details, and Paléologue concluded that the King had advised caution.

The anxious Minister kept the soft pedal down at Fez and continued his belated efforts to mend the wires to Berlin. His old friend Luzzatti informed Monts that France was prepared to give any satisfaction suggested by Germany which would not too deeply wound her honour.[3] In forwarding the news Monts expressed his opinion that the Morocco campaign was won and that the way was opened for a friendly settlement. The Chancellor replied that a purely Franco-German deal was now impossible, since Germany had taken her stand as the champion of the treaty rights of all the Powers. In informing Radolin of the approach and his reply, Bülow attributed Delcassé's risky policy to the encouragement of England, and suggested that Rouvier should take the initiative in proposing a Conference. Another attempt to reach Germany was made by Eckardstein, now a private individual, who visited Bülow in Baden at the request of friends of Rouvier, and vainly suggested a friendly declaration so drafted as to force Delcassé to resign.

[1] Maurois, *Edouard VII et son Temps*, 215.
[2] Lee, II, 342–3.
[3] *D.D.F.* VI, 447–51 and 461–2 and *G.P.* XX, 362.

On May 7 Rouvier told Radolin that he could not propose a Conference. Delcassé, he added, was now more pliable.[1] He was, however, annoyed to hear of the approach to Germany through Luzzatti, and complained that the Foreign Minister was as reserved with his colleagues as with the Ambassador. The Premier regarded war as out of the question, but if it came England would certainly not intervene. The King had spoken most peacefully during his visit to Paris. On receiving the report of Betzold, his secret envoy to Berlin, Rouvier observed that it was best to mark time in Morocco. Since Delcassé had become more accommodating it would be difficult to remove him—it might take weeks or even months. For the last week the Foreign Minister had done his utmost in St. Petersburg to prepare the way for peace with Japan, and if he succeeded he could not at once be dismissed. He was no longer, however, a free agent, for policy was controlled by the Cabinet. Fearing that Rouvier after all might shirk a breach with his colleague, Radolin reminded him that the situation was grave, and that good relations were only possible with a Foreign Minister whom the German Government could trust. The Premier replied that he would let the Chamber act in due course. At a dinner at the Élysée Doumer, the President of the Chamber, and other influential politicians told the Ambassador that they disapproved Delcassé's policy.

Surrounded though he was by enemies, he had no intention of throwing up the sponge. His conviction that Germany was bluffing was shared by his two ablest and most trusted collaborators, Paul Cambon and Barrère, whom he summoned to Paris for consultation. Lansdowne's offer of support in the event of a German demand for a Moorish port seemed a favourable omen, and it was agreed that he should be asked whether he would aid France if she were attacked by Germany on account of Morocco. A meeting was held at the Élysée on May 15, at which the President, the Premier, the Foreign Minister and the two Ambassadors were present.[2] Delcassé explained that he had received important information as to the intentions of the British Government, and Paul Cambon filled in the outlines. The impression which they produced was that an alliance was within reach. Rouvier listened in silence, and then said to the Ambassador : " Je vous en prie

[1] G.P. XX, 371–4.
[2] Barrère, "La Chute de Delcassé," Revue de deux Mondes. August 1, 1932, and Paléologue, 327–8.

instamment, ne continuez pas cette négotiation. Si les Allemands la connaissaient, ils nous déclareraient la guerre." On returning to the Quai d'Orsay Barrère angrily remarked to Paléologue that Rouvier's cowardice would cost France dear.

Two days after this dramatic conference, Lansdowne made the proposal for continuous consultation which has been quoted in a previous chapter. The statement appeared to Cambon so important that he resolved to secure its confirmation in writing by the expedient of a private letter to the Foreign Secretary. The plan worked even better than he anticipated, for the reply of May 25, as he interpreted it, went further than the conversation of May 17. " Il résulte de ce document", he wrote to his chief on May 29, " dont les termes paraissent très étudiés, et qui n'a certainement été expédié qu'avec l'approbation du Premier Ministre et peut-être du Roi, que Lord Lansdowne reconnaît m'avoir spontanément offert de discuter par avance les mesures à prendre en vue de toutes les éventualités.[1] Mais dans la déclaration que j'avais transmise à Votre Excellence, il n'était question d'une proposition de concert que dans le cas où nous aurions de sérieuses raisons d'appréhender une aggression injustifiée. Le Principal Secrétaire d'État rectifie sur ce point, en leur donnant une portée plus large et plus prochaine, le sens de sa déclaration. Ce n'est plus à une entente en cas d'aggression qu'il nous convie, c'est à une discussion immédiate et à un examen de la situation générale. Une réponse à de pareilles avances est fort délicate ; se taire c'est décourager un bon vouloir évident et se donner des airs de reculer. Accepter la conversation, c'est entrer dans la voie d'une entente générale qui constituerait en réalité une alliance, et j'ignore si le Gouvernement de la République serait disposé à nouer de pareils accords."

Cambon believed that an alliance was in sight, and Delcassé shared his opinion. But could they stretch out their hands and seize the glittering prize, with Rouvier's veto echoing in their ears ? It was impossible. The Ambassador suggested a temporising reply, and his chief followed his advice. " I fully appreciate the importance of Lord Lansdowne's reply to your private letter of May 24", he telegraphed on May 30.[2] " Tell him that it has given me great satisfaction, that I too am of opinion that the two Governments should more than ever show one another their entire confidence, and that I am

[1] D.D.F. VI, 557-8.　　　　[2] ibid. VI, 563-4.

ready to examine with him every aspect of a disquieting situation." The King of Spain was in Paris, but he would inform the President and the Premier at the first opportunity.

Instead of conveying this message to Lansdowne, the Ambassador addressed a remarkable personal letter to his chief.[1] A conversation of such a character could not be entered on without all the consequences having been envisaged and without Rouvier's assent. " You remember his last words as we left the Élysée : Surtout ne vous concertez pas ! Unless he has completely changed his mind, it seems to me difficult for you to respond to overtures which, as I told you in my despatch of May 29, will lead us to an alliance. What could I reply to Lord Lansdowne if he proposes a meeting of the chiefs of staff of our armies and navies in view of formidable eventualities ? We should expose ourselves to such a suggestion if we entered too readily on a general conversation. You would certainly not be followed by your Cabinet colleagues nor by public opinion, and you would be accused of preparing war. I therefore think it prudent to reply in terms sufficiently cordial not to discourage Lord Lansdowne's good will, and vague enough to avert proposals for immediate co-operation. The visit of the King of Spain to Paris keeps you so busy that nobody expects instant replies to all pending questions."

The Wilhelmstrasse was growing impatient, and on May 30 Bülow informed Radolin that further action was needed. Delcassé, despite his fair words, was unchanged. The experience of seven years had shown that an improvement of relations was impossible while he was at the helm, and they might even grow worse. He had used every opportunity to display his hostility. His high-handed Morocco policy was not in the interests of France, and could only be explained by some foreign influence which desired to produce acute tension between France and Germany. Since it would be difficult for Radolin to speak to Rouvier with the necessary sharpness, the task was entrusted to Miquel, the First Secretary, who was about to leave Paris for another post. Miquel saw the Premier on May 30, and complained of five instances in which Delcassé had shown unfriendliness, among them the Baghdad railway and Morocco. He concluded with the blunt declaration that the situation could best be relieved by a change of Minister. Rouvier replied that the difficulties were immense,

[1] *D.D.F.* VI, 573.

but that he realised a change in the situation was required. Delcassé could not retire at present, as he was fitted to render great services in the restoration of peace between Russia and Japan. Moreover he, the Premier, was now looking after foreign affairs. " Je ne puis faire tomber M. Delcassé sur un froncement de sourcils de l'Allemagne, on me le reprocherait toujours, toujours." He half-heartedly defended the Moroccan policy on the ground that Delcassé considered the question as purely Mediterranean in character. The conversation was friendly, and the Premier expressed his thanks for the communication ; but there was no indication of an early move.

The gravity of the situation was continually being hammered into the Premier, and on June 3 Radolin was informed that at the close of the visit of the King of Spain the Cabinet would decide. Rouvier had at last made up his mind to act, for he was thoroughly scared. He invited Delcassé to meet him at the Élysée on June 5 in the presence of the President, emphasised the danger, and asked how he proposed to deal with it.[1] The Foreign Minister replied that the best plan would be to send some cruisers to Tangier to bring the Sultan to reason. To Rouvier's remark : " That would be war with Germany", he replied : " Do not believe it, it is all bluff." The Premier rejoined that his own information was precise, and that there was no bluff. He would bring the issue before the Cabinet, and if the majority supported Delcassé he would resign. The position of the latter was weakened by a telegram from Barrère on June 4, reporting a threat by the German Ambassador in Rome to the Italian Foreign Minister.[2] Taillandier, he declared, had presented the Sultan with an ultimatum. If French troops crossed the Moroccan frontier, German troops would march into France. " M. Delcassé nous mène à la guerre", said Rouvier to the President. " Demain j'obligerai le Conseil des Ministres à choisir entre sa politique et la mienne. Demain l'un de nous deux aura quitté le pouvoir." The words were repeated to Delcassé by the President, who urged his friend to accept some approach to Germany. It was too late. Delcassé replied by repeating the Premier's words : To-morrow one of us will have resigned.

When the Cabinet met on June 6, the Foreign Minister declared that Germany was bluffing and that France ought

[1] G.P. XX, 407–9. This was Rouvier's version.
[2] D.D.F. VI, 585–6 and 593–4.

therefore to resist.[1] England offered an alliance, which
should be promptly accepted. If Germany really desired war,
her fleet would be of vital assistance. " Weigh well the
decision you are about to take. To-morrow, if she sees us
falter and tremble before the insolence of William, she will
not trouble about us any more. She will soon arrange a
reconciliation with Berlin at the expense of our colonial
empire." The Ministers listened in silence, and the speaker
realised that his appeal was in vain. Rouvier replied that
Germany was not bluffing. " She is disturbed and humiliated
by your encirclement of her. In our Morocco dispute she
sees an excellent occasion to break the ring, and she is prepared
for extremities. Besides she knows that England has recently
offered us a military and naval alliance." " How does she
know ? " interrupted Delcassé ; " in London only the King,
Balfour and Lansdowne are in the secret, and here I have only
told the President and yourself." Rouvier blushed under the
innuendo. " All I can tell you is that Germany is aware of
the English offer. A few days ago Bülow sent a friend of his
to tell me confidentially that, if we accept the proposal of the
British Government, Germany will declare war." In a melo-
dramatic voice he proceeded : " Are we in a condition to
sustain a war against Germany ? No, no ! Even with the aid
of the British fleet we should be in for a worse catastrophe
than in 1870. We should be criminals to indulge in such an
adventure. France would not recover." Delcassé expected
Loubet to speak, but the President, though his heart was
filled with grief, sat silent.[2] There was little debate, for the
whole Cabinet sided with the Premier.

Delcassé's report of this memorable occasion may be
supplemented by the far more detailed account drawn up the
same day by Chaumié, the Minister of Public Instruction.[3]
The Cabinet met at ten, but it was nearly eleven before the
President entered, followed by the Premier and Foreign
Minister, both very pale. England, declared the latter, had
suggested common action against Germany. Written notes
had been exchanged. He read the latest of them, and argued
for the conclusion of this alliance. Germany was doubtless
a menace, but he believed it was bluff. She did not wish for
war, according to his information and the opinion of all the

---

[1] Delcassé described the proceedings on his return to the Quai d'Orsay,
Paléologue, 350–2.
[2] Combarieu, 317.   [3] D.D.F. VI, 601–4.

French Ambassadors. " If we refuse her offers, take care lest England, who for the moment desires to co-operate with us to destroy the navy and ruin the commerce of Germany, whose competition she fears, does not shortly turn towards Germany, leaving us isolated, exposed to attack, in danger of losing the fight in Europe and of being despoiled of our colonies."

Germany, replied Rouvier, deeply resented the affront of her isolation, and she had chosen the Moroccan affair to make her protest.   She was aware of the pourparlers with England ; she knew it was a favourable moment to attack, and his information left no doubt that her menaces were very serious. He had been warned that, if they signed the formula of co-operation with England, Germany, from whom the secret could not be kept, would cross the frontier without a declaration of war.   Was France ready for a fight ?   Clearly not. The Eastern forts needed repair, munitions were incomplete, the covering troops were below strength.   Anarchist propaganda had affected the soldiers.   Recent strikes suggested difficulties in mobilisation and, in the event of a defeat at the opening of the campaign, risings in Paris and other towns. They could easily understand that England, unafraid of invasion, should wish to push France ahead.   Their combined fleets would be victorious and Germany's commercial ports would be destroyed ; but meanwhile France would be invaded, and the struggle on land would be very unequal if not disastrous.   The country would not understand being plunged into such an adventure in consequence of disagreements about Morocco.   To fight in such conditions of inferiority would be an indefensible gamble.   If they were attacked they would defend themselves to the utmost, even if they stood alone ; but he would never provoke aggression and expose his country to such perils.   When Delcassé reiterated that Germany was bluffing, the Premier gave details of Bülow's declarations as conveyed to him by a responsible agent.

The debate was over and the Cabinet was called on to decide. Each minister in turn was asked his opinion, and in every case the verdict was for Rouvier.   The deciding factor was the recognition that France was unready for war.   Delcassé promptly resigned.   The Premier, in accepting the resignation, assured him that the divergence of opinion could not make them forget his great services, and gave expression to their gratitude and enduring friendship.   The meeting closed with an appeal by Rouvier to the Minister of War to strengthen

the national defences, and to his other colleagues to raise the
moral level of the country. Chaumié ended his report with
the words : L'heure a été vraiment tragique. No wonder that
when the fallen Minister returned to the Quai d'Orsay there
were tears in his eyes.

Four days later Delcassé called on the British Ambassador.[1]
He attributed his fall entirely to German influence and German
gold. He had been ready for commercial concessions if
Germany were willing to discuss the Morocco question, but
not to yield political or territorial rights. The German
Government, however, had been unwilling to deal with him.
What they required was his head, regarding the man who had
negotiated the Anglo-French understanding and encouraged
the idea of an understanding between England and Russia as
an obstacle to their schemes. To give advice and furnish
military advisers to the Moorish Government infringed no
German right. The Spanish Government had suggested that
Spain, France and England should decline the Conference in
identic terms. If these three countries held together, he did
not believe in a German attack. Moreover Italy had disinterested herself in Morocco. Delcassé, however, found but
few public defenders, for men of all parties believed that he
had led his country to the brink of the abyss. Déroulède sent
a message of encouragement from his exile in Spain, and
Drumont hailed him as the only French Minister since 1870
who had dared to look Germany in the face. Testimonials
from such firebrands were not helpful ; but the support of
Stéphane Lauzanne in the *Matin* and of André Mévil in the
Echo de Paris were like water to a thirsty man. An interview
in the *Gaulois* on July 12 repeated the arguments he had used
to his colleagues, and in the autumn the *Matin* published a
series of articles by Lauzanne purporting to give Delcassé's
version of the events preceding his fall.

Rouvier was fiercely attacked by the friends of the fallen
Minister, but his decision was inevitable.[2] Germany had
treaty rights in Morocco, and the project of an international
Conference to consider an international problem was not so
preposterous as to require France to risk her life on its rejection. Moreover, even if Delcassé had possessed a better
juridical case, he had sinned against the cardinal principle that

---

[1] B.D. III, 78.
[2] This was also the view of the Belgian Minister in Paris. *Zur Europäischen
Politik*, II, 71–6.

diplomacy should never outpace military preparations.
Germany may have been bluffing ; but equally she may not.
France was utterly unready for war. The Lansdowne letter,
which was his trump card, contained no promise of armed
support. Even if it had, British ships could not have saved
Paris. Moreover the Russian fleet had been annihilated in
the Pacific a few days before the Cabinet of June 6. Germany
had all the best cards in her hand, and she was determined to
use them. Delcassé was denounced not only by his old foe
Jaurès but by eminent publicists of the Right. In a resounding indictment Hanotaux complained that his successor had
abandoned the tradition of Thiers, Gambetta, and Ferry in the
vain search for a new system.[1] " At attempt was made to
satisfy everybody by giving way everywhere. We know the
results. On the Nile, in China, in Siam, in Madagascar, at
Constantinople and throughout the East, in Egypt, in Newfoundland, in Tripoli it is a story of abandonment and retreat.
Our attention was devoted to Morocco, but was it wise to
select a moment when our ally was engaged in a terrible
struggle ? We presented ourselves to Europe as petitioners.
Italy, England and Spain profited by our impatience to
obtain all they could. We distributed realities, we harvested
promises." Delcassé's policy, echoed René Millet, was
lacking both in foresight and frankness. " Four Powers had,
or believed themselves to have, interests in Morocco. It is
evident that if three of them received satisfaction and the
fourth was kept out, the latter would not be content. Moreover he spoke of pacific penetration, influence, preponderance,
instead of saying clearly that we wanted a Protectorate.
We were always talking of independence with a mental
reservation."

There is no real answer to the complaints of unskilful handling of Germany, whose sensitive pride, rough methods and
military prowess were known to all the world. Clemenceau
charged Delcassé with inflicting on France the greatest
humiliation she had ever suffered.[2] Though this censure is
excessive, no statesman of the Third Republic made a grosser
miscalculation. On the other hand it is unjust to ignore his
historic achievements. Profoundly convinced that Germany
would one day attack, and fully conscious of her superior

---

[1] Preface to René Millet, *Notre Politique Extérieure.*
[2] July 20, 1909, in answer to Delcassé's attack on the naval administration of
the Clemenceau Cabinet.

strength, he determined to be prepared.   " The noble aim of
his policy", declares Barrère, his life-long friend and collaborator, " was the independence of France, the legitimate liberty
of a great people.   He conceived and carried out the plan of
freeing his countr from the subjection to Germany which
had weighed on he : for half a century."   The reconciliation
with Italy and England changed the face of Europe, and a
man can render no greater service to his country than to
change foes into friends.   The Russian alliance bore the
double strain of the *Entente Cordiale* and the Japanese war.
The door leading to Morocco was opened, and the assent of
Spain was purchased at a moderate price.   If the last years of
peace may be described as a bloodless conflict between the
Dual and the Triple Alliance, the net effect of Delcassé's
activities was to strengthen the former and weaken the latter.
There were six Great Powers in Europe, ranged in opposing
groups.   Hitherto France had been one of two.   Henceforth
she was one of four.   Despite the humiliations of his *début* and
his exit, he left his country incomparably stronger, for the
major portion of his work endured.   When the storm burst
in 1914, he consoled himself with the reflection that France
was no longer defenceless and that his labours had not been
in vain.   If the German declaration of war was the fulfilment
of his fears, the collaboration of England and Italy was the
harvesting of his dearest hopes.

N

BÜLOW

CHAPTER III

BÜLOW

I

NATIONAL tradition, which counted for so much in England and France, could mean little in Germany, for Germany only became a nation in 1871.[1] Henceforth it was the task of her statesmen and her soldiers to hold fast the prize that they had won. From the civil war of 1866 to the common triumphs of Sedan and Versailles was a span of five short years. But in that testing-time of heroism and sacrifice the gulf between North and South, between Protestant and Catholic, between Hohenzollerns and Wittelsbachs was bridged. The demon of separatism was exorcised, and a tolerant federalism reconciled the minor states to the hegemony of Prussia. Internally the work was complete. Bismarck, like Cavour, had cemented the edifice of national unity by blood. The perils of the new Empire lay beyond the frontiers—perils of the future, not of the day. France was prostrate, and the surrender of the Rhine provinces was the symbol of her defeat. The benevolent neutrality of Russia, which had been secured in advance by Prussian support of her Polish policy, had helped to keep Austria in check. Italy had hardly begun to count, and England was a friend. The eviction of Beust from the Ballplatz and the visit of Francis Joseph to Berlin in 1872 proclaimed that the Hapsburgs recognised accomplished facts. The Iron Chancellor bestrode Europe like a colossus, and the Dreikaiserbund revived the epic memories of the Napoleonic era. Never again was Germany to occupy a position of such unchallengeable strength as during the first seven years of the Hohenzollern Empire.

The supremacy of Germany rested on her capacity to keep France indefinitely in quarantine, for not even Bismarck could provide his countrymen with " natural frontiers". The loss of Alsace and a portion of Lorraine was an agonising wound which only the dream of the *Revanche* enabled her to bear. So

[1] The best general surveys of German policy are by Brandenburg, *From Bismarck to the World War*; Hammann, *The World Policy of Germany*, 1890–1912; and Oncken, *Das Deutsche Reich und die Vorgeschichte des Weltkrieges*. Reventlow, *Deutschlands Auswärtige Politik*, 1888–1914; Stieve, *Deutschland und Europa*, 1890–1914; Lenz, *Deutschland im Kreis der Grossmächte*, 1871–1914; and Wahl, *Deutsche Geschichte*, 1871–1914, are also useful.

long as she stood alone she was too weak to hit back, but
what if one day she were to find friends and allies? There was
a hint of change in 1875 when the rattle of the German sword
brought the Tsar and Gortchakoff to Berlin; and in 1879 a
growl of the Russian bear drove Bismarck to Vienna. When
the Dual Alliance was followed by the Triple Alliance of 1882
and the Roumanian Alliance of 1883, the Iron Chancellor again
felt solid ground under his feet. Yet the trustful relations with
St. Petersburg were never restored. The new Dreikaiserbund
of 1881 was shipwrecked on Bulgarian rocks, and the secret
Treaty of Reinsurance, though better than nothing, was a
poor exchange. When Bismarck fell in 1890 Holy Russia had
already overcome her shrinking from Republican France, and
the lapse of the pact of 1887 removed the last obstacle. Napoleon used to say that he was afraid of nothing but a hungry
Paris. It was the *cauchemar de coalitions* which had kept
Bismarck awake, and with his disappearance the danger began
to materialise.

The Franco-Russian alliance was the first break in the Bismarckian system of insurance of the status quo. After twenty
years of impotence France had escaped from her cage. The
Triple Alliance was stronger than its new rival, but it was no
longer supreme. Now that the wire to St. Petersburg had
been rashly cut, it was all the more necessary for Berlin to
maintain the friendship of England unimpaired. For while
England remained friendly, France and Russia would scarcely
risk a conflict with the Central Powers. Caprivi grasped the
situation, but the launching of the Kruger telegram shortly
after his fall undid his patient work. For the first time since
the foundation of the Empire the spectre of British hostility
hovered over the Wilhelmstrasse; and Italy, apprehensive of
her undefended coasts, informed her allies that she could take
no part in a conflict with England on the opposite side. Almost at the same moment Japan was estranged by a summons
to disgorge the continental fruits of her victory over China.
Russia was a rival and was openly playing for her own hand.
France was her ally and dared not lag behind. But why, asked
the Japanese, should Germany join in the game? " We shall
remember", observed a Japanese statesman with the eloquent
brevity of his race. The Bismarckian tradition of limited
liability was breaking down, and the waves were beginning to
lap over his dykes. Austria was not so strong as she looked.
When Marschall left the Wilhelmstrasse for Constantinople in

1897, the international position of Germany was ominously weaker than when he had entered it in 1890. But it was still possible for his successor, if a skilful and cautious pilot, to steer the ship safely through the shoals and rocks.

Bülow brought to his work a width of culture and a range of diplomatic experience possessed by none of his predecessors or successors.[1] Himself the son of a Minister of Foreign Affairs, he grew up under the eye of the Iron Chancellor, a friend of Herbert Bismarck and a *persona grata* at Court. Five years in the Paris of Gambetta were followed by four years at St. Petersburg, and in 1888 he became his own master at Bucharest. His transfer to Rome in 1893 restored him to the capital where he had served his apprenticeship and to the country of his talented wife. When Marschall lost favour the brilliant Ambassador was summoned home. The appointment was of peculiar significance, since Hohenlohe, the Chancellor, was losing grip with advancing years. Bülow declares in his Memoirs that he took office with the conviction that Germany had little to gain by a war and much to lose. A localised struggle was almost unthinkable, and a world war would be a gamble. Every year in which peace could be honourably preserved was a gain for a country steadily increasing in population and economic strength. How could the peace desired and required by the German people be maintained? The answer was obvious—Germany must give no provocation, but at the same time allow nobody to tread on her toes.

The new Foreign Minister entered on his task under the brightest auspices. He enjoyed the affectionate confidence of William II, and no urgent problem clamoured for solution. The relations of Germany with her allies were good, with France and Russia correct, with England a little better than in the previous year. Russia was busy with her plans in the Far East, and her new pact with Austria put the Balkan question in cold storage for a time. Russia and Germany, remarked Muraviev to Bülow, should restrain their respective allies from committing irreparable follies. France was occupied with her activities in West Africa and her ambitions on the Upper Nile.

---

[1] Bülow's Memoirs have provoked innumerable protests. The most important is *Front wider Bülow*, edited by Thimme. Spickernagel, *Fürst Bülow*, contains useful letters. Sigmund Münz, *Fürst Bülow, Der Staatsmann und der Mensch*, is a personal study. Morrow, "The Foreign Policy of Prince von Bülow," *Cambridge Historical Journal*, IV, 63–93, is a useful summary. Tardieu, *Le Prince de Bülow*, gives a French view.

The forward policy of Paris and St. Petersburg was a potential challenge to the interests of England, who in consequence moved closer towards the Triple Alliance. Germany's hands, it seemed, were free, and she might, if she wished, stride boldly forward along new paths. It was the task of statesmanship to relate the prizes to the risks. Since the hostility of France was incurable, common sense dictated that at any rate Russia and England should not be simultaneously antagonised. If *Weltpolitik* was to be the order of the day, two courses lay open—the exploitation of Asiatic Turkey and the creation of a first-class fleet. The former was bound to alarm Russia ; the latter, however legitimate, would inevitably estrange England. The maxim of limited liability pointed to a choice between the two. The wise tradition was flung aside, and the rulers of Germany, overestimating her strength, determined to pursue both policies at once.

II

The way had been prepared for a forward policy in Turkey by the military mission of Von der Goltz and by the Kaiser's attitude to the problems of Armenia and Crete. While British statesmen of both parties were denouncing the organised massacres in Constantinople and Asia Minor, and a wave of horror swept over the Continent, the ruler of Germany gripped the hand of the Great Assassin. In the Cretan revolt and the Greco-Turkish war his sympathies were openly on the side of the Mussulman Power. With Palmerston and Disraeli at the helm Turkey had found a Big Brother in England, but their successors were loudest in the clamour for reform. The office of Patron was vacant, and Germany strode forward to snatch the prize. *Weltpolitik* demanded *Realpolitik*, and the Kaiser had no scruple in paying the price.

When Marschall reached his post on the Bosphorus in November 1897, he was received with open arms.[1] The imposing, self-confident and yet tactful Ambassador won and kept the confidence of Abdul Hamid, explaining that whereas other Powers aimed at weakening and partitioning Turkey, Germany alone desired not only to keep her intact but to increase her strength. " Things are simpler for the German Ambassador than for his colleagues", he wrote on August 6, 1898.[2] " The firm basis on which we stand in Constantinople

[1] *G.P.* XII, ch. 83. [2] ibid. XII, 569.

is the sincere and hearty friendship of the Sultan for His Majesty the Emperor, and his confidence in the honourable character of German policy.   And with it goes his admiration for the German army as the bulwark of authority against radicalism and revolution, and his trust in the fortunes of German industry."   The Ambassador certainly held the best cards, for the interests of the two countries appeared to coincide.   Together they might achieve great things.

The time of waiting, reported Marschall on April 9, 1898, was nearly over,[1] for the Sultan was eager to extend the Anatolian railway in the direction of Baghdad.   The Wilhelm-strasse was inclined to hold a little aloof ; but with the Kaiser's spectacular visit to Constantinople, Palestine and Syria in the autumn of 1898 all opposition was swept away.   Among its attractions, as Bülow pointed out to his master before they started,[2] was the diminution of the prestige derived by France from her historic Protectorate over the Catholics in Turkey. The well-timed and well-staged journey was triumphant beyond all expectations, for never had a Christian monarch been so acclaimed.   The climax was reached in the resonant declaration at Damascus ;   " May the Sultan and the three hundred million Mohammedans in different parts of the world who revere him as the Caliph rest assured that the German Emperor at all times will be their friend."   On the following day the Kaiser laid a wreath on the tomb of Saladin.   The tour and its results were described by the Foreign Minister for the benefit of Prince Henry.[3]   " Not only our ideal, but our material interest will benefit", he concluded.   " Wide horizons for German industry and commerce are opened up."   Bülow, however, was less intoxicated by the plaudits and the pageantry than his romantic master, for his nature was fundamentally unadventurous, and his references in the Reichstag were cool enough.[4]   Fantastic motives for the journey had been sug-gested.   Germany, he explained, sought no special political influence in Constantinople such as one or other Power had exercised in past times.   She made no claim to the Protectorate of all Christians, only of German nationals.   It was precisely this policy of limitation on which the stability of her position in the Turkish capital was based.

The first-fruits of the Imperial mission quickly appeared. In January 1899 the Sultan gave the Anatolian Railway Com-

[1] G.P. XIV, 464–6.   [2] ibid. XII, 610–1, June 4.
[3] ibid. XII, 578–80.   [4] Reden, I, 31–40, December 12, 1898.

pany a concession to build a commercial port at Haidar Pasha,
on the Asiatic side of the Bosphorus, and at the end of the year
the Company received permission to continue the line via
Konia to Baghdad and Basra.[1] It was a triumph for Marschall
and still more for Georg von Siemens, the head of the Deutsche
Bank, who, like List and Moltke before him, had visualised the
political and economic importance of railway development in
Turkey. " Since the return of Your Majesty from the Holy
Land", wrote Bülow to his master in March 1899, " this plan
has been continuously discussed between the Foreign Office
and Siemens.[2] He was told not only that we had no objection
to the extension of the Anatolian system, but that we were
absolutely ready to foster the plan in every way and to give it
vigorous support in Constantinople." The Baghdad concession and the Turcophil policy of which it was the fruit raised
problems in which other Powers were closely involved, and the
outlines of a grandiose coalition began to emerge. Since the
lapse of Bismarck's secret treaty with Russia the Austrian
alliance had increased in importance, and the realm of the Hapsburgs now appeared in a new *rôle* as the bridge between Germany and Turkey. Railway communication from Hamburg to
the Persian Gulf, financed and controlled in the main by the
Central Powers, with the prospect of a stronger and richer
Ottoman Empire at the Eastern end, introduced fresh possibilities and new apprehensions into the international game. It
was the task of the rulers of Germany to secure that the laurels
won at Constantinople should not wither in their hands.

On March 24, 1899, the Russian Ambassador announced that
his Government felt some disquiet at the concession for a port
at Haidar Pasha.[3] Bülow suavely replied that German aims in
Turkey were not political but purely commercial. Germany
was becoming more and more industrialised and she needed
markets. When the Ambassador remarked that Constantinople had always been a *noli me tangere* for Russia, and that for
religious reasons she could not surrender her influence in the
Balkans, the Foreign Minister rejoined that Germany had not
got and would not get in her way in the Balkans, the Black
Sea or the Straits. On the other hand Russia could not
possibly claim the whole Turkish Empire as her exclusive
domain. The Ambassador admitted that she would rather
see German than exclusively English enterprise in Asia Minor,

[1] Earle, *Turkey, The Great Powers, and the Baghdad Railway.*
[2] *G.P.* XIV, 474–6.   [3] ibid. XIV, ch. 95.

and explained that the vital question was the security of the Black Sea and the Straits. No assurance from Berlin could dispel the apprehensions of St. Petersburg. On April 5 Muraviev remarked to the German Ambassador : " What is this concession of yours at Haidar Pasha ? [1] You Germans are always pushing your economic interests in those regions, and I cannot help fearing that one day they will collide with ours." Bülow argued that German economic enterprise in Asia Minor should be a bond of union with Russia, not a cause of estrangement. Russians were afraid, replied the Ambassador, that economic interest might grow into a political hegemony, which must in time lead to an antagonism hitherto unknown. Russia had no intention of excluding Germany from Asia Minor, in which, as in the Far East, the two countries could walk hand in hand. The time of alliances was past, but an arrangement might be made. Bülow replied that he could say neither Yes nor No, but would await more concrete proposals. Asia Minor was big enough for both. The Kaiser regarded friendly relations with Russia as the first principle of German policy. He aimed at no exclusive influence in Constantinople, and Germany felt sure that Russia would not grudge her elbow-room for economic expansion elsewhere.

A few days later the Ambassador returned to the charge.[2] He had no doubt as to the loyalty of German policy, but he wished it to be understood in Berlin that the Straits were and would always remain a vital question. Russia desired the maintenance of the Turkish Empire so long as possible, but it would not last for ever. If and when it fell to pieces she could not tolerate another Power in the capital, and the Straits were the keys of the Black Sea. There should be a written agreement, in which Germany would give assurances concerning the Straits and receive a free hand in Asia Minor in return. " The German advance in Asia Minor must bring Germany and Russia nearer together." He added that he was speaking for himself, and that if Muraviev learned of his proposals too soon he would wish to checkmate them out of jealousy. An agreement should be reached, after which they must consider how to secure the Tsar's assent.

At their next meeting Osten-Sacken explained that his chief was so jealous and distrustful of his Ambassadors that he either ignored their suggestions or misrepresented them to the Tsar.[3]

[1] G.P. XIV, 478.   [2] ibid. XIV, 541–3.   [3] ibid. XIV, 546–9.

The proposal must therefore be made through the German Ambassador. Bülow rejoined that Germany was ready at any moment for a pact or alliance with Russia, or with Russia and France, on condition of a mutual guarantee of the territories of the contracting parties. That would be impossible for France, replied the Ambassador ; and when the Foreign Minister rejoined that at any rate a Russo-German agreement on these lines was feasible, he was silent. In reporting the conversation to Hatzfeldt in London Bülow expressed his doubts as to whether he was merely speaking for himself. The suggestion of a German initiative could not be considered, and a binding agreement with Russia was impossible till France, her ally, abandoned the *Revanche*. Moreover an agreement about the Straits would have a point against England, and could only be considered in return for a guarantee of the territorial status quo. Bülow's caution was approved by Marschall, who reported that, despite the temporary diversion in the Far East, Russia kept steadily in view the gradual dissolution of Turkey.[1] Any measures tending to strengthen Turkey were therefore distasteful to her ; yet Germany should go steadily ahead.

A final effort was made by Muraviev at the end of June.[2] Russia was the leading Power in Turkey, he declared, and she could exert the strongest pressure. The existing situation suited her, since she had no desire to see Turkey too strong. If a collapse were to come she would exercise her exclusive claim to Constantinople, and she must watch that no other Power gained a dominating position on the Bosphorus. German activity in Asia Minor would increase the wealth of the country and therewith the power of the Sultan to a point which might be uncomfortable, if not dangerous, for Russia. It was time to delimit their respective spheres of influence in order to avert a clash of interests. England, he added, was not irreconcilable, and if Germany declined to meet his wishes, he would look elsewhere. The rather dictatorial tone confirmed Bülow's disposition to avoid entanglements. Russia's demands, he wrote to the Kaiser, bore no relation to her offers.[3] If she betrayed the secret, as she doubtless would, Germany would lose the friendship of Turkey and incur the enmity of England. If she pressed for assent, the onset could be checked by stipulating for publicity and a bilateral territorial guarantee. The only result of these conversations was a clear warning that

[1] *G.P.* XIV, 485-9.   [2] ibid. XIV, 549-54.
[3] ibid. XIV, 558-60.

German enterprise in Asia Minor was regarded with suspicion in the Russian capital.

In November the Tsar, accompanied by Muraviev, visited Potsdam for a few hours on his way home from a holiday at Darmstadt. Nowhere, he observed to Bülow, were German and Russian interests opposed, but Germany must consider Russian traditions.[1] She must not appear to desire to eliminate Russia, either on the political or the economic plane, from the Near East, with which she had been connected for centuries by national and religious ties. Muraviev's tone was equally friendly. Russia had no objection to railways in Asia Minor, and preferred German to English exploitation ; but she hoped that none would be built which directly threatened her strategic or financial interests. If Germany were to communicate her plans in advance, the aspirations of the two countries could be reconciled. He was asking not for any kind of pact, but for friendly conversations. Bülow declared himself pleased with the results of the visit, and was relieved that he had neither to accept nor to decline a written agreement. The two parties, however, were no nearer to one another when the preliminary concession of the right to build a railway to Baghdad was signed on December 23. In reporting his success Marschall declared that the Russian Embassy in Constantinople had been officially neutral during the long negotiations, but that attempts had been made from the British side to arouse the suspicions of the Sultan.[2] It was clear that the new policy in Turkey would require to be conducted with exceptional skill if the Baghdad project was not to be checkmated by the machinations of St. Petersburg.

From the meridian of Berlin the first Hague Conference was merely an incident in Russo-German relations.[3] The Tsar's manifesto of August 24, 1898, on the limitation of armaments was a disagreeable surprise. It would be best, wired Bülow to Hatzfeldt, if the plan, which concealed a real danger of war, were wrecked on the opposition of England without Germany taking the lead. The Kaiser greeted the move with jocular contempt as a bad joke, attributing it to the anxieties of Russian finance. " Honour will henceforth be lavished on you by the whole world ", concluded his reply to the Tsar, " even should the practical part fail through difficulties of detail. My Government will give the matter its most serious attention." No one dared to decline the invitation, and Bülow,

[1] G.P. XIII, 227–31.   [2] ibid. XIV, 504–5.   [3] ibid. XV, ch. 100.

like Hohenlohe, was anxious to stand well with St. Petersburg. His instructions for Münster, the chief German delegate, were nevertheless cynically frank. " That we have no intention of binding ourselves in the question of military armaments in any direction", he began, " I need hardly say." The other Great Powers, he added, would doubtless take the same line. Equally unacceptable was the plan of a Court of Arbitration, which involved the abdication of the *rôle* of a Great Power. Here again Germany could probably leave the opposition to other Powers. Open antagonism to Russian suggestions should be avoided wherever possible.

Bülow's desire was shared by the chief Russian delegate and President of the Conference, who visited Berlin on his way to the Hague. His task, explained Staal confidentially, was to avoid a fiasco for his sovereign and his country. Regarding the Conference as his own work, the Tsar would deeply regret its failure and would hold other Powers responsible. As a believer in good relations with Germany Staal was most anxious that she should not expose herself to such a charge. Paris and London, and possibly Vienna, would rejoice at the opening of a breach which would tighten the bonds of the Franco-Russian alliance and bring Russia nearer to England and Austria. Bülow tactfully replied that Münster would go hand in hand with the Russian delegate in all matters, so far as the security of Germany and the fundamental principles of a conservative Monarchy allowed. The Kaiser's annotations on his report expressed the real mind of the German Government. " The apprehensions of antagonism arise from the fact that the whole Conference is more or less directed against our military development, which Russia wishes to check in order to keep us in a subordinate position. She is short of money. . . . I will take part in the Conference comedy, keeping my sword at my side."

The policy of inaction proved easy enough to apply, for the Conference was doomed from the start. The chief item in the programme, the limitation of armaments, presented no difficulties for it received no support. The doctrine of unfettered national sovereignty, combined with the suspicions and ambitions of the Powers, rendered the organisation of Europe impossible. Even a permanent Court of Arbitration was too much for Bülow, who argued strongly against the " democratisation " of foreign policy. While Münster pleaded from the Hague for a conciliatory attitude, Holstein, who counselled intransigence, won the day.   The German attitude, however, aroused no resentment at St. Petersburg, where arbitration was contemplated only in trifling affairs.   When Bülow was sounded as to a German initiative on the immunity of private property at sea in time of war, he replied that he would welcome a general recognition of the principle, but that in the absence of unanimity there was no need to take the lead.   The German delegates, he explained to Münster, should meet unacceptable Russian proposals with the argument that they were too general in form.   The German Government could not think of giving way on questions of importance out of politeness to anybody, but its representatives should always try to find a bridge of honourable retreat for the servants of the Tsar.

On June 21 the Foreign Minister reported to his master on the situation at The Hague.   The German delegates had, so far as possible, worked hand in hand with the Russians according to orders, and had tried to prevent the Conference being a spectacular failure.   The vague and harmless Russian plan of arbitration in individual cases had been revolutionised by Pauncefote's scheme of a permanent Court, to which certain categories of disputes would be automatically referred.   In opposing the latter Germany found herself alone ; but the concessions made to her standpoint left little more of the original plan than the name, and it was likely still further to be watered down.   As a result hardly any change would be made, and therefore it could be regarded as innocuous.   It was, moreover, very much better than incurring the resentment of Nicholas II.   In commenting on the report the Kaiser remarked that he accepted the nonsense in order to save the Tsar's face.   " But I shall continue in my practice to trust solely in God and my sharp sword."   None of the Great Powers was ready to part with any portion of its armed strength or to fetter its policy ; for rampant nationalism was the order of the day, and the disdainful utterances of Germany's rulers may be paralleled elsewhere.   The Conference was premature.   Yet no Government made so little effort to conceal its hostility to its avowed purposes, and no other Great Power contributed so little to the meagre harvest that was reaped.   Shedding no tears over its failure, Bülow rejoiced that an awkward corner in Russo-German relations had been turned.

III

In Western Europe at the time of Bülow's appointment to
the Foreign Office Anglo-German relations were improving
while Anglo-French relations were growing steadily worse.[1]
The storm of anger aroused by the Kruger telegram gradually
subsided, though its rumblings never died entirely away.
German support in financing the reconquest of the Sudan
from the Egyptian treasury was warmly appreciated in Downing Street, where the prospect of trouble with Russia in the
Far East and with France in tropical Africa enhanced the
importance of a friendly Berlin.   Despite the assertions of
Tirpitz and his school, commercial competition never seriously
affected either the popular sentiment or the official diplomacy
of England.   On July 31, 1897, Hatzfeldt reported that Salisbury, speaking with a friendliness that he had not shown for a
considerable time, declared that he would always be glad to go
with Germany.[2]   A political understanding with France was
utterly impossible.   If the mood lasted, commented the Ambassador, a satisfactory arrangement in Samoa seemed within
sight.   The attraction of Germany was much stronger in
Chamberlain and the Duke of Devonshire than in the Prime
Minister, and the seizure of Port Arthur by Russia in March
1898 rekindled British Russophobia into a flame.   In the middle
of March Salisbury left for the Riviera owing to ill-health,
and Balfour took charge of the Foreign Office.   Though less
impulsive than Chamberlain, he desired some sort of rapprochement with Berlin, for the sky was filled with clouds.   In an
informal conversation with Hatzfeldt on March 25 at the house
of Alfred de Rothschild—as ardent a champion of Anglo-
German co-operation as Eckardstein himself—Balfour declared that in the great political questions the two countries
were separated by no conflicting interests, and expressed the
wish for a better understanding.[3]

Four days later Chamberlain and the Ambassador were
invited to meet at the same hospitable table.[4]   Trouble

---

[1] Meinecke, *Geschichte des deutsch-englischen Bündnisproblems*, 1890–1901, and
Willy Becker, *Fürst Bülow und England*, 1897–1909.   Eugen Fischer, *Holsteins
Grosses Nein*, takes Eckardstein's *Lebenserinnerungen* rather too seriously.   Cp.
Gerhard Ritter, *Die Legende von der verschmähten englischen Freundschaft*, 1898–1901;
the essay on Holstein in Gooch, *Studies in Modern History*; and Theodor Wolff,
Das Vorspiel, 91–6.
[2] *G.P.* XIII, 31–2.
[3] ibid. XIV, ch. 91, 195–6, March 25.
[4] ibid. XIV, 196–9.

threatened in the Far East and in West Africa, explained the Colonial Secretary. The Government desired to give up its policy of isolation and reach an understanding with Germany and her friends. If she would stand by England now, England would stand by her if she were attacked. He was indeed ready for a treaty with the Triple Alliance, and time pressed. Chamberlain's report to the Cabinet is to much the same effect.[1] " I said that, as far as I knew, there was no question between the two Governments which affected any important interest, and they were all absolutely trivial in comparison with the great issues involving our relations with other nations. It seemed to me that on these greater issues the interests of Germany were really identical with our own. The conversation then became more definite, and in the course of questions and answers the following suggestions were evolved. That an alliance might be established by Treaty or Agreement between Germany and Great Britain for a term of years. That it should be of a defensive character based upon a mutual understanding as to policy in China and elsewhere." Though the talk was understood to be entirely unofficial, the prestige of the strongest personality in the Cabinet gave it unquestionable significance. Never before had a British Minister, officially or unofficially, dangled an alliance before the German Empire.

Bülow wired a chilly reply.[2] The weak point of an Anglo-German pact, he pointed out, would be that it would only bind the Cabinet that made it. A change of public opinion might leave Germany in the lurch, for the British ally could always walk out by the back door. On the other hand every German statesman realised that a diminution of England's power would encourage the foes of the Treaty of Frankfurt, and if such a situation arose no treaty was necessary to secure the aid of Germany. Till that moment arrived her neutrality would secure the neutrality of others, on the principle that one sword kept the other in the scabbard. Time was against England. In ten years Russia would be stronger and perhaps less disinclined to take part in a war between England and France. The elaborate argument breathes profound suspicion of the value of England as an ally, and displays a curious complacency as to the foundations of German strength.

Three days after the first conversation Hatzfeldt visited the

[1] Garvin, *Life of Joseph Chamberlain*, III, 259–60.
[2] G.P. XIV, 199–202.

Colonial Office and explained the views of his chief.[1] Chamberlain replied that England could be trusted to keep her word, that parliamentary ratification could easily be obtained, and that secret articles might accompany the published treaty. The object of the understanding would be, not to deprive Russia of the advantages in China which she already possessed, but to preserve the rest of the country for the commerce of the world. Germany's sphere of influence could be extended in the hinterland of Kiaochau. Chamberlain's report supplies more details relating to China.[2] Asked by Hatzfeldt how he proposed to prevent further aggression, he suggested that the two Powers might say to Russia : " You have got all you say you want. We are ready to recognise your position, but you must go no farther. The rest of China is under our joint protection." In addition to extending her protection over Shantung and its hinterland, Germany, by agreement with China, might raise an army under German officers. England might do the same in the centre and south. Thus, if Russia attempted further aggression, she would have to confront not only a war with two great European Powers, but also the defensive forces of China organised and led by European officers.

Bülow was no more attracted by the second interview than by the first. He continued to doubt whether Parliament would approve, and shuddered at the situation which would arise if it refused.[3] Germany would have been caught in an attempt, without any visible necessity, to ally herself with Russia's arch enemy. " At the present time Germany, who is confronted with no immediate or prospective danger, has no reason to shoulder the risks of an alliance." Moreover public opinion, owing to the press feud of recent years and the uncompromising attitude of Downing Street in colonial questions, was predominantly anti-English. " The great mass of the German people do not at the present moment believe that they are threatened from the East. It would therefore be no easy task to justify a change from enmity to comradeship and an alliance which automatically stamps Russia as our foe." Under present circumstances he could make no promises, but the future was left open. " In the long run England will not escape the struggle for existence, and when it comes she will find no other ally and no better friend than Germany." A hint should be dropped to Chamberlain

[1] G.P. XIV, 202–4.   [2] Garvin, III, 263–6.
[3] G.P. XIV, 204–7.

not to complicate the rapprochement of the future by the rough handling of smaller issues.

When Hatzfeldt told Balfour that the Wilhelmstrasse doubted the acceptance by Parliament, the Minister confessed that he himself could not be sure.[1] It was a peculiarity of Chamberlain, he added confidentially, to wish to advance too fast. He agreed that the duty of the moment was by mutual consideration in little things to prepare opinion in both countries for future co-operation. The Ambassador gathered the impression that the failure of Chamberlain's approach was not altogether distasteful either to Balfour or Salisbury. Bülow was delighted with Balfour's words, which he contrasted with Chamberlain's endeavour to lead Germany along dangerous paths.[2] The Kaiser, who was only informed of the conversations after they had taken place, welcomed the revelation of England's insecurity and hoped for further advances at a later stage. " With a friendly England we have another card against Russia in our hand, with the prospect of securing from her colonial and commercial advantages. It will be Hatzfeldt's difficult task to prevent the postponement of a formal alliance being felt as a snub, and to convince England of our cordial desire for fruitful co-operation." In annotating his master's telegram Bülow stated his price. " The indispensable condition of an Anglo-German alliance in the present European situation is its extension to Europe, in plain language the guarantee of our territories." Till then Germany must stand uncommitted between England and Russia, the tongue in the balance, not the pendulum swinging from side to side.

Bülow's cautious attitude never changed ; but his impressionable master, under the stimulus of a visit from Eckardstein, now clamoured for an alliance on a wider basis than had hitherto been proposed. The news was communicated to Chamberlain on April 22 by Eckardstein, who added that, in his master's belief, Austria and Italy would eagerly join in the arrangement.[3] The basis would be a mutual guarantee of territory, and the Kaiser recognised that England should have a free hand in Egypt and the Transvaal. German policy, however, was controlled, not by the Kaiser, but by Bülow and Holstein, and there is no perceptible advance in the instructions for a further meeting of Hatzfeldt and Chamberlain.[4] The Ambassador was to emphasise that the neutrality of Germany by itself would

[1] G.P. XIV, 207–8. [2] ibid. XIV, 208–9.
[3] Garvin, III, 271–2. [4] G.P. XIV, 218–21.

probably suffice to guarantee England against a war with
France and Russia.   Thus England had no need to buy the
neutrality of France, since it was a corollary of the neutrality of
Germany.   And the latter was cheaper to purchase than the
former.   " All we ask is that in the process of extending her
own dominions England should grant us some compensations."
Hatzfeldt's brief was embodied in a single sentence.   " French
neutrality depends on German neutrality, which depends on
England's policy, above all in regard to particular issues."
Hatzfeldt had wired that the interview was sought by Chamberlain, whereas the latter's report states that the invitation came
from Eckardstein.

When the two men met on April 25 Chamberlain reiterated
his arguments for an alliance, explaining that he only spoke for
himself.[1]   Hatzfeldt replied that in neither country was public
opinion ripe ; that the approval of Parliament was uncertain ;
that rejection would provoke a Franco-Russian attack ; that
German neutrality automatically held France in check ; and
that the best preparation for an alliance, in the event of a
change in the political situation, would be a friendly settlement
of all minor questions.   Russia, rejoined Chamberlain, would
continue her advance in China, and Germany could not allow
the hinterland to Kiaochau to fall into her hands.   His plan
was that England and the Triple Alliance should bar the way.
If the natural alliance with Germany was not to be had, an
understanding with Russia or France was not impossible.   A
settlement with Germany or any other Power about minor
matters was not worth having without a general understanding.
His words left Hatzfeldt in no doubt that in case of a refusal he
was ready for a deal with France or Russia, and that no colonial
concessions would be forthcoming in the absence of a political
agreement.   In face of this plain speaking the Ambassador
assured Chamberlain that there were no insurmountable
obstacles to an eventual understanding.   The ambitious
Minister, he concluded, was eager to score a success before
Salisbury's return ; but he resolved to tell the Prime Minister
everything.

Chamberlain's record of the conversation, though much
shorter, makes it clear that nothing more could be done.[2]
" If, he said, the negotiations failed, or the results were not
accepted by Parliament, and the Russian Government became
aware of what had been attempted, it was certain that they

[1] G.P. XIV, 221-6.   [2] Garvin, III, 273-7.

would attack Germany and would be assisted by France. . . . I said that I gathered that he thought any attempt to secure a direct defensive alliance between Germany and England was premature. He assented, but said the opportunity might come later. I reminded him of the French proverb *le bonheur qui passe.*" On the following day Eckardstein expressed to Chamberlain his great regret that the interview had been indefinite. The Kaiser had told him that an alliance with England would be the best thing in the world. " I said that I was of course sorry, as personally I desired that an arrangement might be found possible, but that there was now nothing more to be done."

Bülow fully approved Hatzfeldt's language, which indeed faithfully reflected the instructions from Berlin.[1] " The utmost we can do is to let Chamberlain believe that there are no insurmountable obstacles to a future understanding." No danger threatened from Russia, and the possible refusal of Parliament to approve a settlement would leave Germany exposed to her wrath. The time for discussing an Anglo-German alliance would only arrive if Russia threatened German interests and if England realised that France could not help her against the Tsar. When the illusion of a choice of allies had been shattered, Anglo-German relations would improve. For the moment there was nothing more to be done. The Kaiser's annotations on Hatzfeldt's report of his last conversation show that he was now of the same mind as the Wilhelmstrasse. John Bull was feeling uncomfortable about Russia and was looking round for help. Chamberlain's promises were not enough.

In forwarding his memoranda to Salisbury, who had now returned, Chamberlain noted that in every case the initiative came from the German side.[2] He felt, however, that England was powerless to resist the ultimate control of China by Russia, and that our isolation was a great disadvantage in negotiating with France. The country, he believed, would favour a treaty with Germany. Hatzfeldt also reported to the Prime Minister, but without going into details. " His business", wrote Salisbury to Chamberlain, " was evidently to throw cold water. He hinted that if we wished for an alliance we must prepare the way for it by amiability in other matters. . . . I quite agree with you that under the circumstances a closer relation with Germany would be very desirable ; but can we

[1] *G.P.* XIV, 227–9.   [2] Garvin, III, 278–80.

get it ? " When the two men met at the Cabinet next day Chamberlain told his chief that the Kaiser expected a mutual defensive arrangement, of course including Alsace-Lorraine and, he assumed, Egypt and Afghanistan. " He said that if Eckardstein came to me again I might say that the Government were prepared to regard the idea favourably. He agreed that any agreement should be a public one."

Despite Salisbury's words to his colleague, his reading of the situation was very different. " We know that we shall maintain against all comers that which we possess", he declared in a memorable speech on May 4, " and we know, in spite of the jargon about isolation, that we are amply competent to do so." Undeterred by this snub Chamberlain gave public expression a week later at Birmingham to his desire for a change of policy. Since the Crimean war England had had no allies and no friends. " All the powerful states of Europe have made alliances, and as long as we keep outside those alliances—so long as we are envied by all and suspected by all and as long as we have interests which at one time or another conflict with the interests of all—we are liable to be confronted with a combination of Great Powers." If the policy of isolation continued, the fate of the Chinese empire would probably be decided without regard to our interests. If, on the other hand, a policy of the open door was to prevail, we should not reject the idea of an alliance with those Powers whose interests most nearly approximated to our own. The speech echoed round the world, but it produced no concrete results. On June 2 Salisbury observed to Hatzfeldt that Powers should not attempt a formal agreement till the necessity arose.

Chamberlain's undisguised hostility to Russia increased Bülow's disinclination to grasp his outstretched hand. The best policy, he wrote to his master, was to keep a free hand, alienating neither England nor the Franco-Russian group.[1] A letter from the Tsar to the Kaiser, after receiving a highly coloured account of the discussions with Chamberlain, confirmed his conviction that he had acted wisely. Three months ago, wrote the Tsar, England had made many tempting proposals, which, as their purpose was suspect, had been promptly refused. The revelation, commented the Foreign Minister, was a new proof of the untrustworthiness of England, demanding even greater circumspection. Vague general agreements with her should be avoided and only con-

[1] G.P. XIV; 248-9.

crete questions discussed. The British offer to Russia, need-less to say, was misrepresented by the Tsar, and it was the seizure of Port Arthur which had interrupted the discussion. Of this Bülow was unaware. But even had he felt more con-fidence in British policy, he would none the less have rejected the unwanted gift.

At this moment Lascelles remarked to Bülow that the relations of England and Germany had greatly improved in the last year.[1] Referring for the first time to the recent discussions in London he declared that Chamberlain, whose influence was increasing, had spoken in good faith. He was not sure, how-ever, that public opinion and Parliament would' at present approve an alliance. Before English wishes could be realised, rejoined the Foreign Minister, three conditions must be fulfilled. There must be a certainty of acceptance by Parlia-ment. Secondly, Germany was situated between France and Russia. France's aims were well known, but Russia had no reason to support them so long as her position in Asia was unchallenged by Germany. If an Anglo-German alliance was made with a point against Russia, what security could England provide against her resentment ? Thirdly, England must be more accommodating in colonial affairs. He could not understand why she grudged Germany everything. If relations were to be permanently improved, British policy must remember the principle : Live and let live. That Bülow was unwilling to throw himself into the arms of Eng-land without counting the cost is intelligible enough ; but there was something more than caution in his cool response to the advances of Chamberlain. He knew far less of England than of the other Great Powers, and Russia loomed larger in his field of vision. He was much more anxious to avoid the loss of her favour than to win and keep the confidence of the mistress of the seas. Two months later, on receiving the Kaiser's report of a conversation with the British Ambassador at Homburg, he congratulated his master on his exposition of German policy.[2] He had made it plain that he would never pull English chestnuts out of the Russian fire *pour les beaux yeux de John Bull*, and that England could not help Germany in a war with Russia. He had preserved Germany's relations with Russia intact, a consideration of the first importance for the safety of the realm. Germany had no desire to goad

[1] G.P. XIV, 253-5. Bülow's report is dated July 11.
[2] ibid. XIV, 339-42.

England into war with Russia, but such a war was ultimately inevitable. By careful management of both England and Russia, the Kaiser could appear at the celebrations of Queen Victoria in the following year as *arbiter mundi*. It was a courtier's vision and nothing more ; for the Kaiser was one day to find himself falling between two stools.

Meanwhile the Foreign Minister was entirely satisfied with the situation. In a Reichstag survey of the world at the end of 1898 he sang a paean to the Triple Alliance, which he compared to a fortress in time of peace.[1] The trees on the glacis grew higher year by year, but in case of need it could be made ready for action without delay. The Alliance rested on a sure foundation. It was the outcome of the historical development of three great states, combining close cohesion for external purposes with complete autonomy. Each of its members had the same interest in its continuance : each would lose in equal measure if it ceased to exist. And since it aimed solely at the maintenance of the status quo, it served the interests of all other states and the cause of European peace.

IV

While neither Bülow nor Salisbury desired an alliance, the wish of the Wilhelmstrasse for co-operation in particular issues was gratified in the Treaty of August 1898, which divided the Portuguese colonies into British and German spheres of influence.[2] The finances of Portugal were in more than ordinary confusion, and early in June Soveral was instructed to raise money on the security of the revenues of Mozambique and Angola. The financial problem had a political aspect, for Delagoa Bay and the railway to the Trans-vaal were objects of first-class importance both to London and Berlin. The German claim to be consulted in the event of the alienation of Portugal's rights in her colonies had been known to the British Government for years, and the recent collapse of the Spanish Empire suggested the possibility that another weak Power might also prove unable to hold its distant possessions. Hearing of the Soveral-Chamberlain discussions, the German Ambassador asked on June 14 on what conditions Soveral proposed to raise the money. Salisbury replied that he did not know, and referred him to Chamberlain. He added that

[1] *Reden*, I, 37-8.
[2] *G.P.* XIV, ch. 92 ; *B.D.* I, ch. 2 ; and Garvin, III, 307-23.

he desired to maintain the best relations with Germany, and would report any steps which might concern her rights or legitimate interests in the Portuguese colonies. England was bound by treaty to guarantee the integrity of Portuguese possessions, and she had the greatest interest in averting a collapse. Hatzfeldt rejoined that a unilateral procedure by which Portugal's sovereign rights in her colonies passed into English hands would produce the worst impression in Germany. The Prime Minister declined to admit that the British Government could not furnish financial aid without a preliminary agreement with Germany, but was otherwise conciliatory. England, he explained, was interested not in Angola but in the East African coast, where Chamberlain feared that Germany had designs on Delagoa Bay. Hatzfeldt believed that he would keep the promise to inform him of an agreement, but was afraid that he might not trouble to secure Germany's preliminary assent. " How false and untrustworthy Lord Salisbury is ! " commented the Kaiser. " That is not the way to entice us to an alliance."

Fearing that an agreement between Soveral and Chamberlain might be reached at any moment, Hatzfeldt favoured co-operation in a loan secured for Germany on the customs of Angola and for England on those of Delagoa Bay. Bülow approved the suggestion, but added that Angola should be supplemented by the northern part of Portuguese East Africa. Without a moment's delay Hatzfeldt made the suggestion to Salisbury, who replied that it required careful consideration. Bülow was now thoroughly alarmed. The German Ambassador in Lisbon was ordered to tell the King of Portugal that the German Government had learned of negotiations which would involve a complete revolution of the economic and therewith the political position of Portugal, and that it must consult with other Powers with a view to establish an international financial control. An invitation to co-operate in this and other matters was sent to Paris ; but a Cabinet crisis was in progress, and the desire of Hanotaux to work with Berlin was not shared by his successor Delcassé. Hatzfeldt was instructed to counterwork an English monopoly, but to favour a delimitation of spheres of interest.

On June 21 Salisbury informed the Ambassador of the decisions of the Cabinet. The question of assisting Portugal with a British loan was purely financial and only concerned the two Governments. If, however, the status quo became impossible and Portugal was compelled to part with her African colonies, that would be a subject for full discussion with Berlin. Hatzfeldt challenged the contention that a British loan was not the concern of any other Power; for conditions, he understood, were to be imposed which transformed a financial operation into a political issue. Salisbury replied that Portugal would probably retain her colonies for centuries, and that it was therefore premature to discuss an eventual partition. Since, however, Germany had raised the question, what would she demand? He would ask for instructions, replied the Ambassador, and meanwhile he could only express a personal wish for Angola and North Mozambique.

Bülow telegraphed instructions to London which reveal his annoyance at Salisbury's chilly attitude. In ignoring Germany in colonial questions, he complained, England relied on her supremacy at sea and on the fact that neither Russia nor France would support Berlin. They would change their attitude, however, if Germany raised the question of Africa as a whole. She had watched England enter Egypt without envy and had helped her to establish her position, but she expected a reward for her services. If England now proposed to lay hands on another considerable slice of Africa and virtually ignored the German claim to reciprocity, it would damage not only the interests but the prestige of Germany, who would be driven to resist. It would therefore be to England's advantage to concert her plans of African expansion with the Wilhelmstrasse. To yield her a free hand in Delagoa Bay would be painful to the German people, who had for years felt sympathy for the Boers. In return Germany must ask for northern Mozambique, the Portuguese section of Timor, Walfish Bay, and South Angola. Salisbury rejoined that the demands were very large, and that the value of Delagoa Bay was overestimated in Berlin. Hatzfeldt interjected that modifications were not ruled out. It would be painful for Portugal, continued Salisbury, and disagreeable to British opinion to divide up the inheritance while the owner was still alive. In a further discussion he inquired if Germany would be willing to surrender her right of exterritoriality in Zanzibar. The Ambassador was unable to answer the unexpected question. The Prime Minister then remarked that Germany's wish for northern Mozambique was natural, and that she might perhaps receive the larger part of Angola. The situation in Portugal, however, was at present too confused to make definite plans. His whole manner, reported Hatzfeldt, indicated that he had now decided in principle on a friendly compromise.

On July 13 Salisbury communicated the terms approved by the Cabinet. A British loan should be secured on the customs of southern Mozambique and northern Angola, a German loan on those of the remaining parts of the two colonies. If these districts were to be abandoned or surrendered, the two Powers would have first claim in their respective spheres. Hatzfeldt complained of the omission of Walfish Bay and asked for our good offices in obtaining Portuguese Timor, to which Salisbury replied that the surrender of exterritoriality in Zanzibar and Pemba should also be discussed. At this moment an entirely unexpected event occurred. Soveral announced that in view of all the difficulties his Government had abandoned the idea of a loan on the security of her colonies, and would try to manage without foreign help. In dealing with a stronger Power this would have brought the Anglo-German negotiations to an end : but since the capacity of Portugal to extricate herself from her embarrassments was doubted, the exchanges between Berlin and London continued without a pause.

At this point Hatzfeldt communicated the German terms, and, in surveying alternative concessions, mentioned for the first time the English share of Samoa and the Tonga Isles. On the following day Salisbury reported the result of the Cabinet deliberations, which seemed to threaten the continuance of the negotiations. The surrender of Samoa or Tonga was virtually impossible, at any rate without the consent of Australia ; and his colleagues, led by Chamberlain, attached greater importance than himself to Walfish Bay, which could only be exchanged for such an equivalent as Togoland—a suggestion greeted with loud laughter by the Ambassador. Hatzfeldt expressed his keen regret at the probable loss of opportunity of hearty accord. Germany could not stand alone ; if England withheld her friendship, she must turn to Russia. It was now clear that both sides had gone a little too far ; yet no agreement was in sight when the Prime Minister left for his summer holiday. On August 11 Hatzfeldt found Balfour, who took charge of the Foreign Office, in such a friendly mood that he expected a pact in the next few days. Balfour strongly emphasised his wish to spare the susceptibilities of Portugal. It was almost impossible to enter into such an agreement as was contemplated without suggesting that the contracting parties desired the eventual dismemberment of her colonial empire. It was, nevertheless, the earnest wish of the British Government to maintain her integrity. Hatzfeldt replied that his Government was equally anxious to maintain the status quo. A week later Balfour presented drafts of a public and private Declaration, which, to the disappointment of Hatzfeldt, made no reference to Timor ; but he was convinced of Balfour's sincerity and good will. Timor, came the response from the Wilhelmstrasse, was indispensable. It was promptly restored to the programme, and on August 30 the treaty was signed.

The preamble defined the objects as the avoidance of international complications, and the preservation of the integrity and independence of Portugal. If she asked for a loan at some future time on the security of the Customs revenue of Mozambique, Angola and Portuguese Timor, the signatories should have the right to join in providing it. The revenues of southern Mozambique and part of Angola were to be assigned to the British portion, those of northern Mozambique, the rest of Angola, and Portuguese Timor to the German share. A " Secret Convention " of the same date carried the agreement a good deal further. If " unfortunately " it proved impossible to maintain the integrity of the Portuguese Empire, the signatories agreed to oppose the intervention of a third Power by a loan on the security of the revenues of Mozambique, Angola and Timor, or by the acquisition of territory. Henceforth each would advance no claims in the zone allotted to the other. If Portugal renounced her sovereign rights, the signatories should enjoy commercial equality in each other's spheres. A " Secret Note " of the same date was added to secure equality of treatment. If either party obtained a cession of territory or special privileges in its allotted sphere, they should not become operative until similar grants of approximately equal value were accorded to the other. In informing Soveral of the conclusion of the treaty, though not of its terms, Balfour expressed his earnest desire that, if Portugal were to contract a loan, there should be neither loss nor diminution of her sovereign rights, still less any cession of territory.

In congratulating Hatzfeldt on his handiwork Bülow sketched out what he described as the second part of the South African problem. A settlement with Portugal must be reached before Paris could take a hand in the game, and it was for England to suggest the means. Balfour must not underestimate the importance of the *fait accompli* in facing the inevitable friction with France. Rapidity and silence were the chief needs in the negotiations with Portugal, for in a few weeks Franco-Portuguese discussions would be resumed. Hatzfeldt spoke to Balfour of the possibility of Portugal, in ignorance of the treaty, obtaining a loan from France on the security of her colonial customs, adding that France had already been sounded. This might be avoided if Soveral was informed that the intervention of a third Power could not be admitted, and that England and Germany were ready to raise the necessary loan. Balfour referred the matter to Salisbury, who exploded in a contemptuous minute. " They are not content to wait for events to give them their share of Portuguese territory, but wish to force the pace of destiny. I do not think that it is possible to make such an intimation to Portugal till we know the sort of financial terms Germany is disposed to give. They will be of the Shylock school."

The forecast was not fulfilled, for Portugal, contrary to German hopes, abstained from a foreign loan. Thus the treaty elaborated with so much care remained not only a secret but a dead letter. The signatories had embraced a shadow. Moreover, a year later, when the South African war had transformed the situation, the Anglo-Portuguese secret Declaration of October 14, 1899, confirmed the ancient territorial guarantees, and Portugal undertook not to permit the importation of arms destined for the Transvaal.[1] The so-called Windsor Treaty was not communicated to the German Government till 1913, when a fresh discussion of spheres of influence in the Portuguese colonies began ; but it was quickly discovered by Bülow, who pronounced it in flagrant antagonism to the spirit of the treaty of 1898.[2] This would only have been the case if the British Government, like the German, desired the collapse of the Portuguese empire. Thus the discussions of Anglo-German co-operation in Africa bore as little fruit as the recent exchanges regarding an alliance. The treaty was not an achievement of which either party had reason to be proud.

Bülow shared the healthy appetite of his countrymen for possessions overseas. A partition of the Philippines among

[1] G.P. XIV, 359, note. B.D. I, 88–99.
[2] Bülow, *Erinnerungen*, I, 274.

several Powers, he wrote to the Kaiser during the Spanish American war, was a possibility ;[1] and during the negotiations concerning Portugal Hatzfeldt mentioned Samoa.[2] A few weeks later the death of Malietoa left a disputed succession. Since 1889 the islands had been under the joint control of England, Germany and the United States ; but such a settlement could hardly be expected to last. On the death of the king Bülow instructed Hatzfeldt to sound Balfour as to the possibilities of partition.[3] Balfour rejoined that the Australians would object to a German settlement, and Salisbury, on being consulted, made the same reply. At the end of the year, in discussing colonial problems with Lascelles, Bülow confessed that Germany would never succeed in colonial enterprise without the assistance and good will of England.

The outbreak of civil war in Samoa in January 1899, in which the German officials on the spot championed one claimant to the throne and the British and American supported a rival, compelled the three Powers to act ; but action without agreement was perilous. The Kaiser asked Lascelles whether the time had not come for partition. Hearing that Washington was more inclined to such a policy than England, Bülow suggested to Hatzfeldt that they should negotiate first with America behind the back of England. The Prime Minister indeed was in no mood to meet the Germans half way. When Hatzfeldt argued that a change was imperative to avoid further conflicts, he was told that the situation must become worse before Australia could be reconciled to partition. " Salisbury will do nothing for us", he complained, and the Prime Minister's despatch to Lascelles of March 2 tells the same tale. Hatzfeldt, he reported, had more than once urged partition of the islands or buying out Germany with compensation elsewhere. Neither alternative seemed practicable. The Ambassador, he added, had always shown an unaccountable eagerness on this question. A ray of hope for the Wilhelmstrasse came from Rhodes, who, during his visit to Berlin for African purposes of his own, promised to work for partition.

In March British and American ships bombarded the hinterland of Apia, the capital, which was being attacked by Germany's candidate for the throne, and landed sailors, some of whom were killed. The German Consulate was damaged and German subjects suffered. The Samoan kettle had at last

[1] G.P. XIV, 249, June 5, 1898. [2] ibid. XIV, 299, July 20, 1898.
[3] ibid. XIV, ch. 76 and B.D. I, 107–131.

boiled over, and the policy of drift stood condemned. The German suggestion that a High Commission should be sent to take control of the situation was promptly accepted in Washington. Bülow told Lascelles that he did not care who was king of Samoa, but he felt strongly that the Samoan question should not be allowed to impair the excellent relations of the two countries. The islands were of very small value, but unfortunately public opinion had been led to believe that they were of importance to Germany. Lascelles wired that the extreme importance attached by the Kaiser and the German public to the Samoan question did not appear to be fully realised in England. Bülow despatched an emotional telegram to his master. President McKinley had accepted the proposal of a High Commissioner, while no reply had come from London. England, he believed, was the driving force in the recent explosion, America the tool. " Apparently the English wish to use the Americans to elbow us out of Samoa." He had instructed Hatzfeldt to explain that the friendly attitude of Germany in all questions since the preceding summer could not continue, in view of the disappointment and excitement of German opinion, unless more consideration was immediately shown. England, he recommended, should be asked for a categorical declaration that she would only introduce changes in Samoa with the assent of Germany. " If she breaks her agreement with Germany, your Majesty cannot reply to this act of illegality and direct discourtesy by a declaration of war, but would withdraw your representative." It was a fresh proof, he concluded, that oversea policy was only practicable with a sufficient fleet, a sentiment which evoked the Imperial comment : As I have been preaching to the asses in the Reichstag for ten years !

Bülow made no secret of his exasperation. Recent events in Samoa, he complained to Lascelles, constituted a very serious threat to the good relations so lately established. Many Germans, especially among the Colonial party, were opposed to his policy of a good understanding. The strong feeling about Samoa was perhaps exaggerated, but it could not be ignored. Salisbury replied that an impression existed in England that Germany had been trying to force America and England out of Samoa. For the moment the tension was relieved when he consented to the German demand for unanimity among the three Commissioners, instead of decisions by majority as he preferred. His earlier sympathy for Germany,

wrote Hatzfeldt to Holstein, had veered to its opposite, chiefly
on personal grounds ; and Fashoda had increased the arrogance of England to a point at which she believed that she was
invulnerable and could do whatever she wished.   Washington,
however, was tired of the controversy.   Rhodes, fulfilling his
promise to the Kaiser, attempted to pour oil on the troubled
waters ; and Chamberlain, with South Africa on his hands,
stood for conciliation.   The Commission took over the
Government in April, disarmed the inhabitants, and withdrew
two months later after completing its work.

Bülow's anger continued to smoulder.   The Samoa question, he wrote to Hatzfeldt, meant much less to England than
to Germany.   The former possessed good harbours in the
neighbouring Fiji, while for the latter the name Samoa denoted
the starting-point of her colonial efforts.   Yet instead of
consideration, England had hitherto displayed open hostility.
Fortunately Chamberlain and Balfour were more reasonable.
In a temperamental letter to his grandmother the Kaiser
complained bitterly of " the most unhappy way in which Lord
Salisbury has treated Germany in the Samoa business. . . .
There is no man more deeply grieved and unhappy than I am.
And all that on account of a stupid island which is a hairpin
to England compared to the thousands of square miles she is
annexing right and left every year unopposed. . . . The Government of Lord Salisbury must learn to respect and to treat us as
equals."   The angry Queen referred this outburst to Salisbury,
who replied that the Emperor had had his way in everything
and that he failed to understand the complaint.   He also told
Hatzfeldt that he would be happy to remove misunderstandings
when the Emperor visited England, since nothing was further
from his intention than to pursue a policy hostile to Germany's
legitimate interests.   Bülow welcomed the polite message as a
triumph for his master.   Salisbury's acceptance of the King of
Sweden as arbitrator in regard to compensation for damage
in Samoa confirmed the good impression, and the Kaiser
telegraphed to the Queen that he hoped to pay her a visit in the
autumn.

The Samoa problem, telegraphed Bülow to Hatzfeldt, would
have to be satisfactorily solved before the proposed visit could
be made.   The best solution would be the partition of the
islands, England to have Savaii and the Tonga group.   If
Salisbury rejected such a deal, the cession of British New
Guinea or the Solomon Islands might be proposed.   Salisbury

declined the plan of Upolu for Germany and Savaii for England, but approved the Ambassador's proposal to submit the fate of the two islands to an arbitrator. The Kaiser was willing to accept arbitration only if the party to which Savaii was assigned were also to receive the Tonga group and Savage Island. At their next meeting the Prime Minister, without rejecting the idea of arbitration, suggested money compensation to whichever party obtained Savaii; and a lengthy despatch shows that he was convinced by the argument of the Commission that the system of joint rule must end. "Samoa and the Transvaal", he wrote to Chamberlain on September 18, "are not wholly disconnected at least in the mind of the German Emperor."[1] German policy since Bismarck, replied the Colonial Secretary, had always been one of undisguised blackmail. He expected that the opportunity would be seized to press Samoa. He was bound to remember colonial feeling. "But I have also to consider the general policy of the Government, and I cannot doubt that at the present time the Transvaal question is of much greater importance to us than any other. . . . If therefore you think it necessary or desirable to pay the price for the Emperor's support—or neutrality—I shall make no objection on my own account, and we must face the colonial indignation as best we can." Chamberlain's mind was moving precisely as Berlin anticipated, and the conversion of Downing Street was effected, not by the arguments of the Wilhelmstrasse, but by the belligerence of the Boers.

At this point Eckardstein saw Chamberlain, and explained that intransigence in Samoa would compel a new orientation of German policy. The Colonial Secretary bitterly accused Germany of trying to make capital out of England's growing embarrassments in South Africa, but he added that he realised that good relations with Germany were more important than Samoa. England, he suggested, should have Upolu, the chief Samoan island, and Germany should have concessions in West Africa. Bülow repudiated the idea of using the South African crisis as a means of pressure, since he had put forward no fresh demands, though he hinted that the visit of the Kaiser could only be of use after Samoa was out of the way. Salisbury accepted the King of Sweden as arbitrator on the possession of Upolu and Savaii, and Hatzfeldt reported that he had at last become more pliable. Bülow's hopes rested in

[1] Garvin, III, 334-5.

P

South Africa, for if the crisis blew over England, he believed, would make no concessions in Samoa or anywhere else. Eckardstein and Chamberlain met frequently and strove hard for a settlement, but Hatzfeldt and Salisbury, in Eckardstein's phrase, were still playing hide and seek. Both sides were waiting to see which way the South African cat was going to jump.

Despite the shadow of war Salisbury seemed to Hatzfeldt on October 6 to have fallen back into his old obstructive ways. He raised difficulties, complaining that Germany asked too much and that he must have about a fortnight to consider the latest suggestions. The Prime Minister was equally dissatisfied with the interview. The Ambassador, he reported, had urged his views with extraordinary vehemence, plainly hinting that the friendship of Germany was at stake ; and it was not Salisbury's way to be intimidated by threats. On October 8 Bülow spoke to Lascelles with great earnestness. Samoa was the only question which separated the two countries, and a settlement, after coming within sight, was again postponed. Neither side was in a yielding mood. When Chamberlain asked Eckardstein if the German Government could not give some sign of sympathy with England as a means of reassuring public opinion, Bülow replied that its attitude in the South African crisis was strictly neutral and absolutely loyal. Compared with that of the French and the Russians it might even be described as friendly. After the Samoan troubles in the spring it was extremely difficult to take up such an attitude, and it was impossible to go further till a satisfactory settlement of the Samoan question had been reached. Salisbury's latest conversation with Hatzfeldt was so discouraging that the invitation to represent British interests in the Transvaal in the event of war was declined.

At this moment Kruger's ultimatum cleared the air. In conversations with Eckardstein Chamberlain, who now virtually took command, sketched out two alternatives—Germany to be bought out by concessions in other Pacific islands and in West Africa, or England to leave Samoa in return for a price. Eckardstein carried the alternatives to Berlin, where opinion was divided. The former was, materially speaking, the better offer, and Bülow was ready to accept it. But the Kaiser and Tirpitz, dreaming of a German fleet, were against him. German opinion, wired Bülow to Hatzfeldt, would be deeply stirred by the surrender of the islands, and equivalent compensations would be of no avail. The acceptance of the British offer to leave Samoa brought the end within sight, and after some haggling about the compensation, which included the Tonga and the Solomon Islands, the agreement was signed on November 14. Germany obtained Upolu and Savaii, while Tutuila fell to the United States.

It was a bitter pill for Salisbury and Chamberlain to swallow, and nothing but the outbreak of war could have overcome their resistance. Though Bülow owed his victory to the Boers, it was hailed as a personal triumph. " You are a real magician", wired the Kaiser, " granted to me quite undeservedly by Heaven in its goodness."[1] Bülow and Harzfeldt sent Chamberlain through Eckardstein a warm message of gratitude for his help, without which the settlement would have been impossible ; and the Foreign Minister looked forward to the pleasure of making the Colonial Secretary's acquaintance on the forthcoming visit of his master to England. Chamberlain replied that he hoped the agreement would do much to unite the two countries in closer bonds of friendship. It had been a sharp tussle, but it had ended without bitterness ; for it is the recognised practice to take advantage of the luck of the deal. Chamberlain liked being squeezed as little as his chief ; but the Samoan controversy left his desire for a working partnership with Germany unimpaired. Bülow could congratulate himself on his good fortune, if not on his skill. As he looked round Europe and the world at the end of 1899, he had no reason to be dissatisfied with the situation of his country or with his own commanding position in the state. When the Reichstag approved the purchase of the Caroline Islands from Spain, he was rewarded with the title of Count in gratitude for adding a jewel to his master's crown.

V

The relations of the Transvaal Government to the Outlanders digging for gold had grown steadily worse since the Raid, and in the spring of 1899 war was in the air. The sympathies of Germany and Holland were with the little Boer Republic, but both Governments worked for a compromise. Realising that the Kruger telegram was a costly blunder, Bülow did his best to sponge the slate. On the eve of the

[1] Bülow, *Erinnerungen*, I, 283.

Bloemfontein Conference he counselled the Dutch Government to advise Kruger to avoid intransigence, since the issue of a conflict was not in doubt.[1] Kruger replied that, while ready for far-reaching concessions on the franchise, he was prepared to fight for his independence. Salisbury was informed of the *démarche* and expressed his thanks. Three months later, when the sky was darker still, Bülow sent a second and almost identical warning through the same channel. Neither Germany nor any other Great Power, he explained, could help. " For our part, with sincere sympathy for the Boers, we should wish to prevent Kruger playing into the hands of the war party, and driving towards a conflict which could only end in one way." A fortnight later he despatched a third warning to Pretoria. Salisbury, he reported on Hatzfeldt's authority, desired to avoid war ; but war was inevitable if Kruger insisted on the abandonment of suzerainty.

At home the press was urged to moderation on the ground that, as the other Powers did not dream of quarrelling with England about South Africa, Germany could not expose herself alone. On the other hand, while Germany must not appear to be exploitingEngland's difficulties, a skilful diplomacy should be able to secure a satisfactory settlement of pending questions, above all Samoa. That England was beginning to realise the value of Germany's good will appeared in a warm letter of the Queen to her grandson, expressing a wish that the Empress and Bülow should accompany the Kaiser on his visit. Since Kruger had ignored Germany's advice, her course was clear. When war broke out on October 9, Dr. Leyds planned a visit to Berlin, but was told that the Foreign Minister would be unable to receive him. From this attitude of cool neutrality Bülow never swerved. It was obvious that far more advantage could be obtained by friendly relations with England than by championing a hopeless cause. What chance had the Boers against the British Empire ? And what could a Power without a fleet do against the mistress of the seas ? Sentiment, and if necessary popularity, had to yield to common sense.

" The mere fact that the Emperor comes to England is a great event", telegraphed Bülow to Hatzfeldt on the eve of the journey ; " it suffices for the time to render any anti-English coalition impossible." He was not exaggerating, for the abandonment of the Boers, so deeply resented by the German people, was thus proclaimed to the world. Since the Kruger

[1] G.P. XV, ch. 101.

telegram the Kaiser had not crossed the Channel. Now, four years later, with a formidable war on their hands, the hosts were eager for the guest. Nobody in England was afraid that the Boers would win ; but the hostility of France and Russia was notorious, and Bismarck was not the only statesman to suffer from the nightmare of coalitions. The visit passed off to the entire satisfaction of both parties. The troublesome Samoa dispute was out of the way, and the British people gratefully welcomed its distinguished guests at a moment when the rest of the world was frowning on its deeds. The Queen and the Prince of Wales spoke with warmth on the need of friendly co-operation. Salisbury lost his wife on the day the Kaiser landed, but the British Government was amicably represented by Chamberlain and Balfour. When the former reiterated his desire for a general understanding with Germany and America, the Kaiser cautiously replied that it presented certain difficulties. The tradition of England was against formal alliances, and Germany's excellent relations with Russia imposed limits on her action. The wisest plan was to pursue the policy of special agreements.

Bülow, who knew little of England, received an authoritative exposition of her policy. All parties, declared Balfour, desired co-operation with Germany and, if possible, with America as well. Germany's wishes as regards England, replied the Foreign Minister, were rather negative than positive. She wanted and asked nothing, desiring only that there should be neither misunderstandings nor friction nor provocation. Balfour accepted the programme as his own. There was no envy of Germany's economic advance, for England was rich and energetic. In the economic field she stood closer to Germany than to France and Russia. He would not object to German contractors building the Anatolian railway, for England did not dream of obstructing Germany in Asia Minor. When he complained that the German press was much more hostile than the English, Bülow replied that the *Times* correspondent in Berlin was the greatest mischief-maker of all.

Far more important was the conversation with the Colonial Secretary, who reiterated his conviction that the two countries must sooner or later reach a general understanding. England needed Germany, and Germany might one day need England. That was not the case at present, replied Bülow. Germany and Russia were on very good terms. France was no longer

thinking of the *Revanche*, and Fashoda was a more recent
memory than Sedan.   The peace of Germany did not seem to
be menaced, whereas England's vast empire exposed her to
danger at more than one point.   Russian influence in China,
Chamberlain continued, was growing rapidly, and England
needed German and American support to withstand it.   She
wanted nothing more in Asia than she possessed, but she
would not consent to be driven out of China and Persia by
Russia.   It was her interest to keep China, Persia and Turkey
intact as long as possible.   Germany's commercial aspirations
in Asia Minor would not be thwarted if she would display
friendliness at other points.   Co-operation with America was
a cardinal principle of his policy.   France was on the decline,
and it was impossible to do business with her.   Complaints on
both sides of the attitude of the press followed, and Chamberlain showed displeasure at the proposed strengthening of the
German fleet.   Salisbury did not desire an alliance with Germany or any other Power, as he did not wish to tie his hands.
Balfour, on the other hand, leaned to a general understanding
with Berlin.   In a second conversation with the Kaiser
Chamberlain went a little further.   He expressed a wish that
English capitalists should share in the Anatolian railway, as he
would prefer the German to the French and Russians
in Asia Minor.   England, he added, wished for Tangier, while
Germany could find compensation on the Atlantic coast.

Bülow was impressed with his visit and his hosts.   " The
country breathes wealth, comfort and contentment, confidence
in its powers and its future. . . . It is physically and morally
sound. . . . Beyond doubt opinion in England is far less anti-
German than opinion in Germany is anti-English.   So those
Englishmen are the most dangerous for us who, like Chirol and
Saunders, know from personal observation the sharpness and
depth of German dislike of England.   If the English public
realised the present feeling, it would seriously alter its views of
England's relation to Germany.   Possessing a strong fleet and
keeping on good terms with Russia and England, German
policy should await the inevitable developments with patience
and self-control."   The warmth of the welcome and the eagerness of Chamberlain had not modified the attitude of the
Foreign Minister in the slightest degree.   Relations had
improved under the impact of the South African war, and the
anticipated clash with Russia would make them better still.
Time, he was convinced, was on the German side.   Describing

the visit in his Memoirs, Bülow recalls an impressive conversation with Hatzfeldt.[1] The experienced Ambassador warned
him to be careful with Chamberlain, who, in his desire to win
the South African war, naturally wished to make Germany a
buffer against Russia and France. "We cannot blame him,
but we must not let ourselves be pushed beyond a certain line,
for, after all, Russia is nearer to Berlin than England." Hatzfeldt, adds Bülow, was no enemy of an Anglo-German alliance.
If his chief could secure it on an acceptable basis, he remarked
with a smile, he would congratulate him, for Bismarck himself
had failed. Regarding a treaty with firm guarantees and equal
obligations as unprocurable, he advocated a policy of friendliness without entanglements. Bülow adds that this attitude
was shared not only by his master and himself, but by Hohenlohe, Holstein, Richthofen and all the higher officials of the
Wilhelmstrasse. Moreover could Edward VII, who loved the
French and hated his nephew, have been trusted to play the
game?

The *détente* was dramatically announced by Chamberlain
at Leicester on November 30, when he spoke of "a new triple
alliance" or understanding between England, Germany and
the United States. The Colonial Secretary believed himself
to be making a declaration authorised by Bülow, who, he
wrote to Eckardstein, had greatly impressed him. "He
expressed a wish that I might be able at some time to say
something as to the mutual interests which bound the United
States to a triple understanding with Germany as well as Great
Britain. Hence my speech yesterday which I hope will be not
unsatisfactory to him." The comments of the press, not only
in Germany and the United States but also at home, furnished
instantaneous proof that he had gone too far. The German
and American peoples desired friendly and if possible cordial
relations with England, but they desired nothing more. A
single incautious word had undone much of the benefit of the
Windsor visit, and Bülow's response turned the defeat into a
rout. In the first great speech of his life, while commending
the Second Navy Bill to the Reichstag, he reviewed the relations
of Germany with the world.[2] Quoting Salisbury's memorable
observation that the strong states were growing stronger and
the weak ones becoming weaker, he declared that Germany
could not and would not stand aside while others were cutting
up the cake. While the English spoke of Greater Britain and

---

[1] *Denkwürdigkeiten*, I, ch. 20.   [2] *Reden*, I, 88–97, December 11.

the French of Nouvelle France, and the Russians were opening
up Asia, Germans had a claim to a Greater Germany, not in the
sense of conquest but by the peaceful extension of her trade
and its bases.

After friendly references to France, Russia, and the United
States the Foreign Minister came to the most important part of
his speech. " As regards England, we are ready to live with
her in peace and harmony on the basis of full reciprocity and
mutual consideration. But just because our international
position is now favourable, we must utilise it to secure ourselves for the future." They all hoped that the future would
be peaceful, but nobody could be sure. New questions
arose which might subside as quickly as they came, but they
might also become acute. " We must be secured against
surprises on the sea as well as on land. We must have a
fleet strong enough to prevent the attack of any Power—I
emphasise the word attack, for with the absolutely pacific
character of our policy it could only be for defence." In the
pursuit of her oversea interests, however, Germany must not
forget that her centre was in Europe, where her security was
based on the Triple Alliance and good relations with Russia.
She was exposed to plenty of envy, both political and economic.
There were individuals and groups and perhaps peoples who
preferred the days when, despite her culture, she was looked
down upon. " These times of political impotence and of
economic and political humility must not return. To use the
words of Friedrich List, we will not be the serfs of humanity.
But we shall only remain on the heights if we realise that without power, without a strong army and a strong fleet, there is
no salvation. . . . In the coming century the German people
will be hammer or anvil."

Instead of applauding and echoing Chamberlain's desire for
a triple partnership, Bülow made no reference to the speech
which had echoed round the world. Moreover his emphasis
on the solidity of the Triple Alliance, the friendship of Russia,
and the need for a large fleet indicated a standpoint in which
co-operation with England played no part. Chamberlain's
suggestion of an alliance had overshot the mark, especially at a
time when German detestation of British policy in South
Africa was at its height, and Bülow had said nothing at Windsor to encourage such a plan. He might, however, have
welcomed the spirit of a declaration which he had partially
inspired and have found warmer words for the nation whose

honoured guest he had so lately been.   The Colonial Secretary
was humiliated, incensed and distressed.   " I will say no more
about the way in which I have been treated by Bülow", he
wrote to Eckardstein, who tried to explain away the Reichstag
utterance.[1]   Further negotiations on the alliance question, he
added, must be dropped.   All had been going so well, and
Salisbury was in agreement as to the future of Anglo-German
relations.   Bülow never quite lived down the impression that
the *charmeur* was not a man of his word.   He was not responsible for the Boer war, which for the time prevented the
working partnership of which Chamberlain dreamed, and he
was right in keeping the wires to St. Petersburg in good
repair.   But it was a costly error not to nourish the tender
plant of Anglo-German understanding sown at Windsor.

In the closing week of 1899 the *Bundesrath*, a German mail
steamer, was held up outside Delagoa Bay and taken as prize to
Durban, though no contraband was on board.[2]   The Foreign
Minister naturally asked for immediate release, but Salisbury,
while promising inquiry as quickly as possible, declared that a
definite answer might not be ready for some time.   At this
moment a second German ship was held up and examined.
Immediate release was demanded, and Bülow described to
Hatzfeldt the anger of the German people.   " I cannot conceal
from your Excellency that the brutal conduct of the English
commanders against the two steamers, and even more the
slackness with which the Government has treated our representations, has produced the worst possible impression and
forced us to the conviction that Lord Salisbury fails to realise
the importance of the matter."   Hatzfeldt was instructed to
point out that such a question of slight material importance
might prove more inflammable than many weightier matters.
" We shall treat questions of honour as vital questions.   If our
relation of benevolent neutrality involves public submission to
illegal and inconsiderate action it cannot continue, and we must
look for another combination which it would be easy to find."
Before Salisbury was ready with a reply, a third steamer was
seized.   Bülow now asked for arbitration or a mixed commission.   Salisbury informed Hatzfeldt that one of the ships was
already released and another would follow, but he heard that
contraband had been found on the *Bundesrath*.

The Foreign Minister postponed the inevitable debate in the
Reichstag for a day or two, and on January 10, 1900, Salisbury

[1] Eckardstein, II, 125.   [2] *G.P.* XV, ch. 102.

promised to do his best to avert the repetition of such incidents. He blamed the excessive zeal of young commanders and the failure of the Durban authorities, despite his urgent orders, to report on the cargo of the *Bundesrath*. Three days later Bülow was informed by Lascelles that the ships could not be released without examination by a Prize Court. The Wilhelmstrasse was exasperated, and Eckardstein received an alarming telegram that the Kaiser was considering the despatch of an envoy. The crisis ended with the news that no contraband was found on the *Bundesrath* and that compensation would be paid ; and a promise was given that within a certain radius no more ships should be seized. Salisbury expressed his gratitude for Bülow's willingness to compromise and the great importance he attached to Germany's friendship. " Our people have committed a stupid blunder", remarked Devonshire to Eckardstein. The anger of Germany at the seizure of her innocent vessels was understood a few years later when British merchantmen were held up by Russia in the Japanese war.

The storm passed, but the sunshine of Windsor had disappeared. Metternich, who arrived in London to represent the ailing Hatzfeldt, reported a long conversation with Chamberlain on March 18. After the Leicester speech, complained the latter, Bülow had given him the cold shoulder. Metternich tried to explain the Reichstag declarations, and quoted some recent words of his chief about the Colonial Secretary : " Like all big men he is ahead of his time. What is not yet may yet be." Passing to the recent crisis Chamberlain said that he had only learned from the Blue Book of the sharp notes that had been exchanged. He had been bombarded by Salisbury with appeals for rapid action, and he had done his utmost. The peremptory tone of the German notes was very wounding, and it was a mistake of Salisbury to publish them. Despite his annoyance, continued Metternich, he still regarded the Emperor and Bülow as friends. In commenting on the report, Bülow expressed his regretful surprise at the publication of the Blue Book, which could only serve to excite British opinion. Thus a further portion of the ground gained at Windsor was lost, and the threatening tone of the Wilhelmstrasse was attributed to British embarrassments in South Africa, then at their height.

Though the initiation of the *Flottenpolitik* was due to William II and its execution was entrusted to Tirpitz, it impinged on the sphere of foreign policy at many points. In accepting office Bülow was well aware that one of his main duties would be to foster the project his master had at heart. The task had no terrors for him. He was genuinely convinced that the growth of German commerce and oversea possessions required a navy to defend them. Moreover the importance of sea-power as a factor in national strength had been recently illustrated in the Spanish-American war, emphasised in the writings of Mahan, and brought home to the German people by the seizure of the *Bundesrath*. To play her full part in the life of the world, to increase the value of her good will, to heighten the disadvantage of her enmity, a powerful fleet seemed essential for Germany. Diplomacy without armaments, declared Frederick the Great, was like music without instruments. *Weltpolitik* was the order of the day, and a fleet was regarded by all the Great Powers as one of the major conditions of success in that perilous game. Germany had as much right to build ships as anyone else. An invincible army had sufficed for Bismarck, with his maxim of limited liability. It was not enough for his successors, for whom Europe had become too narrow a stage.

In commending the Second Navy Bill to the Reichstag Bülow argued that the world had rapidly changed in the last few years.[1] In England the age of Gladstone was over and the age of Imperialism had begun. German foreign policy aimed both at the maintenance of peace and the dignity of the Empire. Diplomatic skill must be supplemented by material strength. The weakness of one Power was a temptation to others to impose humiliations which the German people could not accept. Official relations with other countries were excellent. But popular passions counted for more and more, and material means for the safeguarding of peace must be available. This cautious and conventional utterance para-phrased the celebrated Preamble to the Bill, which announced that Germany must possess so strong a fleet that war, even for her most powerful opponent, would involve too great a risk. The Bill which became law on June 12, 1900, contemplated the construction of thirty-four battleships in sixteen years.

The argument that Germany must follow the example of other Great Powers seemed unanswerable, but it clearly involved a risk of trouble with England. Unlike Holstein, Bülow was undismayed, for he trusted in his own skill. He was convinced that a conflict would never come :

[1] *Reden*, I, 118–20.

i. " If we built a fleet which could not be attacked without very grave risk to the attacking party.

ii. If we did not, beyond that, indulge in undue and unlimited shipbuilding and armaments, and did not overheat our maritime boiler.

iii. If we allowed no Power to injure our reputation or our dignity.

iv. If we allowed nothing to make an irremediable breach between us and England.

v. If we kept calm and cool, and neither injured England nor ran after her."[1]

Bülow's task, as the Kaiser and Tirpitz used to tell him, was to steer his country through the danger zone. While the fleet was building and before it was strong enough to defend itself, there was the possibility that a certain Power might attack. When the Chancellor inquired at what stage the danger of an unprovoked attack would pass away, Tirpitz replied that the most critical time would be about 1904 or 1905.[2] The fleet would then be so strong as to evoke jealousy and alarm. After that period Germany would gradually emerge from the danger-zone, for the English would realise that an attack would involve too grave a risk. To understand Bülow's policy in the early years of his rule we must bear in mind the double obligation imposed by the *Flottenpolitik*— on the one hand to avoid war with England at almost any price, and on the other to prevent any arrangement, however superficially attractive, which would fetter the development of naval power. For the Kaiser, however changeable in his moods, never varied in his determination to go down to history as the creator of a mighty fleet.

From the beginning of the South African conflict Bülow and his master were resolved not to burn their fingers. When the French Ambassador informally suggested a common front against British expansion, William II replied that he could not abandon neutrality since he possessed no fleet.[3] His Foreign Minister was equally cautious. When the Russian Ambassador inquired as to Germany's attitude towards a joint protest in the event of England seizing Delagoa Bay, Bülow replied by asking what France would do, explaining that while England could inflict little damage on Russia, she could gravely injure

---

[1] Bülow, *Imperial Germany*, 46-7. [2] *Denkwürdigkeiten*, I, 412-3.
[3] *G.P.* XV, 406-8.

Germany, who possessed an extensive trade and an inadequate fleet. Osten-Sacken retorted that Russia could not allow a British occupation of Delagoa Bay and the complete strangulation of the Boers, and suggested the despatch of French, Russian and German ships to the bay. On the following day the Ambassador asked the Kaiser his view of the English fleet, quoting Admiral Makaroff's opinion that it was as inefficient as the army, and adding that three smaller fleets could deal with it. In view of England's aggressiveness and universal unpopularity, could not a coalition be formed? The Kaiser replied that he could not join it, and that he would only abandon his neutral attitude if driven to it by intolerable provocation. The situation in Persia, continued Osten-Sacken, was becoming more complicated, and Russia might be compelled to intervene in the interest of peace in Asia. In the event of her being seriously involved, could she be certain that Germany would not attack her flank? The friendly relations of the rulers and the peoples, replied the Kaiser, excluded such a possibility. To the question what Germany would do if England occupied Delagoa Bay, the Kaiser replied that he had not considered the matter. It was a searching interrogatory, and according to Bülow's report his master was a model of reserve. The Russian Ambassador's report on the other hand quotes the Kaiser as saying that Russia alone could deal England a mortal blow, and that if ever the Tsar attacked India he would mount guard over his European frontiers.[1]

Whatever temperamental indiscretions William II may have permitted himself in conversation with Osten-Sacken, Bülow's neutrality never varied. " The German policy towards England", he wired to Eckardstein on February 7, 1900, " is so loyal that only utter prejudice and injustice could misinterpret it." On March 3 the Russian Ambassador officially proposed the mediation which he had discussed academically on January 13. France, Germany and Russia should engage in friendly pressure to end the war and prevent the annihilation of the Dutch Republics. Bülow replied that it was for the Tsar to take the initiative. Germany must avoid all danger of complications with other Great Powers, particularly Naval Powers, so long as she was not sure of the attitude of France. A mutual guarantee of their European possessions for a long term of years would be essential before she could consider the

[1] Lee, *King Edward VII*, I, 761-7.

proposal. On receiving this reply Muraviev explained that Russia's motives were purely humanitarian, and that her material interests in Africa were too small even to sound the British Government alone. Such a step would be best taken by the three Powers. " As regards a mutual guarantee of possessions, the long negotiations involved would destroy the purpose of the rapid termination of the war." The Kaiser informed the Prince of Wales of the Russian *démarche*, and received his cordial thanks. " You have no idea, my dear William, how all of us in England appreciate the loyal friendship which you manifest towards us on every possible occasion."

The request of the Boer Republics for the friendly mediation of the Powers with a view to the restoration of peace evoked the reply that Germany would co-operate when both sides desired it. The Kaiser informed the Queen and the Prince of Wales, who responded in grateful telegrams, and even Salisbury was appreciative. A few days later the Queen of Holland urged the Kaiser to take the lead in a joint representation to England, adding that she was sure that Russia and France would co-operate. The Kaiser replied that the South African Republics were not worth a war, and that France and Russia were as indisposed to fight as Germany. On hearing from London that it was believed in Paris that Germany was urging France and Russia to intervene, while making exorbitant demands for herself, Bülow wired to Metternich that it was a lie. On the contrary more than once suggestions had been made from various quarters to secure German aid in creating an anti-English Continental group. How correct were the rulers of Germany was shown in the summer when the Kaiser declined to receive the Boer deputation which travelled to Berlin ; and when Kruger fled from South Africa in the autumn he was warned off Berlin. The unpopular decision was defended by Bülow in the Reichstag on the ground that the interests of Germany demanded a cool neutrality. " We are not called upon to play the part of Don Quixote and to tilt at English windmills everywhere in the world."[1] At this period he was informed by the police that an attempt might be made on his life by some fanatical champion of the Boers.[2] Fortunately he had good nerves. He disapproved his master's action in conferring the order of the Black Eagle on Lord Roberts, the conqueror of the Boers, which was decided without seeking his advice. He never pretended to

[1] *Reden*, I, 168, December 10, 1900. [2] *Denkwürdigkeiten*, I, 473.

approve the action of England, but he saw no reason to put spokes in her wheel.

The correctitude of the Wilhelmstrasse in regard to South Africa facilitated co-operation with England in the Far East. The suppression of the Boxer revolt by international action left a number of delicate questions behind. When the seizure of Port Arthur proclaimed Russia's domination of Northern China, England began to regard the Yangtze valley as her peculiar sphere. Her attitude aroused the suspicions of France, Russia and Germany, and on June 30, 1900, Bülow advised his master to approve its neutralisation.[1] The Kaiser discussed the matter with the Prince of Wales and Lascelles at Wilhelmshöhe, and explained that Germany desired commercial equality for all on the Yangtze. Salisbury had no objection, since England stood for the open door ; but he proposed to extend the arrangement beyond the Yangtze to include " the ports of the rivers and littoral of China." Hatzfeldt pointed out that such an extension would annoy Russia, who would object either to commercial freedom in Manchuria or to evacuating the province. Salisbury retorted that he had no intention of infringing Russian interests, which were in the the interior of Manchuria. Agreement on a draft treaty proved difficult to secure, for British hostility to Russia was not shared at Berlin.

The treaty signed by Salisbury and Hatzfeldt on October 19, 1900, embodied a compromise in the first clause. " It is a matter of joint and permanent international interest that the ports on the rivers and littoral of China should remain free and open to trade and to every other legitimate form of economic activity for the nationals of all countries without distinction, and the two Governments agree on their part to uphold the same for all Chinese territory as far as they exercise influence." The signatories declared for the territorial integrity of China, and agreed to discuss action for the protection of their interests if a third Power were to obtain territorial advantages. Eckardstein reported that, while welcoming co-operation in China, some of the British Ministers feared that Germany would refuse to stand up to Russia. The forecast was quickly fulfilled, for a Russian concession in Tientsin, on which it was feared fortifications might be erected, filled the British Government with suspicion. Berlin was sounded as to a joint inquiry at St. Petersburg, but preferred to make friendly

[1] G.P. XVI, ch. 105.

inquiries of her own, and learned from Lansdowne that British anxieties were unfounded.

A larger issue arose with the announcement in Bülow's speech of March 15, 1901, that the Yangtze treaty did not extend to Manchuria and that Germany had no essential interest in that province. The declaration was provoked by the development of events since the Boxer rebellion.[1] When the rising spread to Manchuria, Russia occupied parts of the country, declaring that she would withdraw when order was restored ; but her increasing indisposition to co-operate with the Powers created the suspicion that she had made a secret treaty with China amounting to a Russian Protectorate in Manchuria. In January 1901 the *Times* published details of a pact infringing the Yangtze treaty to which Russia had conditionally adhered, and confirmation arrived from the Far East. Germany was not much interested, since the Yangtze treaty, she believed, had no concern with Manchuria, and Lamsdorff was informed that German interests would be unaffected if Russia were to occupy Manchuria, or to proclaim a Protectorate.

Lansdowne sent for Eckardstein to tell him that the Russo-Chinese agreement concerning Manchuria concluded with the Chinese General commanding in Manchuria was about to be ratified. Would Germany join England in supporting Japan in a protest at Pekin against the ever-extending Russian encroachments ? Bülow was ready to tell China that, in the opinion of Germany, she should not at present make treaties concerning territory or finance with any Powers. Lansdowne was delighted. Japan, however, wanted more, and at her request England added that " in the opinion of H.M. Government any such agreement as that reported to have been concluded with regard to Manchuria would be a source of danger to the Chinese Government." Germany, on the other hand, was determined to avoid antagonising Russia, and was careful not to associate herself with Japan, whose ambitions in Korea were no secret. It seemed less dangerous to repudiate the British interpretation of the Yangtze treaty than to lose touch with the Tsar.

VI

Despite Bülow's chilly response to Chamberlain's overtures in 1898 and 1899, the Colonial Secretary made a further attempt

[1] *G.P.* XVI, ch. 106.

at the opening of 1901 to reach a firm understanding with Berlin.[1] During a visit to Chatsworth he assured Eckardstein that the time for isolation was over; that England desired to settle all pending questions, especially Morocco and the Far East, in co-operation with the Triple or the Dual Alliance, preferably the former; and that failing the Triple Alliance she would turn to France and Russia. Bülow's attitude remained unchanged. The initiative, he telegraphed to Hatzfeldt, must be left to England. He had no fear of a pact between England and the Dual Alliance. Germany and England might conceivably co-operate one day in defence of their vital interests, but this was not the time.

This attitude of reserve was impressed by the new Chancellor on his master when he hurried to the deathbed of Queen Victoria. England had been moving away from isolation and towards Germany since 1898. She must not be repulsed, but a premature arrangement must be avoided. "English embarrassments will grow in the coming months, and therewith our price will rise." Germany must play for time. "It would be a masterstroke if Your Majesty succeeded in leaving the English their hope of future intimacy without prematurely binding ourselves. The threatened rapprochement with the Dual Alliance is only a nightmare invented to frighten us." His Majesty should be careful not to suggest that Russo-German relations were in any way strained. Bülow's advice to his master to make himself agreeable and keep his hands free seems to have been loyally obeyed. It was a private, not a political visit, explained the Chancellor to the Reichstag.[2] If such human feelings fostered friendly relations between the countries, so much the better. "Of course full and lasting equality of status between the German and the English people is the condition of all co-operation." There were many points of friction, but also many points of contact. The change of ruler had made no difference. "To-day, as before", he concluded, "our foreign policy is determined neither by love nor hate, neither by dynastic considerations nor by family ties, but solely by coolly-weighed interests of state." Like his master, he followed a national policy defined as follows: "Good and friendly relations to all Powers which desire to live with us in peace and friendship, but full preservation of our political and economic self-sufficiency and independence, to which the German people,

[1] G.P. XVII, ch. 109, and B.D. II, ch. 10.   [2] Reden, I, 185–90, March 5, 1901.

Q

by its struggles, its work and its cultural triumphs, possesses an unalienable right."

When Eckardstein reported a proposal by Lansdowne for a defensive arrangement in the middle of March, Bülow replied that Germany welcomed the suggestion but must consult her allies.[1] England might approach Austria direct, and, if Goluchowski approved, Germany would be ready for negotiations. His instructions to Hatzfeldt included the association of England with the Triple Alliance—the *casus foederis* to arise if either were at war with two enemies—and the sanction of Parliament. The negotiations were rather unreal, since the proposal, according to Lansdowne, came from Eckardstein, not from himself. Accepting Eckardstein's version, however, as he did, Bülow was never for a moment tempted by the bait. As he saw it, the problem was simple enough. Germany was on good terms with Russia, and England was not. An Anglo-Russian war seemed extremely probable. Why should Germany be dragged in ? To the end of his days he contended that the only possible reply to a British offer, official or unofficial, was to spread the risk by inviting England into the Triple Alliance. If she came in, well and good. If she declined, Germany and her allies could stand alone.

Nobody in England desired to join the Triple Alliance, and neither side was willing to advance beyond academic discussions to the written word. There is, indeed, a certain air of mystery over the whole story. Each Government believed the other to have taken the initiative on March 15, whereas it was probably taken by neither. The absence of Imperial *marginalia* suggests that the Kaiser was unaware of some of the most important documents, and we cannot be sure that Bülow himself knew all that which passed between Holstein and Eckardstein. Holstein was mistaken in imagining Salisbury to be the mortal foe of Germany. But he was correct in believing that so long as he remained in office an alliance was impossible, and after the Premier's uncompromising Memorandum of May 29 the discussions could have but one end. When the summer holidays were over, neither party reverted to the subject. In their first and last discussion on December 19 Lansdowne and Metternich, the successor of

---

[1] On the publication of *B.D.*, vol. II, Meinecke supplemented his book by an essay, " Zur Geschichte der deutschenglischen Bündnisverhandlung von 1901," in a Festschrift for Hans Delbrück entitled *Am Webstuhl der Zeit*.

Hatzfeldt, agreed that nothing could be done. If a defensive alliance between the British Empire and the Triple Alliance were ruled out in London, no minor proposal would be considered at Berlin. The Wilhelmstrasse had never wavered in its terms. There seemed no reason why it should, for it believed that Germany held the strongest cards. France was the only enemy. Russia would only become hostile if she were actively obstructed in her expansionist ambitions or if Germany, without any compelling cause, joined hands with her traditional foe.

Bülow cannot be justly blamed for refusing an alliance never officially proposed by the British Government, and he rightly desired not to impair such confidence in Germany as Russia still entertained. The weakness of the Colossus had not yet been revealed on the Manchurian battlefields. Yet who will assert that the rulers of Germany turned the friendly sentiments of Chamberlain and Lansdowne to the best account during the anxious years when we had South Africa on our hands ? The importance of British friendship was insufficiently recognised at Berlin, and no sustained attempt to secure it was made. The Kaiser had moments of doubt, and he was not informed of all the moves in the game. Despite the frank warnings of Chamberlain, the Wilhelmstrasse airily dismissed the possibility of a British rapprochement with France or Russia and played for time, confident that England would one day find herself in urgent need of aid. The forecast proved a ruinous miscalculation, and the prophets were in large measure responsible for its failure. If they could make no direct response to Chamberlain's advances without endangering their relations with Russia, they should at least have avoided the alienation of the British Empire by their subsequent policy on sea and land. The Boer war would not last for ever. The friendship of Russia—the ally of France and the rival of Austria—was precarious. And perhaps England after all might have more than one string to her bow.

When the struggle with the Boers was drawing to a close a lively controversial exchange revealed and inflamed the hostility of the two peoples. In arguing the need of stronger measures in South Africa, Chamberlain declared that the British Government would be able to find precedents for their action in the record of the nations who were now talking of barbarism and cruelty, though they would never approach what those nations had done in Poland, in the Caucasus, in

Bosnia, in Tonkin, and in the war of 1870.[1] Metternich was
instructed to complain to Lansdowne, who replied that no
provocation had been intended in the Edinburgh speech.[2]
The insult to the German army, as it was considered to be, was
passionately resented by public opinion, and the Chancellor
was deeply annoyed. The provocation, he wrote to Metternich, was undeniable. No German Minister had spoken of
England except in a tactful way. The speech complicated the
task of the German Government, which would nevertheless
continue its policy of friendliness to England. It was in
England's own interest not to make it too difficult for Germany,
all the more since no other Power had displayed such good will
and proved of so much use during the Boer war.

In addressing the Reichstag at the opening of 1902 the
Chancellor made a stinging reply.[3] If a Minister felt compelled
to defend his policy, he would be wise to leave other countries
alone. If foreign examples were quoted, the greatest care
should be exercised. If not, there was a danger not only of
being misunderstood, but of wounding the feelings of other
people, even if unwittingly as in the present case. It was
entirely intelligible that a people identified with its glorious
army like the Germans should revolt against the attempt to
challenge the heroic character and the moral foundations of the
wars of unification. " The German army stands far too high
and its scutcheon is too clean to be affected by unjust judgments." When Frederick the Great was told that he himself
and the Prussian army had been attacked, he replied : " Leave
the man alone, and calm yourselves ; he is biting on granite."
Chamberlain retorted that he had nothing to retract or to
explain. He had not attempted to give lessons to a foreign
statesman, and he would accept none. The official controversy ceased, but it had stirred public opinion in both countries
to the depths. Henceforth Bülow was *persona ingratissima* in
England and Chamberlain in Germany.[4] The only comfort,
wrote Metternich to his chief, was that it could not get worse,
and that the extreme embitterment must be followed by exhaus-
tion and therewith improvement.

Bülow was quite impenitent as to his share in the encounter.
Chamberlain had attacked, and he had been forced to reply.
The account was now even. In a letter to Metternich two
months after his speech he noted an improvement in German

[1] October 25, 1901.   [2] *G.P.* XVII, 194.   [3] *Reden*, I, 241-2.
[4] Cp. Chirol, *Fifty Years in a Changing World*, 295-7.

feeling. Moreover, despite the sympathy with the Boers as the weaker side, Germans, unlike other great peoples, did not desire the weakening of England, which would upset the balance of power to the disadvantage of Germany. The darkest cloud in the sky was the British press, above all the Berlin correspondent of the *Times*. The Chancellor took the situation a little too calmly. When the Boer war was over Chamberlain spoke to Eckardstein in hot anger.[1] He had been mistaken in his efforts for Anglo-German co-operation and would not try again. All classes, at home and throughout the Empire, were filled with such hatred towards Germany that every Ministry would have to reckon with it. The Kaiser's coming visit to England would not alter it, for the causes of estrangement were too deep.

VII

The termination of the South African war in May 1902 stopped a running sore, and the retirement of Salisbury was welcomed in Berlin. The Kaiser discouraged a visit of the Boer generals on learning that it would be resented in England, and the prospect of co-operation in Venezuela seemed to show that the Governments at any rate were on amicable terms. At the opening of 1902, Bülow had informed his master that a pacific blockade was desirable, that the United States would not object, and that England would probably co-operate in exerting pressure.[2] Action was postponed till Prince Henry's visit to the United States was concluded and the heat of the summer was past. The omens were not very favourable, as the Kaiser discovered when he met Balfour, Lansdowne and Chamberlain at Sandringham in November.[3] In vain did he remind the latter that his Chancellor was denounced in Germany as pro-English and nicknamed Lord Bülow. The angry Colonial Minister believed himself to have been tricked, and his resentment had spread to the people. " He alone counts in England, and he has every class behind him. The Ministry dances to his tune, and does nothing important without him, still less against him. In these circumstances it is vital to hold in our press, for they will not stand much more, and in foreign policy to avoid needless friction." The welcome of King

[1] *G.P.* XVII, 221–5, September, 1902.
[2] *G.P.* XVII, ch. 112. Cp. Ilse Kunz-Lack *Die Deutsch-Amerikanischen Beziehungen*, 1890–1914, ch. 2.
[3] *G.P.* XVII, 115–7.

Edward, he continued, was as hearty as ever, but a distinction was drawn between himself and the German Government. Much patience and tact were needed, and the press must hold its tongue. " If not, very grave consequences will ensue. So caution ! They have thirty-five battleships and we have eight." Chamberlain's hostility, replied Bülow calmly, was very regrettable, but he forgot three things : Salisbury's systematic unfriendliness, the indefensible seizure of German mailships, and the Kaiser's friendly services during the South African war. The German press had recently displayed greater moderation than the English, and he would do his best to keep it in the same path. He would also strive to co-operate with England so far as this was possible without antagonising Russia.

After a joint ultimatum to Venezuela on December 7 the blockade commenced. Bülow wished the German naval force to be small, in order to counteract the legend in the British and American press that Germany was the ringleader in the business of coercion. Germany had in fact accepted the British plan of a belligerent blockade in place of her own milder proposal of a pacific blockade. In addition to the seizure of ships, three vessels were sunk by German guns in the course of joint operations. The sinking, reported Metternich, caused the press to complain that Germany had acted with needless violence, for England had no wish for drastic steps. Lansdowne feared a cooling of Anglo-American relations, foretold sharp criticism in Parliament, and proposed arbitration by the United States on the financial claims. The British Government, commented Metternich, was not strong enough to swim against the stream. Never had he known such bitterness against a foreign nation. It arose mainly from the attitude of the German people in the Boer war. " It would be useless to hold out our hand for reconciliation. It would simply be rejected." Throughout his long and honourable term of service Metternich neither concealed disagreeable facts nor failed to indicate the policy to which in his opinion they pointed. The atmosphere in Washington was equally electric. The President and himself, declared John Hay to the German Ambassador, had full confidence in Germany, and were determined not to intervene ; but a speedy settlement was highly desirable, for the public and Congress were excited.

At this moment an unfortunate incident of the blockade increased the tension on both sides of the Atlantic. A German ship was fired on from a Venezuelan fort, which in return was bombarded and destroyed.   It was in vain that the Germans argued that an English or American admiral would have acted in the same way.   The tide of feeling was running strongly against Germany, for it was instinctively felt that she was more intransigent than her British partner.   On February 11, 1903, Lansdowne warned Metternich that, if Germany was uncompromising in her demands and England was thereby compelled to continue the blockade, an outburst of feeling on both sides of the Atlantic would occur which might produce grave consequences.   Metternich fully concurred and advised his Government that intransigence would bring danger for Germany as well as for the British Government.   Agreements were signed with the three blockading Powers on February 13, and the blockade ended just in time to avert an embarrassing debate   at   Westminster.   Anglo-German   relations   were emphatically worse at the end of the partnership than at the beginning.   Moreover, opinion in the United States, where the Manila incident of 1898 was unforgotten, had shown itself suspicious, and the Ambassador reported Roosevelt's doubts as to Germany's respect for the Monroe Doctrine.   The chief result of the Venezuelan adventure was to reveal and increase Germany's unpopularity throughout the Anglo-Saxon world.

Lansdowne's friendliness and British hostility were manifested anew shortly after the liquidation of the Venezuela affair.   Though Germany had secured the concession in principle for the Baghdad railway at the end of 1899, the undertaking was so vast that it required all the help it could find.[1] England preferred German to Russian influence beyond the Bosphorus, and indeed welcomed its appearance as a makeweight against her rival's advance in Persia.   In the rivalry of the British lion and the Russian bear the Wilhelmstrasse saw an excellent chance of carrying the line to the Persian Gulf. The only danger, reported Marschall from Constantinople, threatened from Russia, who might exert pressure which the Sultan could not resist.   " Downing Street", wired Bülow to Marschall on February 12, 1900, " is glad to see us deeply involved in Asia Minor.   They hope to secure in us powerful allies against Russian expansionism.   We have no reason to destroy this hope, which perhaps opens a way without complications to Koweit."   The prospect appeared very promising, for the Turks naturally resented Russian attempts to block

[1] G.P. XVII, 114.

the development of their estate. It was finally agreed that Russia might build railways in the north of Asia Minor. She was assured that the Baghdad railway was never planned as a political undertaking, and that the co-operation of other nations placed its purely economic character beyond all doubt.

With the Irade of January 16, 1902, sanctioning a concession of ninety-nine years and a kilometric guarantee, the project entered on a new stage. The triumph was followed by a series of disappointments, for the beneficiary was left to carry the burden alone. At the opening of 1903, Gwinner, Director of the Deutsche Bank, found Lansdowne hostile, though admitting that if the line was to be built England had better co-operate. Further discussions removed his objections, but the English press exploded in anger at the rumour of an agreement. Balfour shared Lansdowne's desire for co-operation, and Metternich reported him as saying he would rather resign than refuse. But the clamour was too much for the Prime Minister. "Opinion in and out of Parliament", reported Metternich, "is against any new agreement with the German Government. There is a morbid tendency to believe that the British Government is influenced by Germany, and inclined blindly to carry out all her wishes." The only antidote was abstention. Leave the Englishman alone for the present, and he would one day wish to have his say about the shortest route to India.

Balfour's announcement on April 23 that the Government had decided against co-operation was received with unconcealed regret in Berlin. It was all the more deplorable, wrote Bülow to his master, since the British financiers and the British Government alike were in its favour, and had capitulated to the outcry of the press. Lascelles made no secret of his regret, and the Kaiser wrongly attributed the fiasco to Russian intrigues. After the German rebuff the Russian campaign pushed steadily forward, and a rival line from Van to Baghdad was discussed. "While the Russians ask for our support in their Balkan policy", commented Mühlberg, "they are doing their best to ruin the darling project of the Kaiser." In October the French Government declined official co-operation, though French capital retained its interest in the scheme. When the Emperors met at Darmstadt in November, Lamsdorff confided to Bülow that he was convinced of the purely economic character of the line, but that he was faced with an opposition of which Witte was the chief. The negotiations had not been conducted by the German Government, but their failure was none the less a blow to its prestige. The antagonism of Russia was no surprise, and France might be expected to follow in her train. But the opposition of England was a further disquieting illustration of a shift in the wind. Germany, it seemed, would have to build the Baghdad railway alone if it were to be built at all. Venezuela and Baghdad were a warning that she would have to move very carefully if the wire to London was not to be damaged beyond hope of repair.

VIII

If Bülow was largely responsible for the estrangement of England, the loosening of ties with Rome can scarcely be placed to his account. The process of disintegration began before his appointment to office when, in 1896, Italy intimated that she could not join in a war in which England and France were ranged against her allies.[1] Though Germany and Austria declined to acknowledge this unwelcome declaration, it remained on record. At the opening of the twentieth century the causes which had turned the steps of Italy in 1882 towards Berlin and Vienna had ceased to operate. When the Franco-Italian reconciliation took place after the fall of Crispi, the Triple Alliance lost its *raison d'être*. The structure remained outwardly intact, for there was no pretext for its termination. Moreover every one recognised the truth of Count Nigra's aphorism that Austria and Italy must be either allies or enemies. The Franco-Italian *détente*, however, could be neither prevented nor undone. All that the Wilhelmstrasse could do was to mediate in the recurrent friction between its partners. As Visconti Venosta observed to Bülow, Austria and Italy were two horses very apt to bite each other. It was the task of the coachman, in other words of the German Chancellor, to make them run in double harness.[2] The difficulty increased with the accession of Victor Emmanuel, whose hostility to Austria was unconcealed.

Bülow's first public comment on the new orientation was provoked by a speech of the Italian Foreign Minister on December 14, 1901. The relations between Italy and France, declared Prinetti, had become so friendly that declarations relating to their respective interests in the Mediterranean had been exchanged which revealed complete identity of aims.

[1] Pribram, II, 110-2.   [2] *Denkwürdigkeiten*, I, 609.

The Chancellor had already been informed of a satisfactory exchange of opinions about Tripoli, and he took the announcement of an agreement calmly.[1] The Triple Alliance, he assured the Reichstag, was in excellent health, despite the hopes of certain people that it would die.[2] It was an insurance society, defensive in character and thoroughly pacific in aim. It did not exclude good relations between its members and other Powers, and Germans had no need to worry about the Franco-Italian agreements. "In a happy marriage the husband must not be jealous if his wife for once has an innocent dance with another man. The main thing is that she should not elope, which she will not do if she is best off where she is." Franco-Italian agreements on certain Mediterranean questions were in no way opposed to the Triple Alliance. Its makers had only needed to think of their European frontiers, whereas their successors embraced the whole world in their vision. "If then the Triple Alliance is no longer an absolute necessity for us, it remains extremely valuable as an extra guarantee for peace and the status quo, in addition to the fact that it is a very useful connecting link between states which, owing to their geographical position and their historical traditions, ought to be good neighbours. Germany must be kept so strong that her friendship is of value to all and her hostility a matter of indifference to none." It was an adroit pronouncement, neither censuring an ally nor touting for favours, but gently indicating that Germany was not dependent on Italy for her safety.

The change of front in Rome complicated the problem of the renewal of the Triple Alliance, for Italy's demands rose after her rapprochement with France.[3] Prinetti insisted on a satisfactory settlement of pending commercial questions as a preliminary condition. The negotiations concerned Vienna far more closely than Berlin, for the Wilhelmstrasse was less interested in details than in keeping the alliance alive. Bülow, however, had no intention of making himself too cheap. In a frank conversation with the Italian Ambassador he explained that, so far as Germany was concerned, Italy had an absolutely free hand in Tripoli.[4] The treaty with Italy, he continued, was not essential for Germany. If necessary she could find support and compensation elsewhere. For many reasons

[1] G.P. XVIII, 508–510.
[2] Reden, I, 243–5, January 8, 1902.
[3] G.P. XVIII, ch. 122, and Pribram, II, ch. 5.
[4] G.P. XVIII, 746–7, and 523–4.

isolation would be less dangerous for her than for Italy. As a German he desired the renewal of the Treaty as an old and well-established arrangement. He desired it also as a friend of Italy, for whom it was a question of existence, and who in its absence would become completely dependent on France. He was ready to renew on two conditions. Firstly Italy must declare that she had made no agreements with other states which diminished the defensive value of the alliance. Secondly it must remain unchanged so far as Germany was concerned. As regards Balkan issues, she would probably accept any agreement reached between Vienna and Rome. The German Government had no desire to hustle ; but if the negotiations were spun out his master's suspicions would be aroused, with consequences that could not be calculated. It was a grave warning, very different in tone from the seemingly good-natured chaff in the Reichstag a few days before. Yet it produced little effect in Rome ; for at Prinetti's elbow stood the wily Barrère, and far-reaching designs were afoot of which Italy's allies were not informed.

Prinetti's attempts to alter the text of the third treaty of the Triple Alliance concluded in 1891 were resolutely opposed both in Vienna and Berlin. At a meeting with the Italian Foreign Minister in Venice at the end of March the Chancellor explained that, however excellent the Italian proposals, any change in the treaty would open the door to suspicions which would endanger the tranquillity of Europe and might disturb the peace of the world, to say nothing of the shock to the reciprocal confidence between the sovereigns and the Cabinets. With these plain words the hopes of Prinetti and Barrère for a modification of the pact disappeared. In two directions only were the Central Empires willing to meet the wishes of their restive ally. A vaguely worded protocol promised commercial advantages, and an Austrian secret Declaration gave Italy a free hand in Tripoli and Cyrenaica.[1] After six months of struggle and strain the fourth treaty of the Triple Alliance, binding the parties for six years, was signed at Berlin on June 28, 1902. The Central Empires had succeeded in their main desire of renewing the treaty unchanged. But the partnership was weakened by the stubborn conflict, and the temper of the Italian Government was not improved by the refusal to accept its demands. Moreover a day or two after the signing of the treaty Delcassé announced in the Chamber that Italy

[1] Pribram, I, 220-35.

could under no circumstances join in an attack on France. This momentous declaration revealed the existence of a recent assurance from Prinetti, the text of which remained a secret for many years.[1] Not till the following spring did Bülow publicly comment on an announcement which indicated that henceforth Italy stood with one foot in each camp.[2]

The renewal of the Triple Alliance without modification, began the Chancellor cheerfully, showed that it was not a purely temporary arrangement but corresponded to the fundamental interests and needs of the three states. It imposed no other fetters on the internal and external development of its members than those required for the maintenance of the status quo and therewith of peace. " I can hardly think of any alliance in history at once so pacific and so strong, so enduring and so elastic." The renewal had presented certain difficulties, for it had enemies not only in Austria and Italy but elsewhere. He was not referring to any foreign Government but to the foreign press. To counterwork these machinations he had insisted during the negotiations that it should retain its defensive character without any weakening of its structure. " We hold fast to our obligations to our two allies with German loyalty. But we also have every possible pledge that in all cases hitherto envisaged in the Triple Alliance our partners will stand steadfastly by us." When Delcassé had declared that Italy was not bound to take part in an attack on France, he had doubtless only intended to say that the Triple Alliance had a defensive character. That was common knowledge in Germany, and it was satisfactory that France should realise that it threatened nobody. Once again the Chancellor had shown how skilfully he could skate over very thin ice. Yet the makers of the Franco-Italian entente must have smiled when they read this reassuring bulletin.

Bülow was well aware that he was fighting a losing battle. When the Kaiser and his Chancellor visited Victor Emmanuel in Rome in May 1903, the host explained that, though Italy needed the friendship of France for many purposes, it would be a grave danger to depend on her alone.[3] The young King, however, like his Montenegrin wife, was notoriously Austrophobe, and the growth of irredentism caused alarm in Vienna. On a visit to Vienna in September Bülow was informed by Goluchowsky that things could not continue as they were.

[1] Pribram II, 244–7.   [2] Reden, I, 437–41, March 19, 1903.
[3] G.P. XVIII, 613–16.

Another time he would only renew the Alliance if Italy promised to check the irredentists and to curtail her activities in Albania. Goluchowsky's thoughts turned longingly to a revival of the Three Emperors' League, and Francis Joseph lamented the loss of King Humbert, the loyal friend of the Triple Alliance. In all three capitals the cracks in the structure were becoming audible and visible.

At the opening of 1904 the pulse of the Triplice beat so feebly that it could hardly be felt. The Anglo-French reconciliation, synchronising with a growing estrangement between London and Berlin, drew Italian sentiment and interest ever further away from the Central Powers. Worse still was the approaching visit of the French President to Rome, in return for Victor Emmanuel's journey to Paris in the previous year. If the projects discussed in the French and Italian press were adopted and the relations of Italy to Germany ignored, Bülow warned the Italian Ambassador, it would be the death of the alliance.[1] Germany could not loyally shoulder all the dangers and burdens of the partnership with Italy if her conduct towards France made it a sham. He had heard from French sources that she had promised France neutrality in a Franco-German war. Private assurances counted for nothing against public demonstrations. If Italy's continued alliance with Germany were not mentioned during the visit, he would have to tell the German people that it had virtually ceased to exist. The Italians, he telegraphed to the German Ambassador in Rome, must be reminded of the dangerous results of losing the support afforded by the Triple Alliance, and thus be prevented from turning the flirtation with France into a lasting *liaison*. The festivities for Loubet must not be more imposing than they had been for the Kaiser.

Monts, who was incensed by the disloyalty of the Italian Government, carried out his instructions without flinching.[2] Tittoni promptly promised that the Triple Alliance would be mentioned in the King's toast; but when the Ambassador further demanded the abandonment of the proposed naval demonstrations at Naples, the Minister demurred. " My impression", wired Bülow, " is that the Italian statesmen do not yet fully realise the gravity of the situation. A reception such as is being prepared for Loubet destroys all the advantages

[1] *G.P.* XX, ch. 142.
[2] Monts, *Erinnerungen*, throws light on his years in Rome and his relations with Bülow.

of the alliance with Italy, leaving us with all its disadvantages and dangers. An Italy which declares so openly for union with France is no longer a useful ally. Indeed our policy would gain in flexibility if we were free from our treaty fetters. It would lighten our task both abroad and at home. If this is to be averted the celebrations must be drastically curtailed and the alliance with Germany must be emphasised by the King." Monts, who never minced his words, declared that Italy must choose between the Naples festivities and the Triple Alliance. Tittoni and Giolitti, he reported, did not seem to believe that Germany was in earnest, and behind the Ministers stood the stubborn determination of the King. To the Italian Ambassador in Berlin Bülow declared categorically that the conduct of the Ministers and above all of the King during the visit of the President would decide whether the alliance was to survive. At this moment a meeting between the Kaiser and Victor Emmanuel at Naples brought about a slight *détente*. The toasts were satisfactory, but the King's deep suspicions of Austrian designs in the Balkans were revealed. The despatches of Monts emphasised the *rôle* of the King, who was dominated by a blind hatred of Austria.

The French President, accompanied by Delcassé, arrived in Rome on April 24. The King's toasts in the capital and at Naples ignored the Triple Alliance, and the host, usually so reserved, treated his guest with effusive cordiality. It was in vain that Monts complained that the flirt had become a *liaison* and that the promises of the Foreign Minister had been broken. In the Ambassador's view the King was the ringleader, even more than Barrère. Bülow's declaration to the Italian Ambassador that Germany might revive the Three Emperors' League made little impression in Rome, and a telegram from Tittoni, communicated by Lanza, was equally ineffective in Berlin. No political agreement between Italy and France, it ran, had been made or was planned. There was no ground for such an agreement, for no question was pending, and a general political pact could not be reconciled with the spirit of the alliance, "to which we desire to remain true". In a speech to the Chamber at the same moment Tittoni declared that the alliance with Germany did not exclude friendly relations with France. It mattered little at this stage, however, what he said, for deeds spoke louder than words. Bülow comforted himself with the reflection that Italy was weaker than Austria, and that the loss of Savoy and Nice was a

reminder that French help had its price. In case of war
Italy would certainly not co-operate, but it would be better
than nothing if she remained neutral. How far she had
drifted from her anchorage was to be revealed anew at
Algeciras. Bülow knew he was beaten ; but no German
statesman could have held her back, for a rapprochement
with France was clearly in her interest. Henceforth she
skilfully got the best of both worlds.

IX

While England and Italy were slipping away, a new apple of
discord began to complicate the relations of Germany with
France. At the turn of the century it was generally recognised
that the Moroccan problem would before long engage the
attention of the Chancelleries.[1] England desired Tangier,
observed Chamberlain to the Kaiser in November 1899, and
Germany could find compensation on the Atlantic coast.
When the French occupied Tuat in 1900 Bülow expressed his
apprehensions, and Delcassé explained that it was merely to
open up the Sahara and protect trade routes. The situation was
intermediate, and German interests, Bülow believed, would of
be best served by postponing the liquidation of Morocco.
Hatzfeldt, on the other hand, urged co-operation with
England, since Germany could do nothing on the coast against
her veto. Moreover, in the absence of an agreement, England
might act alone or reach an arrangement with France. Germany, he advised, should tell England that she must be consulted in any settlement of the question, for when the Boer war
was over she would be so swollen with pride that she would be
more difficult to handle. Chamberlain was ready, and urged
Germany to make a proposal to Salisbury ; and Hatzfeldt
advised a claim for the earmarking of the South Atlantic coast.
Salisbury, however, avoided speaking of Morocco, and it
seemed undesirable to invite a snub.

A new chapter opened with the Moroccan missions in the
summer of 1901. Germany, declared the Chancellor, must for
the present play the sphinx. After the Kaiser had warmly
expressed his desire to see the country remain intact, the
Wilhelmstrasse advised the envoy to keep in with France and
to substitute railways and telegraphs for isolation. Taking
no action was not a purely negative policy, for France was

[1] G.P. XVII, ch. 113.

unlikely to seize her prey while unaware what Germany and England would do. Momentary alarm was felt when in January 1902 Metternich reported negotiations between Chamberlain and Cambon on colonial questions ; but in the summer Delcassé assured Lansdowne that he had no plans in Morocco. Thus the danger of an Anglo-French agreement concerning Morocco ceased to trouble Berlin until King Edward's visit to Paris in 1903.

On March 13, 1904, Delcassé outlined the scope of the coming agreement to the German Ambassador. On April 6 Lascelles announced the approaching pact, and at Lansdowne's request explained that it was not directed against Germany. Bülow replied that he had not supposed it was. Germany, he added, was glad to see England and France liquidate various differences, since that served the interest of peace. On the day after the signature of the treaty, he instructed the Wilhelmstrasse to have it discussed in the press without annoyance or jealously as a new symptom for the peaceful shaping of the world. In reply to a question in the Reichstag on April 12 his tone was friendly and composed.[1] " We have no reason to suppose that the Anglo-French Colonial agreement is pointed against any other Power. It appears to be an endeavour to remove a number of differences in a spirit of a friendly understanding. From the standpoint of German interests we have nothing to object. Strained relations between France and England are undesirable if only because they would endanger the peace of the world, which we sincerely strive to maintain. As regards Morocco, the kernel of the arrangement, we are in essence only interested in the economic sphere. It is therefore of importance for us that tranquillity and order exist there. We must and shall protect our commercial interests in Morocco. We have no reason to fear that they will be ignored or infringed by any Power." Nothing could be more satisfactory to British and French statesmen than this conciliatory utterance, and the consent of Germany to the Khedival Decree was secured without very much difficulty.

Despite its smooth words the Wilhelmstrasse felt that German interests had been rudely ignored. Morocco, wrote Holstein, was one of the few countries where the commerce of Germany could compete on equal terms.[2] Railway and other schemes were afoot, and the French system of virtual monopoly

[1] *Reden*, II, 74. [2] *G.P.* XX, ch. 145.

would be fatal to her hopes. Even worse would be the loss of prestige if the Government looked on with folded arms while national interests were being given away. " We have long believed that France would seek an understanding with the interested Powers. As far as Germany is concerned, that is not the case. If we let ourselves be trampled on in Morocco, we invite similar treatment elsewhere. Not for material reasons alone, but even more for the sake of prestige must Germany protest against the intended appropriation of Morocco by France." The only question was at what moment and in what form the protest should be made. With this reasoning Bülow entirely agreed. He had a good legal case and was determined that it should prevail.

Action in Morocco, wrote the Chancellor to Radolin on July 21, involved far-reaching consequences and required careful thought. It was improbable that England would take her obligations of diplomatic support very seriously, and the negotiations between France and Spain would doubtless diminish French preponderance in Morocco. France had paid England a good price and completely ignored Germany. The commercial activities of Germans in Morocco had increased so rapidly that it was vital to prevent a French monopoly. How, he asked Radolin, ought Germany to proceed ? In two ways, replied the Ambassador. She could ask France what guarantees she proposed to offer for the preservation of her commercial interests. That would be the simplest method ; but he did not like approaching France, since France had herself made inquiries as to the wishes of England and Spain. A more energetic course would be to provoke an offer of compensation by action in Morocco and by stiffening the Sultan's back. France would then learn that Germany, whose silence was already making her uncomfortable, could become a great nuisance. " As Your Excellency is convinced that England's diplomatic support will not amount to much, we should have a free hand, whereas Anglo-French opposition could easily compel us to retreat."

The attitude of England, as the Ambassador realised, was a vital factor, and on August 15 Metternich explained the views of his countrymen to Lansdowne for the first time. France was aiming at a monopoly, which Germany could not accept. Free markets were becoming rarer, and she possessed treaty rights in Morocco. Equal opportunity was in the general interest. She might very soon be compelled to defend her

R

commercial rights in Morocco against France, and she was therefore anxious to know whether England would afford diplomatic support to France under Article IX of the treaty. British Governments, replied Lansdowne, disliked dealing with questions of principle before a concrete case arose. Article IX, however, involved no support of an infringement of the treaty rights of third parties. France, he believed, intended to move very cautiously and to avoid complications with other Powers. Metternich's impression was that the Foreign Minister would strive to limit rather than to extend the obligation in concrete instances. On the other hand German control of a harbour on the Atlantic would probably be opposed. Where treaty rights existed, concluded the Ambassador, Germany could safely take a strong line. But while England would do nothing to accelerate the penetration of Morocco, she would equally do nothing to risk her good understanding with France. If any Power attempted a political challenge to France, British diplomacy and above all British opinion would be ranged on her side.

The policy of the sphinx was continued throughout the autumn, and no more notice was taken of the Franco-Spanish treaty of October 3 than of the Anglo-French treaty of April 8. But the mission of the French Minister to Fez ended the period of watchful waiting.[1] Kühlmann, the energetic young Chargé d'Affaires in Tangier, advised plain speaking to stiffen the Sultan, and the German Consul in Fez received instructions from the Chancellor. German and French interests were not identical, and Germany had not been consulted by France as to changes in Morocco. If the Sultan asked whether Germany would support him, he was to state that she could not declare war against France on account of Morocco. Kühlmann replied that the Moors desired only moral support, since the majority of the Powers represented at Tangier stood for the open door.

The arrival of Taillandier in Fez at the end of January 1905 stimulated the Francophobia of the Sultan, which Vassel, the energetic German Consul, did his best to encourage. Bülow's plans seemed to be working out satisfactorily. The French Cabinet was unwarlike, he telegraphed to Kühlmann, and the French people had no wish for a costly struggle in Morocco which would denude the German frontier of troops. "The future is always obscure, but it is extremely improbable that, if

[1] G.P. XX, ch. 146.

the Sultan, surrounded by the representatives of about ten million Moors, defends his sovereignty and independence, France would risk a war in Morocco with a silent Germany on her flank. In any case he will realise that the first step on the slippery surface will be decisive." Meanwhile the less noise made by German diplomacy, the better. Pursuing his policy of pulling the strings in the background the Chancellor strove to secure American support. Germany, he wired to Washington, had no covetous aims in China, Morocco or anywhere else. " Nowhere do we seek to acquire territory. We merely aim at preventing a change of the existing situation to our detriment." English business men were afraid of losing the Moroccan market. France, feeling isolated, was proceeding cautiously. If Washington and Berlin simultaneously displayed interest for the open door in Morocco and for an improvement of conditions independently of France, the question would be quickly and peacefully solved. Roosevelt politely replied that Americans would not allow their country to be entangled in an issue of which they knew nothing, but that the American Minister in Morocco would keep in touch with his German colleague.

Convinced that France would not fight, that French ambitions were deeply resented by the Moors, and that England could not repudiate her maxim of economic equality, Bülow at last determined to throw his hat into the ring. It was decided in February and announced in March that the Kaiser would shortly visit Tangier. " Your Majesty's visit", he wrote, " will embarrass Delcassé, upset his plans, and foster our economic interests in Morocco." *Tant mieux*, commented the Kaiser. But when he learned of the preparations for a political demonstration he wired that it was very uncertain whether he would land, that he was travelling incognito as a tourist, and that there should be no audiences. To change the programme, rejoined the Chancellor firmly, would be a triumph for Delcassé. " If the diplomats inquire about Tangier and Morocco ", ran his instructions to the Wilhelmstrasse, " please do not reply, but wear a grave and impassive look. We must for the present be like the sphinx which, surrounded by inquisitive tourists, reveals nothing." " We waited ", he explained to Metternich, " till the Moroccan Government asked if it was true that France, as the French Minister informed the Moroccan Government, was the mandatory of all the Powers." That the French Minister had made any such claim he stoutly denied, but the story was believed at Berlin. The strength of the German position, in Bülow's words, lay in the fact that she asked no privileges for herself, and strove merely for the equal status of all nations. When Bebel complained in the Reichstag that German policy in Morocco had changed, he replied that the attempt to alter the juristic position of the country and to close the open door came from another quarter.[1]

Bülow's detailed recommendations for the visit were telegraphed to Lisbon on March 26. Delcassé, he reminded his master, had completely ignored Germany in his Moroccan plans. The Kaiser should therefore make no reference to France, and should greet the French Chargé without a word. Germany's aims should for the moment be left unspecified. An alliance with the Sultan was impossible, but moral support was essential. He proceeded to sketch out declarations which the Kaiser should make—that he desired no Moroccan territory and that Germany claimed commercial equality. If asked whether she would intervene in a war between Morocco and France, he should reply that he must reserve his decision. All eyes, he concluded, were directed towards Tangier. It was a great responsibility for the Kaiser, who had no relish for his task, and who was not even furnished with a carefully prepared brief. At the eleventh hour he tried to avoid the ordeal on the pretext that the rough sea rendered landing a little dangerous ; but he yielded to pressure and carried out the programme with great spirit. His declarations, couched in rather uncompromising terms, made it clear that Germany regarded Morocco as a sovereign Power, not as the pawn of France.

When the demonstration was over the next step in checkmating the French advance was the summoning of a Conference. On March 27 Bülow asked Kühlmann to ascertain from Harris, the *Times* Correspondent in Tangier, whether England would be likely to agree to a Conference summoned by the Sultan.[2] If so, it would be the simplest way of maintaining the status quo with some ameliorations. If not, the plan was impracticable. The Sultan and his advisers, came the reply, desired to answer the demands of France by referring them to a Conference if Germany approved. When Italy asked to be consulted if Germany negotiated with France about Morocco, the Chancellor replied that he had no such intention, as other Powers were also concerned. Germany, he added

[1] *Reden*, II, 209-10.   [2] *G.P.* XX, ch. 147.

with some severity, reckoned on Italy's approval of her policy. " The attitude of Italy in this question, where dignity and interest point in the same direction, will govern Germany's attitude to Italian questions later."

On April 4 the Chancellor congratulated his master on the Tangier demonstration and cheerfully analysed the situation. German policy was the open door and no territorial claims. America would support the demand for commercial equality, and England would take care not to oppose her. Austria would approve, and probably Italy as well. Russia was engaged in the Far East. It was therefore out of the question that the Conference would play into the hands of France. After thus scanning the horizon he encouraged the Sultan to summon a Conference at Tangier. When Hammann, head of the Press Department of the Foreign Office, remarked that it would be a great achievement to break the Anglo-French Morocco pact by this method, the Chancellor noted : " That we do not desire, or at any rate we reveal no such aim. We only want to defend our rights in Morocco." To Hammann's request for guidance if war came in sight he replied : " No shrinking and no cowardice." The Sultan was to be encouraged not to yield to France nor to abandon the Conference. Italy was to be told that Germany would help her to secure Tripoli when the psychological moment arrived, subject of course to her loyalty to the Triple Alliance. Spain was ready for a Conference if England and France approved it.

The German leaven was beginning to work in Paris no less than in Fez. On April 13, yielding to the wishes of Rouvier, Delcassé informed Radolin that if there was a misunderstanding he was ready to clear it up. He had waited too long, and the Ambassador replied that separate negotiations were undesirable. The prospect of thwarting and even overthrowing Delcassé seemed bright, since Rouvier was known to disapprove his policy. Nothing could now deflect Germany from the course on which she had entered at Tangier. French control of Morocco was to be averted, but Germany would ask nothing for herself. When Tattenbach suggested that a portion of Africa could be secured by an agreement with France, Bülow quoted the Kaiser's declaration of territorial disinterestedness to the King of Spain in 1904. Rouvier himself, who disliked the idea of a Conference, suggested a general cleaning of the slate on the Anglo-French model of 1904, but there was no response. Germany, explained Bülow to his

Italian ally, had taken her stand on the principle of collectivity, and to abandon it was now impossible.

The Chancellor saw no reason to doubt the success of his strategy. "We waited long enough till we took up a position", he wrote to Radolin on May 4. " Now we have done so, we must not lose credit, which a Government needs as much as a private firm. I feel sure Rouvier understands the situation." The only course was to slow down French action and to reserve the future. Morocco would continue to decay, and France would lose nothing by delay. Delcassé's prestige alone would suffer. His policy of haste and of ignoring Germany was unintelligible, especially at a time when Russia's hands were tied. The only possible explanation appeared to be the prompting of England. Could not Rouvier himself take the initiative of calling a Conference ? It would neither partition Morocco nor prevent its decay. Rouvier felt unable to adopt the suggestion, and, though he desired to dismiss his Foreign Minister, he could not hurry as his colleague possessed powerful friends. The Wilhelmstrasse, however, was unrelenting, for the goal was in sight. On May 30 Miquel, the First Secretary of the Paris Embassy, informed the Premier of the Chancellor's accumulated grievances. Germany was not bluffing, and the situation might become dangerous. The best solution would be a change at the Foreign Office. Rouvier replied that the existing situation could not continue, but that it would be difficult to get rid of Delcassé at the moment. Pressure on the Premier was kept up, and on June 3 he sent a message that he would act after the departure from Paris of the King of Spain. The blow fell on June 6, when Delcassé found himself without support in the Cabinet and resigned.

At this moment of apparent triumph Bülow accepted from his grateful master the title of Prince which he had previously declined. Looking back on the crisis long afterwards, he explains that he played for high stakes because he knew he could win.[1] " It was not the magnitude of our commercial and political interests in Morocco which decided me to advise the Kaiser to resist, but the conviction that in the interest of peace we could no longer swallow such provocations. I desired war with France as little at that time as before and after, if only because I knew that any serious conflict would involve a world war. But I did not hesitate to confront her with the issue of war because I trusted to my skill and strength to pre-

[1] *Denkwürdigkeiten*, II, 108.

vent it, while at the same time overthrowing Delcassé in order to frustrate the aggressive plans of French policy, to strike their continental sword out of the hand of Edward VII and the war party in England, and thus simultaneously to combine German honour with peace and to enhance German prestige." He adds that the elimination of Delcassé preserved the peace for several years. It was an optimistic interpretation of an episode in which, in the long run, Germany lost far more than she gained ; for both France and England angrily resented the blow of the mailed fist and drew closer together in alarm.

X

While the Wilhelmstrasse was preparing its challenge to Delcassé, a fruitless attempt was made to mend the wire to St. Petersburg so rashly cut when Bismarck fell. The struggle in the Far East provided the opportunity, for the attitude of Germany was of vital importance to Russia, and the dazzling victories of Japan enhanced the value of her good will. The seizure of British merchantmen by Russian ships roused England to indignation, which boiled into fury at the outrage on the Dogger Bank. Japan and England, telegraphed the Kaiser to the Tsar on October 27, 1904, might demand the cessation of the coaling of the Russian fleet on its way to the Far East.[1] Germany, Russia and France should form a combination which the Anglo-Japanese group would hardly dare to attack. The angry Tsar, convinced that there had been foul play in the North Sea, telegraphed his approval of an arrangement by the three Powers " to abolish Anglo-Japanese arrogance and insolence ", and invited the Kaiser to supply a draft. " As soon as it is accepted by us, France is bound to join her ally. This combination has often come to my mind. It will mean peace and rest for the world." The draft of a defensive alliance between Germany and Russia against attack by a European Power was promptly sent to St. Petersburg. The Tsar returned the document with emendations, on which the Kaiser commented in a long letter. Bülow was thrilled with the prospect of success. " If Paris or London had the least notion of the contents of this letter, they would do their utmost to frustrate the German-Russian alliance, which removes the possibility of a Russo-French-English alliance." It was too good to be true, for on reflection the Tsar felt

[1] G.P. XIX, ch. 135.

bound to consult his ally. But to tell France, as the Kaiser complained to the Tsar, would be to tell England, who might proceed to launch an Anglo-Japanese attack on Germany. If the Tsar insisted, it would be best to abandon the pact. On the other hand he could not continue to coal the Russian fleet without a guarantee of aid in the event of war with England. There was no time to be lost, and France must know nothing till the coaling convention was signed. To this limited demand for a promise of support if a conflict arose from the coaling of the fleet Lamsdorff consented. He had no alternative, for Russian ships required German coal; but he did not share the German apprehension that England would fight, and on this ground he attempted to postpone the discussion of details.

At the close of 1904 Bülow asked Metternich whether in his opinion a defensive alliance with Russia would increase the probability of an English attack. The Ambassador replied that England had no such thoughts, but that many Englishmen believed Germany to be contemplating an attack on their country. A chauvinistic agitation designed to carry through a new Navy Law would involve serious danger. An alliance with Russia for the duration of the war would also be clearly directed against England, and hostility would increase. " There is no danger of war in the existing situation, but from the moment that we make Russia's cause our own it would arise. We obtain an ally who has till now been defeated and who could not possibly help us in a war with England." If such a one-sided arrangement were to be made, it must remain secret at any rate till the end of the struggle in the Far East, and France must not share in the entente. The Tsar's proposal was inspired by his anger at the Dogger Bank incident, and his mood might change. The continuance of benevolent neutrality was the wisest policy. Rarely has a despatch contained so much wisdom and truth, and it was not without effect in Berlin. The Kaiser wrote to the Tsar that France must not be informed till an arrangement was reached, and that, if he insisted on telling her, the project had better be dropped. The Tsar very properly refused to act behind the back of his ally. " A negative result after two months hard work ", wrote the Kaiser to his Chancellor. " My first rebuff ! " He attributed the failure to Delcassé, who must have got wind of the negotiations.

The annihilation of the Russian fleet in May 1905 brought

peace within sight, and encouraged the German Government to revive the discussion of a pact. In 1904 the initiative came from the Tsar : in 1905 it was the Kaiser who proposed a meeting " as simple tourist", and the Tsar chose Björkö for the rendezvous.[1] The Kaiser asked for a copy of the defensive alliance proposed in 1904, and Bülow begged Holstein for his advice. Support for Russia in the peace negotiations, he added, was out of the question ; but the Tsar might be so far won over that Witte and Lamsdorff on the termination of hostilities would be unable at once to engineer a Russo-Franco-British entente, at which King Edward and Clemenceau were aiming. Holstein counselled that the Kaiser should wait till the Tsar renewed his initiative, since a Russian refusal would damage relations. To the Chancellor's query whether France should only be informed when agreement had been reached, he rejoined that it was no longer necessary. Rouvier had succeeded Delcassé, and Russia's increasing dependence on French money rendered concealment impossible. The Tsar should be reminded that if Germany joined the Dual Alliance she would always side with Russia, who would thus have her way, whereas England as the third party would always go with France. England was working for an Anglo-French-Russo-Japanese grouping, and Russia needed Germany to preserve the equilibrium.

The Björkö pact was signed on board the *Hohenzollern* on July 24, 1905. If one of the signatories was attacked by a European Power, its ally would aid it in Europe. The treaty would become operative on the conclusion of the Russo-Japanese war, when the Tsar would invite France to come in. Nicholas II, still deeply incensed against England, embraced his guest with the words : " You are the only man in the world I entirely trust." The pact, however, was not in the form prepared by the Wilhelmstrasse, for the promise of aid was confined to Europe. " Do you think that the addition ' *en Europe* '," wired the horrified Chancellor to Holstein when he heard the news, " renders the treaty useless, since in Europe Russia could not help us against anybody with her worn-out fleet and could not help us against England with her army ? Shall I refuse my signature and thus cancel the treaty ? Or would it even thus be of value in loosening the Dual Alliance ? " Its value, replied Holstein, would be greatly diminished, for in the event of an Anglo-German war Russia would not be

[1] *G.P.* XIX, ch. 138, and Bülow, *Denkwürdigkeiten*, II, ch. 9.

pledged to attack India.   It would be useless, however, to ask Lamsdorff to remove the unfortunate words that were so useful to Russian interests, especially as they were inserted by the Kaiser himself.   Bülow wired his regret to his master.   " The only thing the English really fear is a Russian attack on India." The Kaiser defended his handiwork.   Without the limitation, he argued, Germany would be pledged to co-operation in Asia, and a Russian march on India, he was assured, was only a dream.

Bülow was not pacified.   " A treaty in which the possibility of a Russian advance in Asia is expressly excepted is less calculated to prevent an English attack on Germany."   He refused to accept responsibility and sent in his resignation, which provoked an emotional outburst from his master.   He had thought to lighten his Chancellor's heavy burden, and all he got was a few cool lines and a resignation.   " To be thus treated by my best and most intimate friend without any reasonable ground has been such a frightful blow that I am quite broken. . . . You are worth a hundred thousand times more to me and the Fatherland than all the treaties in the world."   He had carried out Bülow's policy in Tangier, contrary to his own wishes and at the risk of his life.   He could not survive his resignation.   " I appeal to your friendship, and let me hear no more of your resignation.   Telegraph ' all right ' and I shall know you will stay.   For the morning after your resignation would find me dead.   Think of my poor wife and children."   It was the most dramatic testimonial that a German Chancellor ever received.   The resignation was withdrawn, and the Kaiser was persuaded that the words *en Europe* were a mistake.   Bülow was anxious to secure their omission by a direct appeal to the Tsar, but he was dissuaded by Holstein.   An attempt from the German side to alter the treaty would encourage Lamsdorff to propose changes too, and would probably lead to the loss of the treaty, of which he was no friend.   Witte, on the other hand, who visited the Kaiser on his way home from the peace negotiations in America, favoured a Russo-German-French combination to prevent England dominating the world.   For this purpose France must be treated with consideration.   The Kaiser informed Witte, with the Tsar's consent, of the making of the Björkö pact, which he welcomed with tears of joy.[1]

[1] Witte's *Memoirs*, ch. 14, should be checked by Korostovetz, *Graf Witte*, ch. 7.

The addition of the words *en Europe*, which had caused such a flutter at Norderney, was of no real importance, for the project was doomed from its birth. When Lamsdorff saw the Björkö treaty he pointed out that it was incompatible with the Dual Alliance. The difficulty which had prevented success in 1904 proved no less insurmountable in 1905. A genuine Russo-German partnership was equally impossible with or without France. The Björkö pact was to come into force at the conclusion of the Japanese war, but on October 7 the Tsar suggested that it should be postponed till the French view could be ascertained. It was a polite method of announcing his desire to back out of his engagement. "What is signed is signed", replied the Kaiser sharply, though he added that he was ready to consider modifications. The Treaty, he argued, did not conflict with the Franco-Russian alliance ; and France had left Russia in the lurch throughout the war, whereas Germany had helped her in every compatible way with neutrality. The latter was true enough, but the Russian Government had made up its mind.

On November 23 the Tsar wrote that there was not much chance of winning over France at present, and proposed a Declaration that the pact should be inoperative in the event of a Franco-German war. "That is the thanks for our attitude in recent years", commented the angry Kaiser in forwarding the letter to Bülow. If the Franco-Russian alliance was purely defensive, replied the Chancellor, it would not conflict with the Björkö pact, and the Tsar's Declaration was therefore needless. Such pleadings and recriminations were now in vain. The Tsar wired that the alliance with France was indeed defensive, but that the Declaration must stand till France accepted the Pact. With the ending of the war Russia's need of Germany disappeared, and the road was clear for a rapprochement with England. It was a deep mortification to the Kaiser, who had seen for a moment the mirage of a European combine under his leadership to keep England in her place. Thus ended the attempt to undo the disastrous mistake of 1890.

XI

When the golden dawn of Björkö melted into the light of common day, Morocco again became the main preoccupation of Berlin. Satisfaction in Germany at the fall of Delcassé had been qualified by the rumour that England had offered France armed support in the event of war. A further disappointment was the discovery that the conciliatory Rouvier was not his own master. The chief offender had gone but the Quai d'Orsay remained. Three days after Delcassé's fall the Premier begged Germany not to press the Conference, which he envisaged as the humiliation of France.[1] The humiliation, commented Bülow, had been on the side of Germany, and she could not throw over the Sultan. France was wavering between surrender and intransigence, and if she thought that the Kaiser had altered his attitude there would be trouble. Accordingly Radolin informed Rouvier in very serious tones that Germany stood with her whole strength behind the Sultan to preserve his independence and the status quo if the Conference were declined. The tension was relieved when the anxious Premier hinted that participation would be easier if the programme were discussed in advance. Meanwhile Italy's delay in accepting the Conference revealed how little Germany had to expect from Rome. " If Italy fails us in the relatively unimportant Morocco question", wrote the angry Monts prophetically, " that is a foretaste of what we may expect in really serious times. It seems as if the Triple Alliance, so far as Italy is concerned, has outlived itself."

The Chancellor accepted the suggestion that the programme should be discussed. There would have to be real though limited reforms, he explained to Tattenbach, since Germany had obstructed the French scheme ; but the battle was not yet won. Rouvier argued that the Conference would be dangerous without an agreement and useless if it had been reached. He was unable to accept without a clear understanding on the proposed reforms. " Rouvier is now trying to force on us Delcassé's programme as his own ", telegraphed Bülow in annoyance to the Kaiser. He desired no conflict, but he had been talked over by the Delcassé group. The Chancellor told the French Ambassador that he was surprised and distressed, and that he could not anticipate the decisions of the Conference. The situation, he added, was serious, and it was a mistake to play with fire. He had never spoken more gravely when Delcassé was at the Quai d'Orsay. In addition to his official reply he sent a private message to Rouvier. The Moroccan Government had offered Germany a position which would make her mistress of the situation. If an understanding with France proved impossible, she would claim a free hand.

[1] G.P. XX, ch. 148.

At this point Roosevelt urged France to accept a Conference and Germany to be considerate. Jean Dupuy, the intimate friend of Rouvier, assured Radolin that the Premier had not changed his opinions and regarded a lasting understanding with Germany as his chief aim. The recent note had been drawn up in the Quai d'Orsay, and he had not realised that it failed to carry out his intentions till it was pointed out to him by Dupuy. Even now he explained that unconditional acceptance at German dictation would destroy the Ministry. When the Conference opened, replied Bülow in conciliatory tones, Germany would be one of several members. It was not intended as a snare for France. The reforms would probably succeed as little as in Turkey or even less. In that case a new situation would arise, and an understanding with France would be easy. In reporting his conversation with the French Ambassador to Radolin the Chancellor added that German policy desired to meet France as far as possible, since Germany regarded the improvement of her relations with France as more important than her interests in Morocco. On the same day that this despatch was written Rouvier accepted the Conference ; and, after a further sharp tussle about the wording, the declaration of July 8 pledged the signatories to three principles—the independence and integrity of Morocco, commercial equality, and reforms under international auspices.

The next step was to formulate a programme for the Conference, and for this purpose Dr. Rosen was sent on a special mission to Paris.[1] Since the Pact of Björkö, which had just been concluded and which contemplated the adherence of France to the Russo-German defensive alliance, Bülow kept the soft pedal down. The fewer details settled in advance, the better. Germany desired the Conference to meet at Tangier, but she accepted the French preference for Algeciras. The Kaiser, at all times a moderate on Morocco, was anxious for an agreement, but both parties were suspicious. Even Dupuy lamented that the promise of friendliness if France accepted the Conference had not been fulfilled, and the experts, Révoil and Rosen, complained of each other's intransigence. On September 16 Radolin warned the Wilhelmstrasse of the danger of a *crise de nerfs* if the negotiations were either broken off or prolonged. The Chancellor telegraphed to Radolin to complain of the French press and ended with a threat. " If

---

[1] *G.P.* XX, ch. 149, and Rosen, *Aus einem diplomatischen Wanderleben*, I, 148–226.

the French imagine that they can intimidate or humiliate us by threats, that is a dangerous game which may lead to war." There should be *ni vainqueurs ni vaincus*. The declaration defining the programme of the Conference was signed at last on September 28.

Bülow had evicted Delcassé and secured a Conference,. but the goal was not yet in sight. It was essential to avoid isolation.[1] " If in a question in which we have taken our stand we have the majority or all the members against us, threats will be useless, for our position, after all that has happened, would be almost ludicrous. We must therefore concentrate on essentials and decide how to secure the support of other Powers in our views." The first task was to reassure his allies. " We pursue no separate advantages ", he explained to Rome and Vienna, " but only freedom and economic equality." It sounded innocent enough, but the relatively simple problem of reforms in Morocco had become hopelessly entangled with the graver issues of national prestige. In a discussion with the high officials at the Wilhelmstrasse on Christmas day the Chancellor reviewed the situation. He did not wish to humiliate the French, but equally he could not accept humiliation. For instance a French mandate for West Morocco would mean war, and the French must be informed of that fact in good time. Instructions were now sent to Radolin. " Our endeavour at the Conference will be towards a peaceful agreement in which both sides are satisfied for the time. We do not aim at a diplomatic triumph over France, and we could not admit a French triumph over us. We demand in Morocco nothing beyond the open door for all nations, and on this we cannot yield. If France accepts it fully, the success of the Conference is assured." The same line of thought was embodied in the instructions to the German delegates. Germany must have control of the police in one of the ports, but she should never stand alone or merely receive the support of Morocco.

Though convinced of the justice of his cause and the modesty of his demands, the Chancellor was uneasy about the forthcoming trial of strength. He assured Lascelles that he had no wish to inflict humiliation on France.[2] The situation indeed was even less favourable than he thought. He counted on Rouvier's good will and suspicion of England, but after six months at the Quai d'Orsay the Premier was no longer in a

[1] *G.P.* XXI, ch. 151.   [2] *B.D.* III, 217–219.

yielding mood. "I have had enough of German intrigues and recriminations", he exclaimed to George Louis, the Permanent Under-Secretary, in November.[1] "If the Berlin people imagine they can intimidate me, they are mistaken. I will yield nothing more, come what may." At the end of the year he told Paléologue that the English alliance was indispensable, and that he should instruct Cambon to resume the secret pourparlers. France had now the stronger cards, for the Japanese war was over and England was a friend.

The news from London was not encouraging. On January 3, 1906, Grey quoted Lansdowne's warning to Metternich in the previous summer on the probable consequences of an unprovoked attack, adding that in his opinion the British people would insist on aiding France if she were involved in war on account of the Anglo-French treaty. Metternich summarised the British view with his usual accuracy. England was anxious to avoid trouble but she was loyal to France. " The Morocco question is regarded by everyone here as a trial of strength with the Anglo-French entente, and our Morocco policy as an attempt to smash it. Hence the determined opposition." The appointment of Visconti Venosta as the leading representative of Italy seemed like a gleam of sunlight at Berlin. " He regards the Triplice as a necessity for Italy, and he is not anti-Austrian", wired the Chancellor to Radowitz, the chief German delegate, who was instructed to get in close touch with the veteran statesman. Bülow's information was not up to date, for Visconti Venosta's appointment had been urged by Barrère himself. The attempts to secure the support of Washington for an acceptable compromise were zealously continued, and Henry White played a conciliatory part in the discussions.[2] But neither Roosevelt nor anyone else could tilt the balance in favour of Berlin.

At the end of the first week of the Conference of Algeciras, which opened on January 16, Radowitz reported in a hopeful strain.[3] The atmosphere seemed friendly, and the hope of the French and British press that Germany would be isolated was unrealised. " So far it is clear that our endeavour to win the confidence of all the Powers who stand for equal rights and the preservation of common interests in Morocco has proved a success." The Chancellor was encouraged and relieved.

[1] Paléologue, 410, 420.
[2] Nevins, Henry White, ch. 16, and Dennis, Adventures in American Diplomacy, ch. 19.
[3] G.P. XXI, ch. 152, and Tardieu, La Conférence d'Algésiras.

"Now we no longer need fear isolation", he wired back. "I hope that in approaching great decisions you will secure solutions compatible with the dignity of the Empire, which His Majesty laid down in Vigo and later in Tangier, namely the economic equality of all the interested Powers and the prevention of the preponderance of a single Power in questions where it would render economic equality a sham."

The optimistic mood of the Wilhelmstrasse melted away when the Conference came to grips with the crucial question of the control of the police in the ports. Visconti Venosta acted rather as neutral than an ally; Goluchowsky remarked to the German Ambassador that Morocco was not worth a war; and Nicolson emerged as a valiant henchmen of France. Bülow was at length fully aware of his difficulties, but, with Holstein behind him, he had no thought of lowering his flag. Germany and the Powers sharing her interests, he explained to the Italian Foreign Minister, were on the defensive. They were asked to make place for France. "We have recognised her claims to a privileged position in the frontier districts, despite their doubtful legality, in the expectation that it would secure the solution of the other aspects of the Moroccan question on the basis of equality of status. There is no reason for further retreat. The principles of sacrificing one's interests, simply because they block the path of another Power, might involve such dangerous consequences that the failure of the Conference would be the lesser evil." Thus the French proposal to entrust the police to French and Spanish officers was rejected. When Grey defended the project Metternich retorted : "He who has the police has Morocco." To Witte's complaint that German policy seemed to aim at a humiliation of France, Bülow replied that the French claim to control the police would be a defeat for Germany. To Witte Morocco seemed a trifle compared with the desirability of Franco-German-Russian co-operation : to Bülow it was a symbol of Germany's determination not to be thrust aside.

A further cold *douche* was administered by a declaration from Francis Joseph to the German Ambassador. A vote on the police, he believed, would find England, Spain, Russia and probably the United States on the side of France, with Italy at best folding her arms. Such a division and the resulting failure of the Conference would lead to a new grouping of the Powers, Russia separating herself from the Central Empires and joining England and France. It was urgently desirable to avert such a catastrophe. Goluchowsky sought for a compromise, but the tide was flowing away from Berlin.[1] Italy could no longer be reckoned a friend. The Björkö honeymoon was over, and Russia was looking to Paris for a loan. England followed where France led, even with doubts in her mind. Spain recognised that she could secure more from France than from Germany. " All the miserable and degenerate Latin peoples", wrote the angry Kaiser, " are becoming mere instruments in England's hands to assail German trade in the Mediterranean. Not only have we no more friends among them, but they detest us." The fall of the Rouvier Ministry stiffened the attitude of France, and American sympathies for Germany faded away.

Holstein refused to surrender ; but Bülow who, like the Kaiser, had no stomach for a fight, took the rudder out of his hand. The Mystery Man of the Wilhelmstrasse declared after his fall that he had no responsibility for policy beyond March 12, when the Chancellor accepted an Austrian compromise on the police ; and he lived to confess that his own policy had been a mistake since his chief shrank from war.[2] Germany was now fighting a rearguard action, and by the end of the month agreement was reached. Bülow and his master put the best face on the settlement, and an Imperial telegram gave Austria, the brilliant second, a pat on the back. But it was impossible for them to conceal the fact that their Conference was a failure. Their prestige had been diminished, not enhanced. Their weakness had been revealed. Germany and Austria were alone. For the first time England, France and Russia walked hand in hand. Italy was obviously lost. The French advance in Morocco, though slowed down by the Act of Algeciras, was not checked. Delcassé had gone, but his policy survived.[3]

On April 5 the Chancellor defended his Moroccan policy before the Reichstag.[4] " Was it our duty or our desire to fight about Morocco ? No, gentlemen, not about Morocco. . . . We have there no direct political interests or aspirations. . . . But we have economic interests in an independent, rich and undeveloped land. We were signatories of an international convention embodying equality of status. We derived from

[1] G.P. XXI, ch. 153.
[2] Von der Lancken, *Meine Dreissig Dienstjahre*, 54-7.
[3] See the eulogy of Barrère, " La Chute de Delcassé, Le Duel d'Algéciras," *Revue de deux Mondes*, January 1, 1933.
[4] *Reden*, II, 303-6.

S

a commercial treaty most favoured nation rights. To allow these matters to be settled without our assent was a question of the prestige of German policy, of the dignity of the German Empire, in which we could not give way. . . . Our aim was to show that Germany could not be treated as a negligible quantity ; that the basis of an international treaty cannot be shifted without the assent of all the signatories ; that in an economic area, independent and of great importance, the door must be kept open for foreign competition." Concessions had been made during the Conference for the sake of peace ; but there had been no surrender of the two governing principles of the open door and the maintenance of German prestige. It had been rather a difficult mountain to scale, and parts of the road had been dangerous. The Conference had resulted in a settlement equally satisfactory to Germany and France and useful for all civilised nations. " I believe we can now look to the future with greater confidence." After the close of his speech the Chancellor, overcome by the labours and anxieties of the crisis, fainted away, and only reappeared in the Reichstag in the late autumn.

The strain of Morocco was followed by a perceptible *détente* in Western Europe. Bülow's claim that the five years between Algeciras and Agadir were the sunniest period in Franco-German relations is excessive.[1] Yet the French were fairly satisfied with the position in Morocco, and the British Cabinet, having loyally fulfilled its obligation of diplomatic support to France, was not unfriendly to Berlin. The meeting of Edward VII with his nephew in August 1906 was pleasant enough, and in September Haldane, the new British Minister of War, was warmly welcomed in Berlin. Fisher, it is true, desired to destroy the German fleet before it became dangerous, but he dared not reveal his guilty thoughts to the Government. France marked time in Morocco, and Clemenceau, who became Premier in the autumn of 1906, seemed in a conciliatory mood.

On November 14, 1906, Bülow surveyed the European situation in his first public utterance since his collapse in the Reichstag.[2] The speech was intended to be reassuring, but it conveyed pointed warnings to Paris, London and Rome. Quiet, normal and correct relations with France were possible, though intimacy was ruled out. Co-operation in the economic field was a possibility, and perhaps here or there a colonial

[1] *Denkwürdigkeiten*, II, 212.   [2] *Reden*, II, 306–348.

agreement. There was no desire to interfere with her English friendship. The Franco-Russian alliance had made for peace, and he hoped it would be the same with the *Entente Cordiale.* " Good relations between Germany and Russia have done the Franco-Russian alliance no harm. Good relations between Germany and England are equally compatible with the *Entente Cordiale* if it pursues peaceful aims. Without good relations of the Great Powers to Germany it would be a danger for European peace. A policy aiming at the encirclement of Germany, at the formation of a ring of Powers with a view to isolate and paralyse her, would be of evil omen for European peace. Such a grouping is impossible without exerting a certain pressure. Pressure produces counter-pressure, and from pressure and counter-pressure explosions occur." Germany would never begin a war, and she did not dream of possessing a fleet as strong as the English.

Passing to Italy the Chancellor complained of her press but not of her statesmen. She and France had made certain arrangements about Morocco which were not incompatible with the Triple Alliance. " All serious Italian politicians are too clear-sighted and patriotic to wish to steer the ship of state out of the quiet harbour of the Triplice with its safe anchorage into the stormy sea of new groupings, a voyage of adventure without a compass. So long as Italy remains loyal to the Triplice she contributes to the preservation of peace for herself and others. If she deserted it or pursued an ambiguous policy, that would increase the chances of a general conflagration." Russia's negotiations with England concerning Central Asia caused no alarm, for he would have to go a long way back to find a period when Russo-German relations had been so good. Germany had no reason to fear isolation. " A people of sixty millions with an army such as ours is never isolated so long as it remains true to itself." It was the greatest Parliamentary effort of his life, closely modelled in substance and spirit on Bismarck's incomparable survey of 1888, which ended with the proud boast : We Germans fear God and nothing else in the world. For the moment the barometer seemed fairly steady, but the improvement was only on the surface. The Crowe Memorandum, drawn up at this moment, reveals the growing resentment and suspicions of the British Foreign Office. England and Russia were busily engaged in removing their differences, and an incident might at any moment revive the smouldering embers of Franco-

German antagonism. The military and economic strength of Germany was waxing day by day, but her rulers were not so certain that time was on her side. Even the obsequious Bülow could no longer suggest that his master was, or might become, *arbiter mundi*. And the Kaiser himself, realising the futility of the Morocco policy, began to think about a change of Chancellor.

The failure of the second Hague Conference of 1907 to achieve substantial results was a measure of the European *malaise*.[1] Marschall, its outstanding figure, correctly defined it as a Conference on International Law. That it was nothing more was due to the selfishness and timidity of the Great Powers. In conversation with the Kaiser in August 1906 Edward VII denounced the approaching Conference as humbug; and the Russians, who had urged limitation in 1899, excluded it from the programme of 1907. Alone of European statesmen Campbell-Bannerman pleaded earnestly for a step in advance, but the hostile reception of his appeal proved that it was in vain. The German Government, which had been genuinely alarmed in 1899, had no fear in 1907 of an excess of zeal. On April 30 the Chancellor defined his position in the Reichstag.[2] It was useless and even dangerous to discuss limitation until there was a good hope of agreement. Germany would therefore take no part in a discussion. If others cared to do so and something practical emerged, he would carefully consider the scheme. The platonic resolution moved by Sir Edward Fry gave dignified burial to the only question that made it worth while to summon a Conference, and Europe continued to drift towards the precipice.

XII

1907, the year of relative tranquillity, ended with the Kaiser's visit to Windsor and an Anglo-German *détente*. Though the Duke of Connaught, who had met Bülow in Karlsruhe, had invited him to accompany his master, a sharp attack in the *Times* rendered it impossible, and Schön, the Foreign Secretary, came in his place. Grey regretted the attack, but he was relieved that the Chancellor, whom he thoroughly distrusted, did not come. The visit gave the greatest satisfaction to both sides, and co-operation in the Baghdad railway was again discussed after an interval of four years. The improvement,

[1] *G.P.* XXIII, chs. 157–62.   [2] *Reden*, III, 32–6.

however, was only on the surface, for the construction of the German fleet went merrily forward. While William II was still on English soil, a new Navy Bill reduced the life of battle-ships from twenty-five to twenty years and increased the size of replacements.[1] At the opening of 1908 Grey announced in a speech to his constituents that England would have to increase her fleet, and the press was up in arms. The Kaiser's well-meant but injudicious letter to Lord Tweedmouth, written without the knowledge of his Chancellor, who greatly regretted its despatch, widened the gulf.[2] A mocking fate seemed to rule over Anglo-German relations, each successive *détente* being followed by a fresh blunder or misunderstanding. The Baghdad negotiations, so hopefully planned at Windsor, were frustrated by the Wilhelmstrasse on the ground that Germany would be outvoted in a Conference *à quatre*. King Edward's visit to Reval in June put the seal on the Anglo-Russian reconciliation, and rumours of agreements hostile to Germany fostered the conviction that the Fatherland was being hemmed in.

Metternich's despatches kept Bülow accurately informed of British opinion. In a comprehensive review of the situation on the occasion of the visit of President Fallières to London in June, he emphasised the strength and popularity of the Entente.[3] Englishmen, he added, desired neither alliances nor wars. There was no hostility to Germany, but there was a growing fear. The recent bitterness had gone, but the increase of the German fleet prevented confidence. The latest navy law ended the rapprochement initiated during the Kaiser's visit. Metternich described Grey as " an honourable and peaceful opponent, but an opponent none the less."[4] Lloyd George, on the other hand, ardently desired to reduce naval expenditure and to use the savings for social reforms. He urged the retardation of shipbuilding, and counselled Metternich to use the time while a pacific Liberal Government was in power.

No German Government, replied Bülow, could submit to a demand for unilateral limitation of armaments.[5] Moreover Germany was unfortunately exposed to the possibility of a French attack. If England would promise neutrality in such an event, retardation in shipbuilding would be facilitated.

[1] Tirpitz, *Politische Dokumente*, I, ch. 2, Die Zweite Flottenkrisis.
[2] *Reden*, III, 118–21.   [3] *G.P.* XXIV, 68–76.
[4] ibid. XXIV, 110.   [5] ibid. XXIV, 117–9.

268 BÜLOW

Metternich was instructed to point out the baselessness of British fears, since Germany had no intention of attempting to rival the British fleet. Unfortunately the Chancellor could do little to dispel British apprehensions, for his master's pride was involved. He describes in his Memoirs how earnestly and how vainly he pleaded in 1908 for a slowing down of the pace.[1] When Hardinge, who accompanied King Edward on his journeys, spoke seriously to the Kaiser at Cronberg in August on the inevitable effect of the *Flottenpolitik*, he met with an angry rebuff.[2] It was the first and the last time that the British Government officially suggested an agreed limitation. When Lloyd George during his visit to Germany later in the same month proposed a visit to Norderney, Bülow replied that it would be connected with the shipbuilding controversy, and would arouse hopes in England which could not at present be fulfilled.

The Chancellor explained his attitude in a remarkable letter to the Kaiser which, behind the courtier's phraseology, betrays a change of key.[3] " I beg Your Majesty not to doubt that I support Your Majesty's naval plans with heart as well as head. I know that the creation of the fleet is the task which history assigns to Your Majesty." In public and behind the scenes he had energetically sponsored all the naval programmes. Yet, just because he was so anxious to carry them out, he desired to shield the growing tree from storms. Unlike the Kaiser, he believed the English might fight if they felt sure that Germany's naval armaments would be continued *ad infinitum*. Thoughts of war in England were not confined to the hotheads. The alarm went deeper than that. Metternich reported the desire for an arrangement to avert a large increase in ship-building, and, though the Ambassador did not suggest an immediate German invitation to an official discussion, the door of hope should not be closed. " If we categorically and for-ever reject any understanding about the fleet, even in the many unofficial private conversations which every Ambassador must have, the ill-feeling in England will wax in geometrical progression. A real danger of war would arise, and England would build more than ever. The prospects of a peaceful development of events are more or less bound up with the Liberal Cabinet." The Chancellor's letter ended on a note of high confidence. " Your Majesty may rest assured that if

[1] *Denkwürdigkeiten*, II, 319–21. [2] *G.P.* XXIV, 125–9.
[3] ibid. XXIV, 148–51.

the storm beyond the Channel breaks, I shall not collapse. In Your Majesty's service I shall do my best to inflict many casualties. But Your Majesty should also understand that I am striving to shape events so that Your Majesty's lifework may be accomplished with God's help. The task is to get through the next few years."

In September Bülow reported to Metternich a conversation with his master about the Cronberg interview.[1] Confronted with the thorny question of the fleet the latter had answered more sharply than would have been the case in other circumstances. He explained to Bülow that he had no desire to build beyond the existing programme, and indeed for financial and military reasons he could not do so. Tirpitz, added the Chancellor, would be glad to discuss the naval question with British experts, but did not see how he could visit England without exciting attention. " He seemed to me not wholly disinclined to an agreement with the English on shipbuilding. But he thought the existing programme could hardly be modified, since the Reichstag and public opinion would not understand it. Moreover English policy and the press would have to be more friendly, for the German people would reject concessions due to pressure. If a *détente* were achieved, an agreement on shipbuilding, which would banish the fears of both parties, would not be impossible." Thus Tirpitz, like the Chancellor and unlike his master, was no longer wholly unaffected by the arguments of Cronberg.

While the rulers of Germany were secretly discussing possibilities in a new tone, the tide of excitement in England rose higher. The *Daily Telegraph* interview presented a picture of an Anglophile ruler and an Anglophobe nation. The speech of Lord Roberts in the House of Lords in November, wrote Metternich, would scarcely have been possible a year before.[2] " It is not the economic development of Germany which makes our relations to England worse from year to year, but the rapid increase of our fleet. Germans resident in England know this as well as the Englishman himself." Stirred from his complacency by the Ambassador's reiterated warnings, the Chancellor wrote to Tirpitz as he had never written before.[3] Everyone who had been recently in England reported lively apprehensions, groundless though they were, of an attack by the German fleet, and the idea of a preventive war was being

[1] *G.P.* XXVIII, 17–21.   [2] *G.P.* XXVIII, 17–21
[3] ibid. XXVIII, ch. 220.

voiced in the English press. " It is extremely probable that this idea will gradually permeate the English people, just as suspicion of our intentions in regard to the fleet has taken root. As a responsible statesman I must face the grave question of our attitude towards such an eventuality. I must therefore ask Your Excellency whether Germany and the German people can look forward to an English attack with quiet confidence."

The Grand Admiral took time to consider his reply. In view of the great superiority of the English fleet, his answer was in the negative. His task had been defined in the preamble to the Navy Bill of 1900—to build a fleet strong enough to avert an English attack. Only a powerful battle-fleet could keep the peace—not the submarines and mines recommended by Admiral Galster. That this policy involved a danger-zone had been known from the start. While Metternich advised a slowing down of pace, Tirpitz pressed for the execution of the programme with iron energy. The danger of war had diminished, not increased, as the fleet grew in strength, and large circles in England were now afraid of it. It would soon be so strong that to attack it would be a formidable risk. Hostile feelings were not the same thing as danger of war, and the former had probably come to stay. Bülow's annotations on the letter show him unconvinced. In the event of war would not Germany, he queried, be on the defensive? If so, would not coast defences, mines and submarines be more useful than battleships? Should not the time-table be slowed down in the next three years? Could not three battleships be laid down annually instead of four, followed by three annually instead of two, thus leaving the total unchanged but diminishing the immediate strain? The writer was at last alive to the peril of war and defeat, and he was impressed by the campaign of Admiral Galster for a different type of naval armaments.

The Chancellor returned to the charge in a second letter on Christmas Day 1908, elaborating the views expressed in his notes on the first. Since the British fleet was and would remain greatly superior, would the German fleet be able to challenge it to battle? Tirpitz had not answered that question. If it was reduced to the defensive, would not the improvement of coast defences, increase of mines and a powerful submarine fleet, be wiser than to concentrate on the increase of battleships? Political reasons also pointed to a slowing down of the time-table. Whether the cause of England's hostility was the navy or commercial competition was a secondary consideration.

There it was.   " Our duty is to seize every opportunity compatible with our self-respect to diminish English apprehensions, and to enable us to pass safely through the dangerous years."   He proceeded to propose the substitution of three for four battleships in 1909–11, making up the number in 1912–1914.   The Admiral's rejoinder was uncompromising. The Chancellor's plan, he declared, would be interpreted at home and abroad as a surrender to British threats.   Their success would lead to fresh humiliations, and the danger of war would increase.   To reduce the programme from four to three annually was also needless, since there was no danger of war : if there was, it would be too small a concession to avert attack.   If such an alteration of the Navy Law were to be pressed, he would resign.

The Chancellor withdrew the proposal for slowing down the programme, and confined himself to other points of the case.   Tirpitz had spoken of English threats.   There had been none.   The argument that the plan involved humiliation to Germany stung the Chancellor to wrath, for he was as good a patriot as the Admiral himself.   " I have never dreamed of doing or suggesting anything derogatory to our national dignity.   That would be in complete contradiction to my attitude during the last twelve years in all instances and in all situations."   Tirpitz at last showed some sign of advance. He admitted that if a diminution of programmes on both sides were to be suggested, it would not be rejected out of hand, as that would look too bad.   But Germany must not be the only party to make sacrifices, for she alone was threatened.   He would accept a ten year arrangement to build not more than three capital ships annually if England limited herself to four. " This proposal of Tirpitz is a new fact," noted Bülow on the letter.   " If he thinks this is the right course, he should go to England and try to reach an agreement on this basis. . . . He should remember that, so long as England is alarmed by the German fleet, we are up against her everywhere, which greatly complicates our foreign policy."   The Chancellor had taken a long time to learn his lesson, but he had learned it at last.

In a final letter to the Admiral Bülow replied that England would reject the 4 : 3 proportion as incompatible with the Two-Power standard and as insufficient to remove her fears. Moreover Germany would require political assurances as well. If England raised the question of naval armaments again

Germany should express her readiness for an agreement in return for a policy of friendliness, especially in the event of hostilities elsewhere. He concluded his letter by recapitulating the reasons for the correspondence. For years England had opposed Germany and made difficulties for her everywhere. That was all the more regrettable as the *Revanche* still lingered in France and Panslav tendencies in Russia. The cause of British hostility was the growth of the fleet. Since Tirpitz admitted that Germany could not resist an attack, it was the duty of the Chancellor to consider how to steer safely through the danger-zone. It was now the Admiral's turn to object. In view of the growing British hostility and the great superiority of the British fleet, it was the duty of Germany to arm to her utmost capacity. It was impossible to barter the reduction of armaments for a political concession. A promise of neutrality in the event of Germany being at war with a third Power would be almost useless, and would not prevent England herself declaring war. Thus ended the long correspondence without agreement and without practical result. The Chancellor had at last been converted to Metternich's view that the *Flottenpolitik* had produced a dangerous situation, but it was too late to remedy the mischief. A wiser statesman, with a deeper knowledge of England, would have realised in good time what the effect of such a policy must be ; and, if he had decided that the distant goal outweighed the temporary risk, he should have sought to strengthen the international position of his country in other ways.

The visit of King Edward and Queen Alexandra to Berlin in February 1909 produced a momentary *détente*.[1] Bülow assured Lord Crewe that it was an error to suppose that Germany was building her fleet against England, adding that she must be ready to defend herself against other lands as well ; but such polite assurances had long ceased to carry weight. The conversations, which were friendly enough but without significance, led the Chancellor to believe that it was not the time to discuss the fleet. It was desirable, he wrote to Tirpitz, that the *Flottenverein* should not agitate for a further increase. At this moment Metternich reported that the British Government believed Germany to be secretly accelerating her programme : they were seriously alarmed, but had not asked for an explanation. The Chancellor replied that no acceleration was contemplated. The statement produced no effect, since the

[1] *G.P.* XXVIII, ch. 221.

Cabinet preferred the information of the British Admiralty. Grey unofficially suggested an occasional exchange of information, but Bülow stiffly replied that since precise declarations were not believed such a plan would be useless. When, however, Asquith and Grey suggested inspection by the respective Naval Attachés, he advised acceptance as a means of calming opinion in England. Tirpitz was also prepared for inspection within certain limits, but the Kaiser refused his consent.

On March 29 the Chancellor spoke on foreign affairs for the last time.[1] Beginning with a warm reference to the royal visit, he declared once again that Germany had no intention of competing with the British navy. Her fleet was solely for the defence of her coasts and commerce. The programme was public property, and there was no intention to accelerate. Germany had nothing to hide. All rumours to the contrary were false. Negotiations for the limitation of navies were fruitless till a practical basis could be discovered. Informal conversations between Englishmen and Germans had taken place, but no English proposal had been made which could serve as a basis for official negotiations. These assurances failed to allay suspicions in England, where the Conservative party gave notice of a vote of censure on the Government for the inadequacy of its programme. The Parliamentary attack was repulsed, but the Opposition triumphed when the Government ultimately decided to lay down eight capital ships in the programme of 1909-10.

Grey's speech, which emphasised the gravity of the situation, also expressed a wish for a naval understanding. The Kaiser was ready for a 3 : 4 proportion, but not for a recognition of the Two-Power Standard.[2] Bülow hoped that the panic in England would quickly subside and that discussions might then begin. He reported his master as ready for a naval understanding only if combined with a comprehensive agreement, such as a promise of neutrality or a colonial pact. The Kaiser added that he had no thought of building up to the English level, and that the gap would always remain as it was. England was not the only nor indeed the principal opponent at sea. He had no wish for a race of armaments, but the programme must be carried out. Bülow informed Metternich that their master had no objection in principle to an agreement

[1] *Reden*, III, 179-98.
[2] *G.P.* XXVIII, ch. 222.

on the pace and range of shipbuilding. The idea of an understanding, he added, had gained ground in Germany; but a naval agreement would only be possible and fruitful as part of a political rapprochement.

On June 3 a conference was held in the Chancellor's palace, which Metternich was summoned from London to attend. The chairman opened with a warm tribute to the Ambassador's courage in describing the grave situation as it was. England was afraid, and serious people talked of war. Diplomacy alone could not remove the apprehensions. Slowing down on both sides, with a colonial agreement and a neutrality pact, would be the best way out. Relations with England were the only black cloud on the horizon, which otherwise was brighter than it had been for years. After Metternich had reiterated his familiar contention that the *Flottenpolitik* alone was the cause of the tension, Tirpitz argued that commercial competition was the root of the trouble, and that the latest excitement was Fisher's work. England should make suggestions, and Germany should quietly wait. The Chancellor contested his analysis and repudiated his conclusion. The cloud over the North Sea was a thundercloud. He was for slowing down and for renunciation of supplementary laws. The discussion, in what may be described as a Crown Council, revealed the Chancellor as the pupil of Metternich and Tirpitz as the leader of the intransigents. Three weeks later, in his last despatch to London, Bülow indicated that a naval agreement was possible in combination with a friendlier orientation of British policy. But it was too late to bridge the gulf, which, as he had at last come to realise, yawned beneath his feet, for three days later he resigned. It is astonishing that so clever a politician, with such a mentor as Metternich, should have taken so long to face realities, and his countrymen were doomed to suffer bitterly for his neglect. In a farewell conversation with the British Ambassador he declared that the idea of war was almost unthinkable.[1] If therefore there was no sense in being enemies, why could they not be friends? It was too late to ask such questions. He had had his chance of winning the friendship of England, and he had signally failed.

XIII

The last phase of Bülow's reign was the most anxious that he had ever known. For two years following the Conference of

_____
[1] *B.D.* VI, 279-80.

Algeciras there was no serious trouble in Morocco. Pichon
was at the Quai d'Orsay, determined to avoid friction if he
could. " If I had been Minister three years ago ", he confided
to Radolin on October 17, 1907, " there would have been no
troubles in Morocco.[1] I should have nipped them in the bud.
Delcassé let himself be carried away. Si vous saviez que de
mal j'ai à resister aux poussées continuelles des différentes
personnes influentes qui veulent me forcer la main ! " The
most pacific Minister, however, cannot prevent the occurrence
of incidents which frustrate his plans. On September 27,
1908, three German deserters from the Foreign Legion were
arrested in Casablanca while attempting to board a German
ship, and two German Consular officials accompanying them
were maltreated by French soldiers.[2] Both Governments
endeavoured to moderate the press, for both parties were at
fault, the one in helping deserters to escape, the other in using
force against officials. " Our shield is not clean", noted
Bülow on October 5. Both sides were ready for arbitration,
but the versions of the incident differed and tempers began to
rise. The Chancellor sharply complained of French pro-
crastination, demanding the release of the deserters and
satisfaction for the mishandling of the officials. The French
Government, he added, must be made to understand the
gravity of the situation. On the handling of this painful and
dangerous affair depended not only the further development of
the whole Morocco question but the relations between France
and Germany. The tension was at length relieved by the
discovery that the conduct of the German officials had been
incorrect, and by a personal appeal of Francis Joseph to the
Kaiser, at the wish of France, to settle the affair. An arbitration agreement was signed on November 24, and in the
following spring the Hague Tribunal declared both parties to
have been at fault. The Chancellor had striven to avoid a
conflict ; for, as he explained to the bellicose Crown Prince, to
give France a lesson would involve a war with England and
Russia as well.

The Casablanca incident increased instead of diminishing
Bülow's desire for a liquidation of the Moroccan problem.
" When Radolin says that at present we must leave France in
peace", he wrote to the Kaiser at the close of the year,[3] '
quite agree. When things have calmed down a bit we will try

[1] G.P. XXIV, 247.　　　[2] ibid. XXII, ch. 180.
[3] ibid. XXIV, 464-5.

for an agreement." He had not long to wait, for Pichon desired a *détente* as much as himself. A month later Jules Cambon was busily engaged with the Wilhelmstrasse, and on February 9, 1909, a pact was signed.[1] Germany declared her political disinterestedness in Morocco, and the two Powers pledged themselves to co-operation in the economic field. The agreement provided a breathing space, if not a solution, and it was welcomed with a sigh of relief not only in Berlin and Paris but in London and Vienna. For Europe was entangled in the Bosnian crisis, and the Powers desired to have their hands free to deal with its emergencies.

While Goluchowsky, mindful of the organic weakness of the Hapsburg Empire, preferred to let sleeping dogs lie, Aehrenthal was determined that Vienna should count for at least as much as Berlin. The Dual Alliance was in his view an equal partnership, not a meek acceptance of inferiority. Driven out of Germany and Italy by force of arms, Austria could find an outlet for her energies in the Near East alone. The Balkan peninsula, he believed, was big enough for the ambitions of two Great Powers. Austro-Russian co-opera-tion in the Balkans, however, which began in 1897 collapsed in January 1908, when he obtained from the Sultan a concession to build a railway through the Sanjak of Novibazar. A few months later he decided to proclaim the annexation of Bosnia, and on September 5 he informed Schön, the Foreign Minister, of his intention.[2] On September 26 he wrote fully to the Chancellor, concluding with a pointed reference to Algeciras : " We reckon with complete confidence on the support of Germany, who has received proofs that we stand by our friends at critical moments."

Bülow's comments on the momentous decision were written in no cheerful mood. It would probably lead to the indepen-dence of Bulgaria and the union of Crete with Greece. But, as Aehrenthal had secured the consent of Russia, it was impossible to resist. " Our position would indeed be dangerous if Austria lost confidence in us and turned away. So long as we stand together we form a *bloc* which no one will lightly attack. In Eastern questions above all we cannot place ourselves in opposition to Austria, who has nearer and greater interests in the Balkan peninsula than ourselves. A refusal or a grudging attitude in the question of the annexation of Bosnia and Herze-govina would not be forgiven. The old Emperor and official

[1] *G.P.* XXIV, ch. 182. [2] ibid. XXVI, ch. 193.

Austria see in the possession of these provinces a compensation for the loss of Italy and Germany." All that the Wilhelmstrasse could do was to suggest that the feelings of Turkey should be considered as far as possible, and that the Balkan States should not be encouraged to attack her. The Kaiser, deeply incensed that he had not been consulted and fearing that the annexation would be a signal for plundering the Turk, denounced it as robbery ; but he agreed that nothing could be done. Aehrenthal had the whip hand and Berlin knew it. Holstein, though in retirement, was still in close touch with the Chancellor, and helped him to make up his mind.

The angry protests of Marschall, who watched the work of years crumbling into ruins, failed to move Bülow from his position. " I am far from underestimating the value of our friendly relations with Turkey.[1] But in my opinion Marschall goes too far when he advises us to sacrifice or at any rate to jeopardise our alliance with Austria for the sake of this friendship. In view of the importance which leading circles in Austria attach to this matter, our alliance would indubitably be badly shaken and suffer an irremediable breach if we showed ourselves untrustworthy friends and did not stand loyally at her side. In the present world constellation we must be careful to retain in Austria a true partner, all the more since the Vienna Cabinet in recent years has repeatedly given proof of its loyalty, occasionally without considering its own interests." The Chancellor, indeed, had no choice. Moreover he believed that the confidence of the Turks rested on stronger foundations than Marschall admitted, and that they could be made to understand that Germany dare not oppose her ally.

Since it was no use crying over spilt milk, Bülow strove to limit the range of the catastrophe. The Turks were assured that the German Government had not been consulted. The first task, he wired to the Wilhelmstrasse, was to secure the future of Turkey. " The real cause of the activities of the Bulgars and Greeks lies in the military weakness of Turkey. That is where the lever must be placed, and she must be reorganised to offer better resistance to future storms." The press should understand that Germany had no interest in playing a prominent *rôle*. " In Balkan questions we are third parties. . . . We are not directly concerned. Mindful of the Bismarck tradition we shall try to localise a war in the Balkan peninsula if it breaks out. We remain friends of Turkey and

[1] *G.P.* XXVI, ch. 195.

particularly of the Young Turks." A Conference made as little appeal to the Chancellor as to Aehrenthal himself. Germany and Austria would probably be outvoted by Russia, England, France and Italy. He did not believe in the danger of war in the Near East. Russia could not face the Austrian army, and the war cries of Serbia and Montenegro need not be taken too tragically.

In view of Iswolsky's visit to Berlin at the end of October on his way home from the Western capitals, Aehrenthal wrote a private letter to Bülow explaining his action and communicating the more important documents.[1] The Chancellor advised his master to avoid political discussion with his visitor, and to refer him to his Ministers. " My idea too ", commented the Kaiser. " I will let him do the talking "—a difficult resolve which for once he faithfully carried out. The Russian Minister spoke angrily of Aehrenthal and almost despairingly of his own position. He begged for pressure on Austria to allow the annexation to be discussed at a Conference and to grant territorial compensation to Serbia and Montenegro. The alternative, he argued, was the breaking loose of Serbs and Montenegrins, the whole Balkan peninsula in flames, an Austro-Russian conflict, and finally a world war. Bülow explained that Germany could neither put pressure on Austria nor leave her in the lurch—a reply which earned the cordial gratitude of Aehrenthal. Having determined his course, he backed up his ally in every capital. When Tittoni urged him to moderate Aehrenthal, threatening resignation and the break up of the Triple Alliance, he was warned not to offend Vienna. " Italy can only be the ally or the enemy of Austria. The end of the alliance would mean the first step towards a conflict in which Italy would risk her all. . . . I say that, not only as Chancellor, but as a confessed friend of Italy." Orders were given to the Ambassador in St. Petersburg to explain the situation to Iswolsky if he complained of his reception in Berlin. As Russia had so demonstratively advertised her intimacy with England since the Reval meeting, Germany could not leave Austria in the lurch.

On October 30 Bülow replied to Aehrenthal's private letters. " I know from Herr von Schön that you have come to doubt whether the unsavoury conditions in Serbia can last. I have confidence in your judgment, and moreover in this particular matter I recognise that you can estimate the conditions better

[1] G.P. XXVI, ch. 196.

than I. I shall therefore accept your final decision as dictated by the circumstances." Hitherto the Chancellor's policy in the Bosnian crisis had been beyond cavil, but at this point loyalty degenerated into subservience. Such was the attitude of the statesman who in 1914 was to blame his successor for following the Austrian lead. In both cases the Wilhelmstrasse was a brilliant second to the Ballplatz. The horse and the rider had changed places, with consequences disastrous to both. Meanwhile, desiring to combine support of his ally with the maintenance of peace, Bülow reminded Iswolsky of the advantages to Russia of a bloodless solution of the Bosnian question.[1] For Germany to be a passive spectator of a conflict would be still more difficult than for Russia to recognise the *fait accompli*. It sounds like a faint foretaste of the " diplomatic ultimatum " of the following spring.

On December 7 the Chancellor spoke on foreign affairs in the Reichstag, emphasising both the reserve of Germany in the Eastern question and her unflinching loyalty to an ally.[2] On the same day Aehrenthal wrote another of his revealing private letters. Could Italy be trusted in the event of war ? He would be glad of Bülow's opinion. Would it not be well for Moltke and Conrad to discuss the situation which would arise in the event of her neutrality ? He added that he did not expect her to join the enemy in the event of a Russian attack on Austria. Bülow forwarded a preliminary reply to Monts. After the attack on the annexation by a powerful group of states, Germany had to stand fast by her ally. If she had not done so, Austria would have had to yield. " We should then have found ourselves alone in face of the same group that had humiliated Austria. Her humiliation would be our humiliation." Austria must be strengthened in her self-confidence, not frightened by fears of an Italian attack. To Aehrenthal's private letter he replied in almost effusive terms. He congratulated him on the increasing acceptance and understanding of his policy in Austria and Germany. If Iswolsky continued his misrepresentations, should not the incriminating documents be published ?

Having identified himself with Vienna at the outset Bülow never looked back. While the Kaiser was anxious to meet Russian wishes in the Straits, his Chancellor argued that encouragement of Russia would forfeit the confidence of the Mohammedan world, increase the suspicions of England and

[1] *G.P.* XXVI, ch. 198. [2] *Reden*, III, 154–62.

T

France, and make Austria believe that her ally contemplated
new advances towards St. Petersburg.[1] "No opposition to
Russia's aspirations in the Dardanelles, but no premature and
uninvited offer to help ! " The Tsar realised that the time had
not arrived to raise the question of the Straits, but at the turn
of the year war was in the air, and Germany had a difficult part
to play. "I appeal to our old friendship", wrote Nicky to
Willy ; "if you make them understand at Vienna that a war
down there is a danger to the peace of Europe, then war will be
avoided." Willy replied that he would continue to give counsels of moderation to both sides.[2] Austria was not going to
attack Serbia, but the Balkan states must avoid provocations.
"These small states are an awful nuisance. The slightest
encouragement from any quarter makes them frantic."
These assurances produced no effect in St. Petersburg, where
Iswolsky continued to harp upon Aehrenthal's wickedness and
Austria's aggressive plans.

Bülow warmly welcomed the conclusion of the Austro-
Turkish agreement and the liquidation of the Bulgar-Turkish
dispute. His policy was to keep the ring while Aehrenthal
peacefully settled his difficulties one after the other. He was
never really alarmed, for he knew that Russia was too weak to
fight. The most annoying feature of the crisis was the
estrangement of Turkey. Germany's relations with England
were scarcely affected, since it was realised in Downing Street
that she had to stand by her ally. When Edward VII visited
Berlin in February 1909 Hardinge expressed the satisfaction
of the British Government that the two countries had recently
pursued a parallel course in Balkan affairs.[3] Germany had
naturally to avoid all apppearance of pressure on her ally, but
she had tactfully encouraged a compromise with Constantinople. Bülow replied that Germany desired a strong,
independent, flourishing Turkey. When he added that
Serbia and Montenegro would not dare to fight if Russia
declared that they would do so at their own risk, Hardinge
rejoined that it was too much to ask of the Protector of the
Slavs. The Powers must continue to warn the little states
against a *coup de tête*. If Austria was compelled to take action
against Serbia, she should promise to respect her integrity and
independence.

The hardest nut still remained to crack ; for while Serbia

[1] *G.P.* XXVI, ch. 199.   [2] ibid. XXVI, ch. 200.
[3] ibid. XXVI, 551-3.

clamoured for territorial compensation, Iswolsky dared not raise the white flag. Now that Turkey had been squared, Aehrenthal focused his attention on Belgrad, and the world began to wonder how long his patience would last.[1] Germany declined the proposal from London and Paris to avert the danger by joint mediation, on the ground that peace was threatened from Belgrad alone. On February 20 Aehrenthal privately explained to the Chancellor that he might feel compelled to fight Serbia, for in the middle of March he would insist on her recognition of the annexation. If she agreed, economic privileges would be granted : if she declined, an ultimatum would be launched. The same treatment would, if necessary, be applied to Montenegro. Everything would depend on Germany's influence at St. Petersburg at the critical hour, since a declaration from Berlin would induce Russia to give advice at Belgrad which would avert a war. In forwarding Aehrenthal's alarming letter to his master, the Chancellor reiterated his belief that, even if Austria took up arms against Serbia, Russia would not intervene.

Austria continued her preparations for war, and Aehrenthal threatened to publish the compromising documents.[2] Against the latter menace Iswolsky sought the aid of Bülow, who consented to mediate on condition that Russia strove to hold Serbia in check. " We could ask if Vienna would be ready to notify the Powers of the agreement with Turkey and to ask them to sanction the abrogation of Article 25 of the Treaty of Berlin. If this joint action were taken, Russia would then be able to speak more freely to Belgrad." The telegram concluded by a warning that, if he took no advantage of the offer, Germany would have to let things take their course. Here were the outlines and almost the phraseology of the coming " ultimatum." When the Russian Foreign Minister sent an evasive reply, a telegram to the German Ambassador carefully drafted by Kiderlen brought the dragging dispute to a head.[3] " Tell Iswolsky we are ready to propose to Austria to invite the Powers to accept the abrogation of Article 25 of the Berlin Treaty. Before, however, we approach Austria, we must know definitely that Russia will unconditionally accept. You will inform him that we expect a precise answer—yes or no. We should regard an evasive, conditional or ambiguous reply as a refusal. We should then withdraw and let things

[1] G.P. XXVI, ch. 203.   [2] ibid. XXVI, ch. 204.
[3] Jaeckh, Kiderlen-Wächter, II, 26–9.

take their course. The responsibility for further events would be his alone, after we had made a final sincere attempt to be helpful to him and to clear up the situation in a manner he could accept." Russia promptly capitulated, her *protégé* had to follow suit, and by the end of March the crisis was at an end.

Pourtalès denied that the "yes or no" telegram was a virtual ultimatum, though Kiderlen, who drafted it, boasted that it was. Whatever the intentions of Berlin, the surrender was felt as a painful humiliation. The effect in England was the more deplorable since the two Governments had worked without open disharmony throughout the crisis. Aehrenthal rejoiced at the result of Germany's stroke, and Francis Joseph thanked William II and his Government for their steady support. Bülow was proud of his laurels, the last he was to win ; for his handling of the *Daily Telegraph* incident had lost him the remains of his master's confidence, and in June 1909 he seized the opportunity of a defeat on a financial measure to resign without waiting to be dismissed. Germany, as he told the Reichstag in his last speech on foreign affairs, stood by her ally at a critical moment with "Nibelungen fidelity".[1] The debt of Algeciras had been repaid ; war had been averted ; the strength of the Central Powers had been revealed. As a matter of fact Aehrenthal and Bülow had won and peace had been preserved merely because Russia was not ready to fight. It was a Pyrrhic victory, which contained the germ of future strife.

In his brilliant and malicious Memoirs, dictated after the collapse of the Empire, Bülow contends that he left his country in a stronger position than he found it, and argues that it was the fault of his successors that his beneficent work was destroyed. His complacent reading of the European situation is shared neither by his countrymen nor by the outside world.[2] The Austro-German alliance was in good repair, and for the first time German battleships floated proudly on the North Sea. But the strength of Austria was waning with the growth of racial aspirations, and the price of the High Sea fleet was the estrangement of England. The Moroccan agreement of 1909 was merely a breathing space between Algeciras and Agadir, and France was disinclined to yield to further pressure. Russia, who had turned her back on the Far East and resumed

---

[1] *Reden*, III, 187, March 29.
[2] The attack in Germany began with Johannes Haller's pungent little book, *Die Aera Bülow*, published in 1922.

her interest in the Balkans, was moving instinctively towards a trial of strength with Austria in which Germany was bound to be involved. Indeed, the steady backing from the Wilhelm-strasse throughout the Bosnian crisis encouraged the Ballplatz to take the lead in Balkan questions and to count on the con-tinuance of German support. Italy had ceased to be a member of the Triple Alliance in anything but name, for she had made a secret treaty with France and was about to make another with Russia. To the Young Turks Germany was no longer the Big Brother but the ally of the Austrian despoiler.

For some of these untoward circumstances Bülow was not responsible. Yet the position of Germany was indubitably weaker in 1909 than in 1897, and even a successor wiser than himself would have been unable to repair the mischief that he had wrought or failed to prevent. Powerful though she was in armaments and industry, in organisation and discipline, in numbers and national pride, Germany had shouldered a burden too heavy for her to bear. The Triple Alliance, as fashioned by Bismarck, implied the loyalty of Italy and the hegemony of Berlin. These vital conditions of security and success were no longer fulfilled. Meanwhile the Triple Entente was growing in cohesion and strength. Of the eight Great Powers in the world Germany in 1909 could count on the friendship of Austria alone. Never for a moment throughout his twelve years of office did Bülow desire war or take a step which directly threatened the preservation of peace ; yet he was distrusted in most of the European capitals. His colleague Kiderlen used to speak of him as "the eel". His clumsy handling of England and France was mainly responsible for the increas-ing isolation of which his countrymen complained. That he was seriously handicapped by the blazing indiscretions of his master, the *enfant terrible* of Europe, and by the stark intransi-gence of Tirpitz was his misfortune, not his fault. But these excuses cannot shield him from the arrows of his foes. The abandonment of the sound Bismarckian tradition of limited liability had begun before he was called to the helm. Under his guidance it was thrown to the winds.

ISWOLSKY

CHAPTER IV

ISWOLSKY

I

THE key to the foreign policy of Russia throughout the centuries is the urge towards warm water ports.[1] No country of her size and importance is so badly placed for maritime intercourse with the outer world. Her northern coasts are only available in summer, and unrestricted access to the Mediterranean is barred by the Turks. The first sortie from the beleaguered fortress was the conquest of the Baltic provinces by Peter the Great; the second the attempt of Nicholas I to secure control of the Straits; the third the construction of the Trans-Siberian railway under Nicholas II; the fourth the advance towards the Persian Gulf. Such instinctive movements are " beyond good and evil "; and the historian, like the statesman, must strive to realise their elemental strength.

The latter half of the nineteenth century was the classic age of Imperialism, and Russia took an active part in the game. On recovering from the Crimean war she renewed the struggle with Turkey in 1877; and, though the Congress of Berlin watered down the Treaty of San Stefano, the Turkish grip on the Balkans was loosened, and Russian influence at Constantinople was again supreme. In the 'eighties Skobeleff pushed forward towards India, and the Trans-Caspian railway consolidated the advance. In the nineties the Pacific provinces were linked to Moscow by a ribbon of steel, and the seizure of Port Arthur announced the determination of Russia to dominate the Far East. At the turn of the century her influence became supreme in Teheran, where loans and concessions were extorted from a degenerate Shah. A policy so adventurous and spread over such an enormous front invited antagonism and involved formidable risks. During the half century inaugurated by the Crimean conflict Russia's principal competitor was England, and, though an armed conflict was averted, the lion and the bear found themselves more than

---

[1] No adequate survey of Russian policy since the Crimean War exists. Of the great series of documents designed to cover the period 1878–1917 only the volumes on 1914–15 have appeared.

once within sight of war. British traders feared the loss of markets in the Far East; British soldiers peered with anxiety towards the north-west frontier of India; the guardians of the Balance of Power dreaded a Russian control of the Straits. Next to England the most formidable rival was Japan, whose strength was only realised by Russia when it was too late. Nearer home her "historic mission" in the Balkans was challenged by Austria; and, though Bismarck argued that the peninsula was large enough for both, the delimitation of spheres proved no easy task.

With Germany the old relations of friendship dating from the Napoleonic wars were nearing an end. When Bismarck found himself compelled in 1879 to opt between Russia and Austria, the path was opened to a Franco-Russian alliance. His attempt to make the best of both worlds by the secret reinsurance treaty of 1887 broke down on his fall, and an isolated Russia stretched out a hand to lonely France. The value of the partnership was mainly financial, for the savings of thrifty Frenchmen facilitated expansion and strategic lines. At the turn of the century the Franco-Russian alliance confronted the Triple Alliance on the chessboard of Europe. England stood outside the system of groups, but her sympathies were with the latter.

Alexander III was relatively pacific, but with the accession of his weak-willed son in 1894 the rudder oscillated from side to side. In 1896 a raid on Constantinople was seriously discussed. In 1897 Russia and Austria put the Balkan question into cold storage. In 1898 Port Arthur was seized by the Power which a few months later invited the nations to a disarmament conference at The Hague. Vast though she was, there seemed no limit to her appetite. Under the guidance of Witte she was ceasing to be a purely agricultural state. The revolutionary ferment in the cities was a stimulus rather than a check to adventures abroad. This mood of reckless Imperialism was chastened by the Japanese war, and disaster in the Far East cleared the stage for new performers.

In his unfinished Memoirs Iswolsky[1] describes his career before his summons to the Foreign Office in 1906. After serving in Turkey, Bulgaria and Roumania the young diplomatist had a fleeting glimpse of the United States, and then settled down for a decade as Minister to the Vatican. In 1898 he was transferred to Belgrad and thence to Munich, receiving

[1] His own spelling, v. facsimile, B.D. vol. IV.

his first important appointment at Tokio in 1900. Through-out his three years residence in the Far East he urged a con-ciliatory attitude towards Japan and an understanding on the burning questions of Manchuria and Korea. Convinced that the attitude of the Tsar, Bezobrazoff and Alexeieff was leading straight to war, and undesirous of taking a hand in the game, he obtained permission to return to Europe. He was coldly received by the sovereign and his moderating advice was ignored. He had the reputation at Court, moreover, of being a Liberal, in other words of sympathising with the movement for constitutional reform. But while the Tsar and still more the Tsarina frowned on the audacious diplomatist, the Dow-ager Empress was his friend. The Tsar always consulted his mother on the choice of a Minister to Copenhagen, and in 1903 he was nominated to the post at her wish, with the secret hope of the reversion of the Foreign Office.[1] The Danish capital was a backwater after Tokio, but it was none the less the whispering gallery of Europe. Family gatherings brought sovereigns from London, St. Petersburg and Athens, and with the separation of Norway from Sweden still another throne was filled by a Danish prince. What looked at first like a check to Iswolsky was to prove a stepping stone to the highest place. The adventure in the Far East was bound to fail, and failure necessitated a new course at home and abroad. He impressed every one by his knowledge and energy, and Baron Rosen, his friend and colleague, described him as by far the ablest man in the Russian diplomatic service.[2] The first sign of the change in the ruler's mood was an intima-tion, while war was still in progress, that he was to succeed Osten-Sacken at Berlin. He was also considered for the dis-agreeable task of negotiating peace ; but his candidature, he tells us, was opposed by Lamsdorff, who pressed the claims of Witte.

The outstanding event of Iswolsky's three years at Copen-hagen was his first meeting with Edward VII at the British Legation on April 14, 1904.[3] The King expressed his great satisfaction at the Anglo-French agreement, adding that it encouraged the hope of reaching a similar understanding with Russia, which had always been one of his sincere desires. " I should like the rapprochement between England and France

[1] D.D.F. IV, 109, Nov. 13, 1903, and II, 644.
[2] Rosen, Forty Years of Diplomacy, I, 172–3.
[3] Lee, King Edward VII, II, 283–9.

to serve as the bridge towards this other entente, more difficult no doubt, but even more necessary and desirable. I hope you will transmit the sense of my words and confirm the belief, as far as you can, in my good intentions." The conversation passed to the Far East, and Iswolsky remarked that one of the causes of the war was the Anglo-Japanese alliance. When the King interjected that it was certainly not its purpose, the Minister agreed; but he had witnessed its inflammatory effect on the war party at Tokio. If Japan won, he added, she would become a source of danger for everyone in the Far East, particularly in China. The conversation lasted three-quarters of an hour, the King several times returning to his leading idea—the necessity and possibility of an Anglo-Russian accord. He spoke with absolute conviction, concluded the report, and with warm attachment to the Tsar and his country. The King sent Lansdowne a copy of Iswolsky's record, which the Foreign Minister approved, adding that the observations of the Russian statesman were most interesting and important. "Lord Lansdowne has always understood that he is regarded as a man who may before long play a conspicuous part in the affairs of his country." Writing to the Tsar on May 12, the King expressed his great pleasure in making his acquaintance. "In him you have a man of remarkable intelligence and who is, I am sure, one of your ablest and most devoted servants. . . . My earnest desire, which I am convinced you will share, is that at the conclusion of the war our two countries may come to a satisfactory settlement regarding many difficult matters between us, and that a lasting agreement may be arrived at, similar to the one which we have lately concluded with France." The seed sown at Copenhagen could not germinate while the struggle was in progress ;[1] but it played its part in shaping the policy which Iswolsky pursued when he was called to the helm, a promotion anticipated by the King at the date of the conversation.[2]

The Japanese conflict plunged Russia into a revolutionary ferment. The Empress Dowager, then in Copenhagen, expressed her alarm to Iswolsky, who emphasised the necessity of winning the moderate Liberals. She promised to beg her son for a constitutional charter, and Iswolsky consented to carry the letter to St. Petersburg. He arrived in time to

---

[1] B.D. IV, 188–9.
[2] D.D.F. V, 31, April 16, 1904.   Crozier to Delcassé.

witness the issue of the October Manifesto and the appointment of Witte as President of the Ministry. He counselled
the Tsar to appoint a homogeneous team, and advised his
political friends to support Witte. The attempt was in vain,
and the Minister had to content himself with a heterogeneous
group of mediocrities. Iswolsky, however, had formed ties
with the moderate Liberals who wished to see him Foreign
Minister in a Cabinet formed with their support. Before
returning to his post the Tsar informed him that Lamsdorff,
feeling unable to work the new system, would retire before
the opening of the Duma, and that he was designed as his
successor.

Iswolsky employed a three weeks' holiday in March 1906 to
discuss the European situation with the Russian Ambassadors
in Paris and London. In the former city he also met Muraviev, the Ambassador in Rome. He was delighted to find
himself in complete agreement with them all in regard to the
policy that Russia should pursue—the path which was to lead
to the Triple Entente. His journey coincided with the
closing days of the Algeciras Conference, where England and
Russia co-operated in support of French claims. A few days
after his return to Copenhagen he was summoned home,
arriving on the day of the opening of the Duma. On the
same day the reactionary Goremykin succeeded Witte and the
Cabinet was almost entirely transformed. Iswolsky, he
assures his readers, made a final attempt to remain outside a
Cabinet with which he had so little sympathy, but the Tsar
appealed to him in irresistible terms. At the age of fifty he had
overcome the hostility of his master and had climbed to the
top of the diplomatic tree. A vivid portrait of the new
Minister at the moment of his promotion has been drawn by
Baron Taube's unfriendly hand.[1] Two very different charac-
ters, he declares, met in him—a statesman of broad views and
alert mind, and at the same time a courtier and a snob. His
intelligence was incontestable, his apprehension rapid, his
mind supple, his reading wide, his industry untiring. But
these qualities were accompanied by an almost morbid ambition
to court the high born and the rich at home and abroad, and
by a terror of losing caste through any failure in his clothes,
his carriages, his furniture, his acquaintances and his relatives.
His desire to shine led him, a man of very modest means, to

[1] Taube, *La Politique Russe d'avant-Guerre et la fin de l'empire des Tsars*, 1904–17,
104–19.

hunger for the opportunity to gratify his extravagant tastes. His selfish materialism was as undeniable as his ability. He was no less industrious than Lamsdorff, and intellectually a giant compared with Muraviev. His vanity and affectations, so deliciously described by Harold Nicolson, suggest that a fine intellect was mated with a rather shoddy soul.[1]

Iswolsky came to his post with a definite and far-reaching scheme. " We had unanimously agreed ", he declares in his Memoirs after describing his visit to Paris and London, " that the foreign policy of Russia must continue to rest on the immutable foundation of the alliance with France, but that this must itself be fortified and enlarged by agreements with England and Japan.[2] That was the programme I had resolved to recommend to the Emperor, and I was determined not to accept the post unless I was assured of his entire agreement." The outlines were filled in during a conversation with Taube on the eve of his nomination.[3] He regarded himself as called to " liquidate the heritage of Lamsdorff in Asia " and to make a rapprochement with England. Finally, her hands free at last, Russia was to resume her activities in the sphere of her traditional interests, which she had abandoned for idle dreams in the Far East. Asked for his opinion, Taube approved the first two aims, but uttered a warning in regard to the third, which might involve a quarrel with Germany and international complications. He proceeded to explain that the internal condition, which Iswolsky had failed to realise during his residence abroad, demanded a long period of curative treatment and the avoidance of shocks.

On May 14, two days after his appointment, the German Ambassador in St. Petersburg reported favourably on the new Minister.[4] He quoted an official of the Foreign Office as saying that it was a change not only of person but of system. Hitherto a Minister had trained his successor. Gorchakoff had inherited the ideas of Nesselrode ; Giers was a pupil of Gorchakoff ; Lamsdorff was the right hand of Giers. Iswolsky was an outsider, whose course he could not predict. To Schön personally the change was most welcome ; for Lamsdorff had requited Germany's recent services to Russia with complete indifference to her interests in Morocco. Schön and Iswolsky had been friends at Copenhagen, where the

[1] H. Nicolson, *Lord Carnock*, 216, cp. *Letters of Sir Cecil Spring Rice*, I, 72–3.
[2] *Mémoires*, 91–2.
[3] Taube, 99–101.
[4] *G.P.* XXII, 21–4, cp. Schön's *Memoirs*, ch. 3.

former had learned to respect the latter as a very well-informed and skilful diplomatist as well as an upright and dependable colleague. "He has discussed with me many a delicate question, and I have never caught him in an untruth. I cannot support the widely held view that he loves crooked ways. Without describing him as a tried friend of Germany, I am convinced that he realises the value of a close friendship too high not to keep it in repair. To the French, despite his love of their literature and art, his attitude is objective, and he knows the danger to internal politics of too close an intimacy with the Republic. He hates the English, whose anti-Russian policy, familiar to him from Tokio, he cannot forget." Iswolsky assured his friend that his first visit to a foreign diplomat was to him. As Schön was aware, he had desired to spend some time as Ambassador at Berlin in order to gain the confidence of Germany and master the problems concerning the two countries before becoming Foreign Minister. In accordance with the wish of the Tsar and his own convictions, he would earnestly strive to make relations as friendly as he could. Lamsdorff had meant well, but his handling of the Morocco question had been unskilful. The German Ambassador appears to have taken these utterances at their face value at a time when the new Minister was already deeply pledged to a rapprochement with England. Iswolsky was never a Germanophobe, but he had come to realise that Russia must look to the Western Powers for her safety and her strength.

II

Iswolsky's *rôle* in Russia resembled that of Delcassé in France, for both Ministers succeeded in turning foes into friends. Steps towards an Anglo-Russian rapprochement had been taken during the last months of Lamsdorff's rule, and with the appointment of Nicolson to St. Petersburg one of the cleverest of British diplomatists arrived on the scene to co-operate in the task of reconciliation.[1] Within a few days of Iswolsky's appointment Schön inquired regarding press rumours of an entente between Russia and England concerning their reciprocal interests in Turkey, Persia, Afghanistan and Tibet. Germany, he declared, would welcome any arrangement which did not damage German interests, and she hoped that Russia would not confront her with a *fait accompli*.

[1] The negotiations are fully described in *B.D.* IV.

He added that the Baghdad Railway directly affected German interests. The Minister replied that the tendencies towards an arrangement between England and Russia regarding Asiatic affairs had not yet assumed a concrete form, but that an entente might emerge. Russia recognised German interests in the Baghdad railway and would take no decision in the matter without consulting Berlin. Iswolsky, declared Grey to Benckendorff after hearing his report of the interview, had accurately described the situation. He added that nothing was further from his wishes than to use friendship with Russia to create difficulties with Germany. He reminded the Ambassador that, though he had not made proposals for an entente, the Baghdad railway and the situation in Persia might help towards a general agreement. On the following day he replied to a Parliamentary question that the alleged Anglo-Russian agreement did not exist, but that there was an increasing tendency to deal in a friendly way with questions of common interest.

On May 29 the new British Ambassador called on the Foreign Minister, and opened the momentous conversations which issued fifteen months later in the Anglo-Russian Convention. He had received instructions, he began, to exchange views on Tibet and other important matters. Iswolsky was delighted, all the more since the friendly message from Berlin left the way clear for an Anglo-Russian understanding. Having received a hint from the French Ambassador that he was inclined to take Schön into his confidence, Nicolson suggested that the forthcoming discussions should be strictly private; for the Baghdad railway, in which Germany was particularly interested, would not be included. The British strategy was to put forward its wishes in Tibet and Afghanistan, leaving Russia to formulate her Persian demands. The negotiations began on June 7, when Nicolson communicated the British proposals in regard to Tibet, and Iswolsky asked for time to study the problem. Discussions followed concerning the Dalai Lama, the relations of the Russian Buriats with Lhassa, scientific missions, and the occupation of the Chumbi valley.

After the friendly opening both sides marked time. " While Russia is on the brink of revolution ", wrote Grey to Nicolson on August 10, " it is no good going faster in these matters than is necessary to keep the negotiations alive." Moreover Persia was in a chaotic condition, requiring continual attention to financial and constitutional problems as they arose. On September 7 Nicolson was instructed to state that England would be ready to receive any proposals relating to Persia, but Iswolsky showed no great eagerness in pursuing the negotiations. The long promised draft convention on Tibet had not materialised, and the Ambassador hinted that he would be glad to know in general outline the Russian views on Persia. " He looked blankly at me and said that he had no views at all. This was a little discouraging, so I suggested that perhaps we might soon begin to talk as to Afghanistan. To this he vaguely replied that this would be agreeable, but he did not seem disposed to take up the topic seriously. It is clear that we shall have difficulty in getting him to take the initiative, and I propose to leave him alone for a while on our larger subjects, and endeavour to settle with him the more pressing special Persian questions." It was clearly going to be a lengthy and difficult affair.

On September 23 Iswolsky " unofficially " approached the Persian problem, explaining that he was merely expressing the personal views of the Minister of Finance and himself. The object of any arrangement was to avoid the possibility of collisions. Russia would therefore claim a sphere of influence in the north, at some distance from the British sphere, leaving the rest of the country open to general enterprise. The General Staff, however, might have other views, and Russia might desire to construct railways in her zone for which she would need foreign loans. In a private letter to Grey three days later Nicolson reported more interest in the negotiations, though the Minister confined himself to verbal expressions of his personal views, and even in these he had not gone beyond the vaguest outline. He evidently expected difficulty with the General Staff, though they could be overcome with the support of the Tsar. The Russians were slow to move and hesitated in committing themselves on paper. " I believe that their present weakness renders them more cautious than would perhaps be the case if they were not hampered by their internal difficulties, as they probably fear that we may wish to take advantage of the existing situation to our own benefit. I fully believe in the sincerity of M. Iswolsky, and if I had to deal with him alone I do not think that the course of negotiations would be troublesome, though it might be lengthy."

On October 15 the French Ambassador in St. Petersburg inquired about the discussions, and Nicolson replied that the

broad outlines were being reviewed. Had Nicolson observed
any German tendencies in Iswolsky? Not at present, was the
reply, but it would be foolish to imagine that Germany would
view with complete satisfaction the conclusion of a durable
understanding between England and Russia. Bompard remarked that Iswolsky would break his journey at Berlin,
where he would probably see the Emperor, to whom he was
a *persona gratissima*. It was this journey, in fact, which was
blocking the advance; for Iswolsky was afraid of the frowns
of the Wilhelmstrasse, and he refused to commit himself till
he was sure of his ground. In a frank conversation with
Bertie in Paris he expressed his regret that he could not accept
the invitation of King Edward for political as well as personal
reasons. "If I went to London the newspapers would
conclude that negotiations between Russia and England had
gone much further than they had done. Moreover I might
have to discuss matters which I am not yet prepared to discuss,
and suspicion would be caused in quarters which it is very
necessary for Russia to consider. Before coming to arrangements with England I must find out at Berlin what interests
the German Emperor and his Government consider that
Germany has in Persia, not necessarily in order to allow them
to stand in the way of an agreement with England, but to
avoid a repetition by Germany of her attitude in the Morocco
question and of Russia being placed in the dilemma of France.
I must also ascertain precisely what are the views of the
German Government in regard to the Baghdad railway and
other matters. I require all this information in order to
enable me to judge how far I can go without the risk of
meeting with German opposition. In the present position of
Russia it is essential to consider German susceptibilities."
The Minister had Delcassé's fate before his eyes, and nobody
could blame him for his caution; for Russia was even weaker
in 1906 than France in 1905.

Two days later Clemenceau explained that France wished
Russia and England to reach an agreement, and that she
intended to remain the ally of one and the friend of the other.
Iswolsky replied that he was entirely in favour of an understanding with England, but that the negotiations must not be
hurried. Clemenceau remarked to Bertie that Germany had
evidently prevented Iswolsky's visit to London, and that
William II, who desired to revive the Dreikaiserbund, would
try to make terms with Russia behind England's back. Pichon

also told Iswolsky of the desire of the French Government that Russia and England should be on the best of terms, adding his regret that he was not visiting London. Iswolsky rejoined that a journey to London before a visit to Berlin would make an agreement with England more difficult. The negotiations required great tact, for he had the difficult task of persuading some of his colleagues of the advisability of coming to terms. He was confident of success if he was not hurried, and Pichon believed him to be speaking in good faith. Despite these explanations King Edward minuted : " I shall always regret that M. Iswolsky was unable to come to London this year."

The visit to Berlin was much more important, and indeed it was for this that he had left his desk.[1] He was glad of the decided improvement in Anglo-Russian relations, he told Lascelles, and hoped for a complete understanding, which, however, would require much time and patience, since public opinion in Russia was still very suspicious. He warmly praised Nicolson as the right man in the right place. He had explained to Bülow that an Anglo-Russian understanding would not in any way be directed against Berlin. It would be ridiculous, he added, to suppose that Russia, considering her geographical position and her internal condition, could deliberately seek a quarrel with Germany. The Russian statesman, indeed, emphasised his good will to Berlin a little too much for English taste. " Iswolsky knows that we must be suspicious of his visits to Germany ", wrote Grey to Nicolson, " and I should like him to feel that we must expect some frankness as to what passed between him and the Germans, and some progress with the negotiations, in order to prove to us that the Germans are not putting spokes in the wheel."

Instructed to discover the Minister's views on the Baghdad railway, Nicolson replied that Iswolsky had not made or been asked to make any embarrassing engagements in Berlin. " He is evidently relieved at the removal of the fear which was haunting him that Germany would step in at a given moment and make matters uncomfortable for Russia, and I think that the assurances which he has received have stimulated him to take up the discussions more actively than he has hitherto done. He assured me that he would devote all his energies to the task, and, laying his hand on his heart, he said that he was honestly and sincerely desirous of arriving at an understanding

[1] G.P. XXII, 38–45.

which he was convinced was the right policy for Russia to pursue." He explained, however, that his difficulties were great, since many influential Russians were in no mood for sacrifice. No details were mentioned, but Nicolson thought that he might ask for some concessions in the Near East to strengthen his hands.

In conversation with Lascelles, Bülow described Iswolsky's visit to Berlin. He had known him for many years and had a high opinion of his abilities and straightforwardness. The conversation had been most satisfactory. He had explained that the only object of the anticipated arrangement was to remove certain causes of friction in the East and thus contribute to the maintenance of peace. It was not directed against Germany. The Chancellor was convinced that Russia, as was only natural after her losses in the war with Japan, was anxious to avoid adventures. He added cheerfully that he saw no reason to fear a disturbance of peace in any quarter. Iswolsky had secured the good will of Berlin, but he had more formidable obstacles to face nearer home. When Nicolson expressed a hope that the negotiations would now proceed with reasonable despatch, he repeated that he must be allowed time to overcome opposition to the proposal of spheres of influence. The General Staff, for instance, disliked the idea of abandoning Seistan to British control, and there was a great mass of opinion to be converted to the new orientation. Moreover would not Persia regard zones of influence as disguised partition, and might she not beg Germany to intervene ? He seemed indeed so non-committal that Nicolson asked point blank if the Tsar still favoured an understanding. Certainly, was the reply ; but when the delimitation of spheres came before him, he would naturally consult his military advisers. The conversation was unsatisfactory, though Nicolson believed that the Minister still desired an arrangement. The German Ambassador spoke warmly of Iswolsky's visit to Berlin, and explained that Germany merely desired the open door in Persia. Nicolson repeated these remarks to Iswolsky, who summarised his conversations in Berlin. Bülow had explained that Germany's only interests in that quarter were the Baghdad railway and an open door for her commerce—a declaration which had relieved his mind. A month later Nicolson presented a draft agreement in regard to Persia in the hope of quickening the pace, but the year closed without any definite advance.

" I trust that the Neva climate is not commencing to exercise an effect upon me ", wrote Nicolson to Grey on January 2, 1907, " but I confess to some misgivings as to our negotiations. . . . Though I still feel confident that he is at heart sincere, I am afraid he is beginning to feel the influence of the military party." Iswolsky spoke as if British interests in Tibet were no greater than those of Russia, and he was less inclined to joint action in the troubles at Tcheran. " It seems to me that he is possibly affected by an impression which is gaining ground in St. Petersburg—wrongly I venture to think—that the Government have surmounted all their internal difficulties and are able to take a higher line in our discussions. Again the Japanese negotiations in which Russia must perforce play a secondary part may incline him to be a little stiffer and less disposed to concession in other matters ; and he may be disappointed that we declined to intervene with Japan, and, if I may say so, we were quite right in refusing. Moreover the General Staff may have been somewhat peremptory with him, and pointed out that he should keep his hands perfectly free." At the end of January Iswolsky announced that a small committee, which Benckendorff would attend, was about to discuss various points. The Tsar desired an arrangement, declared Benckendorff to Nicolson, but some people imagined that England had initiated the negotiation in the desire to turn Russia's difficulties to account. He had explained that pourparlers began before the war and were resumed on the return of peace, but of these the General Staff apparently had been unaware. He believed, however, that the opposition of the military party could be removed. Benckendorff, it was clear, would do his best.

On February 1 a Ministerial Council discussed the plan of an agreement regarding spheres of influence in Russia.[1] Till recently, began Iswolsky in opening proceedings, opinion in Russia was convinced that Persia must fall entirely under her influence, that she must advance to the Gulf, and that a trans-Persian railway with a fortified terminus must be built. Events had proved this impracticable, and everything must be avoided which could lead to a conflict with England. The best plan was a delimitation of spheres of influence, and he invited the opinion of the Ministers on the principle before discussing England's proposals. The Council having accepted the principle, the Chairman continued his argument. Such a

[1] Benckendorff, *Schriftwechsel*, I, 1-9.

policy was only feasible if it aroused no objection in Germany, for events in Morocco were a warning. She had already turned her eyes toward Persia, and Russia must make absolutely sure of her Western neighbour by an agreement on their respective interests. The Baghdad railway afforded a basis of negotiations, and the Council must decide whether it would abandon its antagonism. The Finance Minister, Kokovtsev, declared that the rumours of far-reaching German economic plans in Persia were much exaggerated. The objections to the Baghdad railway were as strong as ever, but, since it could not be prevented, compensation should be sought. The Minister of Commerce and the army representatives agreed that the line was inevitable. After approving the plan of understandings with England and Germany, the Council passed to the British proposals, of which the delimitation of zones of influence was the chief. Iswolsky pointed out that Seistan, so vital to the defence of the Indian frontier, must form part of the English sphere.

It was a harmonious meeting, and the Foreign Minister was now as anxious to go ahead as Nicolson himself. The Japanese negotiations were shaping well, and the more conciliatory Japan showed herself, the easier it would be for Russia to yield in the Middle East. Iswolsky, declared Bompard, was radiant and sanguine. He informed Nicolson that he had won over the military party to abandoning Seistan, but added that the Persian question could not be settled till an agreement was reached on Afghanistan, in regard to which Russia feared that the Ameer would fall completely under British influence. A few days later Nicolson handed in the British proposals in regard to Afghanistan. Henceforth the Afghan discussions ran parallel with those relating to Tibet and Persia. Iswolsky explained that Russia must arrange that Germany should not seek concessions in the Russian zone, and that such an agreement would have to deal with the Baghdad railway. " His idea apparently is that Russia should withdraw her obstruction to the Baghdad railway on condition that Germany gives her a free hand in her zone." Here was the outline of the Potsdam agreement of 1911.

At the close of March the French Ambassador remarked that Iswolsky was becoming uneasy about Germany, owing to some ominous references in the German press to isolation. Nicolson replied that he had not noticed any uneasiness in the Foreign Minister, but he agreed that the sooner the discussions were concluded the better. For the relations between the German and the Russian Courts and Governments were exceedingly intimate and cordial, and the influence of the French Embassy had declined. "But while admitting that many motives impel the Emperor and his Government to draw nearer to Germany and to accept as an unfortunate necessity the alliance with France, it seems to me that more powerful factors than personal sympathy will counteract to a great extent the tendency to drift too much into the orbit of Berlin. I have little doubt that it is the present aim of the Russian Government to remodel their policy in the Far and Middle East and to husband their resources and keep their hands free for recovering their position as a European Power." Nicolson's analysis was entirely correct. Iswolsky resolved to cut his losses in the Far East, make friends with Japan, remove British hostility by securing the Indian frontier, and resume an active *rôle* in the Near East. It was an opulent programme, and it is a memorable achievement to have carried it out.

While the fate of the discussions on Persia, Afghanistan and Tibet hung in the balance, both parties enlarged their claims. On March 15 Benckendorff, employing the threadbare formula that he had "no instructions" to speak of the Bosphorus, pointed out that the opening of the Straits to Russia would ensure a good disposition in that country and the success of the negotiations. Having at present no fleet of her own, she would rather that the Straits should remain closed to all Powers than be opened to all. Access to Constantinople might be on the same terms for all, but for her it was essential that the entrance to the Black Sea should be closed to foreign Powers. Unless it could be open for exit to herself without being open to entrance for others, she would leave the matter alone. Since other Powers were concerned an arrangement with England would be platonic, but its beneficial effect on opinion would be very great. Grey replied that he had felt throughout the discussions that good relations with Russia involved the abandonment of the old British policy of closing the Straits against her, which had been the root of the difficulties between the countries for two generations. To settle problems in Asia and then to disagree on some other important matter would undo the good that had been done. It would, however, be difficult to make a formal engagement, and, even if the Cabinet approved, there might be a storm which would damage the prospects of the Asiatic agreement. After consulting his colleagues Grey repeated his observations to Benckendorff. It would be difficult to fit the Straits into the negotiations. Important sections of opinion might be hostile, and though the House of Commons would doubtless follow the Government lead, a party majority would be undesirable. Moreover such a great concession to Russia would lead to a demand for similar agreements about such questions as the Capitulations in Egypt and the Baghdad railway. Thirdly, other Powers had to be considered, among them Germany, who had been told that the present discussions did not concern her. If a pledge were given on the Straits, other Powers might complain that an attempt had been made to settle the matter behind their backs.

Though very far from an integral acceptance of the Russian demand, Grey's reply was gratefully received. It marked a great advance in the relations of the two countries, declared Iswolsky, who agreed as to Grey's three points. " I have rarely seen M. Iswolsky so contented and satisfied ", reported Nicolson, who anticipated that this evidence of good will would facilitate the negotiations. A memorandum by Iswolsky noted with extreme satisfaction that the closing of the Straits was no longer a cardinal point of British policy, and accepted the view that the discussion of the subject should be postponed. The document appeared to Grey not a wholly accurate summary of the discussions, and the British stand-point was further explained in a memorandum of April 27. It was best, he concluded, to let the matter rest for the present : if the Asiatic negotiations succeeded, the Straits question would be much easier to deal with when it came up again. In a final memorandum Iswolsky noted with great satisfaction that in the main the British view agreed with his own, and expressed the hope that when the moment should come to present a concrete proposal it would be favourably received.

The desire on the British side for an enlargement of the scope of the agreement was in like manner declined. British supremacy in the Persian Gulf was unchallengeable, but in delimiting zones of influence in Persia we should have been glad to obtain public recognition of the fact by Russia. On June 6 Grey forwarded a draft preamble containing the statement that " Great Britain has a special interest in the maintenance of the status quo in the Persian Gulf. This clause has been added in view of the strong and explicit declarations of my predecessor on this subject, which is evidently one of paramount importance to Great Britain. It is felt that the omission from the present agreement of any mention of this point would make a bad impression on public opinion in this country, and seriously affect the popularity of the Agreement when concluded. His Majesty's Government therefore press for the insertion of these words in the preamble in order to secure that the Agreement be accepted from the first by both parties with good will." When Nicolson communicated the proposal Iswolsky complained that this was introducing at a very late hour a matter which did not concern Great Britain and Russia alone, and that it was enlarging the scope of the Agreement beyond the limit originally laid down. He did not deny our special interests in the Gulf, but such a clause might lead to embarrassments. " I could see that he was greatly disturbed at our proposal, which he fears will create difficulties with third Powers." In a minute on Nicolson's report Hardinge regretted that it was an afterthought, but added that it was necessary to disarm criticism. Grey wired that he would consider any wording to meet Iswolsky's contention that other Powers might object, and Nicolson was instructed to press his case.

Before he could renew the appeal Iswolsky sent him a very outspoken memorandum. " It is of a nature to completely change the character and scope of the proposed Agreement, which, in its *partie résolutive*, does not at all touch upon the Persian Gulf, in regard to which there has never been any question during pourparlers between Russia and England. A new clause referring to a political question, the importance of which cannot be misunderstood, and which touches very complex interests, would reopen discussions, and might delay the signature, not only of the Convention respecting Persian affairs, but also of all acts connected with all the other questions which have been treated. It should not be lost sight of that, besides Persia, there is also Turkey, to whom belongs more than half the littoral of the Gulf, and who must consider herself as directly interested in the question. There are, moreover, other Powers who would certainly consider themselves injured if an agreement were made without their knowledge." It was very important to avoid provocation of third Powers, and the proposed clause might lead to an incident similar to that created by the Anglo-French agreement in Morocco. " All these reasons move the Ministry for Foreign

Affairs to earnestly beg the British Cabinet to be good enough to withdraw its proposal to mention in the preamble its special interests in the Persian Gulf. It is, moreover, well understood in formulating this request that the Imperial Government does not at all mean to deny those interests, nor to exclude the possibility of examining later on another occasion with the British the question of the Persian Gulf."

In telegraphing the memorandum Nicolson added that he would make a further attempt but feared he would fail. " If we agree to omit the passage, I would propose to inform him in writing that we abandon our proposal in order to facilitate and expedite the conclusion of the agreement, and that we take note of his recognition of our special interests, but that I should say nothing as to reopening a discussion later in regard to them." If Iswolsky absolutely declined the proposed wording, wired Grey, the words " Great Britain has special interests in the Persian Gulf " might be suggested as an alternative, which, though not satisfactory, would be better than nothing. When Nicolson saw the Minister, before the arrival of this telegram, he made a final appeal. The British draft, he pointed out, bound Russia to no action and laid no obligations on her, merely ensuring her neutrality in any discussions or differences between England and a third Power. It was moreover merely a declaration on an incontrovertible fact. He could see no difficulty, and a considerable section of British opinion would regard as defective a Convention which made no mention of British interests in the Gulf. Iswolsky replied that his objection was not on behalf of Russia ; but was England's special interest in maintaining the status quo generally recognised, and what precisely did the status quo mean ? When Nicolson explained, the Minister replied that his arguments might be called in question by other Powers. The Convention as drawn gave no excuse for any other nation to intervene. But would Turkey recognise the status quo in regard to Koweit ? Would Germany be pleased to see a formal assertion of British special interests in the Gulf embodied in an instrument which, she had been told, dealt only with matters affecting British and Russian interests ? It would be leaving the line of safety. If England insisted, he would have to reconsider the whole situation. Nicolson knew when he was beaten, and, to the Minister's immense relief, he gave way. He added, however, that if the agreement were attacked in Parliament, as it was nearly sure to be,

Grey would have to explain the omission of the Persian Gulf.

It only remained to draft the declaration, which took the form of a letter of Grey to Nicolson, dated August 29.[1] After explaining that it had been considered inappropriate to embody a declaration in the Convention, he added that the British Government had no reason to believe that the question would give rise to difficulties. For the Russian Government had explicitly stated that it did not deny the special interests of Great Britain in the Gulf, a statement of which the British Government had formally taken note. The letter concluded by reaffirming previous declarations of policy in regard to the question. Grey was naturally annoyed at his failure to secure a letter for publication, which inevitably exposed him to Parliamentary attack. It was his one great disappointment in the prolonged Anglo-Russian tussle of wits and wills.

Two days later, on August 31, 1907, the Convention was signed by Iswolsky and Nicolson.[2] The most important of the three agreements concerned Persia, which was divided into a large Russian sphere of influence in the North, a small British sphere in the East, and a neutral zone in which the contracting parties were to have equal opportunities. In regard to Afghanistan England declared that she had no intention of changing the political status of the country or of interfering with its internal concerns, and would neither take nor encourage Afghanistan to take any measures threatening Russia. Russia, for her part, recognised Afghanistan as outside her sphere of influence, and promised that all her political relations with that country should be conducted through the British Government. In the third agreement both Powers engaged to respect the territorial integrity of Tibet, and to abstain from all interference in its internal administration.

Nicolson's impressions of Iswolsky had become much more favourable in the course of the long negotiations. " He has acted most loyally to us throughout ", he wrote to Grey on the day after the signing of the Convention, " and I have not detected the slightest attempt to take an unfair advantage. The game has been played most fairly. I was pleased that you sent him a kindly message. He was much gratified." Years later Nicolson declared that no serious cloud had ever arisen between them.[3] Friendly relations between the Minister and the Ambassador were of peculiar importance,

[1] B.D. IV, 501–2. [2] ibid. IV, 618–20.
[3] ibid. IV, 304, and H. Nicolson, Lord Carnock, 217.

for the final justification of the agreement would have to be sought in the spirit in which it was worked. If the test of a good treaty, like a good commercial bargain, is to be found in the equal satisfaction of the two parties, the Anglo-Russian Convention was a success. Russia had secured the recognition of her predominating influence in the largest and richest part of Persia, in return for the surrender of her claims in Tibet and Afghanistan. The treaty was received with mixed feelings. To Witte it appeared a triumph for British diplomacy, making it impossible for Russia to annex Persia. A more favourable verdict is passed by Prince Troubetzkoi, a Russian diplomatist, who applauded the Persian settlement while regretting the one-sided concession in Afghanistan.[1] But neither of these judgments did justice to a memorable achievement.

The Anglo-Russian Convention was the greatest feather in Iswolsky's cap. Considered merely as a balance sheet it spoke for itself; for the advantages secured in Persia were far too substantial to despise, and they were obtained for a reasonable price. Yet more important than the details of the treaty was the fact that a treaty had been made. The clouds which had darkened Anglo-Russian relations for half a century rolled away. The unyielding attitude of England in the Straits was abandoned. The dangerous anomaly of an England friendly to France and hostile to her ally disappeared. The path was clear for co-operation between the three Powers which might lead in time to a Triple Entente. The international position of Russia was immensely strengthened and her prestige dramatically enhanced. It was the happiest moment of the Minister's life. His relations with Berlin were satisfactory, with Vienna still undisturbed. In the Far East he had ended the quarrel with Japan. Had he died in the autumn of 1907, history would have judged that a statesman of front rank had been too early lost to the world.

III

The parallel negotiations with Japan gave far less trouble and took much less time. Iswolsky had frowned on the adventure in the Far East, and he wisely resolved to restore normal relations with the least possible delay. There were no formidable obstacles in the path, for the war had been

[1] Troubetzkoi, *Russland als Grossmacht*, ch. 3.

thoroughly unpopular in Russia and there was no desire in any quarter for another round. Japanese statesmen were also desirous of a rapprochement with a Great Power which would in due course recover its strength. The Treaty of Portsmouth contemplated supplementary agreements, of which the question of fisheries on the Russian coast was the chief. The Foreign Minister, however, dared not display too much *empressement*, and he hoped that the growing friendliness of England might strengthen his hands. Simultaneously to turn two hostile Great Powers into friends was a noble ambition, skilfully pursued and triumphantly attained.

In November 1906 the Russian Chargé in London asked Hardinge, in the absence of Grey, what progress was being made in the Anglo-Russian negotiations, adding that public opinion in Russia was beginning to demand that they should include the Near and Far East.[1] He mentioned the Dardanelles and recognition of the status quo in the Far East, which would have a moral effect on the Japanese, of whose proceedings they were very nervous, and which need not clash with the stipulations of the Anglo-Japanese alliance. Hardinge replied that we should be glad to consider any proposals, but in writing to Nicolson he was all for caution. " As regards any recognition by us of the status quo in the Far East it is very important that we do nothing which might impair the value of the Japanese alliance." Iswolsky, in other words, must pull his own chestnuts out of the fire.

When Benckendorff was in St. Petersburg for the Ministerial Council of February 1, 1907, he explained to his chief that England could not intervene in the negotiations, but that she could perhaps be of use in regard to his wish to ensure peace in the Far East.[2] Iswolsky desired to insert in the coming Convention a declaration pledging both parties to the status quo, and the British Government might perhaps associate itself with such an engagement. Nicolson replied that his Government would welcome a Russo-Japanese agreement maintaining peace in the Far East, but Russia would doubtless first ascertain the views of Japan. Once again British diplomacy declined to expose itself, but as a matter of fact Iswolsky needed no support from without. Witte, among others, sang his praises to Nicolson.[3] He had viewed the appointment with misgiving and surprise, but now

[1] B.D. IV, 254-5. [2] ibid. IV, 272-3.
[3] ibid. IV, 273-4.

that he had seen him at work he was struck with his intelligence, breadth of view, and honesty of purpose. He hoped he would establish a durable understanding with Japan. If Russia could live amicably with England and Japan, Iswolsky would have rendered an invaluable service not only to his country but to the cause of peace. German policy was so erratic and selfish that Russia should try to make terms with these two Powers rather than yield to the allurements of Berlin. Here was high praise indeed from an unexpected quarter. On his return to London Benckendorff emphasised his chief's desire that the agreement with Japan should approach as near as possible to an Entente,[1] and his hope that England would favour it. We should certainly favour a good understanding, replied Grey, though we would not suggest concessions to Japan. The direct object of an Anglo-Russian settlement was to secure the Indian frontier : the indirect object was to be on good terms with Russia, which among other factors required good Russo-Japanese relations. Beyond benevolent neutrality Grey wisely refused to go.

A Russo-Japanese settlement was facilitated by the signing of a Franco-Japanese treaty on June 10, 1907, which was accompanied by the flotation of a Japanese loan on the French *bourse*. It was a major interest of France to rebuild the bridges in the Far East, not merely because her involuntary breaches of neutrality during the war had strained her relations with Tokio, but because she was anxious to rescue her ally from the danger of another desperate struggle. Three days later, on June 13, Russia and Japan reached an agreement on their respective railways in Manchuria ; on July 28 a treaty of commerce and navigation and a fisheries convention were signed ; and on July 30 two political treaties were concluded. Iswolsky had been fighting a rearguard action, and Japan, like other bargainers, took advantage of her superior strength. He complained to the American Ambassador that the Japanese were most exacting.[2] The fisheries agreement, concluded for twelve years, gave her such far-reaching privileges that a critic described them as a camouflaged war indemnity. " Without doubt ", comments Troubetzkoi, " we made great sacrifices.[3] But justice demands recognition of the fact that our fishing industry had never been much developed, whereas the fishing in our territorial waters had long been a vital matter

[1] B.D. IV, 279.   [2] Howe, G. von L. Meyer, 334.
[3] Troubetzkoi, 67–8.

for the Japanese. Mindful of the proverb : ' When one has to part with the head, it is not worth crying about the hairs ', the smaller evil had to be accepted for the sake of neighbourly relations with Japan."

Of far greater importance were the two political conventions.[1] The published document engaged the signatories to respect each other's territories and treaty rights, and to defend the status quo by all pacific means within their reach. The secret document was more precise. The preamble embodied the desire to obviate all causes of friction with regard to certain questions relating to Manchuria, Korea and Mongolia. The first article divided Manchuria into a Russian sphere of influence in the north and a Japanese sphere in the south, the line being traced in an Additional Article. The second recorded Russia's recognition of Japanese domination in Korea. The third recognised the special interests of Russia in Outer Mongolia. If the Treaty of Portsmouth ended the war, the agreements concluded two years later restored friendly relations. It was a statesmanlike settlement, relieving Iswolsky of his anxieties in the Far East and opening the way for the pursuit of vaulting ambitions nearer home.[2]

Japan proceeded with unflagging energy to develop her new territories, and her railway policy caused rumours of another conflict within a few years. But the determination of Russia to avoid complications in the Far East was unchanged. On April 27, 1909, a Russo-Chinese agreement smoothed out administrative difficulties in the zone of the Eastern Chinese railway. Protests from Germany and the United States encouraged China to object, thereby enabling Russia to return to the status quo ante, which was less favourable to Pekin. When in the winter of 1909–10 the American Secretary of State suggested the neutralisation of railways in Manchuria, Russia and Japan declined the proposal, the former preferring the resentment of the United States to that of Japan. The action of America brought St. Petersburg and Tokio closer together, and on July 4, 1910, a treaty was signed by Iswolsky and Motono supplementing the pact of 1907.[3] The first article pledged the signatories to co-operate in regard to the Manchurian railways, the second to uphold the status quo in Manchuria. Article 3 declared that, if the status quo

[1] E. B. Price, *The Russo-Japanese Treaties of 1907–16 concerning Manchuria and Mongolia*, 26–35 and 107–11.
[2] Ssuworin, *Das Geheimtagebuch*, 273–4, August 19, 1907.
[3] Benckendorff, I, 332–5, cp. E. B. Price, 39–58.

were threatened, they would consult on steps for its defence. Six secret articles confirmed the line of demarcation fixed in 1907 and enlarged the rights of the signatories within their respective spheres.   A few weeks later Japan annexed Korea without protest from Russia, whose silence was a recognition that she had ceased to challenge Japanese aims.   Iswolsky had never wavered in his conviction that his country must be freed from an unprofitable entanglement, and he performed the task of liberation with courage and skill.   But surrender in the Far East could only be justified to public opinion by self-assertion nearer home.

IV

Throughout the long process of reconciliation with England, as we have seen, Iswolsky took the utmost pains to avoid offending Germany, and for a time it looked as if he might do more.   Next to the building of a mighty fleet no project was dearer to the German heart than the Baghdad railway, and here at any rate Russia could hinder or help.   On visiting Berlin in the autumn of 1906 he admitted that Russia had hitherto suspected and opposed the enterprise.[1]   He himself was friendly, but to overcome the antagonism he must dispel the fear that the Baghdad railway aimed at bringing Persia into its net.   He contemplated a treaty with Persia by which transport concessions should not be given without Russia's consent.   Would Germany object to such a pact ?   Mühlberg, the acting Foreign Secretary, replied that he believed there would be no objection, but asked for a written statement of Russia's demands from Persia.   Germany's assent would be facilitated if Iswolsky were to repeat his oral assurance not to oppose the Baghdad railway and promised that, if railways were built in Persia, Russia would not thwart their connection with the Baghdad line.   Iswolsky thought these suggestions reasonable and promised a written statement.   He then inquired so pointedly as to Germany's attitude towards the participation of Russia, France and England in the line that Mühlberg scented a campaign on the part of the three Powers to oust Germany from control.

In commending to the Council of Ministers on February 1, 1907, the project of English and Russian spheres of influence in Persia, the Foreign Minister emphasised the connection of

[1] G.P. XXV, 231–4.

the question with the Baghdad railway.[1] An agreement with England could only produce its expected fruits if it aroused no antagonism in Berlin. Russia had hitherto opposed the Baghdad project in every possible way, but the time had come for a delimitation of interests. Kokovtsev, the Finance Minister, while reiterating his conviction that the line would injure Russian trade, agreed that it could no longer be opposed, though Russia should not share in the enterprise. The representatives of the army in like manner maintained their objections on strategic grounds, but professed themselves ready for a deal.

Fortified by the assent of his colleagues Iswolsky handed a draft agreement to the German Ambassador on February 20, 1907.[2] By the first article Russia undertook not to oppose the railway and promised to facilitate the participation of foreign capital. By the second the two Powers agreed to consult in the event of the construction of lines in Persia connecting with the Baghdad railway or of its prolongation on Persian territory. By the third Germany declared that she had no political interests in Persia, that she recognised Russia's special interests in the north, and that she would not seek concessions within a zone to be determined. Marschall, on being consulted, found the draft unacceptable, since Russia conceded nothing beyond recognition of an enterprise which she could not hinder, and Germany was made to declare that she had no political interests in Persia. At the end of June a German counterdraft was despatched to St. Petersburg. The principal change was the explicit mention of a Persian line to be built by Russia to Khanikin on the Turco-Persian frontier, where it would join a branch of the Baghdad railway ; and the denial of political interests in Persia was omitted. Iswolsky was pleased with neither alteration ; but when the Emperors and their Ministers met at Swinemünde in August the problem was not discussed, since the Russian reply was not ready. The Anglo-Russian Convention concluded shortly after revealed Russia's sphere of influence, which surprised the Wilhelmstrasse by its extent.

While Russia was still considering her revised terms, the Kaiser and Schön visited Windsor in November, where hopes of British co-operation were held out for the first time since 1903. For Grey's refusal to share in the enterprise without France and Russia Iswolsky expressed his gratitude. The

[1] Benckendorff, I, 2. [2] *G.P.* XXV, ch. 185.

x

plan, he explained in a despatch to Benckendorff, appealed to Russia as little as to England and France.[1] In addition to the strategic danger the railway, if connected with future lines in Persia, would open that country to the political and commercial influence of Germany. Discussions, indeed, had taken place with Berlin, but no definite result had been reached. The news from Windsor would doubtless be speedily followed by a German approach to the three Powers, and Russia was ready to examine proposals.

At the end of the year Iswolsky at length renewed discussion with the German Ambassador. He intended to draw up a reply to the German memorandum of June. He was anxious to remove all friction in the Persian question, but he wished to be clear about German aims. When Pourtalès replied " the open door for our trade ", he complained of attempts to secure political influence at Teheran through a concession for a German bank and in other ways. Only on the basis of Germany's political disinterestedness could the negotiations be profitably pursued. Germany, replied the Ambassador, would not challenge Russia's political preponderance in the north, but she could not admit an economic monopoly. At this point Iswolsky remarked that he heard that the Baghdad railway had been discussed at Windsor, and that Germany had accepted in principle discussion of the co-operation of English, French and Russian capital. The proposal, replied the Ambassador, had not been and would not be accepted. Foreign capital might participate, but Germany could do without it. The conversation ended with vague assurances of Iswolsky's readiness to give guarantees for German trade in Persia and to consider the junction of a branch of the Baghdad railway with Persian lines. Though Persian questions were often to be discussed between the two Governments, Iswolsky's promised reply to the German memorandum of June 1907 was never sent, and negotiations were only resumed in 1910 by his successor.

V

In dealing with the troublesome questions arising out of Norway's separation from Sweden in 1905, Iswolsky was even more careful to walk hand in hand with Germany.[2] So close

[1] Benckendorff, I, 9–11.
[2] G.P. XXIII, ch. 173, cp. Schön, *Memoirs*, 63–7.

indeed was the association that suspicions of his loyalty were aroused in Downing Street, where at times it looked as if he were playing a double game. It is true that he engaged in negotiations with Berlin which he strove to conceal from his friends in the West. But he was within his rights in endeavouring to gather advantages for Russia whenever he could ; and in the Baltic there was one coveted prize which, if obtainable at all, could only be secured with German aid.

The separation raised the question of the treaty of 1855 between Sweden and the Western Powers, whereby the former undertook not to grant a harbour or any other rights. In the opinion of the British Government the treaty now lapsed, and the obligation should be renewed in fresh treaties with Sweden and Norway. The Swedish Crown Prince supported this plan in conversation with Bülow, who argued that Germany, no less than England and France, should be a signatory of the new pacts. A year later, in June 1906, Norway proposed a treaty to be signed not only by England, France and Germany but by Russia as well, guaranteeing her integrity in return for a promise not to concede territory or sovereign rights to third parties. The Wilhelmstrasse had no objection, and in November Norway presented a draft neutrality treaty with the four Powers. While Germany and Russia agreed in principle, Grey replied that he approved but must inquire what Sweden had to say.

The Norwegian plan was sharply criticised by Iswolsky, on the ground that Norway was to decide which of the signatory Powers she would summon to her aid if her integrity were threatened or attacked. A rival scheme drawn up by Iswolsky and Schön was accepted with slight changes at Berlin, and Iswolsky was ready to propose it to England, France and Norway. It was not however to be described as a Russo-German plan, since that might provoke the Western Powers to evolve a rival draft. Tschirschky explained the German attitude in a letter intended for the Danish Foreign Minister, who had made inquiries. Norway, he wrote, had asked the four Powers for separate undertakings to defend her integrity and independence by arms. Rightly disliking such a far-reaching obligation, Russia had worked out a counter-draft, by which the Powers jointly recognised the integrity, independence and neutrality of Norway without an explicit obligation of armed support. Germany approved the Russian proposal, and was prepared to co-operate in order that England, France and Russia should not act alone. The situation became increasingly involved the more it was discussed. Norway, dissatisfied with the Russian draft, proposed a Scandinavian Neutrality League, which Iswolsky disapproved. And now Iswolsky himself threw a new apple of discord on the table— the cancellation of the treaty of 1856 forbidding the fortification of the Aaland Islands, which he described as an intolerable limitation of Russia's rights and interests. Here was the trump card which henceforth dominated his play. He hoped for Germany's moral support, particularly in calming Stockholm. The Wilhelmstrasse cautiously replied that Germany would not raise difficulties, but that Russia should deal directly with Sweden, taking care to avoid an unfavourable reaction on the neutrality negotiations.

When Norway agreed to a second Russian draft, it was the turn of England to hang back. Nansen, the Norwegian Minister in London, believed that Russia's zeal for the new treaty had made her suspicious, but Grey told Metternich that he could not sign till Sweden was satisfied. Iswolsky complained to Schön of the British attitude. The change, he well understood, was due to Russia raising the question of the abrogation of the Aaland Islands treaty, and had as its object, under the mask of consideration for Sweden, to foster British influence in the Baltic. This attempt, which was opposed to the interests of Russia and other Baltic states, must be resisted. To this end he was ready for the great sacrifice of postponing the question of the Aaland Islands, and thus depriving England of the pretext for delaying the settlement of the Norwegian question.

This grudging withdrawal of an unattainable aim did not remove all the difficulties, for Grey now proposed the recognition of Norwegian integrity without mention of neutrality. The discussions drifted on through the summer of 1907, Sweden loudly complaining of the draft treaty as containing a point against herself. In discussing the question with the German Ambassador on a visit to Vienna in October Iswolsky expressed his eager desire to cultivate the most intimate relations with Berlin, adding that his master shared his wish. People had complained that the recently concluded Anglo-Russian Convention contained a point against Germany. With such a policy he would have nothing to do, and for this reason he had kept the Wilhelmstrasse informed of the negotiations. Wedel urged his visitor to strive for an accord with Sweden, since it was important for Russia to possess the confidence of that country, and struck the familiar note of the co-operation of Germany and Russia in the strengthening of conservative and monarchical interests.

On November 2 England, France and Norway abrogated the treaty of 1855, and the new pact was then signed by Norway and the Four Powers for the duration of ten years. The Powers recognised and engaged to respect her integrity. If it was threatened or infringed by any Power, the four governments engaged after a communication from the Norwegian Government to support it " by the most appropriate means ". Germany signed after explaining to Russia that she was not undertaking an obligation to defend Norwegian independence by arms. Iswolsky, not Bülow, had been the driving force throughout, and he had seized the occasion to convince the Wilhelmstrasse that his reconciliation with England was of strictly limited scope.

The recognition of the integrity of Norway was only one of the international reactions of her separation from Sweden. Before the treaty was ready Iswolsky and Bülow, accompanying their masters to Swinemünde in August 1907, discussed the plan of a pact of the Baltic Powers. According to Bülow the Russian statesman wished to exclude England from interfering in Baltic questions, desired to avoid a discussion of the Aaland Isles with England and France, and hoped by direct negotiations with Sweden to obtain the cancellation of the veto. France would doubtless accept the change, England would have to follow suit, and Germany, he hoped, would render support. Iswolsky produced a draft secret protocol, declaring that the policy of Russia and Germany aimed at the maintenance of the territorial status quo " on the basis of the complete exclusion from the affairs of the Baltic of every foreign political influence." Sweden and Denmark, as Baltic states, might conclude with the two Empires pacts recognising their territorial integrity and assuring the maintenance of the status quo. He reported the conversation to Schön on his return to the capital. He had explained his desire to thwart the British plan of securing influence in the Baltic by connecting the Norwegian treaty with the question of the Aaland Isles. With this object he had dropped the attempt to secure the recognition of Norwegian neutrality and had ceased to discuss with England the Aaland problem. But it would be incompatible with the dignity and the interests of Russia to preserve the veto on fortification. It was not a question of making a strategic base with a point against Sweden or other Powers, but simply the creation of a police station for effective prevention of the smuggling of arms to Finland. He desired to co-operate with Germany in a policy excluding from the Baltic all influences except the riparian states. He proposed to negotiate direct with Sweden about the Islands, relying on Germany's moral support, and only then to ask France and England to accept the abrogation of the treaty of 1856

Iswolsky's memorandum was analysed in the Wilhelmstrasse. The proposed maintenance of the status quo in the Baltic was acceptable, but not the exclusion of the influence of non-riparian states, for the Baltic had never been a *mare clausum*. The plan could only be pointed against England, and German policy was to avoid every needless antagonism to that Power. Russia, moreover, might betray the treaty and put the odium on Berlin, or London might hear of it from Stockholm. Such a clause, moreover, was superfluous, since the guarantee of the status quo by the four riparian states excluded meddling from outside. The Wilhelmstrasse proposed a counter-project of the four riparian states on the model of the Anglo-Franco-Spanish Mediterranean agreement of May 16, 1907, to which other states, especially England, could not object. It could be either a recognition or, better still, a reciprocal guarantee of the status quo. The pact should be public and England might sign, though Russia would probably object. After such a treaty had been concluded, Germany could propose to England a similar treaty for the North Sea between Germany, England, Denmark, Norway and Holland. The plan of two treaties was approved by Tschirschky and Bülow, and the former explained in a despatch to Schön that the suggested German amendments merely aimed at omitting whatever could be interpreted as pointed against England. Tschirschky added confidentially that Germany approved the principle of reserving Baltic questions for the four riparian states, and only objected to its embodiment in a treaty. The negotiations should be pushed on, for an English proposal relating to the Baltic in which England would share was expected.

Iswolsky recognised the objection to the mention of foreign influences, but argued that the Aaland question must be settled before the four Powers bound themselves to the status quo. Tschirschky replied that a separate protocol might declare that the recognition of the status quo should not exclude the abrogation of the Aaland Isles servitude. Iswolsky then suggested that the Norwegian treaty should first be signed, since, till that was done, England might interfere. The Baltic treaty should be kept secret, at any rate for the time. If it were necessary to prevent intervention by a *fait accompli*, such a treaty could be concluded at once and only published after the Norwegian and Aaland treaties were signed.

On October 5, in the course of his holiday, Iswolsky visited the German Ambassador in Vienna. He explained that Russia's honour demanded the recovery of her sovereign rights in the Baltic. Moreover there was notoriously a systematic smuggling of arms into Finland, which could only be dealt with by a military base in the islands. Sweden was annoyed at the Norwegian treaty, but he hoped she would be reassured by the projected declarations on the maintenance of the Baltic status quo. The Baltic belonged to the riparian states, and England and France had no part in its problems. Asked what he thought Sweden would say to the project, Wedel replied that she felt not merely suspicion but fear of Russia and that the military reoccupation of the isles was particularly dreaded. Iswolsky was aware of the suspicion, but he hoped Sweden would be reassured by the Russo-German guarantee of her territory. Wedel expressed the hope to his chief that Germany would do her utmost to secure the assent of Sweden, since the rendering of such eminent service to Russia would be of great value to Russo-German relations.

During the conversation Iswolsky handed to Wedel, for communication to Berlin, a memorandum replying to the German memorandum of August 23, which he accepted but desired to keep secret. His programme was first a secret Russo-German accord on the basis of the German counter-draft, with a special clause or separate protocol concerning the islands ; secondly, an exchange of public declarations by the Baltic States, with a clause relating to the islands in the Russo-Swedish declaration. On October 29 the Russo-German pact was signed at St. Petersburg, declaring for the mainten-ance of the territorial status quo. Sweden and Norway might conclude with the two Empires special arrangements recognising their territorial integrity. Germany undertook not to oppose the abrogation of the Aaland treaty of 1856. The pact was to remain secret till the two Powers decided on publication. When Metternich received a copy he pointed out that it would not please England, who would realise the intention to exclude her influence from the Baltic. When Sweden and Denmark were invited to adhere they should be allowed no time for soundings in London, for England was powerful enough to prevent the pact. Moreover, if she asked to join, she must be refused. Downing Street, he advised, should not be told of the Baltic treaty till the two empires were ready to negotiate about the North Sea, for a North Sea treaty would be sugar on the Baltic pill.

At this moment Sweden suggested in Berlin a status quo pact for the Baltic with Germany and Russia. Germany replied that she would gladly join, and suggested that Denmark should participate, but without mentioning that a Russo-German pact was already signed. Iswolsky was grateful for the news sent from Berlin, and agreed that now was the time to settle with Sweden, who was incensed by the Norwegian treaty. Denmark should be dealt with later as she might prove difficult. On November 26, however, Iswolsky learned from Berlin that the British Cabinet had got wind of the Russo-German negotiations from Stockholm, and that the Wilhelmstrasse advised that England should at once be told. Iswolsky agreed, but declined to hustle Denmark. Schön accordingly wired instructions to tell Grey that on Russia's initiative Germany, following the model of the Mediterranean pact, desired an exchange of declarations by the Baltic States in favour of the status quo in the Baltic. Germany and Russia were already in agreement on the main points. The delay in completion was due mainly to the Aaland question. Germany would be glad if England would join in similar arrangements concerning the North Sea. France, on being sounded, expressed a desire to join; but Pichon added his wish for a Baltic pact in which England and France would share.

With the Baltic treaty incomplete and a North Sea treaty for the first time under discussion it was a veritable tangle. Iswolsky disliked the notion that Denmark should share in both, fearing that it would lead to a guarantee of her integrity and raise the question of the Straits. Metternich reiterated his warning to hurry on the Baltic pact lest England and France should try to force themselves into it, for instance by an omnibus treaty including both seas which Grey preferred but did not press. An escape from the *impasse* was found when Sweden ceased to demand a binding declaration from Russia not to fortify the islands. Russia, on her side, ceased to press for a recognition of her demands in the islands, where the treaty of 1855 allowed her to keep a garrison. Thus after all the Baltic and North Sea treaties were signed simultaneously on April 23, 1908. Satisfaction was general, if not complete. Neither Russia nor Sweden obtained all they desired. Many Englishmen regretted that we were excluded from the Baltic *consortium*. The Danish Foreign Minister welcomed the treaties, while expressing suspicion both of England and Russia. The full story of Iswolsky's dealings with Berlin remained a secret for many years, but he would have seen no reason to blush at the exposure. It was his declared policy to draw closer to England without drifting away from Germany. Both countries could be of use to Russia. The Triple Entente was only beginning to take shape, and regional pacts were the order of the day.

The second Hague Conference provided a further opportunity for Iswolsky to co-operate with Germany. The Tsar confessed that he was cured of his illusions, and his Foreign Minister had as little desire for a limitation of armaments as Bülow or Aehrenthal. In a weak moment, reported Schön in February 1907, Iswolsky confessed that he felt little interest in and sympathy with the Conference.[1] It was an unwelcome legacy from his predecessor, who had committed the error of not leaving the whole matter to America. When his emissary, Professor Martens, returned from his mission to the capitals, he confessed to Nicolson that he was embarrassed by the conflicting opinions of the various governments.[2] England and the United States desired a discussion of the limitation of armaments, to which Germany and Austria were strongly opposed. He regretted that the question had been raised, and he was searching for some way out of the difficulty. The opponents of limitation, and therefore of discussion, carried the day, and the Conference contented itself with trivialities. The main interest of the proceedings was to be found in the grouping of the Powers, and Russia's subservience to Berlin struck every observer. " The Russians ", wrote Eyre Crowe, " whenever there was a divergence between France and Germany, have steadily and ostentatiously taken the German side.[3] The French have realised that they have had no influence whatever over their Russian colleagues. . . . The

[1] *G.P.* XXIII, 127–9.   [2] *B.D.* VIII, 213–214.   [3] ibid. VIII, 287–8.

dominating influence in the conference clearly has been fear of Germany." Disagreeable as Iswolsky's position had been as official patron of a conference which he disapproved, he welcomed a chance of proving his reiterated assurances to Berlin that the rapprochement with England was purely regional in character.

VI

The gratifying situation of Russia after the conclusion of the treaties with England and Japan was too good to last. Iswolsky had taken infinite pains to avoid arousing the suspicions of the Wilhelmstrasse, and in the Baltic discussions he had run with Germany in double harness. Germany, however, was the loyal ally of Austria, and the harmony was liable to be broken at any moment if either Russia or Austria made a move in the Near East. Russia was still too exhausted by the Japanese war to indulge in fresh adventures ; but in Austria a new and vigorous hand was at the helm, and Aehrenthal had no intention of steering his course according to the convenience of Berlin. The exertions of the Powers in forcing through schemes of Macedonian reform in 1903–5 were followed by a relaxation of effort. Projects of railways in the Balkans, however, were discussed, and in January 1907 Aehrenthal mentioned to the German Ambassador that, if certain lines were made, Austria herself would build one through the Sanjak to Mitrovitza—a plan to which the Wilhelmstrasse took no exception.[1] It was not, however, till the end of the year that the Sultan was asked for his permission, not as a step towards Salonika, of which Austria had ceased to dream, but as an economic necessity. Iswolsky was informed in the middle of January 1908, and on January 27 Aehrenthal announced the secret in the Delegations.

The response from St. Petersburg was extremely unfavourable, though the juridical right of Austria was unchallenged. Iswolsky, reported the German Ambassador, did not conceal his annoyance, and his enemies seized on the event as a new weapon of attack. As the political reaction at home grew in strength, interest in the Near East and the desire to realise Panslav aspirations in the Balkans increased. Austro-Russian co-operation in the Balkans had never been to the taste of the chauvinists. Aehrenthal, declared the Minister, had chosen a

[1] G.P. XXV, ch. 187.

most unfortunate moment for the announcement of his plans. "C'est une bombe qu'il m'a jetée entre les jambes." He himself was a keen and convinced supporter of the Mürzsteg agreement and of the Austro-Russian entente, which he considered the only sound policy in Eastern Europe. All the more did he regret that Austria rendered it difficult for him to hold to this course. The proclamation of her economic plans would have the effect of an alarm clock and would stimulate the ferment among the Balkan peoples. She had joined half-heartedly in the Macedonian reforms, he complained, because she desired to flatter the Sultan into support of her economic plans. A Ministerial Council was summoned on February 2 to consider the situation as a whole.[1] Was it possible, asked Iswolsky, to abandon the strictly defensive policy which Russia had hitherto pursued and to defend her interests with the firmness worthy of a Great Power? Russia, replied Stolypin, would be unable to speak in her old tones for several years. Any departure from a strictly defensive policy would endanger the dynasty. Iswolsky swallowed the bitter pill. Though he was shortly to play with fire, he never forgot that he was too weak to fight.

Aehrenthal was annoyed at the complaints, and a personal estrangement began which was to leave its mark on the history of Europe. "Well, our friend Iswolsky has shown himself in his true light", he remarked bitterly to the German Ambassador. "I was prepared for attacks in the Russian press, but I did not expect him to apply bellows to the flame. He has debts and longs for the well-paid embassy at Berlin. . . . If only he would go! But Tcharykow, his probable successor, is even more dangerous, for he is *borné* and entirely Panslav." He would not oppose the counter-proposals of a Danube-Adriatic line suggested in the Russian press. He then referred to his old project of reviving the Three Emperors' League, to which he had tried to convert Russia when he was an Ambassador; but since Iswolsky had been called to the helm he had seen the fruitlessness of the attempt. In view of the latter's pronounced leaning towards England nothing could be done.

It was in vain that Bülow attempted to pour oil on the troubled waters, for the Russian press suggested that Germany had prompted her ally. Iswolsky repudiated the notion of German complicity, but admitted that in other respects the

[1] Pokrovsky, *Drei Konferenzen.*

opinion of the press was shared by the Government. It would be useless to present the note for Judicial Reform, and in the Macedonian question as a whole he would perhaps draw closer to England. That was the result of Aehrenthal's bomb, though he would have preferred to maintain the entente with Austria. After declaring that the Tsar's friendly feelings for Germany were unchanged, he added his own wish that no cloud should trouble Russo-German relations. In any case there could be no thought of a course unfriendly to Germany. The Wilhelmstrasse was not seriously alarmed, and Pourtalès believed that Iswolsky was not the man for a daring move. His notorious vanity, however, was reflected in his policy. He was angry that Aehrenthal had scored an apparent success, and that the work for Macedonian reform, in which Russia had taken a leading part, was threatened with collapse. However sincere his assurances to Berlin, he might be driven in the other direction.

A memorandum by Iswolsky to the Wilhelmstrasse was one shrill complaint. Aehrenthal had not breathed a word at their meeting in October, and he, Iswolsky, had recently assured the Tsar of his confidence and his loyalty. Berchtold had only informed him ten days before the announcement in the Delegations. It would have been easy to give timely notice and to discuss the plan in relation to Russian interests. He saw no way out of the Macedonian *impasse*. Under the altered circumstances to present the note on judicial reform was to invite a rebuff : to let it drop was to increase the danger of the situation. A day or two later he sent a circular despatch to the capitals recommending the Serbian project of a Danube-Adriatic railway. Aehrenthal made no objection, but the atmosphere was strained. " Outwardly ", reported Pourtalès, " the relations of the two Empires do not appear to be seriously clouded, but one cannot resist the impression that the good relations of the two men have suffered a severe shock and will scarcely resume their old character." He thought the Russian anger with Austria entirely natural. Her increase of power was grudged, and the political and economic rivalry in the Balkans, which had been blunted by the Mürzsteg programme, had revived.

Iswolsky poured out his heart to the German Ambassador. " I have always been true to the Entente and have treated Austria with the greatest consideration. I therefore expected her to treat us in the same spirit. Baron Aehrenthal knows

Russia well enough to realise my embarrassment. We too must reckon with public opinion nowadays. If another grouping of the Powers spontaneously arises, Austria is solely responsible, not I. My policy was that of the entente. That was my basis, and trusting in the sincerity of the Vienna Cabinet I was able to pursue a conservative policy in the Balkans despite all the chauvinism at home. The inconsiderate and selfish procedure of Baron Aehrenthal renders this policy almost impossible." Had he mentioned the matter in the previous autumn, an understanding could easily have been reached. He, Iswolsky, had supported the demand for a Danube-Adriatic railway to soothe Russian opinion, but Russia craved no railway concessions in the Balkans and would provide no money. On the other hand she must prevent Austria from securing a pacific penetration of the Balkans by a railway monopoly behind her back, which would inevitably diminish the political influence of other Powers ; and the Sultan must approve a line in which other than Austrian interests were concerned. He begged Germany to support the demand. Iswolsky, concluded Pourtalès, had no desire for a crisis in the Near East, but he was turning more and more towards a change of course as a countermove to Austria's independent action.

Despite his bitter feelings the Foreign Minister addressed the Duma in conciliatory terms. He explained why, instead of protesting against the Sanjak railway, he was prepared to support all useful railway plans. Since Austria agreed to this principle, the Sanjak incident had lost its acute character. The chief task was still the introduction of urgent reforms in Macedonia, for which he had striven with all his might. The most striking feature of the speech was the warm reference to Germany, who, he felt sure, would give the most loyal support to Russian proposals, and with whom cordial relations had never been interrupted for a moment. The Austrian Ambassador was assured that there was no wish to cut the wires. If Austria also desired to maintain them, she should support the Serbian railway project at Constantinople. Aehrenthal disliked it, though he could not say so. Pasitch, he remarked to the Russian Ambassador, was an intriguer and conspirator, and the policy of Belgrad would have to be entirely changed if he was to meet its wishes. He spoke in an aggrieved tone, reported Tschirschky, and Serbia might well be the arena of the sharpening antagonism between Vienna and St. Petersburg.

Neither line was built or even begun, but the incident left its mark on the European situation. Aehrenthal complained that Russia had turned her face towards England. Iswolsky retorted that Austria had broken the gentleman's agreement to co-operate in the Balkans. Both complaints were justified, but on this occasion Iswolsky had the best case. In liquidating Anglo-Russian differences he was performing his plain duty to his country. In concealing his approaching *coup* Aehrenthal played his colleague a trick, and the breach so rashly opened widened into a bottomless gulf.

VII

The Sanjak intermezzo was only one aspect of the dreary drama of Balkan unrest. There was little to show for the Macedonian reforms inaugurated by Lamsdorff and Goluchowsky in 1903, and the ravages of the armed bands operating from the surrounding Christian states grew steadily worse. The reform of justice, an essential item of the Mürzsteg programme, had been left to the last, and in 1907 a half-hearted attempt was made to secure the assent of the Sultan. Abdul Hamid, however, was tired of concessions, and Marschall, the ablest of the diplomatic corps at Constantinople, believed that it was impossible for a Mohammedan ruler to give way. Alone of the leading statesmen of Europe Grey maintained his unselfish interest in the welfare of the Macedonian peasant and was profoundly dissatisfied with the situation. For Russia the Christian subjects of the Sultan were pawns in a larger game.

The rapprochement with England disposed Iswolsky to close co-operation with her in Macedonia, and Aehrenthal's declaration of independence accelerated the drift.[1] Moreover Russian aspirations in the Straits, as he was well aware, could never be realised without her assent. Berchtold, reported Pourtalès in January 1908, did not wholly share Aehrenthal's suspicion of Iswolsky's Anglophilism, and did not at present anticipate an Anglo-Russian agreement about the Balkans. England, he believed, would scarcely scrap her traditional policy in the Straits, and he saw no signs of Iswolsky marching right into the English camp. "No Russian will ever forget Engla d's *rôle* in our last unfortunate war," the Minister had remarked. Iswolsky, added the Ambassador,

[1] *G.P.* XXV, ch. 188.

had always been extremely sceptical in relation to British proposals, and the latest, which concerned the strengthening of the gendarmerie, he had declined. Aehrenthal saw further ahead than Berchtold, for Iswolsky was moving steadily nearer to the traditional foe. In the Ministerial Council of February 2, 1908, he plainly showed his hand.[1] To find a way out of Russia's difficult situation, he declared, was not easy. Under certain circumstances it could be sought in a close approach to England. The British Ambassador had hinted at such a combination with reference to common interests in the Near East. Joint military measures in Turkey were quite feasible. Such a policy was most attractive and under favourable circumstances he would recommend it, as it would lead to brilliant results and to the realisation of the historic tasks of Russia in the Near East. The Anglo-Russian Convention, it was clear, had begun to bear fruit.

On February 8 Pourtalès reported Iswolsky as saying that, as the presentation of the reform note now seemed useless, he would perhaps get into closer touch with England. He assured the Ambassador, however, that he contemplated such co-operation only in regard to the reform of justice in Macedonia. He had no intention whatever of changing the orientation of Russian policy in the sense of a closer association with the Western Powers and with a point against Germany. He merely desired, with the help of England, to escape from the *cul-de-sac* into which the reform movement had strayed, since failure would be a grave blow to Russia's prestige. Now as before he pursued strictly conservative aims in the Near East, and he only laid stress on reforms in the interest of the status quo. Thus Iswolsky, concluded Pourtalès, was not yet thinking of a comprehensive Balkan agreement with England. But on the same day Nicolson reported the almost universal opinion that Russia should abandon her co-operation with Austria and range herself on the side of the Western Powers in Macedonia, since confidence in Austria had been destroyed.[2]

A new chapter was opened in the history of Macedonian reform with Grey's speech of February 28, 1908, which travelled far beyond the reform of the courts. He proposed the appointment of a Christian Governor of Macedonia, who, though a Turkish subject, should be irremovable without the consent of the Powers. The plan was formally presented to

Pokrovsky, *Drei Konferenzen.*   [2] B.D. V., 232-3.

the Great Powers a day or two later. Berchtold and Aehrenthal incorrectly believed that the radical British programme was intended to prepare the way for Iswolsky's more moderate plans. Grey desired his scheme to be accepted as it stood, and he regretted the unwillingness of the Russian Minister to travel so fast. Nicolson reported that he disapproved Grey's idea of grouping the three Macedonian vilayets under a Governor-General. Why not utilise the existing machinery and retain Hilmi as Inspector-General with wider powers? He also disliked the idea of guaranteeing the integrity of Macedonia in return for a reduction of the Turkish troops.

Iswolsky's alternative was presented at Vienna on March 16. "It has nothing sensational", remarked Aehrenthal, "and I feel firm ground under my feet again." The scheme, indeed, aimed at acceptance by the Powers and the Porte. People, confided its author to Pourtalès, would be astonished by his moderation. Its chief feature proved to be the plan of village guards. Aehrenthal agreed that Grey's proposals, above all the plan of a Governor-General, were unacceptable, and Iswolsky was pleased with the Austrian reply. In the field of Macedonian reform St. Petersburg remained nearer to Vienna than to London. Nicolson, who had been full of his praises, now charged him with insincerity. The Minister himself complained that all the Powers accepted his plan except England, who had not replied. The British response led to further negotiations, but even Grey's modified proposals went too far for his taste. His speech in the Duma on April 17 declared that Germany had loyally supported the Russian plan, and that cordial relations with Berlin had not been interrupted for a moment. Harmonious relations with Germany, in fact, were of greater importance in his calculations than the sorrows of Macedonia.

While the Chancelleries were still playing with schemes of reform, King Edward accepted an invitation from the Tsar. Iswolsky assured Pourtalès that he had no idea of a new political departure or of an extension of the Anglo-Russian Convention. He hoped to establish a basis acceptable to all Powers in regard to Macedonia. With Germany he desired, as ever, the most cordial relations. Bad relations with Austria and good relations with England were not to obstruct the wires to Berlin. Such indeed had been his policy since he took office, but events were now to be too much for him. On June 9 King Edward arrived in Reval, accompanied by

Hardinge, whose conversations with Iswolsky began with Macedonia.[1] He would gladly have accepted Grey's first scheme, declared the Minister, if he had seen the slightest prospect of its adoption by the Powers and the Sultan. It would be useless to go beyond his own last note, which he believed Germany would accept. Russia was always in a difficult position as regards Germany owing to her military inferiority. She must therefore give no cause to imagine that an Anglo-Russian rapprochement entailed a deterioration of Russo-German relations. Hardinge replied that the progress of the German navy had created in England a deep and growing distrust. In seven or eight years a critical situation might arise in which a powerful Russia might be the arbiter of peace, and have much more influence in securing the peace of the world than at any Hague Conference. For this reason it was absolutely necessary that the two countries should maintain the same cordial relations as existed between England and France, inspired by an identity of interests of which a solution of the Macedonian problem was not the least. The visit could not possibly be regarded as a provocation to Germany, and Grey had explained that no treaty would be made.

The latest Russian note on Macedonia was discussed in detail, and loans and railways in Persia were reviewed. Iswolsky ended with renewed complaints of Aehrenthal's Sanjak policy. Austro-Russian relations in reference to Balkan problems could not be the same again. Austria, he felt sure, would push the Sanjak line with the greatest energy, and it was absolutely necessary to promote the Danube-Adriatic railway *pari passu*. The Russian Government had only a very small financial interest in the proposed line, but they realised that the completion of the Austrian scheme would involve the Germanisation of Macedonia. He regretted that England had not felt able to support the Serbian railway plan. Hardinge replied that, when it had been presented at Constantinople, Grey would urge Turkey to allow the line. Both concessions or none should be granted. Iswolsky agreed, adding that he would prefer the latter alternative. Hardinge summarised his impressions of the Minister as very able and adroit, but extremely timid. " Although he tried hard to make me commit myself on the Macedonian question beyond the limit of authority given to

[1] *B.D.* V, 237–45.

Y

me, any suggestion which I made to him was at once set aside
as requiring careful study. He was, however, very friendly
throughout." Iswolsky's report of the conversation is much
shorter, though equally emphatic on its favourable character.[1]
No attempt was made by Hardinge to draw Russia into general
political combinations. But despite the sincere desire of the
British Government to maintain the very best relations with
Germany, " one cannot close one's eyes to the fact that, if
Germany should continue to increase her naval armaments at
the same accelerated pace, a most alarming situation might
arise in Europe in seven or eight years. Then, without doubt,
Russia would be the arbiter of the situation. It is for this
reason that we, in the interest of peace and the preservation of
the balance of power, desire that Russia be as strong as
possible on land and sea." Sir Charles, adds Iswolsky,
reiterated this plea more than once, whereby he indicated that
he was expressing the conviction of the British Cabinet.

It was in vain that the Tsar telegraphed to the Kaiser that
the meeting had " changed absolutely nothing." The
Kaiser's chilling reply revealed the alarm of the Wilhelmstrasse.[2] " I sincerely trust that your impression that nothing
has been changed will prove correct by the course of events."
The press, reported Pourtalès, had obeyed orders to speak of
Germany with moderation, and England had seemed rather
the wooer than the wooed. On the other hand the papers
hinted clearly at a diplomatic group capable of resisting the
dictation of Berlin. On his return from Reval Iswolsky
assured Pourtalès that the interview had in no way altered the
relations of England and Russia. No political agreements
had been made. The German representative could have been
present at all the political discussions. His talks with Hardinge related mainly to Macedonia and Persia. Nothing was
at present further from the mind of Russia than a policy of
adventure. She merely desired to remove complications, for
she needed peace. These friendly words failed to shake the
Ambassador's conviction that the bonds had been drawn
closer and that the visit would tend to Germany's disadvantage.
Grey gave similar assurances to Metternich that nothing of
importance had been discussed except Macedonia and Persia.
Neither of the Ministers confessed that pointed advice had
been given to Russia to press on with the restoration of her
military strength. The Triple Entente, indeed, dates not

[1] Benckendorff, I, 11–14.   [2] *G.P.* XXV, ch. 189.

from the Convention of 1907 but from the Reval visit of 1908. The Kaiser watched the drama with angry suspicions. He scented " an anti-German grouping like that before the Seven Years War ", and responded with the formula " strong fleet, strong army, powder dry ! " Aehrenthal described the meeting as bluff, but Tschirschky believed that the wish was father to the thought. The disappointing response to the Sanjak concession from Russia, which he believed himself to know so well, had wounded his pride, and he sought to diminish the importance of the Anglo-Russian rapprochement. Pourtalès summarised the impressions of an eventful month. Iswolsky had tolerated and even welcomed the press attacks on German and Austrian policy, because the failure of his diplomacy in the Sanjak affair and Macedonian reform required scapegoats, which he found in Aehrenthal and Marschall. Moreover German resentment of the Russian press attacks had at last affected his attitude, and he wished to punish the Central Powers by co-operating with England in Macedonia. To win Germany for the Reval projects he hinted that difficulties made by her would drive him more and more into the arms of England. " Very grave diplomatic conflicts will occur ", he had remarked, " if Germany opposes the project and thereby encourages the Sultan to resist the reforms." On the other hand he had no wish for complications, and everyone was aware that Russia was unready for a fight.

Pourtalès informed Iswolsky that Germany could not support reforms which would bring revolutions and endanger peace.[1] The Minister replied that co-operation with England in Macedonia was much more dangerous than with Austria, but that the dissolution of the entente was Aehrenthal's fault, not his. A day or two later he told the Ambassador impressively that the attitude of the Powers to the Anglo-Russian project, which was now ready, would be of the greatest importance for their relations in general. If Germany were to wreck it, he would be driven further towards England. He added that Aehrenthal had compelled him to turn to the Concert instead of to Austria. He had not looked to England, for an English project was there, which, after the Austrian entente had broken down, he was compelled to adopt as a basis of action. Far from being in tow to England, he had spent three months in bringing the project down to a level acceptable to the Sultan and the Powers. He feared that

[1] G.P. XXV, ch. 190.

German opposition to the scheme was inspired by her Ambassador. " J'ai peur de Marschall." The wire to Berlin was showing signs of strain after all. It was the tradition of German policy to support Turkey, and Marschall's brilliant despatches cogently presented the case for going slow. Germany's guiding principle in the Macedonian question must be to prevent or postpone so long as possible a Balkan war, which would gravely endanger European peace. Grey's plans involved a risk of war, and autonomy would not last. An Austro-Russian reform scheme, on the other hand, was a guarantee of moderation. While dismissing the idea of merely blocking the road to reform, Marschall equally rejected Metternich's advice never to oppose Anglo-Russian proposals for fear of fostering an Anglo-Russian entente. Nothing would serve so much to strengthen the Anglo-Russian combination as the discovery that Germans were afraid of it. The message of this able despatch was to let the Anglo-Russian partnership do its worst.

At this moment Iswolsky poured out his heart to the German Military Attaché. He had tried for three months to turn England's unreasonable proposals into reasonable shape. Germany's attitude would decide if the grouping of the three Conservative Powers were to be restored. If she offered support, Austria and Turkey would follow suit. The situation was extremely grave. He had his hands full with trying to hold back the three Balkan states. It was clear that he attached immense importance to the Macedonian issue, which he hoped to use as a lever for strengthening his personal position. A few days later Pourtalès summarised his latest declarations. " Russia's course will depend on Germany. If Germany and Austria support the Anglo-Russian project for Macedonia, Russia can continue on the basis of the entente with Austria and the co-operation of the three conservative Empires. If not, she will be compelled to lean more heavily on England, which would appreciably increase the tension in Europe." He had done his utmost to moderate English proposals, and England would consent to no further reductions.

In the same conversation the Foreign Minister passed to wider aspects of the problem of the Near East. The basis of his policy was the maintenance of the status quo and the balance of power in the peninsula. Far from desiring the collapse of Turkey, he wished her to continue in her present shape as long as possible. He was also opposed to any aggrandisement of the Balkan States, for history showed that the more independent they became the less they cared for Russia. If the liquidation of Turkey proved unavoidable, the equilibrium between the states must be preserved. For Russia to aim at territory or even a dominating influence in Turkey would be a great mistake. Her only dream was of free ingress and egress for her warships and merchantmen from the Black Sea, not for warlike purposes but simply to play a part in the Mediterranean worthy of her position. Her need for an outlet for her trade could be met without the possession of Constantinople ; she would offer all guarantees for the integrity of Turkey and abstention from any preponderating influence in her affairs. When Pourtalès inquired whether the Panslavs would be satisfied with so limited a programme, he cheerfully replied that they were losing their importance.

Neither the English nor the Anglo-Russian reform proposals were ever presented at Constantinople, for on July 23 the Young Turk revolution changed the situation in a flash.[1] Iswolsky, like other statesmen, realised that the Powers must for the present stand aside. He desired, however, the confidential discussion of his last proposals to continue, for he wished the Cabinets to see how moderate was his programme and to have it ready in case of need. He praised the moderation and cleverness of the Young Turks ; but his satisfaction, Pourtalès believed, was feigned, for a strong Turkey would frustrate his dream of the Straits. Meanwhile his policy was to show a friendly face, since a constitutional Turkey seemed likely to be less Germanophil than Abdul Hamid. To the Minister he remarked that the suspension of diplomatic activity in Macedonia was not unwelcome, for it would have been difficult to secure the hearty co-operation of Austria.[2] All projects had now been swept away. When Nicolson doubted if the Young Turks would be fair to the Christians, he remarked that they would doubtless try to avoid the risk of European intervention, and that this was the best guarantee. Of the bolder plans which were now filling his thoughts he gave no hint.

VIII

Incensed though he was by the Sanjak concession, Iswolsky reflected that Austria could still be of use in the realisation of

[1] G.P. XXV, ch. 191. [2] B.D. V, 309–10.

his plans. A lengthy Aide-Mémoire dated July 2, 1908, discussing Balkan railways, the entente of 1897 and Macedonian reforms, contained the following significant sentences.[1] " Nous continuons notamment à être d'avis que la question de la modification de l'état de choses établi par l'article 25 du Traité de Berlin, c'est à dire l'annexion de la Bosnie, de l'Herzégovine et du Sandjac de Novibazar, a un caractère éminemment européen et n'est pas de nature à être réglée par une entente séparée entre la Russie et l'Autriche-Hongrie. Nous sommes prêts, d'autre part, à reconnaître que la même réserve s'applique à la question de Constantinople, du territoire adjacent et des détroits. Néanmoins, vu l'extrême importance qu'il y aurait pour les deux pays de voir les deux questions susmentionnées réglées conformément à leurs intérêts réciproques, le Gouvernement Impérial serait prêt à en accepter la discussion dans un esprit d'amicale reciprocité." In penning these words Iswolsky was unwittingly opening a new chapter in European history.

Aehrenthal replied that, if circumstances demanded the annexation of Bosnia and Herzegovina, Russia would be expected to display a friendly attitude ; that after the annexation the Sanjak would be evacuated ; and that Austria was ready for a friendly discussion of Constantinople and the Straits. Both statesmen were ready for an advance, and on September 16 they met at Buchlau, the Bohemian residence of Berchtold, the Austrian Ambassador at St. Petersburg. While Iswolsky's report remains unpublished we have to reconstruct his utterances from his later declarations and from Aehrenthal's record.[2] Despite their mutual dislike the Ministers appeared pleased, and they parted on friendly terms. Iswolsky, declared Aehrenthal, was a pepper-box, but quite sensible.[3] Unfortunately the date of the proposed annexation was left unsettled, and from this oversight flowed a stream of disastrous results. If Aehrenthal really attempted to conceal his plans, it was Iswolsky's obvious duty to extract them before leaving the house. That the latter was prepared for early action is proved out of his own mouth, for on visiting Schön at Berchtesgaden on September 25 he described the conversations.[4] " He has the impression that Aehrenthal, chiefly for domestic reasons, will soon deal with these problems. Without having secured precise details, he inclines to believe that he will

[1] Ö-U.A. I, 9-11.
[3] G.P. XXVI, 33-4.
[2] ibid. I, 86-92.
[4] ibid. XXVI, 39-43.

announce the plan of annexation to the approaching Delegations." He added that, though it would be a great thing for
Russia to advance towards her goal, the opening of the
Straits for her warships, Aehrenthal's plans involved many
dangers. Annexation would provoke Bulgarian, Montenegrin
and Serbian claims. He would not have dared to set these
great questions in motion, but, if they were raised by Austrian
initiative, Russian policy would work for a comprehensive
and peaceful solution of all the Balkan problems that arose.
After reiterating his sincerest desire to maintain and deepen
the traditional friendship with Berlin, he expressed the surprising opinion that the alliance with France was a grave error
of policy, a cramping bond which Russia was unable to throw
off. The agreement with England, he added, was in no sense
a general rapprochement but merely a regional liquidation.

After visiting the German Foreign Minister Iswolsky
travelled south to meet Tittoni.[1] The annexation of Bosnia,
he explained, was only practicable with the assent of all the
signatories of the Treaty of Berlin. Russia would not object,
on condition that the limitations on the sovereignty of Montenegro were removed and the Straits were opened to the
warships of the States bordering on the Black Sea. It was the
interest of the Triple Alliance, argued Tittoni in reporting the
conversation to Berlin, not to alienate Russia by ignoring her
wishes. So far Iswolsky's plans had worked smoothly
enough. Neither from Germany nor Italy had he heard a
whisper of antagonism to his dream of opening the Straits,
and Austria's consent was already secured. It looked as if
1908 might repeat the triumphs of 1907.

When he reached Paris on October 4 Iswolsky found to his
consternation a letter from Aehrenthal dated September 30,
announcing that the annexation was to be proclaimed on
October 7. The Austrian statesman had indeed fulfilled his
promise of notice, but in the letter rather than in the spirit.
Moreover on October 3 the Austrian Ambassador announced
the decision to Fallières, breaking his instructions in order to
meet the President's convenience, and before Iswolsky had
had time to prepare the ground with his French ally and his
English friends. He reeled under the shock, and he was never
the same man again. With the assent of Russia in his pocket
Aehrenthal had forged ahead, leaving his ruffled partner
panting and gesticulating in the rear. To deny his complicity

[1] G.P. XXVI, 57-9.

was impossible, for Aehrenthal held the proofs. To admit it was to incur the reproach of acting behind the back of his Western friends, of consenting to the sacrifice of Slav interests, and of failing to secure any operative assurance of the opening of the Straits. A further complication arose from the fact that the deal with Austria, though approved by the Tsar, had been concealed from Stolypin and his colleagues, who disapproved it when it was revealed to them.[1]

In an unguarded moment Iswolsky admitted to the Serbian Minister Vesnich that he had foreseen the step and was not surprised, adding that it would not damage Serbian interests.[2] Such complacency proving impossible to maintain, he adopted the rôle of injured innocent. Aehrenthal, he told the British Ambassador, had said that Austria might have to annex Bosnia, but had not spoken of a definitive decision or an early date.[3] Khevenhüller's statement that Russia had consented was an exaggeration. In reporting the conversation Bertie expressed his conviction that Iswolsky was not telling the whole truth, and that everything had been settled except the date. Repeating his tale to Pichon, he argued for a Conference to deal with the situation, a proposal which the Foreign Minister approved. The French Government, however, was naturally incensed at the action of its ally. It was a gross breach of a treaty engagement, complained Clemenceau to Bertie, and an offence to public morality which, if allowed to pass, would form a very bad precedent.

We learn further details of the pilgrim's feverish days in Paris from various witnesses.[4] To the German Chargé he described the European situation as very serious, especially on account of the ferment in Serbia, which he was doing his best to calm. The whole fault was due to Aehrenthal, who was motived by personal ambition. He had indeed spoken of the annexation, but only in the sense of gradually winning the Powers for the project. To the Turkish Ambassador he explained that the infraction of the Treaty of Berlin by Austria and Bulgaria compelled Russia, like Turkey, Serbia and Montenegro, to demand compensation. Russia coveted no territory, but the question of the Straits must be satisfactorily

[1] Tcharykow, Glimpses of High Politics, 269–70, and more fully in Contemporary Review, October 1928.
[2] Boghitschewitsch, Die Auswärtige Politik Serbiens, I, 5–7. He reiterated his arguments to the Serbian chargé in London, ih. 15–7.
[3] B.D. V, 383–6.
[4] G.P. XXVI, 118–34.

settled, since the present position was a crying injustice. The
Black Sea States should have a privileged position, obtaining
free passage for their warships, while the Straits should remain
closed for the rest. Russia wished to restore the arrangements of the Treaty of Unkiar Skelessy. This would obviously benefit Turkey, since it would secure Constantinople
against foreign attack. Iswolsky was building castles in the
air, for the Turkish Government refused to look at the plan.
To the Austrian Ambassador he remarked that he would
shortly propose a Conference, for which he had a majority of
the Powers on his side. The visit to Paris was profoundly
depressing. He had been outmanœuvred by Aehrenthal,
and his laboured explanations were sceptically received.
Serbia learned with angry surprise that he had discussed the
annexation of Bosnia without consulting her interests. He
had indeed found France favourable to a Conference, but what
could a Conference do? What chance was there of the Young
Turks, flushed with easy victory, limiting their sovereign
rights, even if no protest came from the West? He knew
what Paris thought of his methods and his skill. It was in no
cheerful mood that the baffled statesman crossed the Channel
on October 9 to try his luck on the banks of the Thames.[1]

Iswolsky began his conversation with Grey by describing
his discussions with Aehrenthal. He had not consented to
the annexation of Bosnia, but merely exchanged views. He
urged a Conference to deal not only with the breaches of the
Treaty of Berlin but with questions of compensation. Bulgaria had shown no consideration for Russian wishes, and she
should pay for the East Roumelian tribute and the railway.
Serbia might have some rectification of frontier, but not at
Turkish expense. Turkey might be conditionally promised
the withdrawal of superintendence by the Powers in Macedonia and Armenia and revision of the Capitulations. Passing
to the question of the Straits, he brought his heaviest guns
into action. He would not raise the issue at the Conference,
but, if Russia could reach an agreement with Turkey, he
hoped England would not oppose. It had been a difficult
task to secure acceptance of the Anglo-Russian Convention,
and it would be fatal to good relations if she blocked the way.
Moreover his own position was at stake. He would propose
to Turkey that warships of the Black Sea States should have a
right of way through the Straits when Turkey was at peace,

[1] *B.D.* V, 424-44.

though not for more than three vessels at a time and no
others to follow within twenty-four hours. Russia had no
wish for Constantinople. Grey replied that he realised how
critical a moment it was ; that England was most anxious to
work with Russia ; and that she favoured the new régime in
Turkey. The proposal in regard to the Straits differed from
that which they had discussed in the previous year, namely
that Russia should have egress through the Straits, while
other Powers might send warships into the Straits but not
into the Black Sea. He must consult his colleagues. It was
an inauspicious beginning.

The next step was to communicate a programme of nine
points for a Conference to revise the Treaty of Berlin, which
Grey accepted subject to its approval by Turkey and the other
Powers. The Straits were omitted, since his visitor desired
first to secure Turkish consent. Moreover Grey disliked the
one-sided proposal, and to raise the question at this stage would
suggest that Russia had made a deal with Austria at the
expense of the Turks. The programme was generally
approved at a meeting of the Cabinet, after which Iswolsky
saw Grey again. He desired the Conference to meet as soon
as possible, preferably in Rome. His suggestion that invita-
tions should be issued by Russia, England and France evoked
the very sensible comment that Germany should first be
consulted. Grey proceeded to argue not merely against the
latest proposal for the Straits, but against raising the question
at all. The same evening Iswolsky produced a modified
scheme by which in time of war, when Turkey was neutral,
she should give equal facilities to all the belligerents. Grey
replied that he could not pronounce on particular proposals
as the hour was inopportune. The crisis should be settled
without Russia or England seeking advantages for themselves.

The considered reply of the British Cabinet, embodied in
a memorandum of October 14, did little to dispel the gloom.
The opening of the Straits, it began, would not be opposed in
principle. Disinterested co-operation in the solution of the
existing crisis would predispose opinion to a change, but the
consent of Turkey would require to be obtained. A private
letter from Grey on the following day, written at the instigation of his visitor for the eyes of the Tsar, assured him that
he desired an arrangement about the Straits at a suitable time,
which would not place Turkey or outside Powers at an unfair
disadvantage. Some such arrangement indeed seemed to

him essential for the establishment of permanent good will between England and Russia. Disinterested co-operation to pull Turkey through the immediate crisis would be the best preparation for a settlement later on. These assurances were satisfactory as far as they went, and were calculated to strengthen his position with the Tsar ; but they could not at present be divulged, and were therefore useless as a means of restoring his faded prestige.

The Minister had failed in his main object of obtaining support for an immediate opening of the Straits, but his visit to London was not wholly in vain. " I think Iswolsky departed believing in our good faith and good will," wrote Grey to Nicolson. The opportunity had been used to survey the whole field of Anglo-Russian relations. The evil effect on public opinion of the conduct of the Russian Cossack officers in Persia was clearly explained by Grey and Morley ; and Iswolsky for his part declared that the Afghanistan portion of the Convention of 1907 would be regarded as valid without waiting for the consent of the Ameer. At his first interview with Grey and Hardinge he declared that, unless he could bring back something as a sop to his enemies, he was doomed. Stolypin would go too, and they would be replaced by Anglophobe reactionaries, who were very powerful at Court. " There may be some truth in all this ", wrote Hardinge to Nicolson, " but I think that, at the bottom of it all, is the very strong desire to be able to show the world that he has not been entirely duped by Aehrenthal. Although I think that he is greatly responsible for the development in the Balkans, because he did not reject irrevocably Aehrenthal's advances, yet it is evident that we must do our best to support him such as he is." Such words of disparagement reveal how much ground he had lost in Downing Street by his latest escapade.

Our knowledge of the sojourn in London is enriched by the reports of the German Ambassador.[1] At their first meeting Iswolsky expressed his desire that Germany would act once again as an honest broker between Russia and Austria. Two days later he reiterated his wish for German mediation, fortifying it by the approval of the King. Though he would not include the Straits in the programme of the Conference, a satisfactory solution might possibly be found in the course of the negotiations. In a third conversation he suggested that Austria, by an act of generosity, might offer Serbia and

---

[1] G.P. XXVI, 147–69, and 195–6.

Montenegro compensation in the shape of frontier rectifica-
tions, though he did not expect it.   The same demand
appeared in a *communiqué* in the *Times*, the intransigence of
which appeared to Metternich to reveal the return of self-
confidence.   A private letter to the Chancellor summarised
the Ambassador's impressions.   He had had a remarkable
reception, including a dinner at Buckingham Palace.   More
fuss had been made of him than of any foreign statesman,
even Delcassé.   Though he had not got his way with the
Straits he was now definitely in the English camp, and the
press was jubilant over the strengthening of the Triple
Entente.

   Returning to Paris Iswolsky called on the German Ambassador, whom he had not seen during his previous visit.[1]   After
reiterating his angry complaints of Aehrenthal and urging that
Austria should cede Serbia a strip of Bosnia as a *solatium*, he
described his sojourn in London.   There was no idea of a
grouping of the Powers with a point against Germany.   He
had eliminated any topic that affected her, and he was deeply
anxious to live on the friendliest terms.   If only the German
Government would not identify itself too much with Austria,
the disturber of the peace !   He had tried to keep on good
terms with Austria, and had established friendly relations with
Germany.   And now Austria had spoiled the whole game !
He was about to visit Berlin, where he hoped that the Chancellor—" the only real arbiter of the situation "—would
suggest a just and impartial settlement.   It would have
incalculable consequences if, to please Austria, Germany
declined to take part in the Conference.   What interest had
she in humiliating Russia ?   He spoke throughout in excited
tones, and his almost despairing appeal for German aid
revealed his lamentable plight.   " Iswolsky has made a fool
of himself ", commented the Kaiser on Radolin's report, " and
wants to save his face and split our alliance."   At an official
banquet attended by Clemenceau and all the Ambassadors the
atmosphere was reported to be frosty.   Iswolsky was too
clever a man not to know that he had failed.

   After the disappointments of Paris and London, Berlin was
the Minister's last card.   In anticipation of his arrival Aehrenthal forwarded the essential documents to Bülow, who
cautioned his master to avoid politics.   The Kaiser accepted
the advice, to the unconcealed mortification of his visitor.

[1] *G.P.* XXVI, 180-2.

Nor were his conversations with Schön and Bülow more satisfactory.[1] He appealed to Germany's friendship to persuade Austria to allow the discussion of the annexation at the Conference, and to grant territorial compensations to Serbia and Montenegro. A refusal, he argued, might mean a conflagration in the Balkans, a conflict between Russia and Austria, and, to crown all, a world war. His own position was almost desperate. It was all in vain. Germany had no choice but to stand by her ally, and Russia, as all the world knew, was too weak to fight. The luckless pilgrim had not a card in his hand. When he mentioned the Straits, and Bülow inquired how England and France regarded the problem, he reluctantly confessed that they judged the moment inopportune. The only crumb of comfort was the Chancellor's remark that neither the Tsar nor Russia could dispense with the services of such a statesman. But perhaps the flattery was a little too gross to bring balm to his aching wounds.

IX

Iswolsky returned to Russia in no cheerful mood. He was tired in mind and body, reported Nicolson, and complained of his embarrassing position.[2] His visit to London had left most pleasant memories ; but the conversations in Berlin had been disappointing, for the determination of Germany to support her ally in all circumstances had been frankly avowed. If Austria were to attack Serbia the Russian Government might be swept off its feet, despite its desire for peace. Asked if he intended to explain his policy in the Duma, he replied that it was not likely at present. The same picture of bitterness and depression is painted by the German Ambassador.[3] Serbia, declared the Minister, was aflame with anger, and Austria might seize the opportunity for attack ; for Germany was apparently prepared to give her a blank cheque. Pourtalès rejoined that the annexation had not in fact altered the status quo, and argued that since Russia had made friends with England Germany must cling even closer to her ally. A day or two later Nicolson had an audience of the Tsar, in which he sang the praises of Iswolsky in accordance with instructions from the King. The Minister's position at Court was unshaken, for the Tsar believed his story of the Buchlau

[1] G.P. XXVI, 206-9.   [2] B.D. V, 475-81.   [3] G.P. XXVI, 235-9.

interview. In the eyes of the public it was compromised beyond repair, and nobody knew it better than himself.

Iswolsky's anxieties were increased by the visit of the Crown Prince of Serbia and Pasitch to St. Petersburg in the middle of November.[1] Pasitch struck him as an unreliable man who might ignore the moderating advice he had received.[2] Austria, he complained, seemed to be waiting for a pretext to march into Serbia. " With Baron Aehrenthal", he added bitterly, " one must be prepared for anything. I assure you that when I leave the office for a few hours, I am in continual anxiety as to what alarming message will greet me on my return. The condition of nervous tension in which Europe is living is simply intolerable and cannot last." His position was indeed unenviable. There seemed no prospect of dragging his hated rival to a Conference, and at any moment, he believed, the Austrian troops might seize Belgrad. In that event Russia would have to stand aside in humiliating impotence while Serbia was overrun, or to intervene in a struggle which would ruin her finances and very likely provoke a revolution. " Since his return", reported Pourtalès on November 25, " Iswolsky is thoroughly out of humour.[3] He has cancelled his weekly diplomatic reception four times running, and he is little seen in society. Everyone finds him gloomy and preoccupied. He complains of his cool reception in Berlin. He was particularly offended because the Kaiser avoided politics." He was poisoning the Tsar against Germany, added the Ambassador, and something should be done to counteract his influence.

Early in December the Minister again complained that the tension was becoming intolerable, and expressed his desire to Pourtalès for a heart to-heart-talk.[4] " We must see each other oftener ", he began, " the times are too serious." He believed that Aehrenthal and the growing war party in Vienna intended to attack Serbia in March, the most suitable moment for a Balkan campaign. Now was the time for Germany to hold back her ally from a course which threatened to fill Europe with fire and blood. Meanwhile Aehrenthal continued to veto the discussion of the annexation at a Conference. " What will happen next ? I assure you, I do not know. Je suis au bout de mon latin. If I knew I was helping the cause

[1] G.P. XXVI, 268–70.
[2] Pasitch's report of the conversation is in Boghitschewitsch, I, 25–30.
[3] G.P. XXVI, 300–1.
[4] ibid. XXVI, 315–35.

of peace by resignation I would resign. I have told the Tsar as much." The Ambassador's reply brought little comfort. The cause of the recent estrangement of Germany, he explained, was the rapprochement of Russia and England ; not the arrangement about the Middle East or the Reval visit, but because all the world was talking of the Triple Entente. An alliance between Russia, England and France would be a serious danger to peace. Such a ring would be intolerable for Germany, and there would be a formidable demand to break it before it closed. " I can only tell you that Berlin is beginning to regard the situation as serious." The best way out of the crisis was a speedy understanding with Austria. Iswolsky replied that he could no longer negotiate with Aehrenthal. " I am afraid of him. I am convinced that Austria intends to take Serbia." Though he appeared to realise the danger, he held to the idea of territorial compensation for Serbia, particularly a port. The conversation left the controversy precisely where it was.

A few days later the Minister made a belated declaration of his views in a Circular Despatch and a speech in the Duma. In the former, dated December 19, he argued once again that, following the Black Sea Conference precedent of 1871, the modification of the Treaty of Berlin required the assent of all the signatories.[1] The Conference would also have to define the new situation of Bosnia and Herzegovina. In the long awaited speech on Christmas Day the lion failed to roar, fearing that denunciations of his formidable antagonist might provoke compromising revelations. He dealt at length with the annexation, the action of Bulgaria, the plan of a Conference, and the Russian programme. He explained that a protest such as public opinion demanded was prevented by agreements with Vienna from 1877 onwards. On the other hand, since Austria had decided to alter a portion of the Treaty of Berlin which she disliked, it was a right and duty to raise other articles which were disliked by Russia, Turkey and the Balkan States. He demanded compensation for Serbia and Montenegro, but the Straits, the problem nearest his heart, were not mentioned. It was generally recognised that he had skated over extremely thin ice with a good deal of skill, and Grey pronounced the speech very satisfactory. But while it is no way aggravated the danger, it left the tension undiminished and every problem unsolved.

[1] B.D. V, 532-5.

The year 1909 opened in an atmosphere of gathering gloom.
A remarkable conversation with the German Ambassador on
January 15 reveals Iswolsky's dismay at the wreck of his
hopes, not only in the recent attempted deal but over the
whole field of politics.[1]   He was unable to share Pourtalès'
optimistic view that the worst was over.   Aehrenthal was a
menace to peace, and so long as he remained at his post
anything might occur.   It was impossible to negotiate with a
man who broke his word.   " How different it would all have
been if we had kept to the Russo-Austrian entente !   That was
my policy, to which as a pupil of Lobanoff I was deeply
attached.   When Aehrenthal on taking office assured me that
he stood firmly on the foundation of this entente ; and when
in Swinemünde I was convinced that this policy could count
on German approval ; and finally when I had removed the
danger from the English side by the Convention on Central
Asian questions, I believed in the autumn of 1907 that I could
promise my master a long series of peaceful years in the
domain of foreign affairs, which would have afforded Russia
the opportunity of healing the wounds of war and revolution.
All these prospects are destroyed by the policy of a reckless
and dishonourable statesman, whom we regarded here for
many years as a friend of Russia.   Mark my words : the
Eastern Question is insoluble without a conflict.   To postpone
this conflict to the distant future was the merit of the Mürzsteg
entente. . . . It may not come for five or ten years, but it is
inevitable, and the blame of destroying the only possibility of
its indefinite postponement lies on Aehrenthal alone." Russo-
German relations had naturally suffered, and in Macedonia he
had been driven towards England since Austria had left him
in the lurch.   Russians, reported Pourtalès, realised that for
the moment they must accept the situation, but they hoped in
five or ten years to be strong enough to achieve their aims in
the Near East.   Here indeed was a new programme—to
prepare for the coming strife.

Iswolsky was in a very difficult position, wrote Nicolson
to Grey on January 21.[2]   " His Balkan policy is regarded as a
failure ; and the Serbian case will be treated as a test case, by
which to judge whether he will succeed or not in retrieving
the faults of Russian diplomacy.   If we are unable to assist
him, we perhaps need not oppose him.   At the same time I
do not think it very wise on the part of Russia to have gone so

[1] G.P. XXVI, 396-9.   [2] B.D. V, 571-2.

far in the way of assurances to Serbia. Her Minister here has
been told that Russia will do all that is possible to help her,
and preserves her entire liberty of action whatever arrangement may be made between Austria and Turkey. The meaning of these assurances will doubtless be amplified in Belgrad,
and may give rise to hopes which it will be difficult to realise."
The forecast was painfully correct. With his own hand
Iswolsky was filling up the cup of humiliation which he would
sooner or later be forced to drink.

The overwrought Minister was haunted by spectres as well
as by more substantial terrors and foes. The official *communiqué* issued after the visit of King Edward to Berlin early in
February stated that a complete understanding existed between
Great Britain and Germany.[1] This, he complained to
Nicolson, meant that England had joined Germany and
Austria in Near Eastern policy. France had also established
better relations with Germany in regard to Morocco, and
Russia was isolated. In consequence Austria would shortly
present an ultimatum to Serbia, convinced that Russia alone
would object. It was in vain that Nicolson argued that the
British Government had no intention of deserting Russia.
The German Ambassador, rejoined Iswolsky, was impressing
on him almost daily that Germany held close to Austria. The
communiqué announced that England and Germany were entirely
at one, so the trio was complete. A soothing telegram from
Downing Street declared emphatically that there would be no
modification in British policy. Iswolsky declared himself
convinced of the loyalty of the British Government, but he
continued to view the situation with the gravest alarm. If
Austria advanced into Serbia, as he expected, there would
probably be such an explosion of feeling that Russia would
be forced to act, and a European conflagration would ensue.
Nicolson believed that the Minister was speaking the truth,
and that in case of hostilities Russia would probably give
Serbia active support. Iswolsky added that if Russia were
compelled to remain inactive during an Austrian invasion, it
would mean the complete collapse of her present policy, and
she might have to abandon the French alliance and the British
entente. There had been frequent hints from Berlin that
Russia was steering a wrong course and making combinations
which would prove useless at a critical moment. Never
before had he spoken in such a despairing strain. His feelings

[1] *B.D.* V, 596–601, and Benckendorff, I, 27–41.

Z

were further ruffled by a request from France for an exchange
of ideas in view of the danger to peace in a matter not directly
affecting Russia's vital interests.[1]

The first gleam of sunshine shot through the clouds when
Russia's mediation bridged the gulf between Sofia and Constantinople.   Iswolsky proposed that the compensation due
from Bulgaria to Turkey should be paid in the form of a
corresponding reduction of the Turkish indemnity to Russia.
The plan was approved by England, France and Italy, but not
by Germany or Austria, who disliked the prospect of strengthening Russian influence at Sofia.   A further service to Bulgaria
was rendered when Ferdinand visited St. Petersburg at the
end of February and was received as King.   To Nicolson's
complaints Iswolsky replied that it was merely a question of
etiquette; but the political significance of the honour, before
the change of title had been recognised by the other Powers,
was too obvious to be explained away.   For the time it
appeared that the ingenious stroke had secured the return of
the strongest of the Balkan states to the Russian fold.   But
it was a fleeting triumph, as Russia was to learn in 1913 and
again more bitterly in 1915.   Moreover, by helping to secure
the retirement of Turkey from the scrimmage, the settlement
isolated Serbia in the final trial of strength.   Indeed, the
effective assistance to Sofia merely emphasised by contrast the
humiliating incapacity to defend the cause of Belgrad.

Convinced that Austria would attack Serbia with the
coming of spring, despairing of German intervention to avert
the catastrophe, and realising that the signature of the Austro-
Turkish agreement of February 26 secured Aehrenthal a free
hand, Iswolsky at last gave a sharp turn to the helm.   He
informed Nicolson that he intended to urge Serbia to drop
the claim for territorial compensation, as the Powers were
not disposed to entertain such demands; to maintain a
peaceful attitude; and to leave her case in the hands of the
Powers.[2]   He was aware that his action might be sharply
criticised in Russia, but he was anxious to refute the Austro-
German charge that Russia was the sole obstacle to peace.   It
was a step forward, but it was in no sense intended as a
capitulation.   In announcing the change of course to Grey
he asked him to support the demand for economic concessions,
for Serbia should not be left alone to get what she could from
Austria.   The decisive telegram was despatched on February

[1] Benckendorff, I, 43–6.   [2] B.D. V, 636–7.

27,[1] in which she was advised to inform the Powers that she withdrew her territorial claims. Iswolsky's statesmanlike decision, replied Grey, gave Russia a moral claim on the support of all the Powers in securing a satisfactory settlement by diplomatic means. He was delighted by the recognition of his sacrifice and the promise of support; and Nicolson commented that, whether his efforts succeeded or failed, he had adopted a wise and courageous policy in a very difficult situation. In a letter to Grey a few days later the Ambassador denied the charge that he guided Iswolsky and stiffened him against the Central Powers.[2] "I have never urged him to adopt a line which might widen the breach between him and Vienna. As to my 'running him' the idea is ridiculous. We now know each other very intimately, and without vanity I may say that he has confidence in me and doubtless likes to talk over matters with me. But he forms his own judgments and takes his own decisions."

Iswolsky's advice to Serbia to drop her claim for territorial compensation was followed, not by the anticipated *détente*, but by an increase of anxiety. For there were difficulties both at Vienna and at Belgrad which his sudden change of front was powerless to remove. Convinced from the outset that Russia was not in a position to fight, Aehrenthal rightly interpreted the latest move as a confession of weakness. He believed that he had merely to stick to his guns and victory would be won all along the line. The secret session of the Duma on March 8 confirmed this reading of the situation. Members were informed that the army was unready for war, and Iswolsky declared that Russia would not fight if Austria occupied Serbia.[3] The cup of humiliation was not yet full, for Serbia was in no yielding mood, and Aehrenthal threatened the revelation of comprising documents unless he urged her to recognise the annexation. The frightened Minister once more turned to Berlin with a request to avert publication. Bülow replied that he was ready to mediate if Russia would really urge Serbia to yield. Vienna might perhaps notify to the Powers the agreement with Turkey and ask them for the formal sanction of the change. If, however, Russia resisted a joint sanction of the *fait accompli*, Germany must let things take their course. Iswolsky welcomed what he described as Germany's first attempt to diminish the tension, but explained that his influence in Belgrad was exaggerated. Moreover he

---

[1] Benckendorff, I, 47-8.   [2] B.D. V, 664-5.   [3] G.P. XXVI, 655-7.

retained his gloomy conviction that Aehrenthal was only playing at negotiations, and that he would strike at Serbia in the next few days.

A despatch of March 15 from Nicolson, summarising his interviews during the last few days, reveals the Minister's almost desperate plight.[1] He had gone as far as he could at Belgrad. It was asking too much that Russia should urge Serbia to accept the annexation which she had not yet accepted herself. Aehrenthal knew he was demanding the impossible, and was merely seeking to lay the blame for his contemplated action on Russia or Serbia. He had intended giving no further counsel, but, on learning that Vienna found portions of Serbia's circular ambiguous, he had advised her to seek a satisfactory formula. He would not object if she were to recognise the Austro-Turkish protocol, since such a declaration would not alter the position of the signatories of the Treaty of Berlin. " In short ", concluded Nicolson, " he would be prepared for Serbia making a complete submission to Austria-Hungary. . . . The latest line of M. Iswolsky is not a bold one though in present conditions it may be a prudent one. It is unfortunate that, as I fear undoubtedly is the case, Russia held out until recently hopes to Serbia that she would obtain territorial compensations and that Russia would employ every diplomatic and pacific means to secure them for her. It would have been better, and perhaps juster to Serbia, if from the outset the true situation had been explained to her."

After consulting the British and French Governments Iswolsky replied to Bülow's mediatory proposal.[2] While Russia had striven for peace, Austria's claims, he complained, steadily increased and she seemed bent on war. If, however, she invited the Powers by a note formally to sanction the alteration of Article 25 of the Treaty of Berlin, " the Russian Government would deem it a duty to consider this *démarche* with the honest desire to find in it the elements of a solution which would be equally acceptable for all the signatories of the Berlin Treaty." " A refusal ", wrote the Kaiser on Pourtalès' despatch, " a cheeky answer." On the same day Iswolsky explained to Nicolson that an exchange of notes would not supersede a Conference, which he still considered a necessity. The Minister was still kicking desperately against the pricks.

[1] B.D. V, 685-6.
[2] G.P. XXVI, 691-2.

On receiving Iswolsky's ambiguous reply the Wilhelm-strasse launched its thunderbolt without further delay.[1] Before suggesting that Austria should approach the Powers Germany must definitely know that Russia would accept the note. " You will inform M. Iswolsky that we expect a precise answer—Yes or No. We should regard an evasive, conditional or ambiguous reply as a refusal. We should then withdraw and let things take their course." Iswolsky replied that he must consult his master and his colleagues. " If we only had to deal with you ", he added, " it would be simple enough, and I could give the desired clear answer without fear. But who can guarantee that the question put by the Vienna Cabinet will be equally clear and that Aehrenthal does not give it a form which renders a positive acceptance difficult ? " Acceptance, however difficult, was inevitable, and the Tsar's approval was promptly secured. The alternative, telegraphed the Minister to his Ambassadors in London and Paris, was the immediate liquidation of the Bosnian affair or an Austrian invasion of Serbia.[2] " We have no choice." He had no intention, he added, of abandoning his demand for a Conference.

Next day Nicolson found the Minister in agitation and alarm.[3] " M. Iswolsky was perfectly frank. He said the German summons was perhaps not an ultimatum in the sense that it threatened war as an alternative, but it was a diplomatic ultimatum. He would like to have met it differently, but it was necessary to look facts in the face. He thought that for some time past the two Central Powers had combined on their programme, and that they now considered that the moment had arrived for pushing Russia to the wall. The military preparations in Galicia were on a scale which was ominous, the immediate readiness of Germany for war was undoubted." France could not be depended upon. England had been loyal throughout, but she would not fight. Russia alone was unable to face the Central Powers. Aehrenthal was brow-beating Russia through Germany, and he had succeeded. It was useless to disguise the fact. When Nicolson asked whether he could not consult the French and British Governments before making his reply, Iswolsky replied that there was no time. Any delay might be misconstrued and might precipitate a catastrophe. His hands and those of the Powers

[1] G.P. XXVI, 693–5.   [2] Benckendorff, I, 80–1.
[3] B.D. V, 723, 727–9.

were still perfectly free as to a Conference. To the French Ambassador he explained in similar terms that he had been compelled to submit, adding that for some years Europe must accustom itself to the hegemony of Germany. On the following day he again defended his decision to Nicolson. Russia did not want a war. She was just beginning to bring order into her finances, was reorganising her army, and internal unrest was quieting down. A war would throw back all the progress effected, and would probably revive all the troubles from which she had begun to emerge. It was a bitter pill to swallow, but three or four years hence she would be able to speak in a different tone.

Russia's surrender brought the crisis to an end, for Serbia, deprived of her champion, bowed to her fate. Iswolsky's feelings were mixed. On the one hand the spectacular humiliation of his country was an agonising grief to a statesman so patriotic and so vain. On the other hand he was thankful to escape the dreaded catastrophe of war. The peremptory summons from Berlin provided him with a not wholly unwelcome excuse for withdrawing from an impossible position. He had known he was beaten but had seen no way of covering his retreat. Since it was clearly beyond his power to secure compensation of any kind for Serbia or to drag Austria before a Conference, the easiest course was to attribute his capitulation to irresistible pressure from abroad. While Nicolson was haunted by the vision of an omnipotent Germany and the spectre of a disintegrating Entente, Iswolsky was consoled by the thought of the danger he had escaped. Compromising revelations were no longer to be feared, and the wrath of his countrymen could be diverted from his blunders to the treachery of Vienna and the menaces of Berlin.

The German Ambássador was incensed by the " legend " of a German ultimatum, which the Minister encouraged if he did not invent, and never ceased to proclaim that the message he had delivered had a friendly intent. Six months later, in an informal conversation with Sir Fairfax Cartwright at Venice, Iswolsky himself referred to the distorted press accounts of German intervention.[1] Nothing approaching an ultimatum had been delivered. Germany, in fact, had acted in a friendly spirit, and had merely declared that if war broke out between Austria and Russia it would be very difficult for her not to stand by her ally. She had no desire to see such a war,

[1] B.D. V, 809.

still less to see a conflict with her friendly neighbour Russia. In fact, concluded Cartwright, according to Iswolsky's account Pourtalès came to him like a cooing dove bearing a message of peace. It was a remarkable conversation, suggesting that Iswolsky's version of the drama varied with his mood. What never changed was his hatred of Aehrenthal and his unsleeping desire for revenge. His failure and humiliation had been complete. The weakness of Russia was revealed to the world, the Straits remained closed, the Conference never met, compensation for Serbia was refused, the Minister's prestige at home and abroad was shattered, the Central Empires were triumphant, the Western Powers dismayed. Not a stick was saved from the wreck.

X

Iswolsky's mood after the great surrender altered from day to day. On April 6, smarting under British disapproval of his sudden collapse, he spoke bitterly to Nicolson of the necessity for resignation.[1] Two days later he was bright and smiling. He had to go to Munich for an operation, and would be back in about three weeks. " To office or only to St. Petersburg ? " To office, he replied, though of course one could never tell what would happen. Annoyed though he was, Nicolson seized the opportunity of an audience with the Tsar to put in a good word for the Minister. When the monarch remarked that he had been unduly nervous during the crisis, the Ambassador rejoined that every allowance should be made for a man subjected to such a strain. Few people imagined that he would remain indefinitely at his post, but equally few expected that he would shortly resign. While England desired to keep him as long as possible, Germany, like Austria, wished him to go. But, as Pourtalès pointed out, direct attacks would merely strengthen his position.[2] Before his destiny could be fulfilled a decent interval must elapse. He lingered on for eighteen months ; but his self-confidence was gone, and his thoughts shifted towards the prospect of a well paid Embassy in the West.

In June Pourtalès found the Foreign Minister in good spirits on his return to work.[3] He had seen the Tsar, and there was no sign that his position was shattered. Though

[1] B.D. V, 774-8, 781-5.   [2] G.P. XXVI, 601-4.
[3] ibid. XXVI, 810-7.

his bitterness against Aehrenthal was undiminished, he seemed to hanker after a revival of the Dreikaiserbund. " Our agreements with Austria remain, and Russia has observed them to the last comma. Aehrenthal has simply ignored them, and I fear he will continue his ambitious policy." It was clear that he wished Germany to come into the partnership and thereby veto Austrian pranks in the Balkans. A few days later he returned to the theme. The trustful relationship between Germany and Russia, he argued, must necessarily suffer if the former blindly supported her ally in all her expansionist steps. Austria, replied Pourtalès, was not contemplating further moves on the Balkan stage, so far as he and his Government were aware. " Who can guarantee us that ? " asked Iswolsky. " Guarantees we cannot offer", rejoined the Ambassador, " for Austria is a sovereign state." The Minister then reiterated his conviction that Austro-Russian relations must either rest on an understanding in the Balkans or issue in war. It was clear that he desired a German initiative towards an entente of the three Emperors in which the Wilhelmstrasse would hold the Ballplatz in check ; but Pourtalès had nothing to offer, for Iswolsky had nothing to give.

On the eve of a meeting in Finnish waters between the Kaiser and the Tsar Nicolson asked Iswolsky whether the invitation emanated from St. Petersburg or Berlin.[1] The Minister replied that it was difficult to say, for correspondence between the two rulers was very frequent. German methods, he continued, were peculiar and clumsy. They first hit you, and then pretend to be surprised that you were not pleased. Of course Russia must keep on good terms with Germany, but it was not an agreeable or an easy task. Nicolson gathered that no one looked forward to the meeting with much pleasure, except possibly some members of the suite. Despite these gloomy forebodings the visit was an acknowledged success, and the marked cordiality of the Tsar was reflected in the unaccustomed warmth of his toast. In conversation with Schön Iswolsky poured out his familiar complaints of Aehrenthal, who, he had reason to believe, would push on to Salonika in the probable event of fresh complications in Turkey.[2] If he did, war with Russia was inevitable. All through the interview ran the desire that Germany should not only prevent further Austrian adventures but should mend the wires between Vienna and St. Petersburg. Schön's reply that Austria

[1] B.D. IX, pt. I, 12–3, June 6.   [2] G.P. XXVI, 822–8, 834–6.

contemplated no expansive policy appeared to reassure Iswolsky in some measure ; but while Stolypin and others were full of the Kaiser's charms, Iswolsky proved rather a wet blanket.

The impressions of the Minister, recorded in a private letter to the Russian Ambassador in Berlin, suggest more satisfaction than he showed.[1] The Kaiser had avoided politics with him and Stolypin, but he had plainly manifested his friendly feelings for the Tsar. The report of the conversations with Schön agrees closely with that of the latter. A further Austrian advance in the Balkans would produce a still sharper conflict, and, if Germany again gave support, would endanger the peace of Europe. When Schön argued that the new grouping of the Powers compelled Germany to tighten up her alliance with Austria, Iswolsky once more explained that the agreement with England was regional and had no point against Berlin. There was no intention of turning the ententes into alliances, so Germany need have no suspicions of Russia or France. Schön, on his side, expressed his conviction that Aehrenthal had no new adventures up his sleeve. Germany's relations with France had improved, but in regard to England the atmosphere was charged with electricity. On the whole the meeting seemed to Iswolsky most satisfactory. Unfortunately no trustful relations could exist so long as Russia remained the foe of Germany's ally.

Iswolsky derived greater satisfaction from the visit of his master and himself to the Western Powers in August. Having Aehrenthal on the brain he complained of the friendly relations between Paris and Vienna.[2] Pichon explained that France desired to be on the best terms with Austria compatible with the Russian alliance. If a question arose in which the interests of Russia and Austria diverged, she would of course adopt the Russian point of view. In like manner France would expect her ally to support her interests in case they diverged from those of Germany. Subject to that condition the French Government would offer no objection to the better relations which Iswolsky was anxious to establish with Berlin.

After meeting the President of the Republic at Cherbourg the Tsar returned King Edward's visit to Reval by a visit to Cowes.[3] There had recently been some friction in Persia, but the situation had improved and the sun was shining. An

[1] Benckendorff, I, 121–5.   [2] B.D. IX, pt. I, 32.
[3] ibid. 33–52, and Benckendorff, I, 139–42.

important conversation took place on the Admiralty yacht between Iswolsky and Benckendorff on the one side, and Asquith, Grey and Nicolson on the other. After repeating his version of the Buchlau interview, the Russian statesman expressed grave anxiety as to the future. The Young Turk regime would probably fail, and in that case Austria would probably advance to Salonika, while Bulgaria in collusion entered Macedonia, with the promise of an immediate acquisition of territory and the chance of Constantinople in the background. A new Austro-Russian agreement would be useless, for Aehrenthal had broken the old pact. Berlin kept reminding him that he would gain nothing by siding with England, and that, if he did not make arrangements with other countries, Russia would get the worst of it in any fresh troubles in the Balkans. Would England, he asked, regard with indifference an Austrian advance to Salonika? Certainly not, replied Grey; but she would support the Young Turk regime so long as there was any prospect of its success. Grey was glad to find that his visitor genuinely desired to see Turkey strong, since her weakness would encourage the dreaded Austrian advance. The Ministers agreed, however, that Austria was not anxious to make a new move at present nor to become too dependent on Germany. Grey then urged the withdrawal of Russian troops from Persia as soon as possible. At a second interview Iswolsky expressed his pleasure at finding that they were so much in agreement, but he showed no desire for a discussion of details. The question of the Straits was not raised, for the views of Downing Street were well known. The Tsar was in better spirits than Iswolsky; and the Russian press, except the extreme reactionary organs, welcomed the visit as strengthening the Anglo-Russian Entente. There was no sign whatever that Nicolson's gloomy forecast of the previous March was likely to materialise; for so long as Germany stood firmly by her ally, Russia had no choice but to keep her Western friendships in good repair.

On his way home Iswolsky made the acquaintance of the new German Chancellor in Berlin.[1] Hinting that his position was insecure, he assured Bethmann that he had no thought of an anti-German policy, and that Russia had been forced into her present path by the ambition and the trickery of Aehrenthal. Reval was her answer to the Sanjak; but the Entente

[1] G.P. XXVI, 852–5.

with England was regional and excluded all questions of
general policy. Rumours of Germanophobe agreements were
groundless. There were no secrets in Reval. " Il n'y a pas
une virgule qui ne vous ait pas été communiquée." With
Austria the tie was broken and could not be mended. It was
natural that Germany had supported her ally, and her *démarche*
in the spring had been friendly, but the resulting situation was
bad. Austria undoubtedly cherished further expansionist
plans in the Balkans, as could be seen in her approach to
Bulgaria. Russia would not stand anything more, and a world
war might result. He was doing his utmost to avert such a
calamity, hence his desire for the strengthening of the new
regime in Turkey and the maintenance of good relations with
Berlin. He spoke throughout with passionate excitement, as
if hot from his duel with Aehrenthal, and every word breathed
wounded ambition. " I did not form a very lofty impression
of his political abilities," concluded Bethmann. " He is
certainly gifted, but rather sly than wise, and he is so obsessed
by personal ambition that he loses sight of political realities.
In his resentment against Aehrenthal he would be capable of
acting blindly." The visitor's impression of the new Chancellor was more favourable. He found him a man of calm
temperament, he confided to Nicolson on his return, and
well-informed in foreign affairs. Thus the journey ended on
a relatively cheerful note. France and England were friendly
and Germany was polite enough. Yet none of them could
heal the consciousness of failure that was gnawing at Iswolsky's
heart.

The latest and by far the most important of the visits of
1909 was the journey to Racconigi. The relations of Russia
and Italy had grown to friendliness during recent years, and
the latter was now merely a sleeping partner in the Triple
Alliance. Victor Emmanuel had visited St. Petersburg as long
ago as 1902, and the compliment was at last returned in
October 1909. Italy had been annoyed by her exclusion from
the Mürzsteg partnership, and when the Sanjak concession
loosened the ties between Vienna and St. Petersburg she drew
closer to Russia. Though the annexation of Bosnia produced
no official protests south of the Alps it had a bad press. The
significance of the Tsar's visit was enhanced by the demon-
strative avoidance of Austrian territory during the long
journey from Livadia to Turin. The *détour*, Iswolsky assured
Nicolson, was the decision of his deeply wounded master, and

he had vainly endeavoured to secure its modification.[1] " I should doubt if he exercised much pressure on the Emperor to change his plans ", commented the Ambassador drily. The visit was planned to last two days, but the Tsar was so pleased with his reception that he accepted the invitation to stay another twenty-four hours.[2] The importance of the journey was greater than the world imagined, for a secret pact was signed.[3] In the first article the signatories paid homage to the status quo in the Balkans. In the second they agreed in case of eventualities to apply the principle of nationality in the development of the Balkan States, to the exclusion of any foreign domination. In the third they undertook to oppose by joint diplomatic action any activities contrary to these ends, action of another character being reserved for subsequent agreement. By the fourth each signatory bound itself not to make new accords relating to Eastern Europe with a third Power except with the participation of the other. The fifth and last contained the kernel of the pact. " L'Italie et la Russie s'engagent à considérer avec bienveillance, l'une les intérêts russes dans la question des Détroits, l'autre les intérêts italiens en Tripolitaine et Cyrénaique."

The secret was well kept. Iswolsky, reported Tittoni to the German Ambassador in Rome, had declared that Russia aimed at nothing but the maintenance of the status quo in the Near East and the independent development of the Balkan States.[4] Italy, he had replied, pursued similar aims. Tittoni gave the same incomplete information to Vienna. They had reached agreement on the status quo, and if that broke down " the two states will favour the development of the Balkan states on the principle of nationality." Even this partial lifting of the veil aroused Aehrenthal's wrathful suspicions. They had planned, he observed, to divide Turkey's skin among the Balkan states. It was strange that, while Tittoni was about to agree with Austria on a policy of non-intervention in the event of a change in the status quo, he should at the same moment settle with Russia on the mode of intervention in the same eventuality. He would not ask him to explain, but he defined the Austrian standpoint in a written statement to the Italian Ambassador, reserving complete liberty of action in case other Powers intervened in the Balkans. Avarna

[1] B.D. V, 809–10.
[2] Savinsky, *Recollections of a Russian Diplomat*, 168–70.
[3] *Un Livre Noir*, I, 357–8.
[1] G.P. XXVII, ch. 214.

admitted to Tschirschky that the Racconigi *communiqué* contemplated intervention, and Bethmann called the Kaiser's attention to the discrepancy between the Russian and the Austrian policy of Rome. The avoidance of Austrian territory spoke for itself, and participation in a secret agreement with Italy kept alive the animosity between Iswolsky and Aehrenthal. Each appeared to be perpetually plotting against the other. Though the text of the most important part of the pact was withheld, all the world realised that Italy was moving towards the Triple Entente. Savinsky, who assisted in the discussions and drafted the text, describes the Racconigi agreement as the first decisive step taken by Italy to emancipate herself from the yoke of the Triple Alliance.[1] He was mistaken, for the first step had been taken by Prinetti in 1902. Racconigi was the second.

Iswolsky, reported Nicolson, returned well satisfied.[2] His aim was to secure the co-operation of Italy in any future developments in the Balkans, and to encourage a rapprochement between the Balkan States. His conversation suggested that his position was firmer and that he felt secure for some time to come. To the German Chargé he insisted on the admirable relations of Russia and Germany. " And now one of your friends is also a friend of ours." Racconigi indicated a rapprochement with Italy, but within the framework of the existing system of alliances. An attempt to detach her from the Triple Alliance would be not only a mistake but actually a danger. The two leading principles of the conversations, the maintenance of world peace and the status quo· in the Balkans, were those of Germany herself. The only dark cloud in the sky was the estrangement between Russia and Austria, and Vienna took no step to relieve the strain. Iswolsky's declarations had no effect in Berlin, and the Kaiser wondered if he had played a dirty trick and had a bad conscience.

A memorandum of November 4 furnished the Russian Ambassador in Berlin with Iswolsky's official version of a visit which, he declared, had aroused misunderstanding and suspicions.[3] The conception of a community of views and interests of the two countries was not new. " In denying that our rapprochement with Italy has a point against Germany or Austria, I am not expressing the whole mind of the Cabinet : I go farther and say that in our eyes any attempt to upset the system of alliances on which the peace of the world has rested

[1] *Recollections*, 170.   [2] *B.D.* V, 809-10.   [3] Benckendorff, I, 151-4.

for so long would be a grave danger to peace." But this system should not prevent Russia having the most friendly relations with the Powers of the Triple Alliance. With Germany they were excellent, and it was not his fault that with Austria they were otherwise. " If to-day we seize the opportunity of drawing closer to Italy, it seems to us that the cause of peace and general harmony can only benefit, and we feel sure the Berlin Cabinet will share that view." In conclusion he confessed that the Tsar had deliberately avoided Austrian soil, for he was justly incensed by the policy of the Vienna Cabinet. The memorandum produced no effect at Berlin, where the Kaiser wrote scornfully on the document: The object of words is to conceal thoughts. Iswolsky in fact could not have the best of both worlds. What he gained in one direction he lost in another. In drawing nearer to Rome he drifted away from Berlin. Had Germany and Austria learned the whole meaning of Racconigi their comments would have been sharper still.

In the early stages of the Bosnian crisis Bulgaria leaned to the Austrian side. But the Russo-Bulgar alliance concluded in 1902, in reply to an Austro-Roumanian agreement which threatened certain of their territories, was still in being ; and when Iswolsky skilfully liquidated the Turco-Bulgar dispute at the opening of 1909 the old friendly relations were restored. When the Bosnian crisis was over King Ferdinand warmly expressed his gratitude for the Tsar's support and his wish for closer intimacy.[1] As the Russian Minister in Sofia had no instructions, he merely suggested that concrete proposals should be worked out. Iswolsky replied that the Russian Government would gladly await and consider such plans. Nothing is known of further negotiations ; but among the earliest diplomatic revelations by the Bolshevists was a draft treaty dated December 1909, extending the pact of 1902 to meet new dangers.[2] It is unlikely to have been signed, for in 1912 Gueshov speaks of the treaty of 1902 as still in vigour. In any case Iswolsky could flatter himself that he left the wire to Sofia in good repair.

XI

The *Fortnightly Review* of November 1909 contained an anonymous article on Austro-Russian relations in reply to a

[1] Benckendorff, I, 105–6, May 4, 1909.
[2] Laloy, *Les Documents secrets publiés par les Bolsheviks*, 52–8.

previous anonymous article in the September number sharply attacking the policy and tactics of Aehrenthal and setting forth Iswolsky's case. It was an open secret that the author was Dr. Dillon, the correspondent of the *Daily Telegraph*, who had recently visited Aehrenthal and Berchtold. The story of the negotiations preceding the annexation and of the Buchlau interview was told from Aehrenthal's standpoint and contained information which could only be derived from an official source. Iswolsky promptly published a *communiqué* denying that his secret memorandum of July 2, 1908, had proposed the annexation of Bosnia, and Nicolson reported that he was very indignant and offended.[1] He read to the Ambassador the memorandum itself, regretting that he could not publish it as it dealt with the eventuality of a break up of the Turkish Empire. If, however, Aehrenthal pushed him too far, he might have to retaliate. It was most regrettable, commented Nicolson, that the duel continued and that the past was not allowed to slumber. Aehrenthal, though annoyed by Dillon's unauthorised revelations, replied in the *Fremdenblatt* that his declarations to the Delegations were correct, and added that there was no need for further discussion.[2] The incident retarded the *détente* which the interest of both countries demanded, and confirmed Iswolsky's conviction that his rival was not a man of honour.

Berchtold's letters to his chief at the close of 1909 are filled with lamentations over the nerve-racking Dillon dispute.[3] Aehrenthal replied with expressions of sympathy that he had to deal with " this odious Iswolsky." Private feelings, however, had to yield to political considerations. On January 12, 1910, Berchtold called on Iswolsky and spoke for the first time of the *Fortnightly* article. He had deeply regretted the unpleasant incident and would gladly do what he could to ease the situation. Personal satisfaction, replied the Minister, could only be given by a declaration that a certain passage of Dillon's article was a lying invention. This, however, would provoke fresh comments in the press of the two countries and revive the controversy. He was ready to suppress his feelings in the interest of a rapprochement of the two Governments which were at present out of touch. A joint declaration might suffice. Berchtold attributed the change to the influence of the Tsar and the fear of Balkan complications. In a letter to his chief he confessed that his feelings on entering

[1] *B.D.* V, 810–1.   [2] *B.D.* IX, pt. I, 87–8.   [3] *Ö-U.A.* II.

Iswolsky's room were those of a man entering a lion's cage.
The Minister, however, had been extremely polite and the tone
of reproach had been laid aside. Iswolsky's version given to
Nicolson emphasises his wish for peace.[1] " I am ready to
put aside all personal resentments and to seek a frank explanation between the two Cabinets, not on personal incidents of
the past but on future policy. After this it will be easy to
return to normal diplomatic relations." He added that he
would have no secret arrangements with Aehrenthal, as he
had learned their dangers. Any declaration by Austria would
have to be known to all the Powers. Aehrenthal replied that
he was ready to discuss the declarations to be made in the
Delegations and the Duma. They might say that neither of
the *Fortnightly* articles was authoritative and that both contained omissions and errors. He also was ready for an
understanding, which was all the easier since Austria remained
faithful to the principles of the pact of 1897, namely the
maintenance of the status quo in Turkey as long as possible,
disinterestedness and non-intervention in the event of its
collapse. In a private letter he added that Austria must not
appear to be rushing into Iswolsky's arms. The reply produced a favourable impression on the Minister, who expressed
his satisfaction to the English and German Ambassadors.

The mending of the wires proved less easy than it was
hoped, for Iswolsky's Aide-Mémoire of February 9 introduced
new complications. The exchange of views, he argued, could
not follow the precedent of 1897, for all the interested Powers
should be brought in and recent changes in Turkey must be
kept in view. He proposed three points for agreement and
subsequent communication to the Powers : maintenance of
the status quo in the Balkan peninsula ; maintenance of the
new order in Turkey ; the independence, consolidation and
pacific development of the little Balkan States. Here was a
far more ambitious programme than the resumption of contact
hitherto proposed. Aehrenthal replied that for the moment
it was enough for both Powers to announce that the recent
exchange of views had produced a satisfactory result, and that
the Cabinets recognised that the principles of their respective
policies enabled them to get in touch whenever the Balkan
situation required. Neither an exchange of notes nor a
communication to the Powers was needed. Iswolsky rejoined that a simple *communiqué* seemed insufficient, and that

[1] *B.D.* IX, pt. I, 109–10.

it would best serve the cause of peace to associate the other Powers in the principles jointly professed, thus facilitating a prompt exchange of views between all the interested parties in case of need. Benckendorff was instructed to ask for Grey's moral support in overcoming Aehrenthal's opposition to a proposal to which Russia attached great importance. Grey agreed that all the Powers should have the opportunity of associating themselves with the desire of the two Powers to preserve the status quo.[1] If, however, Aehrenthal declined, a solution might possibly be found in its simple communication to them.

Aehrenthal's reply maintained his refusal. Such a course would suggest a formal pact between the two Cabinets, and, since their policies had not changed and the Powers had frequently affirmed their fidelity to the status quo, there was no need for a solemn declaration. He added that he reserved the right of explaining to his countrymen the renewal of diplomatic contact. Iswolsky, he wrote scornfully to Berchtold, wished to play the part of the angel of peace who had brought Austria to accept the liberal principles of Russia's Balkan policy. When Nicolson asked what he intended to do Iswolsky replied that he too must enlighten his public. " I observed that probably he would concert with the Vienna Cabinet as to the communication to be made to the public press, otherwise the versions might differ. His Excellency said that Count d'Aehrenthal had made no mention of any previous consultation on that point, and apparently wished to have complete liberty in the matter. He would, therefore, claim the same liberty. I remarked that this procedure was rather droll, and if the communications did not accord we might witness a fresh press campaign, which would be unfortunate." The dislike and distrust of each other, concluded Nicolson, continued in full force, and indeed had been deepened if possible by the recent attitude of Aehrenthal. On the other hand it was satisfactory that intercourse between Iswolsky and Berchtold had been restored.

The long argument was at an end, and on March 21 Aehrenthal's *communiqué*, which had been shown to Iswolsky, appeared in the press. The object of the negotiations, namely the restoration of normal relations, had been completely attained. There was no reason for communicating the pourparlers to the Powers, since the well-known principles of Austrian

[1] *B.D.* IX, pt. I, 135.

A2

policy in the Balkans remained unaltered. Very different was
the declaration of Iswolsky, for in addition to announcing the
restoration of normal relations it contained the despatches
themselves.[1] He admitted that the procedure was unusual,
but he was following the precedent of Aehrenthal in December
1908 when he published confidential information without
previous consultation. On that occasion Iswolsky had
described the procedure as very incorrect, and Nicolson
regretted that he should now expose himself to the same
criticism. When the Austrian Ambassador complained of the
publication, the Minister replied that he was following
Aehrenthal's example ; and when Berchtold argued that his
chief had to defend himself, Iswolsky rejoined that a similar
reason existed in the present case.

No protest came from the Ballplatz against an incident that
was condemned throughout Europe, but Berchtold and
Aehrenthal gave rein to their indignation in their private
correspondence. Iswolsky's behaviour, wrote the former,
was without parallel.[2] The last weeks had been almost
intolerable. The longer the struggle lasted, the more hostile
and deceitful he had become. The latest manœuvres were
pure hooliganism. Aehrenthal replied by a warm expression
of gratitude for his truly patriotic patience and perseverance.
Iswolsky's game, he added in a despatch, stood nakedly
revealed. On the pretext of danger in the Near East he had
laid a trap for Austria. His plan was to pose before Europe
as the statesman who had curbed her selfish aims and had
underpinned the status quo. He had tried to put pressure on
Austria through other Powers. Finally he had revealed
confidential documents, thereby compromising not his
antagonist but himself. The restoration of normal relations
was satisfactory, but it must not be regarded as a rapprochement. So long as Iswolsky remained at the helm and his
methods were continued, Austria would have to reckon with
latent hostility. Despite the *détente* great reserve must be
shown. Iswolsky's feelings were equally bitter. Once again
he had been worsted in the contest of wills. When Aehrenthal declined to associate the Powers with the restoration of
normal relations he should have dropped the plan, since he
had no means of forcing it through. His tactical blunder took
the bloom off the *détente*, and the publication of the documents

[1] *B.D.* IX, pt. 1, 150–5.
[2] *Ö-U.A.* II, 776–91.

was a gesture of childish revenge. The Bosnian wound was plastered over, but it never healed.

After formally terminating the Austrian quarrel, there was nothing to keep Iswolsky at his post. In July he told Nicolson that he doubted if he would remain long at the Foreign Office, owing to his opposition to the Finnish policy of the Government, of which his many enemies at Court would make the most.[1] IIe would nestle down in some embassy. Vienna and Berlin being excluded and London being so well filled by Benckendorff, only Paris and Rome remained. A few days later the Tsar informed Nicolson that Iswolsky would be appointed to Paris by the end of the year, adding that Russian policy would remain unchanged. In conversation with Nicolson in August the Minister reviewed the situation of his country.[2] In the Far East she stood for peace and the open door. In the difficult problems of Persia the two Governments would have to keep in close touch. In the Near East there were several clouds in the sky. Russia desired to maintain the status quo and to make no difficulties for the Young Turks. Peace was essential for the next three or four years, and she would do nothing, directly or indirectly, to stir up strife. Aehrenthal, however, might have dark schemes, and if the new regime in Turkey were to collapse Russia could not remain indifferent. With the unrest in Greece, Crete and Macedonia, his mind could not be easy and the outlook was unpromising. In home affairs the economic and financial advance was wonderful, and the Duma was safe. The military recovery was less satisfactory. Russia would not regain her strength for a few years : that was why he considered peace so essential for her. Sazonoff would probably succeed him and would continue his policy, and the Tsar would not swerve from good relations with England.

Iswolsky's withdrawal inevitably provoked discussion in the press.[3] The Right had never forgiven him for the British entente, which, it argued, involved Russia in antagonism to the Central Powers. As the entente developed from Algeciras to Reval, Germany drifted steadily away ; for though she had shown her friendship in the Japanese war, Iswolsky had preferred the ally of Russia's foe. The penalty was paid when Germany stood forth in shining armour in the Bosnian

[1] B.D. IX, pt. I, 180, cp. Les Carnets de Georges Louis, I, 118-21.
[2] ibid. IX, pt. I, 194-5.
[3] ibid. IX, pt. I, 215-6.

crisis, and enabled Aehrenthal to vanquish his rival. Organs of the Centre and the Left maintained with equal conviction that co-operation with England had been the wisest course; that the alternative was the hegemony of the Central Powers; that in face of such a supremacy Russia would be powerless to protect the interests of the Balkan Slavs; that the rival of Austria and the ally of France could never be the trustful and trusted friend of Germany.

There is a good deal to be said for both sides of the argument, but most for the latter. The rapprochement with England had begun with Lansdowne and Lamsdorff, and Iswolsky had virtually no choice but to complete the process. England's enmity was disagreeable and potentially dangerous, and if it could be removed it was a duty to remove it. Moreover, since she had become the friend of France, a new and compelling reason for a rapprochement had emerged. The Convention of 1907 had opened up political and economic possibilities in Persia at the cost of moderate sacrifices in Tibet and Afghanistan. Moreover, her friendship might ultimately facilitate the opening of the Straits to Russian warships, that goal so ardently desired and unattainable without her good will. Finally the formation of the Triple Entente gave Russia a range of action and a prestige which had been lacking since her defeat by Japan. A policy of passivity was contrary to her traditions and the wishes of her people; and since the dream of dominating the Far East had faded away, she was virtually compelled to resume her activities in the Near East.

If the balance of argument tends to approval of the main lines of Iswolsky's policy during the first half of his tenure of office, there is no difference of opinion as to his failure in handling the Bosnian problem. He had some right to complain of Austria's furtive action in the Sanjak; but, after his suspicions of Aehrenthal had been thoroughly aroused, he should have been meticulously careful in his dealings with so slippery a diplomatist. There was nothing inherently wrong from the Russian point of view in discussing the annexation of Bosnia in return for an advance in the Straits, but so experienced a negotiator should have realised the need of a clear understanding at every step of the way. The Buchlau interview marks the turning point of his career. Till then his technical skill had been as remarkable as his success. Henceforth he was like a celebrated tenor who has lost his voice. If Aehrenthal was as unscrupulous as his rival alleged, Iswolsky was a dupe without the excuse of a novice. To leave Berchtold's hospitable roof without some agreed record of the momentous conversations would have been unwise even had he placed unlimited faith in the Austrian statesman. The chastisement for his inadvertence was excessive but by no means wholly undeserved. For he had drifted through carelessness into a situation in which it was impossible to advance and humiliating to retire.

The tragedy of Iswolsky's life was that the man who had done most to revive the prestige of his country after the Japanese war should soon after have begun to squander his capital. Having lost the first round of the game, he was condemned to fight a losing battle. Unlike Delcassé, who went down with his flag flying, he condemned himself to ignominious surrender. Henceforth he was a man with a grievance and something of a bore. His undying resentment ranks among the factors which led to the great catastrophe, for the spectacular humiliation of Russia in 1909 rendered a second capitulation impossible. Racconigi was a flicker of light in a darkening sky, but its secrecy prevented anything in the nature of a personal rehabilitation. Though he was still to experience years of exciting activity, the influence he exerted from Paris on the policy of his country has been exaggerated. For four years he had stood in the centre of the European stage, a maker of history. What followed was an epilogue.

AEHRENTHAL

CHAPTER V

AEHRENTHAL

I

THE expulsion of Austria from Italy and the German Federation simplified the task of her statesmen by focusing their attention on the Near East ; and the battle of Sedan convinced them that their losses could never be regained.[1] In the sixteenth and seventeenth centuries Turkey had been the main object of apprehension in Eastern Europe, and when the Turkish flood receded Austria was confronted with a mosaic of Christian states. Moreover, as Turkey waned, Russia grew from strength to strength. The old rivalry with Berlin was succeeded by the new rivalry with St. Petersburg, and co-operation against Napoleon was merely a parenthesis in the long struggle of diplomacy and arms. Neither Power coveted territory belonging to the other ; but the Balkan peninsula, half Turk, half Christian, lay between them as a sort of diplomatic No Man's Land, tempting them irresistibly to peg out spheres of influence.

Russia was superior in size, population, military and economic resources, and from the outset she held two winning cards in her hand. As the leading Slavonic Power she was connected with the Balkan States by ties of blood, and their common attachment to the Orthodox faith provided an emotional link. The antagonism of the Crescent and the Cross came to be embodied in the struggle between Russia and the Balkan Christians on the one side and the Ottoman Empire on the other. The period when Austria was the bulwark of Christendom against Islam was long past, and her place had been taken by the Colossus of the north. Thus her relationship to Russia was not of a simple character like that of France to Germany, but was conditioned by Balkan developments. During the second half of the reign of Francis Joseph his eyes were turned unceasingly towards the East. Germany and

[1] No adequate survey of the foreign policy of Austria-Hungary under Francis Joseph exists. The most important work is Pribram, *The Secret Treaties of Austria-Hungary, 1879-1914.* Sosnosky, *Die Balkanpolitik Oesterreich-Ungarns seit 1866* ; Wertheimer, *Graf Julius Andrassy*, Vol. III ; Redlich, *Emperor Francis Joseph of Austria* ; Wickham Steed, *The Hapsburg Monarchy*, ch. 4 ; Julius Andrassy, *Bismarck, Andrassy and their Successors* ; Schüssler, *Oesterreich und das deutsche Schicksal* ; Baernreither, *Fragmente eines politischen Tagebuches*, are useful. Kanner, *Kaiserliche Katastrophenpolitik*, is a shrill indictment.

Italy came into the picture only so far as it was necessary to cover his flank. England and France were too remote geographically and politically to count for much ; and, alone of the Great Powers, Austria abjured colonial enterprise. Thus the story of her diplomacy during the last decades before the world war, though complicated in detail, is clear enough in its broad outlines. The governing aim of the polyglot empire—a state but not a nation—was to maintain its precarious existence and its freedom of action by preventing the direct or indirect domination of the Balkan peninsula by its northern rival. For only in Eastern Europe was there a possibility of extending its power and its territory.

The Three Emperors' League formed after the unification of Germany was the first sign of an Austro-Russian rapprochement since the estrangement at the time of the Crimean war ; and in the Secret Treaty of Reichstadt Russia bought Austrian neutrality in her Balkan adventures by consenting to the occupation of Bosnia and Herzegovina. The entente collapsed when Austria joined England in substituting the Treaty of Berlin for the Treaty of San Stefano, and in the following year Andrassy and Bismarck created the Dual Alliance as a bulwark against Russian attack. A second rapprochement began with the revival of the Three Emperors' League, concluded in 1881 and renewed for three years in 1884 ; but once again the tender plant withered and died when the Bulgarian revolution of 1885 ranged the two Powers in opposite camps. Kalnoky, like Andrassy, had no desire for war, but he was ready to fight if there seemed no other way of averting Russian hegemony in the Balkans. A third rapprochement occurred when Kalnoky gave place to the cautious Goluchowsky, and Russia's activities in the Far East temporarily diverted her attention from the Balkans. The pact of 1897 ushered in a decade of harmonious co-operation. The Eastern question was put into cold storage, and when action was required by the Macedonian revolt in 1903 the Mürzsteg programme was elaborated and applied. A year later, when Russia was at war with Japan, a secret neutrality agreement was signed at St. Petersburg as " a mark of friendship and reciprocal confidence."[1]

Goluchowsky was as good an Austrian as his predecessors and successors at the Ballplatz ; but in his belief the policy of an Empire racked by internal dissensions should be con-

[1] Pribram, I, 236–9.

ducted on the principle of limited liability. Without denying
that it was capable of a major effort, he had no intention of
trying the experiment. Francis Joseph was growing old, the
nationalities were becoming clamant, and the *Ausgleich* with
Hungary was wearing thin. The wisest course, in his opinion,
was to keep the Triple Alliance in repair and to remain on
friendly terms with Russia. The price of such friendship was
a conservative policy in the Near East, and Goluchowsky, like
his master, was willing to pay it. The watchword of the easy-
going Polish nobleman was Safety First! If the Turkish Empire were to break up the situation might easily get out of
control.

A dramatic change occurred in 1906, when Aehrenthal
succeeded Goluchowsky at Vienna and Lamsdorff gave place
to Iswolsky at St. Petersburg. A third event of scarcely less
importance was the substitution of Conrad von Hötzendorf
for the veteran Beck as Austrian Chief of Staff. Thus in a few
months three champions of the old order were replaced by
younger men who brought novel ideas and a quicker pulse to
their work. Moreover, the face of the world had been transformed during the preceding year by the overwhelming defeat
of Russia. Baulked of her ambition to dominate the Far
East, she was forced back on Europe ; and it was an axiom that
she would resume her historic activities in the Near East as
soon as she recovered her breath. To those who had eyes to
see, the Treaty of Portsmouth was a signal that the Balkan
truce was nearing the end.

Goluchowksy, like Kalnoky, had fallen for reasons of
internal politics, and in selecting his successor the Emperor
never dreamed of changing the course of the ship. His choice
of Aehrenthal was determined by his high repute.[1] Born in
1854 into the family of a Bohemian Freiherr with a dash of
Jewish blood in his veins, he began his diplomatic career as an
unpaid Attaché at Paris in 1877. A year later he was transferred to St. Petersburg, where he remained for five years.
Recalled to the Foreign Office in Vienna in 1883 he worked
under Kalnoky, of whom he always spoke as his master and
friend, and who in turn was attracted by his untiring industry
and ability. Five years later he was sent back to St. Petersburg
as First Secretary, where he remained till his appointment in

[1] Molden, *Graf Aehrenthal*; Olof Hoijer, *Le Comte d'Aehrenthal*; Seton-
Watson, "La Politique du Comte d'Aehrenthal," in *Le Monde Slave*, June 1933 :
Take Jonescu, *Souvenirs*, 65–73.

1894 to Bucharest. At the next vacancy he returned to St. Petersburg as Ambassador, the most important and difficult post in the diplomatic service. He liked Russia and the Russians, studied their literature and history, admired their autocratic institutions, and had no love for the liberal Powers of the West. He was present at the meeting of the rulers and their ministers at which the Mürzsteg programme was drawn up. Respected in society and *persona grata* with the Tsar, he was universally regarded as a friend of Russia and a champion of co-operation. He was even prepared to see Russia in control of Constantinople and the Dardanelles.[1] His despatches were studied with special attention at the Ballplatz, where he was considered to be the coming man. Thus his call to the helm in October 1906 aroused neither apprehension nor surprise.

II

Aehrenthal remained at St. Petersburg during the first six months of Iswolsky's tenure of office, and the change of Ministers in no way diminished his leanings to Russia. The German Ambassador reported his colleague's eager desire for the renewal of the Dreikaiserbund.[2] The way, he declared, was now open. The Tsar realised the failure of his constitutional experiment. The only course was to dissolve the Duma, whatever the risks. It was the interest of the German and Austrian empires to encourage him in his crusade against radicalism. If the mood lasted it would be easy to detach him from the French, and to win him to an alliance with his neighbours for the defence of the monarchical principle and peace. If this powerful partnership were created the three rulers could easily agree on the reduction of armaments, thereby winning the sympathies of the civilised world.

Schön proceeded to pour water into Aehrenthal's wine. The German Government would welcome the renewal of the Dreikaiserbund with delight, but recent experiences of Russia's friendship and gratitude suggested caution. Germany could not take the initiative, nor could she interfere in Russia's domestic policy. German interests demanded tranquillity in Russia, which could only be attained by a

---

[1] Baernreither, 72.

[2] *G.P.* XXII, ch. 160. The great official publication, *Oesterreich-Ungarns Aussenpolitik*, only begins in March 1908.

constitutional regime and speedy reforms. Moreover moral support of a reactionary policy would antagonise Iswolsky, who desired to reconcile the Crown and the Duma. Iswolsky, rejoined Aehrenthal, was an opportunist rather than a Liberal. There was no case for a return to absolutism. A representative assembly with limited powers and a restricted suffrage would meet the need. In reply to Schön's question whether the monarchs should support the Tsar by words or deeds, Aehrenthal explained that he had only the former in mind, though circumstances could arise, such as anarchy in Poland, which might require action. The revival of the Three Emperors' League, commented Bülow on receiving Schön's report, was an old idea of Aehrenthal, and an excellent idea it was. But a German initiative would look like an attempt to detach Russia from France or impede a rapprochement with England. On the other hand the open disapproval by the democratic Powers of the dissolution of the Duma showed the folly of turning to the West. It would be far easier for Austria than for Germany to suggest an alternative course. Aehrenthal was pleased with Bülow's approval of the principle. The Tsar, he suggested, should be encouraged in his firmness by letters from the Emperors. Such a stiffening of the vacillating monarch seemed essential for the peaceful evolution of Russia and therefore for the revival of the league.

The budding activities of Iswolsky increased Aehrenthal's anxiety to move before it was too late. He complained to the German Chargé that the Foreign Minister was steering a new course. Instead of first discussing Balkan questions with Austria, he turned to England. There was nothing to be said against the improvement of Anglo-Russian relations, but an agreement in regard to the Balkans might have dangerous results. If Germany desired agreement with Russia it was only possible through the revival of the League, not through an agreement with Russia and France. Goluchowsky's belated answer was non-committal. With some of Aehrenthal's points he concurred, with others he disagreed. The matter would be discussed with Berlin. Aehrenthal expressed his regret that Germany had taken so little advantage of Lamsdorff's friendship. Though he made no complaint of Iswolsky, he hinted that he would be found less accommodating. He expected an Anglo-Russian understanding, which had no interest for him in so far as it concerned Persia and Tibet ; but Turkey was another matter. Austrian influence in the Balkans would be diminished, and England intended to reopen the Eastern question. Before long Germany might be forced to choose between energetic defence of Turkish interests which would involve great difficulties, or surrendering the Sultan to England and thereby diminishing her prestige.

Aehrenthal's appointment to the Foreign Office shortly after these conversations was welcome news at St. Petersburg. His friend, the influential reactionary and pro-German Schwanebach, was particularly pleased ; and when the German Chargé remarked that his country was also pleased, since Aehrenthal was deemed a true friend of the Triple Alliance, he replied that they might hope the new Minister would strive for a close friendship between the Central Powers and Russia. When Berchtold presented his credentials in the following January, the Tsar spoke in the warmest terms of his predecessor in St. Petersburg, and the new Ambassador promised to work in the same spirit. In his first conversations with the German Ambassador at Vienna the new Foreign Minister reiterated his desire for a rapprochement between the three Empires in the interest both of monarchy and peace. The wish was shared by influential circles in Russia, particularly by Stolypin. Iswolsky was too much in the English camp, though he too expressed his desire to co-operate with the Central Powers. His Anglomania was a danger, for he might allow Russia to be compromised by England in the Balkans and then employ the resulting confusion to secure advantages in Central Asia. He contested Wedel's argument that the prospect of further French loans would hold Russia to her ally. The rapprochement could not and should not be hurried ; but in leaning on the neighbouring Empires Russia would recover her strength and find money as well. The monarchical idea must be kept in the foreground. Even if Russia became a constitutional State the Imperial power should remain, as in Germany and Austria, a deciding factor. Relations with radical France would be automatically loosened, and Italy would be attracted to the monarchical group. It was a spacious panorama with warm tints in the sky.

A few days later Aehrenthal, who had journeyed to St. Petersburg to take formal leave, discussed the Mürzsteg programme with Iswolsky. The conversation, he told Schön, was satisfactory. There could be no doubt as to the sincere determination of the Minister to carry out existing agreements, yet his consideration for England might lead him in a direction unfavourable to Austrian interests in the Near East. He had volunteered reassuring statements about the new orientations, which would contain no point against Germany. He recognised the necessity of close relations with the Central Empires, and sincerely desired to move in that direction. But was his will strong enough to resist the temptation to a liberal policy which would draw him towards the Western Powers ? He would have to be carefully watched and his back occasionally stiffened. In a farewell audience the Tsar declared that a return to the League was a most desirable goal.

Aehrenthal returned through Berlin, where he made a favourable impression. His emphasis on monarchical solidarity, reported Bülow, strengthened the tie with Germany, for the monarchical and conservative strain in him was stronger than in his predecessor. The Three Emperors' League was his ideal, but he did not think it could quickly be realised, and he had found Iswolsky less accommodating than Lamsdorff. His references to the pact between Russia and Austria were vague, and he hinted that Austrian severity towards Serbia would be resented by Russian opinion. It was obvious that he had not complete confidence in Iswolsky. His programme in the Near East seemed to Bülow very sensible. He desired to keep the Turkish Empire intact as long as possible, and therefore to avoid shocks and experiments. For this reason he was opposed to the English plan, already half approved by Russia, of a Christian Governor-General for Macedonia, and he had done his utmost to detach Iswolsky from the idea. The Russian Minister tended to look at the Near East through British spectacles. The German and Austrian Ambassadors should therefore make him feel that he was being strengthened but also in a measure controlled.

From Russia the conversation passed to Italy, which, declared Aehrenthal with emphasis, must be kept within the Triple Alliance. He had exchanged friendly assurances with Tittoni, and, despite his suspicions, would treat the ally with outward friendliness as his master also desired. He hoped that Anglo-German relations would continue to improve, which would encourage Italy's feeling for the Triple Alliance. He summarised his programme as the maintenance of the Triplice combined with fostering the relations of Austria and Germany to Russia, since the co-operation of the three Empires could alone assure the preservation of monarchy. He was optimistic about the internal politics of his country. He was on excellent terms with Francis Ferdinand, and, with the Emperor's assent, intended to allow him more political activity. " Very nice, provided it lasts ", minuted the Kaiser on Bülow's report; and indeed the new Minister, who expressed his satisfaction with the visit on his return to Vienna, appeared to be entering on his work under the happiest auspices. The only cloud in the sky was Iswolsky's Anglophilism. The Russian Minister had suggested an extension of the Mürzsteg programme—a move in the English direction. He had firmly rejected the plan, for the programme in its existing form demanded years of work, and its extension would accelerate the collapse of Turkey. Here then were the three main pillars of his policy at the outset of his course—the maintenance of the Triple Alliance in full vigour, a rapprochement with Russia coupled with the hope of an ultimate revival of the Three Emperors' League, and a conservative policy in the Near East.

III

When Aehrenthal succeeded Goluchowsky the relations between Vienna and Belgrad were embittered by a tariff war.[1] During the prolonged discussions of a commercial treaty Austria complained of systematic unfriendliness, and Serbia retorted that Vienna was out to destroy her economic independence. The new Minister proved more accommodating, and in 1907 a treaty, which satisfied neither side, was signed. In his Annual Report for 1907 the British Ambassador in Vienna, Sir Edward Goschen, emphasised the change of tone at the Ballplatz. " Ever since his Excellency has been in office he has done all in his power to remove the bad feeling in Serbia caused by Count Goluchowsky's policy, and it is well known that he worked very hard to make the Commercial Treaty as favourable as possible to that country. He even insisted for a long time upon giving Serbia the right to export live cattle to Austria-Hungary. The Prime Minister, however, who was anxious at that time to secure the support of the Agrarian party in other questions, was obdurate, and finally Baron d'Aehrenthal had to give way." The new pilot was well aware that friendly relations with Russia required tolerable relations with Belgrad, and the *détente* with Serbia was an item in his project for the revival of the Dreikaiserbund.

[1] B.D. V, 148–67.

A more complicated task was the problem of Macedonian reform. The intervention of the Powers had resulted in the creation of a Gendarmerie under foreign officers and the establishment of a Financial Commission. The third item in the Mürzsteg programme, the reform of justice, had been kept to the last, and the new actor came on the scene when it could no longer be ignored. The judicial scandals of the Turkish Courts were notorious, and the pacification of Macedonia was impossible till reforms were carried out. The Powers, however, differed as to the possibility of reform.[1] In a series of formidable despatches from Constantinople Marschall argued that they could destroy the existing system but could put nothing in its place, while attempted changes would infuriate the Turks. On his first visit to Berlin Aehrenthal was informed of the Ambassador's views, and, while refusing to abandon the project, seemed inclined to temporise. He was anxious to support the Sultan and maintain the status quo so long as possible. The Powers which clamoured for advance were England and Italy, while France was reasonable, and Iswolsky was talking very sensibly. He would be glad if Marschall could arrange for Hilmi Pasha to come forward with plans for the reform of justice. The Austrian and Russian Ambassadors in Constantinople were instructed to suggest a plan ; but the project, as Marschall reported on New Year's Day 1907, was mainly the work of the latter. The scheme was to be considered in Vienna and St. Petersburg, and after receiving the approval of the Mürzsteg partners was to be laid before the Ambassadors in the Turkish capital. When the German Ambassador in Vienna urged Aehrenthal not to hustle the Sultan, the Minister replied that he would have greatly preferred to grant control to the Governor-General and the Civil Assessors. Owing, however, to the pressure of the Western Powers and the customary indolence of Turkey, something would have to be done, though the Sultan's feelings must be considered. Iswolsky was wavering, but he inclined to more radical measures on the English model.

With such divided counsels it was not surprising that the discussion lagged. It was an open secret that the Central Powers were ranged in one camp and the rest in another. During a visit to Berlin in May Aehrenthal asked for support of his conservative policy against the pressure of the British and Russian Ambassadors.[2] He hoped also to win France by

[1] G.P. XXII, ch. 164.   [2] ibid. XXII, 55–6.

depicting the risk of an active policy to her financial interests, and Russia by the argument that in her present weakness the opening of the Eastern question had better be deferred. He proceeded to advocate the linking up of the Bosnian railways with Salonika. Austria by herself could achieve nothing in Constantinople, where the occupation of Bosnia and Herzegovina still rankled. The Wilhelmstrasse promised support of the railway scheme on condition that the Sultan approved, which was all that he had hoped. He then asked Russia if she would content herself with a cautious policy and would refuse to be pushed beyond a certain line. Iswolsky answered vaguely, and the inquiry reached the ears of the English Cabinet, which was annoyed at the suspicion of its policy. About the same time Aehrenthal spoke in gloomy terms of Macedonian affairs to the British Ambassador. It was the first time, reported Goschen, that he had heard him express misgivings or doubt the efficacy of the Mürzsteg agreement.[1]

The plan of judicial reform worked out by the Austrian and Russian Ambassadors in Constantinople was presented to the Ambassadors of the other Great Powers in August. In conversation with the German Chargé Aehrenthal argued that the Sultan, having accepted the Mürzsteg programme, had no right to oppose its execution, and that it was in his own interest to avert the necessity of pressure. In a private letter to Bülow he expressed his belief that Iswolsky, after some vacillation, was pursuing a conservative policy. A day or two after the presentation of the draft scheme a warning note was struck by Kiderlen, who was representing Marschall in Constantinople. The Sultan, he reported, was appealing to Germany to save him from a demand which he regarded as a peculiar humiliation. " I am assured from a well-informed source ", he added, " that our reply will be of great importance in determining his general attitude towards us." The appeal fell on deaf ears ; for Tschirschky, while reserving his official answer, sharply lectured the Turkish Ambassador. Germany had repeatedly advised the Porte to co-operate with the Mürzsteg Powers in regard to judicial reform, but her advice had been ignored. The Sultan now appealed to the Kaiser himself to postpone the demand for judicial reform, which he would consider an infringement of his sovereign rights. The scheme was willingly accepted in Downing Street and more grudgingly at Berlin. It was impossible for Germany to

[1] B.D. V, 203-4.

stand out, for she had promised to accept in principle proposals jointly recommended by Austria and Russia ; and Bülow realised the danger of her finding herself alone.   All she could do was to urge the two Powers to act as far as possible in agreement with Turkey and without measures of coercion. Aehrenthal replied that he too desired to consider the Sultan's feelings.   For months he had vainly implored her to avert pressure by spontaneous measures for judicial reform.   Italy made no difficulties, and Aehrenthal's meetings with Tittoni in Desio and on the Semmering seemed to bring the two Governments closer to one another.

In September the Porte announced a scheme of its own for judicial reform, informing the Powers at the same time that control by foreign agents was unacceptable.   It was a clever move, and Kiderlen at once secured its conditional acceptance by the Ambassadors as an alternative to the presentation of the Austro-Russian scheme.   England, on the other hand, declared the Turkish plan unacceptable as containing no guarantee for its execution.   The new situation was explored during Iswolsky's visit to Aehrenthal at the end of the month.   The two statesmen issued a declaration denying that the delimitation of administrative areas foreshadowed in the Mürzsteg programme aimed at dividing Macedonia into national spheres. Iswolsky was pleased with his reception, but the conversations were not wholly satisfying.[1]   When he urged Aehrenthal to secure Germany's support for judicial reform, the Austrian statesman replied that he saw no need for such a step, since Germany had gone hand in hand with Austria and Russia in the Ambassadors' Conference.   He had no wish to be pushed forward, he confided to the German Ambassador, all the more since the German press seemed so solicitous for the sovereignty of the Sultan.   He had no desire to infringe it, but control of justice was essential, and if the Powers were unanimous the difficulties would not be great.   Unanimity, however, as the Sultan was well aware, did not exist.

While Germany was inclined to retreat, Aehrenthal stuck to his guns.   He told the German Ambassador that he was about to inform the Sultan that refusal to accept the scheme would expose him to the danger of coercion, which would be far more damaging to his prestige.   Meanwhile England was pressing for the appointment of Christian Inspectors of Justice by the Macedonian Financial Commission, which Germany

[1] B.D. V, 215-6.

pronounced to be a clear infringement of the Sultan's rights. While listening to German apprehensions Aehrenthal begged the continuance of support for the Austro-Russian plan. Without it the whole of the reform enterprise would be endangered. The Wilhelmstrasse was annoyed by his stiffness, and Bülow noted that he must be carefully handled. Germany, it should be explained to him, was not seeking privileges for herself in Constantinople ; but it was in the interests of the conservative Powers, above all Austria, not to weaken Turkey too much and drive the Sultan to desperation. The Powers were deeply divided, and Kiderlen bitterly complained of the " intriguing and turbulent " British Ambassador. " I cannot resist the lamentable impression ", he added " that the Austrian Government, instead of using the weakness of Russia to assume the leadership, gives way to her from fear of losing this wonderful entente." Between England who wanted more, Russia who wanted less, and Germany who wanted nothing, Aehrenthal was in a difficult position, as he explained to the German Ambassador. Russia, urged forward by England, was going too fast, but he could not accept a status quo policy in the Balkans. It was not his business to support Turkish misrule, and if the Sultan rejected Austria's advice he must take the consequences. The only way of applying the brake to Russia was by keeping in close touch with her. To oppose her on the Bosphorus would drive her still more into the arms of England, and lead to a coalition of Russia, England and France against the Central Powers.

On December 14, on his way back to his post, Marschall broke his journey at Vienna at Bülow's wish. When Aehrenthal admitted that the proposed note was too hard on the Sultan, he rejoined that he had never had much faith in the reforms, which were powerless to check national tendencies. " You are right ", replied Aehrenthal. " I make you a present of the Judicial Reform and the reforms altogether, for reforms are assuredly powerless against national tendencies. But ' il faut faire quelque chose ' has become an axiom of Russia and England, who are vying with each other in drastic proposals. France and Italy go with them. And yesterday Prince Ferdinand was here, greatly alarmed by the latest outrage in Sofia, imploring me to do something for Macedonia, as otherwise he could not control the situation." Quite apart from the Bulgarian factor it would be a mistake for Austria, by opposing judicial reform in principle, to bring

England and Russia closer together, with the consequence that the two Powers would one day agree about the Eastern Question without and against Austria. Marschall agreed that opposition was impossible for Austria, but added that acceptance was equally impossible for the Sultan, who would be charged with breaking the Sacred Law. Coercion would be necessary, and coercion would probably set the Balkans aflame. The Great Powers would be unable to control events, and intervention would endanger European peace. Another alternative was possible, replied Aehrenthal. The Powers could proclaim their disinterestedness and leave the Balkan States to stew in their own juice. An excellent idea, rejoined Marschall, but not very practicable. Would England witness atrocities in the Balkans unmoved? Would Holy Russia accept the defeat of her Orthodox brothers? Would Italy hold aloof if her interests in South Albania were infringed? Aehrenthal admitted the justice of his arguments and the extent of the danger; but for the time being Austria and Germany could only join the other Powers in regard to Judicial Reform. He cannot have spoken with much conviction, for he was too well informed to be unaware that the game was up. It is hardly fanciful to connect Marschall's visit with the approaching change of course. At the end of 1907 Judicial Reform was as far away as ever, for the Powers were divided and therefore impotent.

The situation was complicated by the fact that the time had come for the renewal of mandates in Macedonia. The request of the Powers brought a demand that the Civil Agents and the Finance Commission should enter the Turkish service. Further notes were exchanged till the Sultan gave way, but the discussion had served its tactical purpose of holding up the larger question of Judicial Reform. On January 21, 1908, Tschirschky reminded Aehrenthal that Germany, though willing to support the Austro-Russian proposals, could not take part in coercion, which was not contemplated in the Mürzsteg programme and contradicted Austria's conservative policy in Turkey. Austria, replied Aehrenthal, would continue her conservative policy, but, as herself a Balkan Power, she had to consider her relations to the other Balkan States. She must always be on the watch lest her dominating position in the Balkans side by side with Russia should be destroyed. For this reason it was impossible to drop the Mürzsteg programme, which embodied the idea of the predominance of the two Powers. Germany was an ally, remarked the Ambassador, and had a right to know how far Austria intended to go in securing the acceptance of the reforms. He desired the maintenance of the status quo, replied Aehrenthal, but he could not bind himself to it. For instance he would not allow the Sultan to cancel his assurances respecting the Finance Commission by mixing it up with Judicial Reform and thus undermine the whole structure. What measures would be necessary could not be decided at present. Meanwhile the Note on Judicial Reform would have to be presented in order to show the Sultan that the Powers could not be intimidated by the threat of refusing the renewal of the Mandates. On the other hand he was ready for compromise on Judicial Reform.

At the opening of February Austria and Russia urged the other Powers to sign the Note on Judicial Reform. But the situation had been dramatically transformed by Aehrenthal's announcement on January 27 that he had asked the Sultan for a railway concession' through the Sanjak of Novibazar. The Ambassadors at Constantinople were empowered to sign ; but, led by Marschall and Constans, they warned their chiefs against signature in the existing form, since Turkey was expected to decline the note and to defy coercion. A compromise suggested by Marschall, by which the reports of the Inspectors should reach the Financial Commission through Hilmi, the Governor-General, was approved by all the Ambassadors and recommended to their Governments in an identical telegram. The new proposal was unacceptable to Iswolsky, who bitterly complained of Aehrenthal's concession for the Sanjak railway. Austria had used the situation created by the fruitless negotiations for Judicial Reform to secure economic advantages in the Balkans. She had been supported by Germany, whose Ambassador at Constantinople was mainly responsible for the failure of the scheme. At the moment when Aehrenthal had scored a great success, Russia could not possibly accept a check to her Balkan policy. She was so publicly pledged to the reform scheme that retreat was impossible. He admitted, nevertheless, that the Note needed modification. Aehrenthal told Tschirschky that the latest suggestion of the Ambassadors was unacceptable to Iswolsky and Grey as well as to himself. He agreed with the latter in desiring the immediate presentation of the Note. While the Ambassadors believed that the renewal of the mandates was only to be secured by its modification, Aehrenthal argued that to withhold it would jeopardise both. He accepted it more-over, in order that Russia and England should not have the field to themselves.

Aehrenthal's pretence that the Sanjak concession and Judicial Reform could be kept in watertight compartments deceived no one but himself. The Sultan had never intended to yield on the latter, and even a sham surrender was now unnecessary. Austria could not beg and threaten at the same time. Moreover, though Marschall denied having said a word to the Turks, his vigorous campaign against the Note must surely have come to their ears. " The relation of the Powers", he reported on February 17, " presents to-day a picture of such complete disunion as has hardly existed in the last thirty years." Iswolsky now realised that to present the Note was to invite a snub, and the document which had been under discussion for many months became waste paper. The Mandates were renewed on March 13, but on the larger issue the Powers were beaten. It would be untrue to maintain that the Sanjak concession destroyed the prospect of success, for success was unattainable ; but it gave Judicial Reform the *coup de grâce*.

IV

Projects of new railways in the Balkans had often been discussed, among them that of a line through the Sanjak of Novibazar to connect the Bosnian with the Serbian systems.[1] The scheme had been proposed by Goluchowsky in 1902 but was dropped in deference to the feelings of Russia.[2] It was mentioned by Aehrenthal in conversation with Wedel in January 1907, though the Ambassador reported that the new Minister had not given such questions much attention at present. A month later a conference at Vienna discussed the railway projects, and decided to seek the help of Germany in the realisation of a programme which included the line to Mitrovitza. On a visit to Berlin in May 1907 Aehrenthal pleaded for the railway. Austria alone could hardly hope to secure permission in Constantinople, where the loss of Bosnia and Herzegovina was unforgotten. Germany promised support for the project if the Sultan approved.

Many months were to elapse before Aehrenthal shot his

[1] *G.P.* XXV, ch. 187.
[2] *Ö-U.A.* I, 6, and Baernreither, 75–8.

bolt. In the last week of 1907 the Austrian Ambassador secured consent to preliminary measures for the creation of a syndicate. The connection of the Bosnian lines with Mitrovitza, he argued, was an economic necessity. He admitted to the Grand Vizier that, when the plan was known, the legend of a march to Salonika would revive. This was nonsense. Austria held to her policy of the status quo, and it was absurd to suppose that her army could advance through the mountainous Sanjak. " Vous prêchez à un converti," rejoined the Vizier, who added that he must proceed with great caution lest he should be suspected as Austrophil. " Austria's step ", commented Marschall in reporting the interview, " is sure to make a great sensation and to excite sensibilities in different quarters. But such a diversion in the Eastern Question is not unwelcome at a moment when the Powers are confronted with a serious crisis in the reform question." Support was promised from Berlin and Paris, though not from London. Italy and Russia were also informed of the plan, and Iswolsky called the attention of the Ballplatz to the danger involved " in the most delicate and friendly way."

On January 27, 1908, Aehrenthal informed the Delegations that the Sultan had been asked to allow preliminary studies for a railway through the Sanjak to Mitrovitza. With the connection of the Bosnian and Turkish lines Austrian trade would tend to flow through Serajevo to the Aegean and Mediterranean. Others, it was hoped, would follow, and before long a direct line would run from Vienna to Athens. " That would be the shortest route from Central Europe to Egypt and India. . . . I count on the support of the Sultan for these undertakings with all the more confidence since the union of the Turkish system with the Bosnian in the north and the Greek in the south will bring new economic vitality to the Macedonian vilayets." It was a momentous pronouncement, travelling in its wide perspectives far beyond the prospect of the short line through a mountainous and thinly populated district. Till now Aehrenthal had played a secondary part in the European drama, but with the speech of January 27 he assumed a position in the centre of the stage which he was to retain for the next fifteen months. In a moment he had become a European figure, for Austria had taken the initiative in a matter of high significance. Though in itself the Sanjak concession seemed a mere trifle, its results were far-reaching. The Austro-Russian partnership in the Balkans, inaugurated in

1897 and extended by the Mürzsteg pact of 1903, was destroyed in fact if not in name. The Concert was flouted when the Ballplatz petitioned for a concession at the same time as the Powers were pressing for a renewal of the Mandates and preparing for a tussle on Judicial Reform. The period of partial subordination to Berlin was brought to an end, and Austria henceforth determined her own policy in the Balkan peninsula with little regard to her partners in the Triple Alliance. Europe discovered that the tranquil era of Goluchowsky was over, and that the polyglot Empire had a pilot who was not afraid to take formidable risks.

Aehrenthal possessed courage in plenty, but he was singularly lacking in judgment and tact. Though he had broken no treaty, his action inevitably produced a chorus of protest. The speech made a painful impression at Constantinople, since the request for a railway concession was accompanied by a reiteration of the necessity of Judicial Reform. Moreover, he had mentioned the project of a line connecting the Greek terminus at Larissa with Macedonian railways, which was peculiarly distasteful to the Sultan. Iswolsky complained bitterly to Pourtalès that a most unfortunate moment had been chosen for the declaration. Yet, however much he stormed or sulked, he knew that he could not act. Aehrenthal knew it too. The rivalry had begun, and for the moment he held the winning cards.

The speech was no less unwelcome in London. Benckendorff, a convinced believer in the Austro-Russian Entente, feared that it must perish unless the two capitals could be reconciled through the good offices of Germany. The *coup*, he complained to Metternich, sinned against the spirit of the Balkan Pact. The Panslav idea was strengthened, the Slav countries, especially Serbia, were estranged, the unity of the Powers in Constantinople endangered, the opposition of the Sultan strengthened, the work of reform undermined. Austria could not ask concessions with one hand and present reform notes with the other. While making no promises to his Russian colleages, Metternich reported his own reflections to his chief. Germany could only mediate if Aehrenthal was frightened into withdrawal. If he stuck to his project, Iswolsky would doubtless move nearer to Italy and England. More damaging than these mutterings was the unconcealed disapproval of Downing Street. " Surely Sir Edward Grey ", remarked Aehrenthal to Goschen, " did not expect me to wait till the end of the reform negotiations before taking the first step to put into effect a railway policy so necessary to our commercial development. I might have had to wait for years."[1] Unimpressed by this argument Grey expressed his regret at the blow to the reform movement in his historic speech of February 28, which was deeply resented by Aehrenthal.[2] He was not the man to take rebukes lying down. " It is a matter that concerns only Turkey and ourselves ", he replied.[3] " Moreover I cannot admit that we have thereby exercised an unfavourable influence on the policy of reform."

In this chorus of denunciation the sympathy of Germany was particularly welcome. In a private letter Bülow suggested that Russia's resentment was artificial, and doubted whether she had any desire for serious conflicts in the Near East. " Our policy is as lacking in provocation as yours. But Germany and Austria form so strong a *bloc* that, if we stand together, nobody will care to challenge us." Aehrenthal sent a grateful message through the Ambassador, and later wrote himself. Austria, he declared, still stood for the Entente with Russia, and was always ready to work for the fulfilment of the Mürzsteg programme. He was in no way pessimistic about the future. " Perhaps Russia will learn from a crisis in the Near East that her wisest policy is co-operation with her neighbour monarchies." There was no hint that his own action had made such a course more difficult. Iswolsky was particularly incensed because Aehrenthal had not mentioned his Sanjak project during their autumn conversations at Vienna. Indeed when rumours began to reach him of Austria's secret steps at Constantinople, he had declined to believe them and had reassured the Tsar. He could not believe that such procedure was approved at Berlin.

On March 3 the Russian Government warmly commended the Serbian project of a Danube-Adriatic railway in a circular despatch, and asked for German support in Constantinople. The Wilhelmstrasse promised friendly examination, knowing that Aehrenthal had no objection in principle to the scheme, though he had views of his own on the route. Russian opinion, however, was too ruffled to be pacified by the acceptance of Serbia's scheme. Iswolsky continued to speak bitterly of his Austrian colleague ; and the Tsar himself, to whom Aehrenthal had been *persona gratissima*, now spoke of him with indignation. Despite his feeling of injury, however, Iswolsky

[1] *B.D.* V, 339–40.   [2] ibid. V 234.   [3] ibid. V, 337.

delivered a conciliatory speech in the Duma.[1] Instead of protesting, he explained, he had encouraged the building of other Balkan railways which Austria also approved. He followed up the speech with an Aide-Mémoire. Aehrenthal had already declared that he had no objection to the Danube-Adriatic scheme, but he was now asked to support it at Constantinople. It was very important that the preparatory studies for the two lines should begin simultaneously. He declined on the ground that the railway schemes, being purely economic, lay outside the scope of the entente, which dealt solely with politics. In informing Tschirschky of his refusal, he explained that he could not place the two schemes in the same category, since the Sanjak plan rested on the solid foundation of the Berlin treaty.[2] Each country should deal independently with Turkey in regard to its economic interests.

The Foreign Minister could hardly look back with satisfaction on his first important achievement at the Ballplatz. The Sanjak railway, which offered neither military nor economic advantages, was never built, for the district was evacuated a few months later ; but the incident left dark shadows behind. A juridically defensible step may be a serious political error. Russia, it is true, had been moving steadily towards England, and was therefore in less need of a Dreikaiserbund. But England and Austria had been on excellent terms, and Aehrenthal had enjoyed the full confidence of St. Petersburg. There was no valid excuse for taking an important decision in the Balkans without consulting his partner. Germany, it is true, had stood faithfully at his side ; but the Wilhelmstrasse began to realise that Aehrenthal, though a greater man than Goluchowsky, was not necessarily a change for the better. He was sincerely grateful for German help, reported the German Chargé ; but he resented any suggestion that he was not his own master. A tendency to rash or at any rate insufficiently prepared action was apparent, and he seemed unable to forecast its effect on the feelings of other people. The argument that he was merely implementing the Treaty of Berlin was unconvincing. In 1907 the Three Emperors' League was a dream : in 1908 it was a memory. Aehrenthal and Iswolsky had learned to dislike and distrust one another. The opening round of the duel had been fought, and a sharper collision was not far away.

[1] Ö-U.A. I, 3-6. [2] G.P. XXV, 369-71.

V

A month after the Sanjak sensation Grey proposed the appointment of a Christian Governor-General in Macedonia independent of the Sultan. His disinterested desire to alleviate the lot of the Macedonian population was not generally shared, and his plans were received with scepticism or open hostility. " I do not believe that they are meant very seriously," wrote Aehrenthal to Bülow on March 11.[1] " My impression is that they may be intended to smooth the way for the more cautious proposals which we are expecting from Iswolsky. We must reckon with the possibility of parallel Anglo-Russian action in the Near East, but I do not think such an unnatural combination will last very long."

Iswolsky pronounced the English programme too radical, and on March 16 he presented a scheme in which the Christian Governor found no place. Aehrenthal had little objection to its modest provisions, but in the communication of them to the Powers he discovered the definite abandonment of the Austro-Russian Entente. The Wilhelmstrasse was delighted. " Iswolsky's brusque step will cure Aehrenthal of his love for Russia ", wrote Schön to Bülow, " and emphasise the value of solidarity with us. He is doubtless a convinced opponent of radical measures which might lead to a violent solution of the Balkan problem. He has not cared to stress his view hitherto through fear of endangering the entente with Russia. This consideration now disappears." The Austrian answer was regarded by Iswolsky as on the whole satisfactory, but the substitution of the Concert for the partnership remained a fact. The discussion of reforms proceeded between London and St. Petersburg, while Marschall fired his broadsides against all proposals, large and small. England, remarked Aehrenthal to Tschirschky, was working towards the autonomy of Macedonia. " But that is not our policy, and we cannot support it." The Anglo-Russian plan, when ready, might be submitted to the Ambassadors in Constantinople, who might work out a collective note. He added with a smile that they would be going on leave, and the discussions could not begin before the autumn. He had clearly lost interest in the matter, for he was flying at higher game.

Aehrenthal was not at all satisfied with the course of events since the Sanjak declaration, particularly with Russia's drift

[1] G.P. XXV, ch. 188.

towards the West and the Reval meeting. The reaction in St. Petersburg, which he believed himself to know so well, had wounded his pride. A certain irritability had developed, and both the diplomatic corps and his own staff complained that official business had recently become much more difficult to transact. Dissatisfaction was also felt in Austrian political circles. The Minister was reproached with being deceived in Iswolsky and for having estranged nearly all the Great Powers. Austria lacked self-confidence, and her preoccupation with domestic politics indisposed her to take a leading part in foreign affairs. Hence the regret at the ending of the Mürzsteg pact, under the shelter of which most Austrians hoped to go on living quietly and without anxiety. The structure of the Monarchy, it was instinctively felt, was hostile to an active policy. The Sanjak concession had brought no laurels abroad or at home.

Among Aehrenthal's troubles was the different attitude towards Turkey adopted by Vienna and Berlin. To strengthen Iswolsky's hands against English radicalism Pourtalès was instructed to say that Germany could not support innovations which would lead to revolution and the danger of war.[1] It was added that Germany felt sure that this standpoint was shared by Austria. Aehrenthal was annoyed, and begged that such declarations should only be made after consultation with Vienna. He feared that the effect would be that, if the Anglo-Russian proposals were rejected, the odium would fall on the Central Empires. Schön was surprised at the complaint and Bülow realised that a new spirit had entered the Ballplatz. Pourtalès was therefore ordered to tell Iswolsky informally that, just as Germany did not hold him responsible for all the doings of France, so he should understand that Austrian policy under Aehrenthal had become very independent, and that it would be incorrect to assume that Germany was behind every Austrian move. Harmony between the Powers, so far as Macedonia was concerned, was restored by the sensational news of the Young Turk revolution. Even Grey, the driving force in the reform movement, decided to wait and see, and his attitude was shared by Aehrenthal.

The visit of King Edward to Ischl on August 12 took place in the momentary lull between two dramatic events. The Young Turk revolution had succeeded almost without a blow, and the schemes for Macedonian reform had been put into cold

[1] G.P. XXV, ch. 190.

388   AEHRENTHAL

storage.   The conversation between Aehrenthal and Hardinge, ex-colleagues at St. Petersburg, was recorded in detail by both parties.[1]   The former began by explaining his policy in the Balkans.   While desiring to further the reforms initiated by Austria and Russia, he had always pointed out that the sovereignty of the Sultan and Mohammedan feeling must be taken into account.   The leading idea of the Mürzsteg programme was with the Sultan, not against him.   Austria had criticized recent English proposals because this was insufficiently recognised, but she would be ready to resume action in Constantinople at a suitable moment chosen by the Powers. Till then a waiting attitude towards the Young Turk movement would be adopted.   Austria held firmly to the German Alliance, which served her own interest and that of European peace.   Hardinge replied that England too would regard a loosening of the alliance as a grave misfortune.   The German Ambassador was told, though the information was not embodied in the report to the Wilhelmstrasse, that Hardinge had described his disappointing conversation on the navy with the Kaiser at Cronberg.   Aehrenthal had replied that he regretted the gathering of this dark cloud, but he was not surprised.   King Edward's policy was disagreeable for Germany and made it difficult for the Kaiser to modify his naval scheme.   If the pace was to be slowed down a different method must be applied.   Perhaps the change in Turkey would facilitate a rapprochement in the Near East which might ultimately diminish the naval tension.   This might be conveyed to the Kaiser and the Chancellor or Foreign Secretary.

Hardinge's report adds some important information. Aehrenthal explained that the policy of Austria, which had given rise to so much criticism, had been inspired not from Berlin but by her own interests. The German Government had been told of the Sanjak project at the same time as the others. The Anglo-German naval rivalry, though not concerning the Austrian Government, was regarded as potentially dangerous. He particularly desired that Anglo-German friction might not affect the friendly relations of Austria and England.   Travelling further afield he inquired if England, in view of recent developments in Constantinople, contemplated administrative changes in Egypt.   It was a question of considerable interest to Austria, faced in Bosnia and Herzegovina with a very similar situation.   It might prove necessary in the near

[1] Ö-U.A. I, 37-9, and B.D. V, 827-30.

future, replied Hardinge, to widen the basis of government in Egypt, but it was premature to decide what measures, if any, should be taken. Bosnia and Herzegovina, rejoined Aehrenthal, being contiguous to Macedonia, the Austrian Government could hardly avoid making some political concessions. Hardinge found Aehrenthal's attitude perfectly friendly, and his anxious references to Anglo-German tension revealed Austria's need of peace. Neither report mentions the subject of French ambitions in Morocco—which a later version describes as having played an important part in the conversation.[1] The impressions of Aehrenthal were less agreeable than those of his visitor. The German Chargé in Vienna reported that the Emperor had treated King Edward very coolly, sharing as he did the displeasure of his subjects at the Reval demonstrations. Aehrenthal himself informed Schön a week or two later that the Emperor and himself had averted an attempt to detach Austria from Germany by an emphatic declaration that the alliance with Germany remained the unchangeable foundation of Austrian policy.[2] A private letter from the German Chargé reported that Aehrenthal had defended the German standpoint in the navy question with something like passion and almost with discourtesy.[3] Had this been true, it must have been mentioned in Hardinge's report. The visit left Anglo-Austrian relations neither better nor worse. Since no attempt was made from the English side to break up the Austro-German alliance, and since Aehrenthal concealed his projects in the Balkans, the conversations at Ischl cannot compare in importance with those at Reval and Cronberg. King Edward's attentions to Iswolsky and Clemenceau at Marienbad after his visit increased Aehrenthal's feeling that the Triple Entente had come to stay and that England was no longer a friend.[4] After nearly two years in office it was impossible to claim that the international position of Austria had improved.

VI

When Bosnia and Herzegovina were assigned to the administration of Austria by the Treaty of Berlin, no limit was

[1] G.P. XXIV, 133-4, note.
[2] ibid. XXIV, 155.
[3] ibid. 135, note.
[4] ibid. 153-4.

fixed to the mandate.[1]   No one dreamed that they would ever
revert to Turkey, and it was generally understood that formal
annexation was merely a question of time.   The energy of
their new rulers quickly raised two backward Turkish provinces to the European level, and Kallay's beneficent activities
were compared with those of Cromer in the valley of the Nile.
Bosnia and Herzegovina were in fact Austrian in everything
but international law, and after the revolt of 1882 the Mussulman inhabitants appeared to be reconciled to their fate.

The annexation of the provinces was the price secretly paid
by Russia in 1876 in the Reichstadt pact for Austrian neutrality
during the Turkish war ; and it was the wish of Andrassy, not
opposition from the Powers, which decided against the
immediate annexation preferred by Francis Joseph when
Austria received the mandate at the Berlin Congress.   Desiring
to avoid friction with Turkey, who would have declined to
cede sovereignty over unconquered territory, he contented
himself with administrative control and the right to keep
garrisons in the Sanjak of Novibazar.   In the Convention of
1881 creating the League of the Three Emperors Austria
reserved the right to annex the provinces whenever she wished.
With the collapse of the League in 1887 the attitude of Russia
became more critical ; and when in negotiating the Balkan
agreement of 1897 Austria reiterated her claim to annex the
provinces and the Sanjak at will and without any discussion,
Russia called a halt.[2]   " The annexation of these two provinces
would raise a more extensive question, which would require
special examination at the proper time and place.   As to the
Sanjak of Novibazar, there would also be the necessity to
specify its boundaries, which, indeed, have never been sufficiently defined."   The firm juridical basis of the question was
to be found in the Treaty of Berlin and nowhere else, but with
the passing of the years the impatience of Austria grew.   On

[1] For authoritative Austrian views of the Bosnian crisis see Pribram, *Austrian
Foreign Policy* 1908–18 ; Friedjung, *Das Zeitalter des Imperialismus*, Vol. II ;
and Fournier, *Wie wir zu Bosnien kamen*.   Stieve, *Die Tragödie der Bundesgenossen*,
and Frankenfeld, *Oesterreichs Spiel mit dem Kriege*, present German criticism of
Austrian policy.   Bernadotte Schmitt's articles in the *Slavonic Review*, 26–30, and
O. H. Wedel's *Austro-German Diplomatic Relations*, 1908–14, illustrate American
opinion.   Seton-Watson, *The Rôle of Bosnia in International Politics* (1875–1914)
is brief but authoritative.   Boghitschewitsch, *Serbien und der Weltkrieg*, ch. 3,
and Loncarevich, *Jugoslaviens Entstehung*, ch. 5, represent different Jugoslav
schools of thought.   Conrad, *Aus Meiner Dienstzeit*, I, 39–174, and appendices,
contains important documents.

[2] Pribram, I, 184–95.

December 21, 1907, a Ministerial Council was held to discuss the provinces in which Burian pleaded for a Diet.[1] Aehrenthal explained that it was impossible without annexation, which might be feasible if other modifications of the Treaty of Berlin were contemplated. Burian returned to the charge in a Memorandum to the Emperor in April 1908 ; but the Foreign Minister, stressing the international character of the problem, still felt unable to move.

In asking support for a Danube-Adriatic line Iswolsky reminded Berchtold of his constant efforts to remain on good terms with Austria and of his defence of her legal right to her claims in the Sanjak.[2] " Ready to continue on this road and anxious not to sever the thread which connects Vienna and St. Petersburg, he considers it indispensable that Baron Aehrenthal should facilitate this task." The latter, after refusing a joint *démarche* at Constantinople, took up Iswolsky's reference to the larger issue. The entente, he argued, had found expression in close collaboration on the basis of the Mürzsteg programme and their common activity in Balkan affairs as the two most interested Powers. Since, however, the latest Russian proposals, substituting the Financial Delegates for the Civil Agents, terminated this relationship, it would be useful to define the entente anew. If Russia declared her fidelity to the principles of disinterestedness embodied in the agreement of 1897, he would gladly accept the formula. For he was anxious to maintain relations of friendship and confidence, convinced that they alone served the monarchical and conservative interests of the two States. After taking time for consideration Iswolsky replied in the famous Aide-Mémoire of July 2, in which he declared his readiness to discuss the questions of Bosnia and the Straits " in a spirit of friendly reciprocity."[3] Despite some debatable passages, commented Aehrenthal, it breathed a spirit of compromise and approach. He would carefully consider the very important proposals. Meanwhile he expressed his satisfaction at the tone of the note.

While he was considering his reply, the Young Turk revolution brought both relief and complications in the Near East. When the Russian Ambassador presented the latest Macedonian proposals, he promised to consider them, pointing out, however, that the situation had radically changed. He

---

[1] Baernreither, 80–1.
[2] Ö-U.A. I, 3–4.   Aide-Mémoire of April 27, 1908.
[3] v. supra 332

hoped Iswolsky would agree that nothing should be done to intensify the crisis by rash interference. In his memorandum of July 2 he had reiterated the principle of disinterestness enunciated in the pact of 1897. The two Governments should now decide to abstain from intervention in the event of complications in the Near East unless by agreement. This arrangement, of course, would in no way affect the progress of the reform scheme. Iswolsky agreed that abstention was the wisest policy.

When the tiresome problem of Macedonian reform was thrust off the stage, the Serbs began to demand that Bosnia and Herzegovina should send deputies to the new Turkish Parliament. On August 7 Aehrenthal wrote to the Austrian Prime Minister explaining the situation created by the revolution, and announcing the momentous resolve which he and Burian had reached in a conversation on the Semmering on the previous day. Austria had no objection to the experiment of a constitutional Turkey, and her traditional policy in reference to crises in the Near East had been watchful neutrality. On this occasion, however, non-intervention might be difficult, for she had garrisons in the Sanjak. An outbreak of anarchy or a massacre of Christians in that district might compel military intervention. If she was not to be drawn into the Turkish drama she must withdraw her troops. This could only be done without loss of prestige by a simultaneous annexation of Bosnia and Herzegovina. The necessity arose from the impossible position of the Government in regard to the granting of Bosnian autonomy and a provincial Diet. Such a Diet, unless preceded by annexation, would increase Austria's difficulties. For these reasons he had decided to ask the Emperor's leave to discuss preparations in a Ministerial Council. " Having obtained this permission I hasten to inform your Excellency, and to beg for your valuable support at a moment so important for the Monarchy." The two Provinces would continue to be ruled as a *corpus separatum* by a joint Ministry under the control of Austria and Hungary.

Two days later Aehrenthal drew up an elaborate memorandum.[1] When the first smart of the Sanjak episode began to diminish, there were signs that Russia did not desire to cut the wire to Vienna and that she would before long attempt a political approach. It came in the memorandum of July 2, which suggested the discussion of larger issues than Balkan railways

[1] *Ö-U.A.* I, 25–34.

and Macedonian reform. He proceeded to argue that the annexation of the Sanjak was undesirable, and that the aims of Austria's Balkan policy would be realised not through Novi-bazar but through Belgrad. Andrassy's eastern policy rested on two fundamental principles—the preservation of Turkey and the prevention of a big Slav state on the southern frontier. The attempt to secure the first by the joint garrisoning of the Sanjak had been a failure ; for it had aroused the suspicions of the Sultan and prevented Austria from pursuing a healthy and economically profitable policy. The second principle could not be attained by the occupation or annexation of the Sanjak. Even were it possible thereby to hold Serbia and Montenegro apart, that would not achieve the main object of a far-sighted statesmanship, namely, in the event of the collapse of Turkey in Europe, to secure safe frontiers towards the south. " Such safe frontiers we shall not obtain unless we decide to grip the evil by the root and to make an end of Great-Serbian dreams. The antagonism between Bulgars and Serbs is already a factor to be reckoned with. Bulgaria is convinced that the road to Macedonia must pass over the body of the Serbian state, and a violent struggle for the possession of Uskub is inevitable. If we support the Bulgarian cause in this conflict and favour the creation of a Great Bulgaria at Serbia's expense, the ground is prepared for us at a favourable moment to lay our hands on the remainder of Serbia. We should then possess the safe frontiers of which I have spoken—an independent Albania under our auspices, a friendly Montenegro, and a grateful Great Bulgaria." Thus the decision to evacuate the Sanjak and to annex Bosnia and Herzegovina was only part of a more ambitious programme in which the ultimate elimination of Serbia was the principal item.

On August 19 a Ministerial Council was held at Vienna, with the Foreign Minister in the chair.[1] He opened with a survey of the new situation which had led to the withdrawal of the Macedonian reforms. Austria was faced with the questions of Bosnia and Herzegovina and of the Sanjak. By the joint garrisoning of the latter Andrassy had desired to support Turkey and to prevent the union of Serbia and Montenegro. This had given rise to the legend of an advance to Salonika, and the garrisons might now at any moment find themselves in trouble. In Bosnia a great civilising work had been achieved, but there was no constitution. With a constitution in Turkey

<hr>

[1] Ö-U.A. I, 41–50.

this would become a burning question, and institutional change was unthinkable without annexation. The Emperor had approved the evacuation of the Sanjak and the annexation of Bosnia. The first task was to agree on the constitutional questions involved, after which the Foreign Minister would decide on the time to act. At this point Beck, the Austrian Premier, asked for light on the diplomatic aspect of the plan.[1] They could be absolutely sure of Germany, replied Aehrenthal in a revealing sentence, for she could now depend on Austria alone. Russia had on several occasions recognised her right to annex the provinces, and he proposed to promise support for the opening of the Dardanelles. Italy had no claim to compensation under the terms of the Triple Alliance. France was busy with Morocco, and no opposition was expected from England. Turkey would of course resist, but her difficulties would make her cautious.

Aehrenthal was determined to push on. " As you see", he wrote to his Ambassador in Constantinople, " we can no longer follow the maxim : *Quieta non movere.* Neither in the Sanjak nor in Bosnia are things standing still, and if we do not act we shall lose control of events." The announcement of annexation would be unwelcome news in Constantinople, but after the first shock relations would improve. For only when a clear situation existed in Bosnia and the Sanjak would enduring friendliness ensue. The evacuation of the Sanjak would be an eloquent proof that Austria wanted no territory from Turkey. The date was not yet fixed, but events might necessitate rapid action lest the hour was missed. The Ambassador was authorised, though not instructed, to sound the Turks, and was asked for his advice on procedure. He telegraphed that soundings would be useless and that rapid action would be best.

On August 27 Aehrenthal at length replied to Iswolsky's memorandum of July 2 and outlined an agreement.[2] " The two Cabinets would remain faithful to their resolution to maintain the status quo in Turkey so long as circumstances permit. They would engage to abstain from all intervention in the Near East except by agreement. If, however, imperious circumstances obliged Austria to annex Bosnia and Herzegovina the Imperial Gove--ment promise a benevolent and

---

[1] Beck's dislike of the project was greater than he revealed during this discussion. Sieghart, *Die letzten Jahrzehnte einer Grossmacht,* 137.

[2] Ö-U.A. I, 59–61.

friendly attitude. The Imperial and Royal Government, on its side, would undertake to withdraw its troops from the Sanjak simultaneously with the annexation and would finally renounce occupation of this territory. The Imperial and Royal Government is convinced that the Cabinet of St. Petersburg would see in this a new confirmation and a striking manifestation of the principle of disinterestedness which inspires the agreement of the two Empires. The Imperial Government having mentioned the question of Constantinople, the adjacent territory and the Straits, we declare ourselves quite ready for a confidential and friendly exchange of views on this subject." The initiative had come from Iswolsky, and Aehrenthal had joyfully grasped the proffered hand.

Political secrets are difficult to keep. By the end of August some German papers were preparing their readers for annexation. At the same moment the Turkish press began to speak of autonomy for the provinces. In conversation with Goschen at Marienbad the Serbian Foreign Minister Milovanovich remarked that he could not believe that Austria would care to open such a dangerous question.[1] Iswolsky pronounced Aehrenthal's memorandum a step in advance, but he needed time to consult his master. Berchtold remarked that a speedy answer was desirable, since events on Austria's south-eastern frontier might force her hand. When Iswolsky asked whether annexation was planned for the immediate future, the Ambassador cautiously replied that the decision depended on circumstances which could not be foreseen.

Count Lutzow, the Austrian Ambassador in Rome, strongly advised his chief against annexation, but his protest was in vain. On September 4 Aehrenthal received a visit from Tittoni in Salzburg, and told him of his plans.[2] The Italian statesman took the news in a friendly spirit, and did not challenge the assertion that Italy had no claim to compensation. When Aehrenthal complained of Serbia's growing hostility and hinted that chastisement might one day become necessary, Tittoni understood the position, but asked for support of the Danube-Adriatic line in which Italy was interested. Aehrenthal promised it, subject to Italy's support for the Sanjak railway and a line on the Dalmatian coast. He was pleased with the interview, and gathered that no opposition from Rome was to be feared. Next day he engaged in a more intimate

[1] B.D. V, 362.
[2] Ö-U.A. I, 72–5.

conversation with Schön at Berchtesgaden.[1] Though he disliked Iswolsky, he began, it would be unwise to cut the wire to St. Petersburg. Austria, however, would have to consider a final settlement of the question of Bosnia and Herzegovina, which could only be found in annexation. The garrisons in the Sanjak would be withdrawn. The idea of an advance to Salonika was given up. If Russia, as he expected, agreed with these plans, he was ready to discuss the opening of the Straits to Russian warships. His maxim was : Better have Russia with Austria and Germany than with England. He proceeded to explain that a further aim of his Balkan policy was the complete elimination of the Serbian revolutionary nest, and asked for Germany's support. Serbia could be given to Bulgaria—a project of which Schön immediately pointed out the dangers.

On September 10 a second Ministerial Council was held at Budapest, in which Aehrenthal reviewed events since the meeting on August 19.[2] The annexation, he believed, would involve no difficulties with Russia. Germany's support was assured, and Schön had expressed surprise at Austria's moderation in regard to Turkish territory. Tittoni had been friendly, and no serious trouble need be apprehended from Italy. The Turkish army was so disorganised that only a protest and perhaps the breaking off of diplomatic relations were likely. After the first shock the relations would probably benefit by clearing up the juridical position. Serbia was preparing trouble in Bosnia, Croatia and Dalmatia, and a conflict in the Sanjak had become more probable. Speedy action was necessary, for a Turkish Parliament might legislate for Bosnia, or a Bosnian Parliament might come into being. This was the last moment that Austria could withdraw from the Sanjak with the air of conferring a favour. If it were lost, an incident might occur necessitating the strengthening of the garrisons. It was agreed that mobilisation should be avoided if possible, both on diplomatic and financial grounds.

On September 15 Aehrenthal and Iswolsky met as the guests of Berchtold at Buchlau in Moravia, and on the following day prolonged conversations took place between the two statesmen without witnesses. Since no report by Iswolsky is at present available, we have to be content with the very full record by

---

[1] G.P. XXVI, 26–9. No report is in the Vienna Archives. Aehrenthal refers to the visit in a speech of Sept. 10 and a letter to Bülow of Sept. 26. Ö-U.A. 79 and 99–102.
[2] Ö-U.A. I, 78–83.

the Austrian statesman.[1] Iswolsky began with his usual complaint that Aehrenthal had destroyed the entente and his familiar argument that he had been driven to a rapprochement with England. After a vigorous counter-attack, the conversation passed to railways, each party promising support to the projects of the other. When the discussion reached the question of the annexation of Bosnia, Aehrenthal pressed for a definite declaration. Iswolsky replied that, if Austria was compelled to annex, Russia would assume a friendly and benevolent attitude. He also recognised the moderation displayed in the renunciation of the Sanjak, adding that the withdrawal of troops would allow a milder judgment on the annexation itself. He would witness the resulting consolidation of the Monarchy without misgivings ; but in giving his consent he could not forget Russian interests and must consider the reactions of the modification of the Berlin Treaty on the Balkan States and the situation in Turkey.

Iswolsky proceeded to formulate his wishes in regard to the passage of Russia's warships through the Straits. She desired no territory in or near Constantinople, but she should be enabled if necessary to strengthen her fleet from her reservoir in the Black Sea instead of by costly construction. He produced a draft formula in which Austria promised a friendly attitude if she were to take steps to secure a passage through the Dardanelles for single warships. Such modification of existing rights would not affect the independence and security of Constantinople, and the same privilege could not be refused to the other Black Sea states. Aehrenthal replied that he would accept the formula if Russia in the meantime had displayed a friendly attitude at the moment of the annexation of Bosnia. The Russian warships must pass separately, Turkey's possession of Constantinople must be unaffected, and the safety and independence of the capital must not be menaced. Iswolsky was delighted, and hoped he could work out a formula which the other interested parties could accept. In answer to a question he said that he had not sounded England ; but, as her interest in the Straits had greatly diminished in recent years, he hoped for success.

The conversation then passed to the Balkan states, in which Iswolsky anticipated great excitement and possibly momentous decisions. Both statesmen agreed that the annexation of Bosnia might lead to the independence of Bulgaria and the

[1] Ö-U.A. I, 86–92.

union of Crete with Greece, and that they would not oppose
such purely formal changes.   On the other hand they would
try to prevent fresh territorial acquisitions by the Balkan
states at the cost of Turkey, since both Powers were interested
in maintaining the Turkish Empire as long as possible.   The
first discord was heard when Iswolsky suggested frontier
modifications at Austria's cost to secure the approval of
Serbia and Montenegro.   Aehrenthal sharply replied that
Austria could not discuss the cession of a kilometre with any
Balkan state, above all with Serbia in view of her policy of
perfidy and intrigue.   Iswolsky might, however, assure her
that, if her conduct was correct, Austria would not oppose
her aggrandisement in the event of major changes in the
Balkans.   For this assurance Iswolsky expressed his thanks.
When he also pleaded for the removal of some of the dis-
abilities imposed on Montenegro by the Treaty of Berlin,
Aehrenthal promised to consider the matter.   Iswolsky
believed that the proposed changes in the Berlin Treaty would
be accepted by Turkey without violent opposition, and counted
on obtaining sanction by negotiations at Constantinople and
elsewhere.   How did Aehrenthal propose to proceed ?   The
revisions, was the reply, would have to be settled by
negotiations with the Powers, in which, of course, Bosnia and
Herzegovina would not be mentioned.   He contemplated a
conference at the finish, preferably of the Ambassadors at
Constantinople, a plan which made little appeal to Iswolsky.
    The momentous exchange ended with a survey of the
European situation.   Iswolsky stressed Russia's need of
peace for at least twenty years.   He had no choice in Reval
except to develop the Anglo-Russian rapprochement, but
Russia had no interest in going beyond the agreements in
Central Asia.   German policy caused him anxiety, both in
Persia against Russia and in Morocco against France.   It was
agreed that he should put the results of the discussion on
paper and send it to Vienna as soon as possible.   To his
inquiry when the annexation was to be proclaimed, Aehrenthal
replied that it depended on reports from Serajevo and Plevlie.
But it was very probable that it would occur in the first days of
October, just before the meeting of the Delegations.   Iswolsky
replied that he would prefer it after his return home in the
middle of October, as he could then direct public opinion.
Aehrenthal agreed that it would be best if his partner were to
be at his post when the annexation took place ; but Austria

was not a free agent, and he could not promise not to act before the Delegations met. In any case he should hear in good time. The Russian Minister expressed great satisfaction with the talk, and Aehrenthal sent a message to Bülow that he was on the whole very pleased with the visit.[1] " Iswolsky ", he remarked to the German Chargé, " was really quite sensible." It would have been more sensible still if the two statesmen had drawn up an agreed summary of the results. That they omitted to do so suggests to Baernreither that neither of them was playing quite fair. A few days later Aehrenthal sent Iswolsky the promised formula in regard to a Dalmatian railway, and expressed the hope that he would soon receive his report of the Buchlau agreements. " As for Bosnia and Herzegovina", he concluded, " I cannot at present tell you the precise date when we shall proceed to annexation. But you can rely on my promise to inform you at the earliest moment." Iswolsky replied that his answer to the last Austrian memorandum, based on the Buchlau interview, had been sent to St. Petersburg for submission to the Tsar.[2]

The next item in the programme was a meeting with Prince Ferdinand at Budapest on September 23 and 24.[3] He would make no difficulties, declared Aehrenthal, if Bulgaria were to realise her wishes, but he could not speak for Iswolsky. Two points, however, should be kept in mind. Firstly, the Prince should avoid a policy of adventure which the Powers could not support. Secondly Bulgaria should not miss a favourable opportunity of realising her legitimate wishes and turning her military superiority to account. " I did not conceal from the Prince ", concluded the report, " that our situation in Bosnia and the Sanjak had become more difficult owing to recent events in Turkey, and that we might therefore soon take decisions on the subject." This document settles the vexed question whether Aehrenthal and Ferdinand were in collusion.

When everything was in readiness for the curtain to rise the Foreign Minister wrote a private letter to Bülow, describing his negotiations. " In showing a disposition to meet Russian wishes I was also moved by the general desire to drive a wedge between Russia and England." Iswolsky, he reported, had expressed a strong desire not to be driven by Austrian and German policy too far into the arms of England. On September 30 he sent his promised announcement to his partner.[4]

[1] G.P. XXVI, 33–4.   [2] Ö-U.A. I, 94, 115.
[3] ibid. 97.   [4] ibid. 115–6.

The proclamation would be made on October 7, and the Chancelleries would be informed on the same day. " In telling you, my dear colleague, several days before the date of October 7, I am firmly convinced, trusting to the spirit of our conversation at Buchlau, that we can count on a benevolent and sympathetic attitude on the part of Russia." It was the last occasion that such friendly tones were to be heard, and the statesmen never met again. By this time the Austrian press was full of rumours, and on October 1 Goschen reported his belief that annexation would be announced to the Delegations in the following week.[1] This was precisely what Iswolsky had expected, as he had confessed to Schön at Berchtesgaden on September 25.[2]

VII·

Within the frontiers of the Hapsburg Empire the annexation was hailed with delight. That it would create temporary excitement abroad Aehrenthal was well aware, but he failed to realise what a shock it would be to the world. He stands out in history as the author of the Bosnian crisis, as Kiderlen remains the man of Agadir. The evacuation of the Sanjak, which he believed would serve as an emollient, passed almost unnoticed, and an unlucky indiscretion of his Ambassador at Paris gave the announcement a peculiarly sinister air.[3] Autograph letters from Francis Joseph to the chiefs of the Great Powers were sent to the capitals for presentation on the eve of the proclamation, which was fixed for October 7. Khevenhüller asked for an audience on the fifth or sixth. Since, however, the President was going away, he was offered the third or the seventh, and chose the former. In reply to the unexpected question which Powers had given their consent, he answered Russia, Germany, Italy. When Fallières remarked that Bulgaria would be tempted to follow suit, the Ambassador, according to his own account, promptly replied that she would do what she thought best and that the event had been long expected. According to the French version, however, he said that it was all arranged and that she would anticipate Austria by a day. This compromising impromptu, whether or not correctly reported, echoed round the world. Aehrenthal wired his surprise that the letter had been presented before the

[1] B.D. V. 371-2.   [2] G.P. XXVI, 39-43.
[3] Ö-U.A. I, 125-6, 237-9.

dates of October 5 or 6 contained in his instructions, and regretted the statement that Russia, Germany and Italy had agreed. It would have been better to say that the Austrian Government confidently assumed that they would take up a friendly attitude. Francis Joseph, who very rarely annotated a despatch, was no less dismayed by the telegram from Paris. " I too ", he wrote, " was equally surprised and distressed, particularly on account of the unfortunate effect which the announcement to the President before the other sovereigns must produce." It was indeed the worst possible start for an enterprise bristling with difficulties.

The world believed that Austria and Bulgaria had conspired to tear up the Treaty of Berlin. On October 2 Grey sent a circular telegram urging the Powers to warn Bulgaria against the declaration of independence which, it was rumoured, she was about to make. When Goschen conveyed the message to Aehrenthal on October 3, the latter professed disbelief in the rumours, adding that he could not take action before he received definite evidence.[1] Prince Ferdinand, he explained, was in Hungary and his Ministers were unlikely to move without him. The rumours had not been confirmed by the Austrian Legation at Sofia, and a premature remonstrance might provoke a crisis. Goschen was incensed by the Minister's evasive statements, and, when the news of Bulgaria's declaration reached him two days later, his indignation knew no bounds. " It is quite incredible ", telegraphed Grey, " that Baron d'Aehrenthal had not arranged with Bulgaria before speaking to you as he did. You and we cannot but feel justly aggrieved at being treated with such bad faith."[2]

On October 6 Goschen informed Aehrenthal that the British Government could not approve of an open violation of the Treaty of Berlin nor recognise an alteration when the other Powers had not been consulted.[3] The Minister expressed astonishment and regret that the annexation should be considered as a violation of the Treaty of Berlin, which accorded rights to Austria without restrictions on her action. Turkey alone, under the Convention of 1879, had a right to protest. When the conversation turned to Bulgaria, Goschen invited him to explain his declaration of disbelief in the imminence of Bulgarian action two days before it took place.

[1] B.D. V, 379-82, 389.
[2] cp. Wickham Steed's memorandum, B.D. IX, pt. I, 776-9, and Ferdinand's version in Madol, Ferdinand de Bulgarie, 110-17.
[3] B.D. V, 398, 445-6.

Aehrenthal replied that he had been worrying about the impression which the news must have caused his visitor. " Well, I give you my word of honour that I had no idea the declaration of Bulgarian independence was so imminent. I knew that it must come in the near future, in a few weeks perhaps, but that it should have been made so soon was a complete surprise to me." When a man gave you his word of honour, commented Goschen in reporting to Grey, one had to accept it. But the disclaimer could only relate to the precise date, for he knew from other sources that the Bulgarian declaration was a matter of days if not of hours. " D'Aehrenthal's diplomacy ", concluded Goschen, " seems to belong to an earlier school than that in vogue in modern days " ; and King Edward wrote on the letter : " I cannot believe in M. d'Aehrenthal's ' word of honour ' statement, as facts belie it." The Foreign Minister's reputation for upright dealing never recovered from this incident.

Before Goschen left to take up his new post in Germany the two men had a final passage at arms. " You people in England are incurring a great responsibility, and the Russians too ", Aehrenthal burst out hotly on meeting the Ambassador at a state banquet on November 5.[1] " The attitude of both countries has been anything but friendly, and all I can say is that if Russia wants war she shall have it." The entire responsibility for the general unrest, retorted Goschen, rested with the Austrian Government. Aehrenthal denied all responsibility. He had done what he ought to have done and what he had to do. Goschen rejoined that he had violated the Treaty of Berlin, despite the Protocol of 1871 which Austria herself had signed. This was a question of fact which could not be gainsaid, and it was sufficient in itself to account for the British attitude of which he complained. After this unpleasant encounter Goschen was thankful to escape from the feverish polemics of Vienna to the calmer waters of Berlin. Aehrenthal liked England as little as he knew her. " Your Sir Edward Grey wants peace ", he remarked to Mr. Noel Buxton ; and when he was warned not to underrate British influence he replied : " What can England to do us ? "[2]

From almost every part of Europe came protests or complaints. It was a blow to the Kaiser's pride that he learned of the annexation from the newspapers ; and, though the German

[1] B.D. V, 484–6, cp. Steed, Through Thirty Years, I, 293–4.
[2] Conwell-Evans : Foreign Policy from a Back Bench, 24.

Government publicly supported the action of its ally, the private comments of the Kaiser and Marschall were severe. Of the Entente Powers France was by far the friendliest, and the President's reply to the Emperor's letter contained no hint of blame.[1] The French Government was more annoyed with Iswolsky, and the Casablanca crisis counselled a soft answer to Vienna. Grey was angry at the breach of the Treaty of Berlin and King Edward at the concealment of the project during his recent visit to Ischl. Scared by the general outcry Iswolsky announced that Bosnia was a question for Europe and that annexation would involve compensations. Turkey formally protested, and a boycott of Austrian goods began ; Montenegro begged for frontier modifications and abolition of the fetters of the Berlin Treaty ; in Serbia there was talk of war. The Minister had thrust his hand into a hornet's nest, but he was undismayed. To England's remonstrance, based on the precedent of 1871, he replied that the annexation was not a breach of the Treaty of Berlin, which had handed over the provinces without limit of time. The sovereign rights of the Sultan were only mentioned in the Convention of Constantinople, and they were a question for Austria and Turkey alone. He was ready to accept a Congress on condition that the annexation was not discussed. Prince Nicholas of Montenegro, who was always complaining of his poverty, might receive a secret gift of half a million francs. The Russian Government was informed that, if Iswolsky continued to challenge the Austrian version of the Buchlau agreement, documentary revelations would be made.

On October 15 Aehrenthal took stock of the position in a private letter to the German Chancellor, enclosing copies of the memorandum of July 2 and his reply of August 27.[2] Since Iswolsky was about to visit Berlin, it was essential for Bülow to know what had occurred. At Buchlau, he explained, they had agreed on non-intervention in Balkan questions without preliminary agreement ; a friendly attitude of Russia if Austria annexed Bosnia and of Austria towards Russian wishes in the Straits ; benevolence in the event of a declaration of independence by Bulgaria and a union of Crete with Greece ; modification in favour of Montenegro of Article 29 of the Treaty of Berlin. After these more or less formal changes, the territorial status quo in Turkey should be maintained as long as possible. Tittoni, added Aehrenthal, was

[1] Ö-U.A. I, 280-1.   [2] ibid. 215-7.

equally friendly. In a letter of October 4 he had proposed, as
a preliminary to the annexation of Bosnia, an agreement between Austria, Italy and Russia concerning the Straits, the
evacuation of the Sanjak, and the relief of Montenegro from
her fetters. This had been accepted on October 6, and Russia
was informed. " I was therefore justified in assuming that
Italy and Russia were won for the annexation. Unfortunately
a remark of Count Khevenhüller, who let himself go too far,
suggested that I should claim to have received their formal
assent." Reports from Paris and London indicated that the
Cabinets were not in favour of meeting Iswolsky on the Straits.
" I think you will agree that it would be well if Russia withdrew the question of the Straits from the programme of the
Conference. That would greatly facilitate the gathering and
the work of the Conference, and it would show Russia that the
opposition to the realisation of her darling wish came not from
us but from the Western Powers who are now in favour on the
Neva." He was quite ready for a Conference, he concluded,
but only after an agreement with Turkey. Fortunately the
Grand Vizier and Foreign Minister were beginning to reconcile themselves to the *fait accompli*. It was an optimistic
letter, more cheerful than the situation justified. The chief
difficulty was not in Turkey but in Russia and Serbia ; and
Russia had powerful friends in the West.

Aehrenthal's desire to avoid war was shared not only by his
master but by the heir to the throne, with whom be kept in
close touch. Nothing was to be gained by it, wrote the Arch-
duke on October 20.[1] Sharp words should be spoken at
Cettinje and Belgrad, but there should be neither mobilisation
nor war. It was quite right of Aehrenthal to damp the ardour
of Conrad. At Iswolsky's request the Foreign Minister told
the Delegations nothing about their discussions ; but he
flatly refused to entertain the proposal for territorial compensations for Serbia and Montenegro. He would facilitate the
economic access of Serbia to the sea, but he could do nothing
more. Meanwhile the Austrian Minister in Belgrad reported
that Serbia was like a madhouse and that every Serb wished to
die for his country. A circular telegram was sent to the
Powers complaining of Serbian military preparations, and
begging them to address pacific advice to Belgrad. Despite
Iswolsky's dread of the negotiations being revealed, he advised
or allowed the Tsar to send a sharp reply to the Emperor's

[1] *Ö-U.A.* 384, 445–7.

letter. " My profound and sincere friendship forbids me to hide the very painful impression caused by the annexation, by a unilateral act which I deeply deplore, of the two provinces confided to the administration of your Government by the Treaty of Berlin." Aehrenthal was indignant at the tone, which showed how ignorant was the Tsar. How could he speak of the painful impression of an act arising out of a Russian initiative ? Aehrenthal was also annoyed that he had kept the Austrian Ambassador waiting a month for an audience and had received the Serbian Crown Prince in St. Petersburg after his bellicose outbursts in Belgrad. " We shall continue to ignore the war cries and war preparations of Serbia so long as our dignity and the security of our territory permit. In the event, however, of aggression or provocations incompatible with the prestige of the Monarchy, we shall vigorously react."

As the weeks passed without signs of a settlement in any quarter, Aehrenthal complained with increasing bitterness of England. It was increasingly difficult, he wrote to Mensdorff, to understand her policy.[1] She was encouraging the resistance not only of the Turks but of Russia and Serbia as well. Everybody was asking whether she desired to see Austria at war with them. If so, war with Serbia was very probable, and England's attitude would be partly responsible. Russia was less likely to fight, for she would have to reckon with Germany as well. Who had forbidden Iswolsky to bring up the question of the Straits ? Had he scored in the Straits, he would have faced Russian opinion. Aehrenthal had expected opposition from England ; but the attitude of King Edward had been a surprise, and Mensdorff should have a frank talk with him. " Our patience has limits, and if the goading of the English press does not cease, the Serbs, led astray and dreaming of support from certain Great Powers, will receive a chastisement." Austria, like England, desired a consolidation of Young Turkey, and was ready for a conference if Bosnia was not discussed. It was unexampled hypocrisy for Iswolsky to demand such discussion when Russia had thrice earmarked Bosnia for Austria, and had taken the initiative in the summer. " I contemplate coming events with the greatest confidence ", he concluded. " I anticipate no major complication, and I begin to believe that a chastisement of Serbia will be needless —that is if England drops her game of irresponsible and malignant provocation." On receiving Cartwright, the new British

[1] Ö-U.A. 536-8.

Ambassador, he excitedly argued that England's attitude to Austria was at the root of the present troubles.[1] He had no official complaint to make of the Government, whose attitude had been perfectly correct; but the attacks of the press, and the encouragement it had given to Turkey and Serbia to resist, were likely, if continued much longer, to end the traditional good feeling. " Baron d'Aehrenthal ", commented King Edward on the despatch, " knowing that he is in the wrong, uses offensive language towards England which, however, does not strengthen his case."

The key to the situation was not in London but in St. Petersburg. The Tsar sent a friendly letter to the Emperor of Austria on his diamond jubilee,[2] and spoke reassuringly to Berchold. He was well aware of the prevailing animosities, but added ; " Ne vous effrayez pas, je sais les repousser." He spoke throughout with remarkable cordiality, and Berchtold was convinced of his sincere desire for peace. On the other hand the press and public opinion were becoming worse and worse. Francis Joseph's letter of thanks to the Tsar for his jubilee greeting was utilised by Aehrenthal for a homily. Throughout his reign, he made his master say, he had striven for friendship and confidence between the two countries, and the pact of 1897 allowed him to pursue a policy of harmonious intimacy with Russia. He had done more than keep the letter of the pact, for he had spared Russia anxiety in Europe during the Japanese war. The annexation of Bosnia indicated no change in the course. " I wish you to know that my loyalty has not failed ; that I have undertaken nothing which has not been sanctioned in advance by your predecessors and recently even by your Government, which offered the extension of my rule beyond the limits I had traced. I must tell you that I have been grieved to see you show suspicion of my designs." Had he asked for the consent of the Powers, Turkey and perhaps some other states would have refused or demanded a price, and war might have resulted from an enterprise designed to postpone sanguinary struggles in the Balkans. Thus Aehrenthal and Iswolsky thrust and parried in the name of their masters, each playing the part of injured innocent.

On December 8 Aehrenthal sent another of his revealing private letters to Bülow.[3] The Chancellor had written to describe Iswolsky's visit, and had forwarded a blank cheque to

[1] B.D. V, 526–30.   [2] Ö-U.A. I, 471, 541–2, 554–6.   [3] ibid. 558–63.

Vienna.[1] The Foreign Minister was grateful for Germany's steady support. The Tsar was friendly, but could he hold his own against his perfidious Ministers and the Pan-Slav press ? Turkish intransigence was being kept alive by England, and the Turks counted on forcing Austria to take over a portion of the national debt. For this demand there was no justification, since the evacuation of the Sanjak was sufficient compensation. The rumour of an anti-Austrian Balkan League, with Turkey as a member, was not to be taken seriously. The Serbs might break out or might provoke Austria to defensive measures. " You were good enough to say that you would leave the decision in regard to ' the unsavoury conditions in Serbia ' to my judgment. I am most grateful for this new proof of your friendly confidence. Our policy is motived by the wish to avoid a conflict with Serbia. We are not, however, inclined to pursue this policy of patience and long-suffering *ad infinitum*. If in the next two months her attitude again gives us cause for serious complaints, the time will have come for a firm decision. You may be sure that I will tell you in good time. In such an eventuality I intend, in order to localise the conflict, to inform the Powers that we are only carrying out an act of unavoidable self-defence, and that we do not propose to infringe the independence and integrity of Serbia and Montenegro. I hope that this declaration, combined with rapid military action, will avert the danger of which I have spoken." The programme postponed the gravest dangers till the early spring. The letter ended with a proposal that the Austrian and German General Staffs should draw up a written agreement on the hypothesis that Italy might be neutral in a European war.

Strong in the support of Germany, who could not afford to thwart her only reliable partner, and holding in reserve certain missiles for Iswolsky's defenceless head, Aehrenthal yielded nothing to his antagonist. A Russian Aide-Mémoire of November 22 accepted the contention that a preliminary agreement should precede the Conference, which, however, should be able to discuss freely all questions on the programme. Aehrenthal recalled the Buchlau agreement that Russia would not only not oppose the annexation but would adopt a benevolent attitude. Mere agreement as to the items of discussion would not remove the danger. The preliminary exchange of views should deal with the most important points, and Russia was reminded that she had repudiated the Batum article of the

[1] *G.P.* XXVI, 224-7, *v. supra*, 278-9.

Berlin Treaty without consulting her co-signatories. Iswolsky asserted that his consent at Buchlau to annexation was conditional on that of the other Powers. Aehrenthal, on the other hand, maintained that his partner had promised a benevolent attitude, merely adding that the other Powers must have their say. Austria had chosen her procedure in regard to Bosnia, as Russia could choose hers in regard to the Straits, and the method selected gave her no ground to ignore the Buchlau pact. Its spirit demanded a friendly attitude in any case, though Russia was free to express her regret that the other Powers should not have been informed.

Though Aehrenthal's decision to annex Bosnia was entirely his own, Bülow's invaluable support entitled him to advise. On December 16 he told the Austrian Ambassador how glad he was that Austria had shown the world that she was not a *quantité négligeable*.[1] He proceeded to urge the greatest consideration for Turkey's economic and financial needs. A loan, in which Germany would doubtless join, would be most acceptable. No step should be omitted to win over Bulgaria, Roumania and Greece, particularly the first. The wisest course was to be firm with Russia and accommodating with Turkey. If Austria and Germany held together they would get their way without war, for Russia was not in a position to fight. On the other hand the Chancellor expressed approval of Aehrenthal's plan of a written agreement between the General Staffs in view of the possibility of European complications.

While the notion of a financial *solatium* to Turkey was making way, the wrath of Iswolsky rose to ungovernable rage. In his Duma speech of December 25 he used the soft pedal, for he dreaded retaliation, but in private he let himself go. The reply of the Tsar dated December 30 to the argumentative letter of Francis Joseph of December 7 was exceptionally shrill.[2] The story of the quarrel was told once again from Iswolsky's point of view, and the Tsar concluded with the words : " Tu comprendras aussi, mon Cher Ami, combien j'ai été personnellement froissé des procédés de ton Ministre." He expressed his painful astonishment that Aehrenthal had now communicated to foreign Governments confidential documents relating to the pact of 1897. Such proceedings rendered confidential relations impossible, and he had therefore instructed Iswolsky to confine the relations between the

[1] Ö-U.A. I, 606–11. [2] ibid. 678–80.

two Governments to official communications. He wrote these lines not only with deep regret but with great anxiety. Austria, he learned, was making military preparations on a scale which suggested that a conflict with her Balkan neighbours was approaching. Such a conflict would place Russia and her ruler in a most difficult position and might provoke a European war. Throughout this long and angry letter, drafted by one hand and signed by another, we hear the fevered accents of a politician fighting for his life. On the same day Iswolsky made to the Ambassador a similar complaint about the revelation of diplomatic secrets, and asked that future communications from the Austrian Embassy should be through the medium of official notes. Aehrenthal bluntly rejoined that he had revealed no secrets. While the Russian and Austrian dogs thus snarled at one another Europe looked on with alarm.

VIII

1909 opened in an atmosphere of tense anxiety, and matters could hardly be left to drift. When Aehrenthal offered Turkey compensation for State property in Bosnia, compromise in one quarter came in sight. Iswolsky's hatred of his rival, on the other hand, was a devouring passion, and the fretful intransigence of Serbia was a running sore. The latter was the gravest of the Minister's many anxieties, for he was determined not to purchase the acquiescence of Belgrad. While Russia, he continued to believe, would bark but not bite, Serbia might at any moment run amok, trusting that the Tsar would be forced by Panslav sympathies to render aid. Aehrenthal reported on the situation in a private letter to his Ambassador in Berlin. He was delighted at Bülow's approval of his policy. If a settlement with Turkey could be reached, England and France would be satisfied and Iswolsky's feverish temperature would fall. On the other hand an Austro-Russian *détente* was impossible while he was at the helm, or at any rate till his Anglophil policy was recognised as a mistake. Meanwhile technical discussions took place between Conrad and Moltke with the assent of their Governments, based on the possibility of war with Russia and the probable neutrality of Italy ; and the military agreement strengthened Aehrenthal's determination not to give way.[1] Cartwright reported that

[1] Conrad, *Aus meiner Dienstzeit*, I, 379-406, 631-4. Kanner, *Der Schlussel der Kriegsschuldfrage*, argues unconvincingly that the Austro-German alliance hereby lost its purely defensive character.

Austria was feverishly preparing for eventualities.[1]   When he
advised Aehrenthal to show the greatest moderation, the
Minister retorted that counsels of moderation were needed at
Belgrad. He did not wish for war, and Austria knew that no
glory or satisfaction could come from fighting Serbia ; but he
could not predict what would occur.

On January 18 Francis Joseph wrote to the Kaiser expressing
his warm gratitude for German support in the Bosnian crisis
and denying the rumour that he was meditating a conflict with
the Balkan States.[2]   " The past bears witness that we do not
think of attacking our unruly Southern neighbours. We
should only take action if Serbia or Montenegro crossed our
frontiers or indulged in public insults. Even then I can
declare that we should not infringe their independence or take
any of their territory."   The same assurance was given in a
letter to the Tsar. No Great Power conscious of its dignity
and its interests had ever shown such long-suffering in face of
insolent provocations by its little neighbours. " I have never
thought of threatening their independent existence, and I
entertain no plan of conquest to their detriment. On the
other hand I am resolved to repel with the utmost energy
aggression prompted by their growing audacity in the pursuit
of chimerical dreams."

It was a relief to Europe when, on February 26, Turkey
formally recognised the annexation in return for two and a half
millions. Bulgaria's dispute with Constantinople was also
settled by a cash transaction with Russian aid. Aehrenthal
now affected to believe that the crisis was at an end. Grey's remark to Mensdorff that the Serbian and Montenegrin questions
still remained to be dealt with provoked an angry retort.[3]
" Your Excellency ", he wired to Mensdorff, " cannot say too
emphatically that for us there is not and can never be a Serbian
or Montenegrin question in connection with the annexation."
Only Crete and the modification of the Montenegrin article of
the Berlin Treaty remained, and in the latter case Austria had
already accepted the change in principle. On the eve of
King Edward's visit to Berlin Aehrenthal explained to the
Wilhelmstrasse that in view of the provocations and preparations of Serbia he could accept no mediation.[4]   He had never
been pliant, and victory seemed at last within his grasp.

The Foreign Minister preferred bloodless laurels, but, as he

[1] B.D. V, 536-8, 555-7.   [2] Ö-U.A. I, 750-1, 777-8.
[3] ibid. 798-9.   [4] ibid. 806-8.

explained to Bülow, war must not be ruled out.[1] The aim of his policy was to consolidate the annexation of Bosnia, and he had no further plans for aggrandisement. A war against Serbia, with its expense and its diplomatic reactions, was not worth while. " Nevertheless the national passions in unhappy Serbia and the vacillating policy of certain Powers in this question have created a situation which may compel us to consider a conflict." The reopening of the Eastern Question owing to the weakening of Turkey had forced Austria to take action, first by the occupation and now by the annexation of Bosnia. " These two acts mean the destruction of the dream of a Panserb state between the Danube, the Save and the Adriatic. Such a state would be controlled by Russia, and would not fit into the peaceful development of Central Europe. In such a critical phase of the life of nations the *ultima ratio* might have to be applied. But I repeat that I should prefer to avoid war with Serbia, both because my goal can be attained without it and because a weakening of Serbia by Bulgaria could be easily arranged."

Austria's relations with Serbia, he intended, should be cleared up in March. He would await the signature of the agreement with Turkey and the Italian elections, and then press for a categorical declaration that she had no aggressive aims and would cease to arm. In return for her compliance she would receive economic privileges. The signatories of the Berlin Treaty would be informed of Austria's action, and would presumably advise Serbia to yield. If satisfactory declarations from Belgrad were unobtainable, an ultimatum would be sent. Montenegro might subsequently be dealt with in a similar manner. His policy was to settle each problem separately by direct negotiation, after which the sanction of the Powers could be given in one way or another. It was most improbable that Russia would fight, even if Austria were at war with Serbia ; but everything would depend on Germany's action at St. Petersburg. A declaration at the psychological moment should lead to the tendering of Russian advice at Belgrad which would make war unnecessary. Here was the programme of the final phase of the Bosnian crisis, and it was carried out almost to the letter. Serbia's opposition was to be crushed. If it came to a conflict parts of her territory would be given to Bulgaria and Roumania.[2]

[1] Ö-U.A. I, 852-7, February 20.
[2] G.P. XXVI, 556-8, February 12.

Aehrenthal welcomed pacific advice from the Powers at Belgrad, but declined to admit mediation. In such direct discussions " between a giant and a mouse " Iswolsky detected grave danger to peace.[1] For different reasons, however, the two men were equally anxious that Serbia should yield. An Austro-Serb conflict in which Russia had to stand aside would be a supreme personal and national humiliation, and Iswolsky lived in dread lest his rival should publish the compromising documents. At this moment a Russian note informed Serbia that the Powers did not favour territorial acquisition. She should avoid all action tending to war with Austria, and should leave the solution of pending problems to the Powers. The advice received general support, and for a moment it appeared as if Serbia was about to yield.

It was a misreading of the situation, for the worst was still to come. Aehrenthal's suspicion of his rival was unabated. When Cartwright suggested that he should now meet him half way, the Minister replied that he was pleased with Russia's action, but added hotly that had Iswolsky kept his engagements the crisis would have ended long ago.[2] Russia, he declared, was trying to make the world believe that she had a right to act as the protectress of Serbia. This was a mad claim, which Austria could never admit. On March 5 he told Tschirschky that, unless by the end of the month Serbia gave the Powers or Austria the peaceful assurances desired, he would send an ultimatum and, if it produced no effect, cross the frontier three days later.[3] On March 8 the Austrian Ambassador in St. Petersburg was instructed to ask for a plain declaration in regard to the annexation.[4] If Iswolsky sought to evade the issue, he was to be informed that the documents in Aehrenthal's hands would be communicated to Belgrad, London and Paris. The terrified statesman requested the presentation of an official note, with a mention of the threat of publication, and begged Bülow to avert the worst. But by this time the German Chancellor was as weary of Russian delays as his Austrian colleague, and his response was to be very different from Iswolsky's expectations.

Serbia's reply of March 10 placed her cause in the hands of the Powers, without asking any compensation, territorial or economic. The new spirit was welcomed in Vienna, but a more precise phraseology was required. The forces on the

---

[1] Ö-U.A. II, 10. [2] B.D. V, 661.
[3] G.P. XXVI, 646–7. [4] Ö-U.A. II, 61–2.

frontier were strengthened, and the impatience of the military authorities increased from day to day. Aehrenthal, declared Tschirschky to Cartwright, undoubtedly desired peace and would continue to show patience towards Serbia, but he was not entirely master of the situation. Public opinion was certainly averse to war, but every one felt that the tension could not be borne much longer. At this critical moment two parallel attempts to avert a catastrophe were made. Grey sought a formula of surrender which would bridge the gulf between Vienna and Belgrad, and Aehrenthal proceeded to exert pressure on St. Petersburg through Berlin. The Powers had welcomed the Austro-Turkish agreement, and Iswolsky had often said that he would not refuse to recognise the annexation. Since no opposition from any quarter was anticipated, why should not the Powers declare that, taking note of the Austro-Turkish protocol which recognised the annexation, Article 25 of the Berlin Treaty was cancelled? Such a formula would clear up the situation in Serbia and ensure peace. Bülow was delighted with the plan and undertook to propose it to Russia. If Iswolsky declined, the German Ambassador would say that the German Government would let things take their course. The final stage of the crisis was at hand, and the Central Empires stood ready for the test.

Iswolsky argued that the Austro-Turkish agreement did not remove the necessity of submitting the annexation to a Conference, which would also discuss the other points of the programme. He had not changed his ground since October; but he told Berchtold that Russia would stand aloof even if Austrian troops entered Belgrad in a *promenade militaire*. Bülow now completed his preparations, and on March 16 Tschirschky showed Aehrenthal the instructions to Pourtalès. Aehrenthal was delighted. If Iswolsky accepted the German proposal, the other Powers would then be asked by Germany to accept the annexation. When Bülow reported that the Powers were willing to send such notes, Aehrenthal would ask them formally to sanction the change. A hitch arose when Iswolsky sent an ambiguous reply. The German Government thereupon drafted a demand for a precise answer and informed Aehrenthal of its text. While Vienna and Berlin were waiting for the fateful challenge and response, Aehrenthal assured Cartwright that he had no intention of attacking Serbia unless provoked beyond endurance. The Ambassador begged for a postponement as long as possible of the dreaded ultimatum,

and asked, though in vain, to be told confidentially when the
patience of Austria would probably give way.
   On March 24 the success of the German *démarche* in St.
Petersburg was reported to Vienna, and Aehrenthal telegraphed
his gratitude.[1] With the surrender of Russia the battle was
won, though skirmishing continued in different parts of the
field. Italy, England and France accepted the invitation with
reservations, and Grey stoutly declined to follow Iswolsky's
example till the Serbian difficulty was peacefully removed.
Aehrenthal's first draft of a declaration was unacceptable ; but
a formula satisfying London, Vienna and Belgrad was finally
agreed on March 28 and presented at Vienna on March 31.
The promise of good behaviour was given only just in time,
for the coercion of Serbia had been decided in principle, and
an article by Friedjung in the *Neue Freie Presse*, written before
her surrender, was designed as the first shot in the campaign.
While Serbia had obtained nothing, Montenegro received the
treaty alleviations to which Aehrenthal had consented from
the first. Nothing more was heard of a Conference. Four
changes in the Treaty of Berlin had been made—in Bosnia and
Herzegovina, the Sanjak, Bulgaria and Montenegro. Other
aspects of the Eastern Question which had found a place in
Iswolsky's Nine Point Programme, including the opening of
the Straits to Russian warships, had to wait. Aehrenthal,
reported Cartwright, had worked hard for compromise in the
final stages, and the Emperor throughout stood firmly for
peace.[2] Nobody, however, imagined that the end of the Bosnian crisis was the end of the trouble in the Near East. Turkey
was still firmly entrenched in Macedonia and Thrace, while
Austro-Russian rivalry was fiercer than ever.
   On the eve of Serbia's surrender Milovanovich, the Foreign
Minister, sat with a few friends in a café at Belgrad, and spoke
in staccato sentences as if thinking aloud.[3] " Our situation is
very difficult. We must give way. Europe demands peace.
The justice of our claims is recognised, yet nobody will help
us to attain them. But Europe too is in a bad way. Violence
will receive its penalty. Europe will not remain long as it is
to-day. In my journey round the capitals I have seen how
much is rotten. How the *débâcle* will occur nobody knows.
Perhaps a social revolution—in Russia first. I may be
wrong. But of one thing I am sure. Bosnia and Herzegovina

[1] *Ö-U.A.* II, 186.   [2] *B.D.* V, 758-61.
[3] Loncarevich, *Jugoslaviens Entstehung*, 304-5.

will not remain long in the possession of Austria. It may be two, three or several years. But I stake my head that by 1920 Bosnia will be free."

IX

" Aehrenthal, I feel sure," wrote Cartwright to Hardinge, " desires to keep quiet and to avoid further adventures after the dangers he has passed through during the last six months, for if a disturbed state of things continues to exist in the Balkans his enemies will be apt to say that these disturbances are due to him and that Austria-Hungary will have no peace until he is driven from office.[1] The peace feeling is very strong here, especially among the lower classes, and he is perfectly well aware of this. Moreover, as he desires to please the Emperor —who above all desires to avoid a war—it is probable that he will use his influence to find a peaceful solution for any problems which may arise in the Balkans or elsewhere. It is rumoured that he wants to be made a Count, and the Emperor is not likely to give him that title if he involves the Monarchy in further expensive complications." It was a correct diagnosis. Aehrenthal was henceforth a pillar of European peace. The Young Turks knew that Bosnia had been lost long ago, and the annexation was a blow less to their interests than to their pride. For the rest of his life Turkey gave no trouble to the Austrian statesman, who, having sown his wild oats, henceforth posed as an unswerving champion of the status quo. With Russia and Serbia the case was very different. Capitulation in face of superior force is always a painful affair. The greatest Slav Power had confessed its inability to defend the claims of its Balkan *protégé*; but Aehrenthal was aware that its strength would gradually revive and that a renewal of the partnership in the Balkans was impossible. The rancorous Iswolsky would naturally dedicate his life to revenge, and, if he were to fall, his successor could scarcely be expected to alter the course. It was evident that Russia could not again stand aloof from a major emergency in the Near East ; and since the Austrian Foreign Minister, like his master, desired to avoid a European war, he strove to postpone an eruption of the Balkan volcano. Aehrenthal after 1909 is like Bismarck after 1871. The Austrian Minister in Belgrad reported the last stages of

[1] *B.D.* IX, pt. I, 2–3, April 15, 1909.

the exasperating feud.[1] The surrender had been accepted with gnashing of teeth. For a time the Government would be cautious, but the hatred of Austria and the Russian hypnosis were too strong to hope for a change of direction. " Every one here is still thinking of vengeance, which can only be accomplished with Russia as an ally. The present attitude of the great Slav Power is attributed merely to Iswolsky's lack of skill." Forgach, however, closed his despatch on a more cheerful note. " Our great aim is achieved. Bosnia and Herzegovina have been incorporated in the Hapsburg dominions without the shedding of blood, and the dangerous Panserb idea is repulsed." Both the Russian hypnosis and the Panserb idea, Aehrenthal agreed, had received a heavy blow ; yet he cherished no illusions.[2] The best and indeed the only way to a *modus vivendi* was to study Serbia's economic interests. To follow up the destruction of her political ideals by making her economic existence impossible would turn all Europe against Austria as the oppressor of little states, and might even lead to the planning of a Balkan League. Relations with Serbia, he concluded, were part of the Southern Slav problem, and could only be dealt with in connection with the treatment of the Southern Slavs in both portions of the Empire. The latter reflection went to the root of the matter, but the Hungarian magnates were too powerful to be overruled.

At the same moment Aehrenthal surveyed the related problem of Austro-Russian relations in a despatch to Berchtold.[3] The failure of Russian policy, first in the Far East, then in the Near East, was due to a misreading of the real situation by her rulers. Perhaps a more realistic course might now be adopted, virtually involving a return to the policy of the Three Emperors' League. Russia's feelings must be spared as much as possible, and he had warned the Austrian press not to describe the annexation as a victory. The recent rapprochement between Rome and St. Petersburg required careful watching, but did not seem dangerous at present. It was an optimistic reading of the situation to which some colour was given by the attitude of Berlin. On May 15 William II discussed the situation with Aehrenthal, urging him to support the new regime in Turkey and resume contact with Russia.[4] He seemed annoyed by British criticism of the *Flottenpolitik*, and hankered after a rapprochement with St. Petersburg for the consolidation

[1] Ö-U.A. II, 238-9.   [2] ibid. 280-1.
[3] ibid. 292-4.   [4] ibid. 334-7.

of peace. Aehrenthal replied cautiously that Austria also desired a rapprochement with Russia, but that nothing could be done while Iswolsky was in command. In the Near East, he added, it would be best to await developments and reserve liberty of action. Now that the Bosnian crisis was over his attitude to Berlin became more reserved. His one desire, reported Cartwright, was to avoid being dragged into hopeless servitude to Germany.[1] To maintain his independence he needed an atmosphere of peace and a restoration of normal relations with the Entente Powers.

Aehrenthal's desire for a period of watchful waiting in the Balkans was not shared by the fiery Conrad, henceforth a thorn in his flesh. After many conversations and letters the Chief of Staff expounded his policy of action in an elaborate memorandum dated July 2, 1909, addressed to the Foreign Minister.[2] It was a mistake for Austria, he argued, to wait till wars were forced upon her. Her duty was to foresee those which were necessary or unavoidable and to wage them directly there was a prospect of success. Such a moment had come in the spring, but it had been allowed to pass. A new situation had arisen, in which he must ask to be informed of Austria's foreign policy. His own view was that her path pointed to the Balkans and the hegemony of the Adriatic. Serbia should be incorporated in the Monarchy, and Montenegro either incorporated or tightly embraced. A sovereign Southern Slav state of the size of Serbia could not be left as a magnet next door to the Southern Slav territories of the Monarchy. In following this course Austria would meet direct obstacles in Serbia, Montenegro and Italy, for Italy also aimed at the hegemony of the Adriatic. She would encounter obstacles in Russia, France and England at a further remove. Despite therefore all momentary assurances of friendship, Serbia, Montenegro and Italy were the first foes to fight. Russia would probably join them; but she might stand aloof if she could be won over by the Central Powers, or if the conflict were waged before she regained her strength. Austria must be prepared for her three enemies at once, which necessitated the maximum strengthening of her forces on land and sea. Serbia and Italy were openly preparing for war and she must do the same. These measures could only be kept secret for a short time, and therefore the blow must be struck without delay. After taking time to reflect on this audacious scheme

[1] B.D. IX, pt. I, 15-7   [2] Ö-U.A. II, 387-92.

Aehrenthal drew up an elaborate memorandum of great power and interest dated August 19.[1] He began by rebutting the charge that a favourable opportunity of waging war against Serbia had been lost in the spring. Since the opposition to the annexation had collapsed, there was no pretext or need for a war. Moreover, if war had been waged, an occupation of Serbia and Montenegro would have been impossible in the existing European situation. Another evil result would have been the interruption of developments in Turkey, and Iswolsky's plan of an anti-Austrian Balkan League, with Turkey as a member, would probably have been realised. Austria's foreign policy was primarily conditioned by the state of Turkey. To pursue Conrad's plans of expansion in the Balkans would provoke a powerful coalition in reply. Neither Russia nor Italy would swallow aggression against Serbia or Montenegro, and they would probably join the hostile group. The results would be catastrophic. In certain eventualities the incorporation of part of Serbia might have to be considered, since she could not be allowed to act as a magnet on the frontier. To prevent this, however, was primarily a question of internal policy. Austria had no reason to raise the Serbian question, since she would not know how to deal with annexed territories. Equally dangerous would it be to strive for hegemony in the Adriatic, where the hands both of Austria and Italy were tied by the Albanian pact.

Passing to Austria's relations with her Southern ally, Aehrenthal admitted that the Balkan policy of the latter had become more active in recent years, believing as she did that the status quo in Turkey was doomed. Tittoni had sought an assurance that the renunciation of the Sanjak was definitive, and that, in the event of re-occupation, Italy should receive compensation. Her right to compensation if Austria were to occupy the Sanjak or any other Turkish territory, he had replied, was recognised by treaty. Tittoni had also asked for Italy to be associated in any coming Austro-Russian negotiations. To this he had returned a cautious reply, having discovered that Tittoni had proposed to Russia a Balkan agreement though without success. "It will be our task to prevent a concrete arrangement between Rome and St. Petersburg. I do not believe that the Russian Cabinet will accept concrete plans, but rather that it merely coquets with Italy in order to exercise pressure upon us."

[1] Ö-U.A. II, 438–46.

Turning to Russia Aehrenthal noted the recent restoration of friendly Russo-German relations as a proof of her pacific intentions. Being unable to pursue an active policy during the next decade, she stood for the status quo in Turkey and would try to prevent the reopening of the Macedonian question. The Young Turks might fail to prevent troubles in Macedonia or Albania, but the revival of the reforms was impracticable. If a Balkan war were to break out, Austria must keep her powder dry and claim to be consulted when the map was redrawn. "In such a new ordering we must work for the maximum aggrandisement of Bulgaria, in such a manner that her rivalry with Serbia remains. In this way Serbia will be driven towards us on condition that we make a mutually satisfactory economic agreement, and that the right policy is pursued in Serajevo and Agram. The union of Serbia, first in the economic and later perhaps in the military sphere, will probably come of itself by the force of events. The same may be said of Montenegro." Possible troubles in Albania should not tempt Austria to a Protectorate or military intervention.

In steering such a careful course, continued the Foreign Minister, the chances of a conflict with Russia and Italy were fairly small unless Italy became aggressive, which was impossible till 1914 when the Treaty came up for renewal, or unless Imperialist aims such as those suggested by Conrad were accepted in Vienna. A commercial treaty with Serbia would allow political relations to become normal. Now the annexation had been carried through, Austria's policy should be one of internal consolidation and the solution of the Southern Slav question within her frontiers. "If we stick to this course, which excludes extensions of territory at the expense of the Balkan Slavs, the Monarchy can scarcely be involved in war with Russia." If a crisis arose in Turkey, Austria possessed in the Straits question a bargaining object of considerable worth. This policy of waiting was in harmony with that of Germany and her pacific ruler. An Imperialist policy would not meet with such cordial support in Berlin as had the annexation, and indeed might arouse a feeling of envy. Wallenstein had advised Ferdinand II to keep a strong army for defence, but if possible to avoid war. The Austria of to-day had the same mission : to maintain the Balance of Power, not to oppose the national evolution of the Balkan States, but to favour the Balance of Power among them with special regard to Roumania and Bulgaria. "Thus the Monarchy requires a strong army, not to settle by a preventive war differences which may one day become acute, but only in case the honour and integrity of the realm are endangered, or its vital interests can no longer be maintained by peaceful means." It was a masterly refutation, though the impenitent Chief of the Staff continued his campaign. If the annexation of Bosnia had kept Europe in turmoil for six months, what effect would Conrad's preventive war have produced? From his policy of watchful waiting Aehrenthal was never to be moved an inch.

For a time it seemed as if Serbia shared his wish for a *détente*. Milovanovich visited the Ballplatz in August and declared that his country desired the best relations with the Monarchy.[1] Now and in future she wished to abstain from all agitation against Austria and Turkey. Serbians desired to maintain the status quo in Turkey; but many of their brothers in race and religious faith lived in the Sanjak, and at some perhaps far distant time she would have to take it. Could Austria give an assurance that she would not oppose such an extension? Aehrenthal refused to commit himself. It was a warning that the calm after the hurricane was not likely to last very long. A few days later Aehrenthal gave a similar negative reply to Bratiano's request to favour compensation of Roumania by Bulgarian territory in the event of Bulgarian aggrandisement.[2] In no quarter was he willing to encourage a threat to the status quo.

In September a Ministerial Council was held to consider the financial situation for 1910, and Aehrenthal, according to custom, opened the proceedings with a survey of foreign affairs.[3] If he had not annexed Bosnia in the previous year, it would have been impossible at a later period. Austria had discovered how few friends she possessed. On the other hand she had shown herself to possess a vitality and strength of will which took the world by surprise. Success was assured only when there was sufficient force to carry a decision into effect. Owing to her improved position she could more effectively help to maintain peace. England's encirclement policy had been resisted, and Austria had shown that she was neither to be treated as a *quantité négligeable* nor to be separated from Germany. "We have reconquered our proper place among the Powers. For the first time the *casus foederis* with Germany had arisen, with satisfactory results." Italy, as

[1] *Ö-U.A.* II, 453-6.   [2] ibid. 458-60.   [3] ibid. 462-5.

usual, was vacillating, but anger was out of place. She was the weakest of the Powers, and she dared not antagonise England. Of the Entente partners France's policy was the most sensible, and she had been of considerable help in the crisis. England now realised that she had gone too far. Iswolsky's revengeful hostility was unconcealed, but Russia was at present unable to fight. In Turkey there should be neither intervention nor attempts at reform. Austria had two great tasks : firstly to maintain the Balance of Power, which necessitated her taking her full part in the Concert, and secondly the pursuit of peace and equilibrium in the Balkans. It was the speech of an architect who looks round in his handiwork and declares : Behold it is good ! He spoke in a similar strain to Cartwright a few days later.[1] He was now more hopeful as to the direction of the Young Turk regime than he had been. There was no cloud between the Central Empires, and Bethmann, if not a man of decision, was certainly a man of peace. Italy was unlikely to leave the Triple Alliance for a considerable time. Never had Cartwright found the Minister in a happier mind.

Aehrenthal's complacency was not without some justification. In the feverish decade before the world war there were two periods during which it was possible to register a steadying of the pulse. The first followed the Algeciras Conference, the second the liquidation of the Bosnian crisis. On both occasions it seemed as if the Powers, wearying of their strife, might live in peace if not in friendship. In both cases appeasement was only on the surface. In the West the antagonism of France and Germany was too deeply rooted to heal. In the east the rivalry of Austria and Russia was too keen to hold in check. Meanwhile every Great Power was piling up the armaments which were both a symptom and a cause of the unrest. Europe was merely a geographical expression. Only bolder measures than any statesman or nation was ready to adopt could have overcome the anarchy that was hurrying them all to their doom.

The Tsar's journey to Racconigi by a roundabout route was an acid reminder of Russian resentments, but Aehrenthal retained his self-control. In a circular despatch he declared that there was no reason, so far as he knew, for alarm.[2] It was already known that Iswolsky, in his attempt to mobilise the enemies of Austria, had long striven for a rapprochement

---

[1] B.D. IX, pt. I, 69–71.   [2] Ö-U.A. II, 519–20.

with Italy in the hope of loosening her ties with the Central Powers. Tittoni's assurances were satisfactory and no written agreements had been made. There was no reason to believe that she had been disloyal to her allies. He had failed to realise how far Italy had drifted away from her moorings, and he went to his grave in ignorance of the Racconigi pact.

At the close of 1909, to Aehrenthal's intense annoyance, the Friedjung trial revived the glowing embers of the Bosnian fray.[1] In an article published in the *Neue Freie Presse* of March 25, 1909, the historian had used documents indicating compromising relations between members of the Croatian Diet and Belgrad. These proved to be forgeries, and the leaders of the Serbo-Croat coalition prepared to vindicate their honour in court. With the Agram treason trial of the summer of 1909 the Foreign Minister had nothing to do; but he was inevitably associated by the public with Friedjung, who had been supplied with materials from official sources. When Forgach expressed his doubts as to the validity of the evidence, Aehrenthal cheerfully replied that the conscientious and experienced historian would have no difficulty in sustaining his charges. He was living in a fool's paradise, for at the end of October Forgach described how a young student at Belgrad named Stephanovich, Secretary of the Slovenski Jug, had brought documents to the Legation since 1907. Every member of the staff had been convinced of their authenticity, though material supplied by other hands was often suspicious. " Stephanovich " was in reality Vasic, a young student of the lowest character. When on the eve of the trial Friedjung informed Aehrenthal that he had been duped by a forger, he was a broken man. The Foreign Minister explained to Milovanovich that the coming trial was a purely private affair, a relic of a past crisis and therefore devoid of political significance. The conciliatory Milovanovich promised to use the soft pedal in Belgrad. Friedjung maintained that the protocols of the Slovenski Jug were genuine and only the signatures forged; but the discovery of foul play broke the back of the defence. As in the Parnell trial a generation earlier, the revelation that certain documents had been forged outweighed the whole mass of authentic evidence.

Incensed at the lack of support from the Foreign Office, Friedjung broke with Aehrenthal. His reputation as a publicist

---

[1] In addition to the Austrian documents see Seton-Watson, *The Southern Slav Question*, and Baernreither, 133–45.

was destroyed by the trial, but the prestige of the Foreign Minister was also compromised. Austrian officials had been duped, and forgeries had been employed in the campaign against Jugoslav nationalists. To the enemies of Austria it seemed a confirmation of the belief in the trickiness of the Ballplatz and its chief. The trial, in which Stephanovich did not appear, ended in a compromise fairly acceptable to both parties, and Milovanovich welcomed the liquidation of a prickly affair. Aehrenthal made the best of a bad job in a circular despatch of January 8, 1910.[1] Contrary to the general belief in foreign countries, he declared, the Government had no part in the trial or the compromise. Austria's representatives abroad were to point out that the material produced in the trial had not been a factor in the decision to annex Bosnia. Austro-Serb relations were now entirely correct, and no political significance attached to the echoes of the past—a view that was accepted by Milovanovich. The trial, he concluded, would not disturb existing relations with Serbia, but, as a final liquidation, would actually improve them. Shortly afterwards he asked Forgach for a full report, in order to judge whether the documents, in spite of criticisms, were genuine or at any rate rested on a substantial basis. Forgach replied at great length, explaining that the value of the greater part of the material was unaffected by the discovery of a few forgeries.[2] If Aehrenthal and Forgach really believed that they had heard the last of the Friedjung trial, they were deluding themselves. The ghost was not so easily laid.

At the opening of 1910 the detestation of Aehrenthal and Iswolsky for one another was as fierce as ever. The former spoke of "ce crapaud," the latter of "ce sale Juif." Two articles in the *Fortnightly Review* had stirred the embers of the Bosnian dispute, and Berchtold's vivid despatches describe the frosty atmosphere of St. Petersburg. On the other hand both statesmen felt the need of restoring normal diplomatic relations.[3] Tension with St. Petersburg, as Aehrenthal was well aware, involved not only the hostility of France and England but dependence on Berlin. Cartwright reported a growing uneasiness in regard to the stability of the Young Turk regime. "I feel certain", he added, "that Count Aehrenthal is most desirous of bettering the relations between Vienna and St. Petersburg without loss of time, as, should

[1] Ö-U.A. II, 641-4.   [2] ibid. 675-82.
[3] Ö-U.A. II, 653-808, G.P. XXVII, ch. 115 ; B.D. IX, pt. I, ch. 72

trouble arise in the Balkans owing to a change of situation in Constantinople, he foresees that the international political outlook in the Balkans would be greatly complicated by the jealousy and misunderstandings which would arise between the Russian and the Austro-Hungarian Governments." Aehrenthal and Iswolsky were equally anxious for the maintenance of peace, at any rate for the present. An olive branch was brought from Vienna to St. Petersburg by Wesselitsky, the well-known London correspondent of the *Novoe Vremya*, and it was not thrust aside. On February 3 Aehrenthal told Cartwright that miracles were not to be expected, but he was glad to say that Iswolsky had shown a disposition to enter into conversation with him—a marked change from the spirit which inspired the Tsar's visit to Racconigi.

A sharp difference as to the method of resuming contact appeared as soon as the negotiations began. Iswolsky was anxious to extract a reassuring formula from his rival which should be communicated to the Powers. Such an assurance Aehrenthal stubbornly declined to give. In announcing the restoration of normal conditions between the two Empires the *Fremdenblatt* of March 21 added : " This welcome result of the negotiations conducted by the two Cabinets, by which Austria-Hungary enters upon relations of confidence with Russia similar to her relations with the other Powers, will not fail to exercise a tranquillising influence on the situation in the Balkans, where all the Great Powers are unanimously working for the maintenance of the status quo. The Vienna Cabinet has no grounds for communicating to the Great Powers the pourparlers conducted between the Cabinets of Vienna and St. Petersburg. Whereas the well-known principles of Austro-Hungarian policy in the Balkans have remained unaltered, no new circumstance has arisen which would give any occasion for a communication." This public rejection of the course which he had pressed so strongly angered Iswolsky, who proceeded to publish the relevant documents without asking leave. Aehrenthal, though naturally annoyed, made no reply and ordered the press to use the soft pedal. " Normal relations " had been restored, but the personal antagonism of the two Ministers remained.

No sooner were normal relations with Russia restored than the Albanian revolt revived the anxieties of the Ballplatz. In a private letter of April 28, 1910, to Pallavicini, the Austrian Minister in Constantinople, who had emphasised the new

energy displayed by the Young Turks and the political significance of the struggle, Aehrenthal expressed a hope that the
Albanians would be neither completely successful nor utterly
crushed, since either result would involve grave consequences
in the Balkan peninsula.[1] A compromise would be best for
everybody. Accordingly the Turks were warned of the danger of concentrating too many troops in the western extremity
of their Empire, and were reminded of Austria's desire to
preserve the status quo.[2] Bulgaria, he pointed out, would
become a dangerous neighbour directly the internal or external
situation of Turkey deteriorated ; and if the Albanians were
savagely repressed they would be unreliable in a future war.
Moreover, the trouble might spread to Montenegro, in whom
Russia took a lively interest. Beyond the giving of advice he
was not prepared to go. Austria, he explained to Tschirschky, warmly desired the continuance and strengthening of
Turkey ; but there would have to be more trustworthy men at
the helm than the present rulers before a response to Turkish
wishes for a rapprochement coud be considered. His attitude
indeed towards every Power except Germany, where Bethmann
possessed his entire confidence, was one of reserve.

The conclusion of a commercial treaty with Serbia was welcomed in both countries, but it led to no political rapprochement. When in July a visit of King Peter to Francis Joseph
was suggested by the Serbian Foreign Minister and approved
by Forgach, Aehrenthal merely replied that he would inform
his master.[3] That the King desired to be received became
known in Serbia, and in October Forgach again pressed for
the " great sacrifice " to be made.[4] A fresh argument for the
reception was found when Masaryk's speeches in the Delegations reopened the unsavoury question of the forgeries. " If
we do not speedily reply to Serbia's request ", wrote Forgach
impatiently, " our policy will reach a *cul-de-sac*. We cannot
get out of the King's visit, and if we now send a friendly
message, for which they have been waiting for months, we
have a powerful weapon to keep the Government up to the
mark in the Vasic affair." The efforts of Forgach were in
vain, for no invitation arrived. Milovanovich was not
unfriendly, but Pasitch and the Radicals were openly Russophil.
The dynasty and the Government, reported Forgach, grovelled
before Hartwig, the Russian Minister, who, as the Turkish

[1] *Ö-U.A.* II, 813-4, 824-5, 843-5. [2] ibid. 855, 863.
[3] ibid. 914-5. [4] ibid. III, 34-5, 72-4.

Minister used to remark, behaved like a "Resident" in Bokhara.[1] The failure of the Serbian Government to repudiate the charges of forgery against the Austrian Legation led Aehrenthal to declare that his confidence in the good will of the Serbian Government was destroyed, and that his action in future would be determined by their deeds, not their words.

The transfer of Iswolsky to Paris in November was hailed by the Ballplatz with delight, and at the end of 1910 Aehrenthal reviewed the situation in a private letter to Bethmann.[2] Relations with Russia were now normal and correct, and they might become something better. Sazonoff was a great improvement on his predecessor, but caution was always requisite with Russian diplomatists. "We shall not run after Russia." In the recent session of the Delegations he had described Austria as territorially satiated, and it was satisfactory that Sazonoff also stood for the status quo in Turkey. On the same day he sent instructions to Berchtold. The disappearance of Iswolsky had removed the element of personal irritation, and Berchtold's pleasant relations with Sazonoff would be of great use. No change, however, in the general tendency of Russian policy was probable, and the greatest caution was needed. "We have not yet seen Sazonoff at work." He had expressed his anxiety during his recent visit to Germany in regard to a policy of expansion by Austria in the Balkans, and this showed that he shared the traditional Russian mistrust. These apprehensions were aired in order to provoke reassuring declarations to which Austria would be tied, while corresponding Russian declarations were not forthcoming. "Our political relations with Russia can only develop on the basis of complete reciprocity." Demonstrations of zeal should be avoided. Happily Austria's international position allowed a friendly but reserved attitude. "Our alliance with Germany has stood the test, our relation to Italy is now most satisfactory, and the clearing of the air by the annexation has rendered possible trustful relations with Turkey."

Aehrenthal was living down his past. At the opening of 1911 Mensdorff reported Nicolson's satisfaction at the admirable relations of the two countries, and his hopes that the health of the Foreign Minister would allow him to continue at the helm, as Europe could not do without him.[3] "I am quite convinced that we ought to wish d'Aehrenthal to remain,"

---

[1] Ö-U.A. III, 109–13.   [2] ibid. 89–94.   [3] ibid. 157.

wrote Grey to Cartwright, " and I trust that he will not be upset."[1] The statesman who had thrown Europe into turmoil was now generally regarded as a pillar of European peace. Nor can there be any doubt as to his sincerity. " While safeguarding the annexation of Bosnia ", he wrote to Pallavicini, " I have been doing my best in the last two years to disentangle the policy of the Monarchy from the thousand chances of Balkan politics.[2] This involves the establishment of friendly relations with Turkey and moral support of her efforts to strengthen herself, though without any positive engagement on our side."

In a private letter to Bethmann Aehrenthal welcomed the loosening of the ties between England and Russia reflected in the Potsdam meeting of the Kaiser and the Tsar, and interpreted Sazonoff's interest in Asiatic questions as involving a status quo policy in the Near East.[3] Turkey had made a bad slip by her needless severities in Albania and Macedonia, and he was advising her to keep sufficient troops in Europe to avoid a surprise in the following year. Whatever happened, he would endeavour to keep out of troubles in the Balkans. His letters and despatches throughout 1911 breathe an ardent desire for tranquillity and conciliation on every side. When Conrad urged a military arrangement with Berlin in the event of Germany being attacked by France and England, he rejoined that it was unnecessary.[4] It was quite enough that Austria should keep Russia neutral by her pledge to defend Germany if Russia intervened. Moreover Bethmann's foremost aim was to improve relations both with England and Russia.

In April King Peter again mooted a visit to Francis Joseph, and this time the Ballplatz courteously replied that it awaited proposals of a date. May was suggested, but at this stage a new difficulty arose. On the plea of delicate health the King proposed to combine his visit to the Emperor with a journey to Paris. This, as the Ballplatz promptly pointed out, was scarcely in accordance with the solemnity of the occasion, since it would look like a mere act of courtesy. The King thereupon promised to return from Budapest to Belgrad before starting for France. When everything seemed settled, violent attacks in the Hungarian press caused the sensitive ruler to propose postponement on the ground that the visit would do more harm than good. That might mean postponing it for years,

[1] B.D. IX, pt. I, 252-3. [2] Ö-U.A. III, 179-180.
[3] ibid. 198-200. [4] ibid. 203-4, 209-10.

replied Pallavicini, who was in charge of the Foreign Office during the absence of Aehrenthal. The list of the King's suite, from which participants in the crime of 1903 had been excluded at Austria's demand, was approved when Francis Joseph had a cold, and the visit was deferred till the autumn. Both parties were secretly relieved when nature intervened; but the opportunity had passed and never returned.

The tension between Vienna and Belgrad could be taken less tragically now that Austro-Russian relations were normal again. In receiving the new Austrian Ambassador at the beginning of June the Tsar spoke with a cordiality unknown since the Bosnian crisis.[1] There was a new situation, he observed, and a clean slate. Sazonoff used almost the same words, and the Ambassador was convinced of their sincerity. The Foreign Minister was pleased with the assurance that Russia desired to bury the past, but determined to await any advances that might be made. Meanwhile, as he pointed out in his instructions for a new Austrian Minister to Sofia, Bulgaria should be wooed as a counterweight against Serbia and as the chief prospective heir of Turkey.[2] Her aggrandisement would be a fresh guarantee of her independence against Panslav influences and pressure. "We must try to build up a capital of confidence and sympathy on which we can reply when European Turkey, despite our support, collapses." Aehrenthal had never lost his heart to the Young Turks, and he realised that the men who had overthrown Abdul Hamid were just as likely to destroy their empire as to keep it alive. All he could do was to exhort other Powers to abstain from adventures and to set a good example himself.

While the Foreign Minister's whole energies were bent on the preservation of peace, the irrepressible Conrad once more returned to the charge. The Turco-Albanian conflict, he argued, with its possible extension to Montenegro and indeed to the whole Balkan peninsula, counselled military preparations. for the Monarchy might be compelled to intervene.[3] To be of use they must be made in plenty of time. A war against Italy waged some years earlier would have strengthened Austria's military position for action in the Balkans, just as war against Serbia in 1909 would have given the Monarchy its proper position in the same quarter. Aehrenthal replied that he regretted the renewal of the old attacks on a policy

[1] Ö-U.A. III, 254–5, 263–4, 257–8.   [2] ibid. 260–3.
[3] ibid. 279–88.

approved by the Emperor and the Governments of both halves of the Monarchy. The Albanian troubles he regarded as Turkey's domestic concern. Were they to spread, Austria would remain passive and other Powers would probably do the same. He had suggested to Italy and Russia a joint communication to Constantinople and Cettinje that, if hostilities occurred, neither would be allowed to alter the status quo. There was therefore at present no need for military preparations. When Conrad retorted that the contemplated warning would involve action if it were ignored, Aehrenthal explained that only diplomatic pressure was intended. The Chief of the Staff was not converted, and the struggle was shortly to break out again more violently in another portion of the field.

X

Aehrenthal had never served in Rome and possessed no first-hand knowledge of Italian sentiment. He accepted the Triple Alliance as the foundation of Austrian policy, and the tension with Russia strengthened his resolve to keep it in repair. The best and perhaps the only method, as he fully understood, was to keep Europe at peace. A Franco-German conflict was almost certain to involve England, and, if England entered the fray, who could answer for Italy ? A Balkan conflagration, again, would inevitably generate friction between the two Adriatic Powers. The Foreign Minister was unaware of the secret pacts with France and Russia, but had he known of them he would doubtless have pursued exactly the same course. There was no love lost between the Governments and the peoples, and the relations of Vienna to Berlin were of an intimacy forever unattainable in Rome. But there were only two possible policies towards Italy—war or trust. An alliance had been made and it had to be maintained. With Russia and Serbia on his hands, it was vital to keep Italy in good humour. Moreover, if Italy were to be lost, he would have to depend more than ever on Berlin.

Soon after Aehrenthal had entered the Ballplatz he sharply repudiated the plan of a preventive war favoured in military circles. " A conflict of this nature would not only be at variance with the traditions of Austria ; it would not be understood in these days when war means the mobilisation of the entire nation. The necessary moral co-operation between army and civil population would be lacking. Moreover I should be at a loss to know the object of such a war. As history has taught us, further territorial acquisitions in Italy would be a disaster for the Monarchy."[1] From this wise policy he never swerved, and his master stood firm in its support. At Desio in 1907 and at Salzburg in 1908 he pledged himself to joint action with Italy in all Balkan questions. He informed Tittoni of his decision to annex Bosnia, though only when his mind was made up, and throughout the crisis Italy's critical attitude was a disagreeable contrast to the unfailing support of Berlin. When Conrad and Moltke discussed the eventuality of a European war in January 1909, it was assumed that Italy would stand aloof. Tittoni wished for an agreement with Russia and Austria as to their respective spheres of influence in the Balkans, and when this proved impossible he negotiated with them separately. The secret pact of Racconigi, of October 24, 1909, was followed by an Austro-Italian exchange of Notes explaining and supplementing Article VII of the Treaty of 1887.[2] Austria bound herself not to reoccupy the Sanjak of Novibazar without a previous agreement based on the principle of compensation. Each signatory also promised not to conclude with a third Power any agreement on Balkan questions without the participation of the other on the basis of absolute equality, and undertook to communicate any proposition from a third Power contrary to the principle of non-intervention or tending to a modification of the status quo in the Balkans or the Turkish coasts and islands in the Adriatic and the Aegean. The engagement was to form part of the Triple Alliance and only Germany was to be informed. The agreement was proposed by Tittoni and accepted by Aehrenthal in order to keep the wire to Rome in good repair.[3]

At the opening of 1910 Conrad informed Aehrenthal of the apprehensions of the German General Staff that, in a struggle between the Central Powers and Russia, France and Italy might stand aside till the former were deeply engaged and then strike.[4] The Germans had decided to prevent such a stab in the back by demanding a categorical announcement of the intentions of France when a war with Russia was in sight. Austria, he argued, was exposed to a similar danger from Italy and should meet it in the same way. It would be still better to utilise any Russian embarrassment to attack Italy, who would

---

[1] Report to the Emperor, April 1, 1907. Pribram, II, 144. Conrad presents his case in regard to the Tripoli War in *Aus meiner Dienstzeit*, II, 171–290.

[2] Pribram, I, 240–3. [3] *G.P.* XXVII, ch. 213. [4] *Ö-U.A.* II, 694, 707–8.

always be hostile to every Austrian development by land and sea. Aehrenthal replied that, in his opinion, Russia was incapable of a policy of action for years to come. If, however, she were to threaten the Central Powers, Conrad's plan of securing a pronouncement from Italy should be adopted. He saw no need to worry, for Russia was weak and San Giuliano, who took office in March 1910, abounded in declarations of loyalty.[1] Aehrenthal, though pleased with these assurances, was not altogether convinced. The Italians, he remarked to Tschirschky, always liked to have two irons in the fire.[2] It cost Italy nothing in quiet times to declare for the Triple Alliance, but it was very unlikely that she would prove her membership by acts if difficulties arose and she had to show her colours. Prolonged conversations in Salzburg and Ischl during the summer confirmed his belief that the Italian Foreign Minister desired closer relations with the Central Powers, a satisfactory result attributed to their solidarity in the Bosnian crisis and the disunion of the Triple Entente.[3]

On returning to Vienna Aehrenthal issued instructions to the Embassy in Rome that trifling complaints should not be presented without orders from home.[4] In October a visit to Racconigi and Turin confirmed his favourable impressions, and Turkey was informed that Italy shared Austria's desire for the maintenance of the status quo in the Near East. In a private letter to Bethmann he reiterated his impression that the King and San Giuliano desired to emphasise the alliance, though the latter seemed to underestimate the strength of irredentism in Northern Italy.[5] The references to Italy in the Delegations in November were equally friendly, and in December San Giuliano spoke of Austria with a warmth unknown for many years. On February 1, 1911, Grey expressed his satisfaction to Mensdorff that Aehrenthal was at the helm, and added cheerfully that the relations of all the Powers seemed to him very good.[6] With such friendly assurances from London and Rome, and with Sazonoff installed at St. Petersburg, it might well seem that the Bosnian storm was over at last.

The sun never shone for long, and at the end of 1910 Tripoli began to cast a shadow over the scene. On December 8 San Giuliano informed his ally of Italy's chief complaints

[1] Ö-U.A. II, 814–5, 834–7, 882–3, 941–3.   [2] G.P. XXVII, 357–8.
[3] Ö-U.A. II, 945–50.   [4] ibid. III, 3.
[5] ibid. 27–8.   [6] ibid. 172.

against Turkey and her demand for redress.[1] Aehrenthal replied with a gentle warning of the danger of any sort of pressure in view of the sensitiveness of the new regime. Austria, he added, had also difficulties with Turkey, and in dealing with them he bore in mind the insecurity of the Young Turks. " The Italians are trying to drag us into their Turkish business ", he complained to Tschirschky. Many of their complaints, he added, seemed to have very little foundation. While the Foreign Minister was beginning to worry about Turco-Italian relations, the Chief of the Staff read the ambitions of Italy in a more sinister way. Writing on January 3, 1911, he reported that she would be absolutely ready for war in April 1912, not merely on land and sea but in the fortifications on the Austrian frontier and the development of strategic railways.[2] He concluded that she was anticipating a political situation at that period which required such a military backing. Aehrenthal parried the thrust with the information that she was thinking of renewing the Triple Alliance before the time was due. In strengthening her armaments she was only following the example of the other Powers, and no doubt she wished to increase the value of her partnership before the negotiations began. Despite this snub to Conrad, Aehrenthal asked his Ambassador in Rome whether he agreed that Italy was aiming at readiness for war in 1912. The Ambassador replied that it was quite untrue of the navy and only partially true of the army.[3] The motive for the preparations, he believed, was the widespread fear of an Austrian attack. In his long reply Tripoli was not mentioned.

Three months after the communication of December the Ballplatz was again informed of Italy's dissatisfaction with Turkey.[4] Pallavicini, who was in charge during the absence of his chief, attempted to throw oil on the ruffled waters. He was not aware, he replied, of any differences between the two countries. In Constantinople, he added, it was widely believed that Italy was seeking a pretext to score a success at Turkey's expense. Any steps tending to confirm the suspicion might lead to an anti-Italian boycott. A naval demonstration might have disastrous consequences and endanger the status quo in the Ottoman Empire. The second hint from Vienna was as futile as the first. The Agadir crisis was interpreted in Rome as a warning of the danger of delay. The spring of

[1] Ö-U.A. III, 99.   [2] ibid. 140.
[3] ibid. 168–71.   [4] ibid. 212–3.

the *Panther*, though it seemed to Aehrenthal a diplomatic blunder, gave the Italian Government the opportunity that it sought.

At the end of July a third and more precise intimation of Italian plans was made at Vienna.[1] Hearing that Turkey intended to prevent the concession for harbour works in Tripoli falling to an Italian, the Government was about to inform her that, if the report was correct, public opinion might compel it to adopt extreme measures. Aehrenthal promised to continue his conciliatory efforts at Constantinople, but hoped that Italy would not proceed to the dangerous measures which had been mentioned. Even an occupation of Tripoli, retorted the Italian Ambassador, would not endanger peace, since Turkey could not resist. The secret was out at last, and Aehrenthal reacted vigorously. It was less the immediate danger of a conflict, he observed, than the far graver peril of its effects on the Powers and the Balkan States. If Italy signalled the overthrow of the status quo at one point, it would be impossible to appeal to this principle elsewhere. In view of these alarming consequences he hoped she would abstain from such pregnant decisions. Turkey was promptly informed of the danger and advised to consider Italian susceptibilities.

Italy's wish to renew the Triple Alliance before the expiry of the treaty period in 1914 was connected, as it now appeared, with her ambitions in Tripoli.[2] On August 3 Aehrenthal informed his master that, as he had learned from Berlin, a renewal without change was desired by Italy, who, however, hesitated to take the initiative. The Austrian Ambassador in Rome attributed the move to the desirability of renewing the treaty before Francis Joseph was succeeded by the unreliable Francis Ferdinand. Aehrenthal was delighted, and Italy's need of the Triple Alliance in some measure offset his fear of the reactions of her Tripoli plan. Aehrenthal and Kiderlen informed the Italian Ambassadors of their readiness to renew the alliance, and the negotiations were formally opened.

On September 26 the Italian Ambassador announced the decision of his Government to take action in Tripoli.[3] France was increasing her territory in Morocco and had promised not to oppose Italian action in Tripoli. When the Tripoli problem was satisfactorily solved, Italy would be fully contented and therefore all the more a reliable member of the Triple Alliance. Aehrenthal promised a considered reply to

[1] *Ö-U.A.* III, 289–90.   [2] Pribram, II, 150–60.   [3] *Ö-U.A.* III, 353–4.

the communication, merely remarking that she could count on good will, but that his fears of an extension of the conflict remained. He advised Turkey, though in vain, to content herself with a protest. He informed the Great Powers that, since his efforts in Rome and Constantinople to maintain peace had failed, it only remained to keep the conflagration from spreading to European Turkey, where they should announce their determination to maintain the status quo. The same gospel of localising the struggle was preached to Italy and the Balkan States. Aehrenthal, reported Cartwright, was furious at the precipitate action of his ally.[1] He felt that he had been duped by his friend San Giuliano just as he—Aehrenthal—had duped his friend Iswolsky over the annexation of Bosnia. Having more self-control than the Russian statesman, however, he kept his resentment to himself.

A Turkish appeal to hold back Italy was naturally declined; but when Italian warships fired on a Turkish torpedo boat at Prevesa Aehrenthal protested with a vigour which surprised and dismayed the Consulta. San Giuliano telegraphed instructions to the fleet not to operate in the Adriatic or to bombard Albanian or Ionian harbours or forts. Aehrenthal hoped Austro-German mediation might be possible when the occupation was complete, and urged Turkey to compromise before the war spread. When the first shock was over the intransigence of the belligerents increased, and he realised that mediation would come best from all the Powers since the risk of failure had increased. On October 23 he invited the Powers to discuss joint action in Rome and Constantinople. This plan was approved in principle, though it was felt that the time had not come.

Despite his anger at the conduct of Italy he turned sharply on Conrad, who had urged that Austria should compensate herself in the Balkans.[2] For years, he complained to his master, the Chief of the Staff had tried to influence foreign policy and had not scrupled to criticise it. " The combating of the policy of the responsible Minister, based as it is on the instructions of the ruler and approved by the two Governments, is more than an anomaly : it would involve the political paralysis of the Monarchy." A similar complaint was made to Francis Ferdinand ; but the heir to the throne was by this time a declared enemy, and in a lengthy audience he denounced him

[1] B.D. IX, pt. I, 307–8.
[2] Ö-U.A. III, 346–8, 466–70.

in passionate words.[1] Aehrenthal, however, strong in the support of the Emperor, triumphed over his adversary, and Conrad was compelled to resign. It was his last victory.

On November 5 Italy notified the annexation of Tripoli, though only the coast and capital were in her possession. Aehrenthal thought it premature and legally unjustifiable ; but it required no reply and there was nothing to be done. The Ambassador at the same time denied the report that Italian warships would cruise off Salonika.[2] Aehrenthal expressed his pleasure, adding that Italy was bound by treaty not to endanger the status quo in the Balkans. Austria, like Germany, had assumed a friendly attitude to her action in Tripoli, though it attacked the principle of the integrity of the Ottoman Empire ; but she could not watch military action on the Aegean coast unmoved. Would he also disapprove a temporary occupation of the Aegean islands ? asked the Ambassador. The Minister replied that he would. Austria could not accept a landing of Italian troops on the coasts of European Turkey or on the Aegean islands, and would regard it as infringing Article VII of the Triple Alliance. Italy was not seriously alarmed, for she believed that none of the Powers would attempt to limit her freedom of manœuvre by force. Aehrenthal's position indeed was unenviable. On the one hand he was eager to keep his partner within the orbit of the Triple Alliance. On the other he did not wish Turkey to feel isolated and to march off into the Russian camp. Austria, he declared, was a more disinterested friend of Turkey than Germany ; for while Germany only desired the integrity of Turkey for her own economic reasons, Austria supported it on the highest political grounds.

On December 6 Aehrenthal explained the situation to a Council of Ministers in a relatively optimistic tone.[3] If the war lasted till the spring, there might be trouble with the Balkan States ; but the Powers favoured the status quo, and Austro-Russian relations were developing favourably. A policy of watchful waiting was all the more necessary since Anglo-German relations were very strained. The crisis was to be expected in three, four or five years. This grave prospect compelled Austria to be prepared, for as a faithful ally she might have to fight at Germany's side. The best preparation was a prompt acceptance of the defence estimates. On the other hand he did not anticipate a conflict with Italy. He

[1] Ö.-U.A. III, 605-6.   [2] ibid. 515-6.   [3] ibid. 641-8.

had no great confidence in her, but there was no ground for open mistrust. To regard her as a dependable friend was impossible, but with skilful steering it was possible to retain her as an ally. In conversation with Cartwright on the following day he was less optimistic.[1] How could a peace be secured which would not leave Turkey too weak to continue as a Great Power? To weaken Turkey would be to disturb the equilibrium in the Balkans and lead to a crash. The Minister was not destined to witness the fulfilment of his prophecy.

Despite his determination to avoid friction, Aehrenthal's difficulties increased as the conflict dragged on. Certain Powers whispered in Rome that energetic naval action was prevented by Austria alone. Italy did not appear to understand the situation, he commented, for she seemed to expect more from her ally than she could give. Austria had lost no opportunity of showing her good will. She was, however, a neutral, and she had to think of her own interests in Constantinople. He understood that the unexpected duration of the war had made Italian opinion irritable and inclined to seek a scapegoat. But Austrian opinion was justifiably excited by Italy's action. She had attacked Turkey without a thought of the resulting embarrassment to her allies, who were champions of the integrity of the Ottoman Empire. Was it surprising that Austrians felt that one day Italy might attack them with equally little warning? On December 19 the Austrian Ambassador in Rome was instructed to speak frankly to Giolitti and San Giuliano, explaining that the Minister claimed the right to free speech after five years of unremitting effort to strengthen the friendship of the two countries.[2] Italy should drop the game of see-saw between the European groups. Since the famous " extra dance " she had taken too many liberties and endeavoured to cover herself in every direction. Such conduct could not command the confidence of her allies. If she desired to continue the advantages of the alliance, she must prove her desire not only in words but in deeds. Never before had Aehrenthal used such firm language. When the Ambassador spoke with the Italian Prime Minister and Foreign Minister at the opening of 1912, they pleaded that the Moroccan crisis had compelled them to take action in Tripoli.[3] After the liquidation of that problem the see-saw policy would end. Every responsible politician was a convinced supporter

[1] B.D. IX, pt. I, 348.   [2] Ö-U.A. III, 701-3.
[3] ibid. 770-3.

of the Triplice. To make irredentists into martyrs would be a great mistake. The conversations produced no result, and the confidence was never restored. Italy, it was clear, would continue to go her own way, regardless of the spirit if not of the letter of the Triple Alliance. Moreover she was at war, and, like other belligerents, she was out to win.

Early in February an affliction of the blood, against which Aehrenthal had struggled heroically for many months, was discovered to be mortal, and on February 17 he died. A cordial autograph letter from his sovereign reached him on his death-bed, too late to bring him solace. For five and a half years he had ruled in the Ballplatz without a rival. There is no evidence that he was ever compelled, like some of his German colleagues, to adopt a policy which he disapproved or to abandon a course which he desired to steer. That he was the biggest figure among Austrian statesmen since Metternich was the verdict of Pichon, the French Minister of Foreign Affairs. That he raised the prestige of Austria higher than at any time since Metternich was the opinion of Cartwright. That he restored her self-confidence is beyond question. Vienna was no longer the poor relation of Berlin, no longer the steed for the German rider, no longer the brilliant second, but an equal partner in the firm. The passion of his life, declares his friend Baernreither, was to restore the prestige of the monarchy. His instinctive sense of its dignity and of its importance was as profound as that of his master. He knew his own mind and had the courage of his convictions.

It would be difficult, on the other hand, to maintain that he left his country in a stronger position than he found it. His triumph was as bright and brief as the rainbow arch. The independence he had won from Berlin was a danger as well as a gain, for it might tempt the Ballplatz to dangerous courses. His outstanding achievement, the annexation of Bosnia, raised more problems than it solved. The storm gradually abated, and the resignation of Iswolsky brought a welcome *détente* with Russia. But the improvement was only skin deep. No serious attempt was made to win the confidence of Austria's Southern Slav citizens. Serbia was not only unreconciled but embittered beyond recall, the relations of Belgrad with St. Petersburg became ever closer, and the Pan-Serb movement grew apace. Despite his exertions Italy slipped slowly away, and the Triple Entente became an alliance in almost everything but name. Austria's best hope lay in the maintenance of peace throughout Europe, and to this aim he devoted the energies of his closing years. But he was fighting a losing battle, for tendencies were at work which he was unable to control. The Anglo-German rivalry filled him with dark apprehensions of a general war. The duplicity of Italy, though he never fully realised its extent, was a menace if not actually a nightmare. Hence his incessant efforts to pour oil on the troubled waters—to renew contact with Turkey, to hold back the Balkan States, to humour his Italian partner while keeping the Tripoli conflagration from spreading to the Near East.

Aehrenthal died too early to realise that it was all in vain. The loosely knit European structure was too fragile to bear such shocks as the annexation of Bosnia. The damage might seem to be momentarily repaired, but the foundations had been undermined. It is idle to discuss whether he would have been able to keep the peace in 1914. It is enough to record that, in attempting to strengthen the Empire which he served with utter devotion, he set in motion forces which were quickly to bring the realm of the Hapsburgs crashing to the ground. For the world war grew directly out of the quarrel between Vienna and Belgrad, a quarrel which he had done more than any other man to foment. There is no more arresting figure among European statesmen of the post-Bismarckian era. Every inch a man ! exclaimed Cartwright, whose distrust had turned to something like admiration. But among his eminent qualities foresight was lacking. He had grasped at the shadow and missed the substance. Herein lies the tragedy of his career.